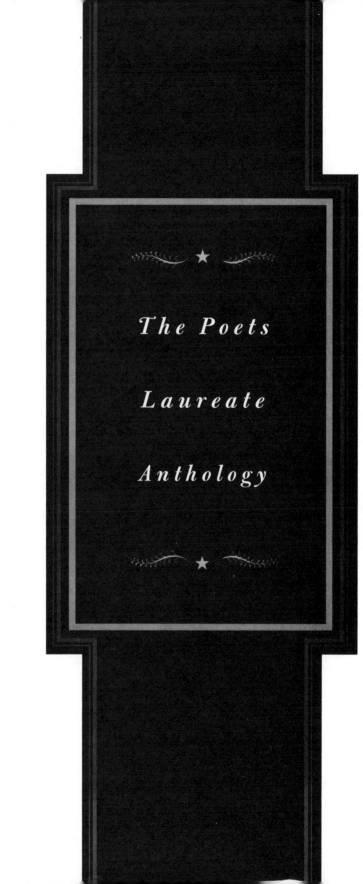

The Poets

Laureate

Anthology

W. W. NORTON & COMPANY | *New York · London*

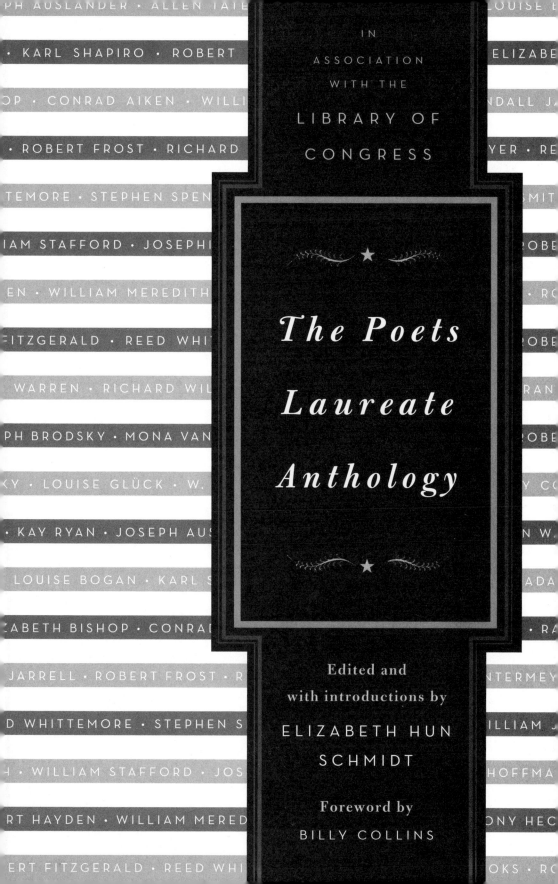

IN
ASSOCIATION
WITH THE
LIBRARY OF
CONGRESS

The Poets

Laureate

Anthology

Edited and
with introductions by
ELIZABETH HUN
SCHMIDT

Foreword by
BILLY COLLINS

For information about special discounts for bulk purchases, please contact
W. W. Norton Special Sales at specialsales@wwnorton.com or 800-233-4830

Manufacturing by RR Donnelley, Harrisonburg
Book design by Chris Welch
Production manager: Julia Druskin

Library of Congress Cataloging-in-Publication Data

The poets laureate anthology / edited and with introductions
by Elizabeth Hun Schmidt ; foreword by Billy Collins. — 1st ed.
p. cm.
At head of title: In association with the Library of Congress.
Poems by each of the forty-three poets who have been named our
nation's Poet Laureate since the post (originally called Consultant in
Poetry to the Library of Congress) was established in 1937.
Includes bibliographical references and index.
ISBN 978-0-393-06181-9
1. American poetry—20th century. 2. American poetry—21st century.
3. Poets laureate—United States. I. Schmidt, Elizabeth.
II. Collins, Billy. III. Library of Congress.
PS591.P63P64 2010
811'.508—dc22

                                        2010021692

W. W. Norton & Company, Inc.
500 Fifth Avenue, New York, N.Y. 10110
www.wwnorton.com

W. W. Norton & Company Ltd.
15 Carlisle Street, London W1D 3BS

2 3 4 5 6 7 8 9 0

 LIBRARY OF CONGRESS

In memory of and with thanks to Evelyn Sinclair and Archibald MacLeish, who both worked at the Library of Congress to support the work of the United States poets laureate.

A poem should be motionless in time
As the moon climbs,

Leaving, as the moon releases
Twig by twig the night-entangled trees

—Archibald MacLeish,
Librarian of Congress 1939–1944, "Ars Poetica"

CONTENTS

POEMS

[signature poems in brackets]

2008–2010: KAY RYAN (1945–)   22

2007–2008: CHARLES SIMIC (1938–) 37

2006–2007: DONALD HALL (1928–) 54

2004-2006: TED KOOSER (1939-)   74

2003-2004: LOUISE GLÜCK (1943-)   85

2001–2003: BILLY COLLINS (1941–)   112

1995-1997: ROBERT HASS (1941-)   171

1988–1990 AND 1963–1964: HOWARD NEMEROV (1920–1999)   262

1978–1980: WILLIAM MEREDITH (1919–2007) 381

1976–1978: ROBERT HAYDEN (1913–1980) 397

1973–1974: DANIEL HOFFMAN (1923–) 419

1971–1973: JOSEPHINE JACOBSEN (1908–2003)   432

1970–1971: WILLIAM STAFFORD (1914–1993)   447

1959–1961: RICHARD EBERHART (1904–2005) 527

1958–1959: ROBERT FROST (1874–1963) 541

1948–1949: LÉONIE ADAMS (1899–1988)   630

1947–1948: ROBERT LOWELL (1917–1977)   639

1946–1947: KARL SHAPIRO (1913–2000)   659

1937–1941: JOSEPH AUSLANDER (1897–1965)   711

FOREWORD

Billy Collins

Becoming the United States poet laureate is a surprisingly straightforward process, especially considering the trumpeting resonance of the title. Unlike the British model, the American version is conferred without ceremony or ritual of investiture. No wreath is bestowed, nor is a cask of dry wine bestowed as is the custom in England. The news, however stunning, is delivered via a phone call from the Librarian of Congress, who congratulates you and talks you through a short list of duties, and after a pleasant luncheon in the Library's pavilion weeks later— poof, you're the new poet laureate. You do get a very nice office, a suite of rooms in the "attic" of the Jefferson Building, where you are apparently free to spend as much or as little time as you please. Located down the hall from the Senate Page School, the office is impressive not only for its elegant period furniture and the spectacular view of the Capitol, but also for the ghosts of all the previous laureates who haunt these rooms and whose photographs stare down at you (well, at me anyway) with expressions ranging from dim recognition to disbelief. *There must be some mistake*, Robert Penn Warren seemed to be saying. *Surely, not him*, Robert Frost seethed.

In place of a royal key, or cape, or coat of arms, the new laureate is presented with a heavy book containing a history of the American laureateship—or "Consultantship in Poetry," as the office was called until 1986—written by one William McGuire and titled *Poetry's Catbird Seat* after a remark by Reed Whittemore, who once described the position as "a job of opportunity, a catbird seat." I had hoped that this heavy book might explain the meaning of the laureateship and make it clear what I now was supposed to do, but this was not the case. The most helpful comment I came across was Howard Nemerov's observation that the poet laureate was expected to devote his tenure to explaining to others what it is exactly that the poet laureate does. Conrad Aiken concurred with Saint-John Perse's description of the job as "not exactly fictitious, but shall we say slightly imaginary." Indeed, apart from giving an annual reading and lecture, it appeared that the poet laureate was free to sit behind his desk and practice the art of Sudoku. "The Consultants," McGuire flatly adds, "were far from idle, but their role remained largely undefined." The most amusing misconception of the laureateship I ever heard issued from a high school student who asked me after a reading, "How many people would have to die for you to become President?"

With no obligation to write "occasional poems," say, on the death of an earl, it seemed that the American laureate was free to write occasionally. Yet many recent laureates had found inventive ways to keep busy. Perhaps inspired by Maxine Kumin's poetry activism in the Washington community and Joseph Brodsky's idea (though Brodsky never acted upon it) of placing poetry books in motels and supermarkets, Rita Dove, Robert Pinsky, and Robert Hass had taken advantage of the opportunities offered by the Library to promote poetry on a national level—to be "a lightning rod for poetry," to quote one description of the office, however painful that might sound. My own contribution was a program called "Poetry 180," the aim of which was to expose high school students to contemporary poems without the attendant pains of explication—a poem a day, one for each of the 180 days of the school year. It was as simple as that. Such boosterism, it should be added, would not have sat well with certain previous laureates, including Louis Untermeyer, who (not warmly) remarked that he "was meant to act as a poetic radiator, radiating a love of poetry over as many miles as possible."

Although *Poetry's Catbird Seat* didn't tell me what a laureate should do, the book contained enough tidbits to appeal to my taste for literary oddity. I discovered, for instance, that Ogden Nash, a reader for Doubleday at the time, was the one who first spotted the manuscript, tossed over the transom, that became Stanley Kunitz's first book of poems. When Ezra Pound was committed to Saint Elizabeths Hospital, Untermeyer proposed an alternative sentence: "life imprisonment in a cell lined with the poetry of Edgar A. Guest." Maxine Kumin would ride her horse, Boomer, for an hour before heading to the poetry office. Senator Edward Kennedy, of all people, introduced Andrei Voznesenskii when he read at the Library, and Daniel Hoffman gave a lecture on Carl Sandburg that bore the intriguing title "Moonlight Dries No Mittens." And speaking of titles, Kumin called one of her lectures "The Poet and the Mule" and was dismayed to see it listed in the evening's program as "The Poet and the Muse" due to a typesetter's understandable confusion. I was surprised to discover that Archibald MacLeish, not the laureate at the time, had accepted Nixon's invitation to write a poem on the occasion of an anticipated moon landing. I already knew that the change in title from "Consultant in Poetry" to "Poet Laureate" was due to the efforts of one Spark Matsunaga, a Democratic senator from Hawaii and war hero, who for twenty-two years tirelessly kept introducing legislation to enact the change until Congress finally relented in 1985; but it was more revealing to learn how various laureates spent their tenure in Washington: Karl Shapiro exploring the library's holdings of esoteric and mystical books, Robert Frost visiting the library rarely but using the title to widen the stage of his own popularity, and Robert Penn Warren hunkering down to write *All the King's Men*.

McGuire's book—which, by the way, deserves updating—provides the best and perhaps the only history of the laureateship, but here in *The Poets Laureate Anthology* this history is told for the first time by some of the very poems that distinguish these forty-three title holders. The anthology offers a generous sample of their work and provides a sweeping aerial view of the shifting ground of American poetry from 1937 to the present. Like any poetry collection, it can be read in any order according to each reader's whims—front to back, back to front, or dipped into anywhere—but editor Elizabeth Hun Schmidt's decision to put the poets in reverse chronological order encourages readers to begin with W. S. Merwin, holder of the office as of fall 2010, and move back in time, stepping plot by plot over the landscape of poetry, arriving finally at the verses of Joseph Auslander, the first to hold the post. This reversal of chronological order may remind readers that literature not only progresses, but it *recedes*; it moves forward toward an unknown future, but it also backpedals toward its origins. Once the Influence and the Influenced trade places on the time line, unusual effects may result. Like the lordly Hudson, poetry flows in both directions.

At first, I planned to describe the arc of this progression from the somewhat dusty poems of Auslander to the spare rhythms of W. S. Merwin or to follow the book's reverse sequencing and travel from Merwin back to Auslander, but I found that the poets in between seemed unwilling to act as stepping stones for my tour, mostly because each is so distinctive. So instead of charting waves of literary change, I am simply going to point to some of the highlights of my perusal of the anthology. Of course, no two readers' tours of these poems will be the same—each will find his or her own delights; each will experience spikes, maybe even valleys; and each may be swallowed whole by individual poems. Here are what might be considered marginal notes pulled from the sidelines onto the page proper.

Straightaway, I admired W. S. Merwin's wonderfully modest, early three-liner titled "Separation": "Your absence has gone through me / Like thread through a needle. / Everything I do is stitched with its color." I have long envied Merwin's ability to transcend punctuation, fully on display here. And I loved Kay Ryan's "Home to Roost" for its perfect balance of silliness and horror accomplished through the image of chickens (not vultures) blotting out the sun—a barnyard apocalypse with a late repetition of its title—now a cliché with teeth. Every one of her poems is a little tower of sonic activity. And how can Charles Simic possibly go wrong when he starts out a poem with "I was stolen by the gypsies. My parents stole me right back. Then the gypsies stole me again. This went on for some time." As in so many of his strange, tactile poems, he leads us into a little world both surreal and real, crazy and scary. In "To a Waterfowl," which echoes the William Cullen Bryant original, Donald Hall is erotic and defiant, barely tolerating hus-

bands, wooing their wives, and challenging the young, while glorify-
ing his own poems and deprecating himself. I liked Ted Kooser's idea
of an ideal reader, a beautiful woman who would rather have her dirty
raincoat dry-cleaned than waste the money on a book of poems, and
indelible is Louise Glück's anti-Romantic assertion that she hates sex
as much as she hates the mock orange flowers that light her yard. Also
stuck to the slope of my memory is Robert Hass's "Then Time," in
which some touching pillow talk between a man and woman wanders
into the deepest human considerations. And Robert Pinsky's "Shirt"
deserves its wide audience for the way it mixes the precise details of
piecework shirtmaking with the criminal horrors of immolation. To
read Stanley Kunitz's "Halley's Comet" was to experience again the
deft way it shuffles together the domestic and the cosmic and to be
reminded of its final image of "the boy in the white flannel gown /
sprawled on this coarse gravel bed" of a rooftop. And Rita Dove's
"Day Star" deserves its place in many anthologies for its empathetic
portrait of a wife and mother who commits the terrible sin of doing
absolutely nothing right "in the middle of the day."

Dipping into the anthology in a few random places is a sure way to
experience the wide variety of voices and styles gathered here. Mona
Van Duyn contributes a lovely sonnet titled "Earth Tremors Felt in Mis-
souri," which cleverly compares love to a sensuous seismic catastrophe.
In "Love Song," Joseph Brodsky's characteristic rhyming is on parade in
a series of seriocomic romantic promises. Richard Wilbur's "A Simile
for Her Smile" has long stood out as a perfectly balanced hinge poem in
which a beloved's smile has the metaphoric power to stop traffic and let
quieter sounds prevail. And Howard Nemerov's wit is fully deployed in
"Money," a mock lecture on American economics, history, and culture
in which he studies a buffalo nickel as Keats had studied his urn.

Some laureates made use of the office to write poems with a social or
political thrust. Robert Penn Warren's mockingbird sings to the presi-
dent, the Senate, and more personally to J. Edgar Hoover. Gwendolyn
Brooks's pool players leave school and die soon; William Meredith writes
a letter to the White House; William Stafford raises his voice against the
murderous policies of the government, vowing in one poem "never to
kill and call it fate." James Dickey drinks from a helmet in a foxhole.

Brooks's ballad of racial injustice, "The Ballad of Rudolph Reed," finds its deserved place. William Jay Smith's "The Pumpkin Field" is part of *The Cherokee Lottery*, a sequence bemoaning the forceful relocation of tens of thousands of Native Americans. Classics such as Richard Eberhardt's "The Fury of Aerial Bombardment" and Frost's "The Gift Outright" need only be given a nod of the head, a bend of the knee.

Poets also kept a steady eye on the natural world. Among the notable poems about animal life is Dickey's fanciful and chilling "The Heaven of Animals," which imagines a place where predation is an eternal state, where the killers kill perfectly and the killed are killed again and again: "They fall, they are torn, / They rise, they walk again." In an earthly version of that meditation, Randall Jarrell describes the snow leopard as "the heart of heartlessness." In another of his poems, a woman at a zoo implores a vulture to change her by investing her with animal power. And Reed Whittemore's "Clamming" is a beautiful example of how to access a large subject (a son) through a small one (clams); it ends with a piece of irreducibly Buddhist advice: "Son, when you clam, / Clam."

The Poets Laureate Anthology contains plenty of surprises, discoveries that may change our notions of how a particular poet's work should be read. But it is clear that editor Schmidt also wants to show our laureates at their best; indeed, some of their included poems have been anthologized so frequently as to become echoes of themselves. William Carlos Williams's red wheelbarrow, Robert Hayden's "austere and lonely offices," Elizabeth Bishop's "rainbow, rainbow, rainbow!" and many other familiar lines and images have achieved a kind of frozen, iconic status. Such may be the price of writing an absolute killer poem. "Household poems" of this order may also take on a much more public tone than the poet intended, and thus the intimacy of what was originally composed may be lost. Plus, placing poets in the context of their public recognition holds the danger of viewing them through a rather polished lens. Enshrined as some of these poets may be, it is important to remember that each of these poems began as a smaller thing— an initiating line, an intriguing image, "a lump in the throat," as Frost put it—not as a contribution to an anthology such as this one with its sober historic title. It is safe to say that these poems were not written to be declaimed to the American public from the balcony of the laureate's office overlooking the Capitol; more likely, they were meant to be uttered quietly to a single reader, or said to no one at all since poems can be what poets say to themselves as they wander from room to room through the houses of their experience. Yet the laureates surely deserve their own anthology, a common place for both the living and the dead to gather. And for us readers, these many poems, so carefully collected here, allow us to tune in to the many voices of our laureates as they talk us through more than seven decades in the life of American poetry.

INTRODUCTION

ELIZABETH HUN SCHMIDT

The journey to the office of the United States poet laureate in the Jefferson Building of the Library of Congress is full of grand passages and unexpected turns, befitting the rich and somewhat vexed history of the state-sanctioned poet here and abroad. On the one hand, few buildings are as glorious a celebration of the marriage of the cultivated mind and the republic as the Jefferson Building, built one hundred years after the signing of the Declaration of Independence in the Italian Renaissance style that Thomas Jefferson believed to be the paragon of stately architecture. No writer has a more august place in which to work. On the other hand—well, good luck finding the tucked-away nook called the Poetry Office on the high floor of its remote wing in the Library, at the end of a narrow unmarked hall lined mostly with rooms set aside for the House of Representatives' teenage pages. You might think our country wants both to flaunt and to hide the fact that the only official job in the arts in the United States is for a poet.

Ambivalence about poetry's place in politics extends back to the earliest writing we have on art and civilization. Over two and half millennia ago, Plato kicked poets out of his ideal republic because their poems distracted philosopher-kings and their charges from ordered, rational thought: "Poetry feeds and waters the passions instead of drying them up. She lets them rule although they ought to be controlled." Plato did make an exception for poets who increased "happiness and virtue" by composing "hymns to gods and praises of famous men." These days many classical scholars argue that we shouldn't take Plato too literally on this one. While it is true, they point out, that Plato dismissed the emotional content of popular sagas like Homer's *Odyssey,* he nevertheless peppers his discourse with poetic flourishes like dramatic personae who speak in pleasing meters and use allusions, complex allegories, and vivid metaphors. Plato well knew, as have most revered politicians, that no one listens to prose that is too literal and didactic. Humans respond to figurative language. We remember sections of speeches because of their striking cadence and imagery. Poets are masters, most of them painstakingly trained, at cultivating such language, and politicians need some poetry in their rhetoric in order to charm, instruct, and lead the masses.

In ancient Greece the laurel was sacred to the god Apollo, patron of music and fine arts, and was used to form a wreath for poets and heroes. In the Middle Ages the Romans publicly conferred the title of laureate upon Francesco Petrarch for his classical scholarship and a long Latin epic he wrote celebrating Italy's connection to the ancient world. But Petrarch is best known for the cycle of intimate love poems he wrote in Italian to the fair-haired, blue-eyed Laura—just the kind of poetry Plato warned us about. The tradition of crowning one exemplary poet settled in England in the mid-sixteenth century, when appointed poets served for life and received a modest annuity from the royal household, sometimes in the form of wine, in exchange for verse delivered on special occasions. In a vitriolic footnote to *The History of the Decline and Fall of the Roman Empire,* Edward Gibbon called for abolishing the practice of tethering "stipendiary poets" to the crown because it made poetry "false and venal." Thomas Gray was the first poet to turn the job down, saying he would rather serve as "rat-catcher to his Majesty." When he was seventy-three William Wordsworth tried to refuse Queen Victoria's appointment but relented after her prime minister struck out the occasional verse clause, promising "you shall have nothing required of you." Wordsworth's brief spell as laureate, however, lives on in Lord Byron's dedication to *Don Juan,* a metered screed rebuking any poet who would sell out and sing before the king. Real poets of the Byronic order don't wear laurels.

When the job traveled to the United States, it had the good fortune to be designed by a poet, Archibald MacLeish, who was appointed by President Roosevelt and served as Librarian of Congress from 1939 to 1944. MacLeish named the post "consultant in poetry to the Library of Congress," partly to distance the job from its imperial associations. While the Librarian still selects our representative poet, the post's $35,000 stipend and the costs of running the Library's literary programs are covered by a private endowment started in 1936 and augmented from time to time with gifts from eccentric donors, like the anonymous one who delivered her $100,000 in a hatbox. In 1986 Congress voted to change the name to "poet laureate consultant in poetry" to increase the post's visibility. Robert Penn Warren, our first official poet laureate, said he had no intention of performing as a "hired applauder" or of writing "odes on the death of the President's Cat."

This brings us back to the Jefferson Building. Several poets have remarked that the post's real perk is the view from the desk in the Poetry Office. Conrad Aiken declared it "the best in Washington," overlooking "the Capitol on one side and the Supreme Court" on the other and "out to river and country too—all Washington." Aiken took full advantage of the lack of a specific job description during his tenure, drifting out for long lunches, strolling among the cherry blossoms, and holding informal, sherry-enhanced discussions with his writer friends in the poetry wing.

Most poets have taken the word "consultant" in their lengthy title to heart. They travel the county, and sometimes the world, giving readings and speaking about poetry; they answer the flood of mail addressed to "United States Poet Laureate" each year; and they devise ways to bring poetry to marginalized communities. And not even a poet can eke out a living on the laureate's stipend. Many continue to work at their day jobs, which usually means teaching, though some have also worked as doctors, executives, farmers, and editors. In the last fifteen years, laureates have harnessed new media and developed dozens of websites, connecting poetry to jazz and environmental causes, piping verse into schools and prisons. A few poets have made it clear to the Librarian that if selected they would continue to live quietly as poets and read only at the start and finish of the Library's annual reading series. "Some of us have chosen to spend a lot of time running around the country lighting poetry bonfires," says Billy Collins, poet laureate from 2001 to 2003, but he notes that "the job can be tailored to each individual's personality."

Perhaps the best indication of a healthy distance between the seat of government and the United States poet laureate consultant in poetry is that no laureate has been asked to read at a president's inauguration since Robert Frost charmed listeners at John F. Kennedy's ceremony in 1961. Kennedy said he asked Frost to read not in order to sing a hymn of praise to his leadership but because Frost's poetry inspired respect for independent thought and the full range of human experience:

> I asked Robert Frost to come and speak at the Inauguration . . . because I felt he had something important to say to those of us who are occupied with the business of Government, that he would remind us that we are dealing with life, the hopes and fears of millions of people. . . . He has said it well in a poem called "Choose Something Like a Star," in which he speaks of the fairest star in sight and says:

> > *It asks a little of us here.*
> > *It asks of us a certain height,*
> > *So when at times the mob is swayed*
> > *To carry praise or blame too far,*
> > *We may choose something like a star*
> > *To stay our minds on and be staid.*

In other words, Kennedy tapped into the very lyrical power Plato urged his audience to resist. Every poet in this anthology writes poems that in countless ways celebrate the freedom we have to write and think and question what it means to live, work, love, mourn, and pursue happiness in America in a particular time—and all flow from Walt Whitman's great 1855 paean to democracy and individualism, "Song of Myself."

No poet who has served as poet laureate changed his or her style in order to sing to the White House. Some have been inspired by their side view of the Capitol to write poems with a discernible political content, to protest war or to commemorate lives lost in conflict, for example. Some have used their perch as a bully pulpit from which to criticize U.S. foreign policy or cuts in funding to the arts or environmental causes. Some write purely from the imagination, set off from anything resembling external reality. All, in a chorus of distinct and memorable voices, fulfill Emerson's quiet maxim on self-reliance, "The eye was placed where one ray should fall, that it might testify of that particular ray." Pragmatically speaking, a poet's very vocation, whether she or he winds up laureled or not, can be seen as a declaration of independence. Stanley Kunitz (poet laureate in 2001, at the age of ninety-five) called poetry the only uncorrupted form of expression because it has no market value—the opposite of Frank Zappa's definition of art, "making something out of nothing and selling it." Perhaps this is why, given all the vexing questions of poetry's place in politics, poets are the only writers leaders want—or fear to have—by their sides. Who has ever heard of a philosopher, historian, novelist, or creative-nonfiction laureate?

The poetry collected in this volume illustrates the idiosyncratic and subjective range of modern American experience: each poem is, as Charles Simic (poet laureate from 2005 to 2006) wrote of lyric poetry, a "snapshot" in which a reader might see herself. Rather than upholding any kind of status quo, the poets in this volume testify in countless voices and styles; as such, this book is a celebration of freedom of speech in motion. But the list of laureates could reflect a fuller span of North American identity. To date there have been few poets of Native American descent and no Latino-American or Asian-American laureates. There have only been three African-American poets selected by the Librarians of Congress—not enough in a country whose traditions of personal narrative and innovative music stem from the sufferings and triumphs of the millions of people displaced and transplanted by the African slave trade.

Above all, the poets that touch down every year or two in the Library of Congress are the gatekeepers of the American idiom. Plato's student Aristotle pushed aside all questions of the just state in his treatise on poetry, which he defined as a "vehicle of expression" employing "current terms," "rare words," and "metaphors." Poets, regardless of temperament or style, work with words. What they choose to do with those words—celebrate or excoriate the state; contemplate a great dinner or a field of flowers; address a lost love, a pinup girl, a scoundrel, a deceased parent, or a beloved child—is between them and their muses. Some poets believe that original use of language can shape the public imagination and thereby influence public values and policy; to some, the greatest expression of liberty is the ability to stand to the side and observe, dream, remember, and testify.

Whatever the case may be, the United States was conceived from the pen of the thirty-three-year-old Thomas Jefferson, entrusted with drafting the first version of the Declaration of Independence (most of which remained unaltered by older statesmen called in to polish and edit) because of his way with words. Our very sense of state emerged from the deft and memorable use of language and the compelling sound of one man's voice on the page. It *is* symbolically fitting, then, that our laureates work when they can find a quiet moment in a building named for Jefferson, set off from but surveying the nation's Capitol.

ACKNOWLEDGMENTS

Books like this contain multitudes. The project began with a call from Martha Kaplan, who came up with the idea for an anthology of work by the U.S. poets laureate with her client and excellent writer W. Ralph Eubanks, director of publishing at the Library of Congress.

Ralph Eubanks and his industrious, cheerful, and patient staff at the Library of Congress were a pleasure to work with. Blaine Marshall helped select the poet photographs and cleared all photo permissions. Evelyn Sinclair, to whom this book is dedicated, was a boundless source of encouragement and information; her prompt e-mails in response to each poet selection and introduction were just what I needed to keep them coming. Patricia Gray in the poetry office answered questions promptly and helped us get many of the photographs for this book. I thank her also for keeping the office of the poet laureate in order. It's impossible to overstate all the help Elizabeth Eshelman provided with her orderly systems for keeping track of our permissions process. This book would not have met our final deadline without her focus and dedication. I look forward to reading *her* writing in books someday soon.

Back in New York this project moved forward, mostly in the summers, with tremendous help from several groups of splendid interns. Lauren Lila Feinberg worked on this book from the very beginning and helped supervise two other interns from Barnard College, Alexandra Loizzo and Alisa Huntley. During the last summer of work, I found a group of young poets and poetry readers who helped me meet our looming deadline. From Sarah Lawrence College, Stephanie Miller helped with introduction and photography research. At the Saint Ann's School in Brooklyn, huge thanks to Catherine Hochman and Liam Lee for their many trips to the library and attention to the order and copyright material for each and every poem. Kimi Lee, Samuel Sullivan, and Evan Walker-Wells were energetic, insightful, dogged, and open to the joy of finding that next marvelous poem. Martin Skobel, famous poetry teacher at Saint Ann's, clearly knows what he is doing. His students are the strongest readers of poetry (they read because they love it) I have encountered in more than a decade of teaching.

It's been heartening to turn this book's manuscript over to the great poetry publishers at Norton, to see the piles of annotated photocopies transform into this beautiful book. Thanks to Adrienne Davich and Alison Liss for helping keep track of the book's many drafts and moving parts, and to Julia Druskin and Nancy Palmquist for ably steering the book toward production. Special thanks to Chin-Yee Lai for the spirited final cover design. And heartfelt thanks to Jill Bialosky for her patience, kindness, and calm, assured leadership throughout the entire process of making this book—and for publishing many of my favorite poets (many of them laureates) with such grace and care.

On the home front I am more grateful than I can say to Eric, Asher, and Silver Liftin, who saw every part of the book emerge and inspired me to stick with it. Thank you for listening to poems, for all of your brilliant suggestions for the cover, for delicious meals, and for your excitement at each stage of this book's development. Sara Goodman and Mott Hupfel, no more huge stacks of books at the beach, I promise. Benno Schmidt, Anne McMillan, Christina Schmidt, Ben and Sara Schmidt, John and Wendy Schmidt, Ralph Schmidt, and Susan Babcock, thank you for your support, cheer, delicious food, and readings of many of these poems in Millbrook after dinner. Helen Whitney, thank you for your attention at the perfect time. I wish my mother and her mother were alive to see this book. Harold and Jeanne Bloom, thanks for tea, cozy meals, for listening and advice about this book's shape and scope. Tom Schmidt helped research and lay out this book's proposal years ago and was the first reader of the last piece of writing for this book, the general introduction. Thanks to Alex Sapirstein, Kay Moffett, Neil Parker, and Caroline Marshall, great friends, great readers.

Deepest thanks to Alice Quinn, the world's most magical first boss, for nurturing the careers of many of the poets herein, both at *The New Yorker* and at the Poetry Society of America, and for arranging the book's PSA reading. Dan Menaker, wonderful non-mentor and friend, encouraged this book from the proposal to the foreword. My colleagues at Barnard College and Sarah Lawrence College provided intellectual nourishment and flexible teaching schedules while I was working on this project. My students have grown used to, and even now encourage, my poetry digressions. It's wonderful to know that the audience for poetry is ever replenishing. Reading sections of Billy Collins's splendid foreword aloud to my kids in that Starbucks in Brooklyn was one of the book's great moments.

Above all, thanks to the poets collected in the volume, gatekeepers of the American idiom, and to the Library of Congress for giving our poets laureate a room of their own in America's greatest library—and for not requiring that they do much of anything while poet laureate.

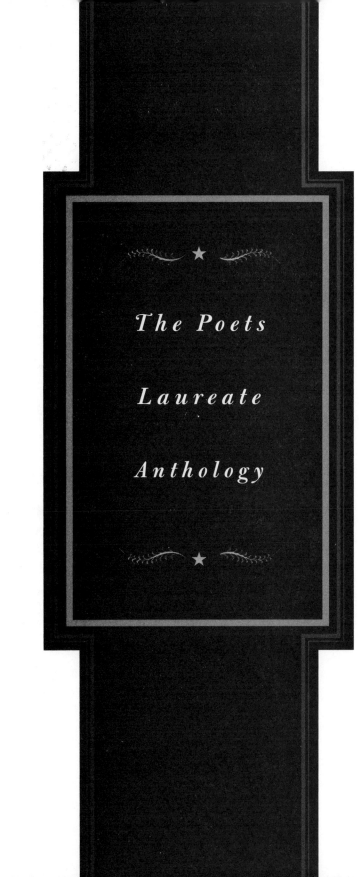

The Poets

Laureate

Anthology

W. S. MERWIN

(1927-)

Poet Laureate Consultant in Poetry (2010-)

Special Bicentennial Consultant (1999-2000),
with Rita Dove and Louise Glück

Prose is about something, but poetry is about what can't be said. Why do
people turn to poetry when all of a sudden the Twin Towers get hit, or when
their marriage breaks up, or when the person they love most in the world
drops dead in the same room? Because they can't say it. They can't say it at
all, and they want something that addresses what can't be said.

W. S. Merwin may be the only poet writing in English whose poems are instantly recognizable by how they look on the printed page. Since the late 1960s, Merwin has written in unpunctuated flowing free verse, often edged with rippling, staggered borders. He writes in an indirect, impersonal narrative voice, making the words and music float on the page and linger in memory with a quiet, numinous intensity. The two-time Pulitzer Prize–winning octogenarian author of more than twenty-five volumes of poetry, two dozen books of translations, eight works of prose, and several verse plays is decidedly unprecious when it comes to sitting down to write. Like Emily Dickinson (another great master of unorthodox punctuation, whose poems are similarly recognizable at first glance), Merwin begins to compose poems longhand, on whatever stray pieces of scrap paper are lying around. In a recent interview with Bill Moyers, he said, "I can't imagine ever writing anything of any kind on a machine. I never tried to write either poetry or prose on a typewriter. I like to do it on useless paper, scrap paper, because it's of no importance. If I put a nice new sheet of white paper down in front of myself and took up a new, nicely sharpened anything, it would be instant inhibition. . . . But if it's something, if I need somewhere to write it down it will be on the back of an envelope, or something like that. Then it's okay. It's just to keep it there so I can find out where it goes from there."

William Stanley Merwin was born in New York in 1927 and grew up in Union City, New Jersey, and Scranton, Pennsylvania, the son of a Presbyterian minister. His earliest poems were hymns he wrote for his father: "As soon as I could write with a little pencil, I was writing these little hymns and illustrating them and I thought they should be sung in church." He received a scholarship to Princeton University and when he was eighteen met Ezra Pound, who told him, "If you want to be a poet you have to take it seriously. You have to work on it the way you would work on anything else and you have to do it every day. . . . you should write about seventy-five lines every day. . . .

And he said, you don't really have anything to write about. . . . At the age of eighteen, you think you do but you don't. . . . The way to do it is to learn a language and translate. . . . That way, you can practice and you can find out what you can do with your language." Merwin has described himself as a desultory student who to this day feels claustrophobic on a university campus: "I spent most of my time either in the university library, or riding in the country: I had discovered that the polo and ROTC stables were full of horses with no one to exercise them." He took off upon graduation and made a living moving around Europe, tutoring the children of wealthy families and translating from many Romance languages. At the same time he was working on his first collection of jewel-like poems, many of them in old verse forms taken from the poets he had been translating. His first book, *The Mask of Janus*, was selected by W. H. Auden for the Yale Series of Younger Poets Prize in 1952. In the late sixties Merwin, a committed pacifist, began to write poems protesting the Vietnam War, and in 1971 he refused to accept the money for his first Pulitzer Prize and published a letter to the *New York Review of Books* saying that he would donate the money to antiwar causes. During this period he used classical legends to explore personal and political themes and began to write in his newly unpunctuated style. Merwin's writing is unified by the recurring theme of man's separation from nature, and its disastrous consequences for the human and animal world.

In 1976 Merwin moved to Hawaii to study Zen Buddhism and ecological preservation. He now lives on an old pineapple plantation in Hawaii, on the edge of a dormant volcano that rises 10,000 feet above the sea. For over thirty years he has worked to restore the land to its original rainforest state, populating it with rare and endangered palm trees. Merwin was once asked what social role a poet plays—if any—in America. He commented: "I think there's a kind of desperate hope built into poetry now that one really wants, hopelessly, to save the world. One is trying to say everything that can be said for the things that one loves while there's still time. I think that's a social role, don't you? . . . We keep expressing our anger and our love, and we hope, hopelessly perhaps, that it will have some effect. But . . . one can't live only in despair and anger without eventually destroying the thing one is angry in defense of. The world is still here . . . and there is a need to pay attention to the things around us while they are still around us. If you don't pay that attention, the anger is just bitterness."

To The Words

When it happens you are not there

O you beyond numbers
beyond recollection
passed on from breath to breath
given again
from day to day from age
to age
charged with knowledge
knowing nothing

indifferent elders
indispensable and sleepless

keepers of our names
before ever we came
to be called by them

you that were
formed to begin with
you that were cried out
you that were spoken
to begin with
to say what could not be said

ancient precious
and helpless ones

say it

September 17, 2001

Separation

Your absence has gone through me
Like thread through a needle.
Everything I do is stitched with its color.

The Way to the River

The way to the river leads past the names of
Ash the sleeves the wreaths of hinges
Through the song of the bandage vendor

I lay your name by my voice
As I go

The way to the river leads past the late
Doors and the games of the children born looking backwards
They play that they are broken glass
The numbers wait in the halls and the clouds
Call
From windows

They play that they are old they are putting the horizon
Into baskets they are escaping they are
Hiding

I step over the sleepers the fires the calendars
My voice turns to you

I go past the juggler's condemned building the hollow
Windows gallery
Of invisible presidents the same motion in them all
In a parked cab by the sealed wall the hats are playing
Sort of poker with somebody's

Old snapshots game I don't understand they lose
The rivers one
After the other I begin to know where I am
I am home

Be here the flies from the house of the mapmaker
Walk on our letters I can tell
And the days hang medals between us
I have lit our room with a glove of yours be
Here I turn
To your name and the hour remembers
Its one word
Now

Be here what can we
Do for the dead the footsteps full of money
I offer you what I have my
Poverty

To the city of wires I have brought home a handful
Of water I walk slowly
In front of me they are building the empty

Ages I see them reflected not for long
Be here I am no longer ashamed of time it is too brief its hands
Have no names
I have passed it I know

　　　Oh Necessity you with the face you with
　　　All the faces

This is written on the back of everything

But we
Will read it together

When You Go Away

When you go away the wind clicks around to the north
The painters work all day but at sundown the paint falls
Showing the black walls
The clock goes back to striking the same hour
That has no place in the years

And at night wrapped in the bed of ashes
In one breath I wake
It is the time when the beards of the dead get their growth
I remember that I am falling
That I am the reason
And that my words are the garment of what I shall never be
Like the tucked sleeve of a one-armed boy

The Asians Dying

When the forests have been destroyed their darkness remains
The ash the great walker follows the possessors
Forever
Nothing they will come to is real
Nor for long
Over the watercourses
Like ducks in the time of the ducks
The ghosts of the villages trail in the sky
Making a new twilight
Rain falls into the open eyes of the dead
Again again with its pointless sound
When the moon finds them they are the color of everything

The nights disappear like bruises but nothing is healed
The dead go away like bruises
The blood vanishes into the poisoned farmlands
Pain the horizon
Remains
Overhead the seasons rock
They are paper bells
Calling to nothing living

The possessors move everywhere under Death their star
Like columns of smoke they advance into the shadows
Like thin flames with no light
They with no past
And fire their only future

For a Coming Extinction

Gray whale
Now that we are sending you to The End
That great god
Tell him
That we who follow you invented forgiveness
And forgive nothing

I write as though you could understand
And I could say it
One must always pretend something
Among the dying
When you have left the seas nodding on their stalks
Empty of you
Tell him that we were made
On another day

The bewilderment will diminish like an echo
Winding along your inner mountains
Unheard by us
And find its way out
Leaving behind it the future
Dead
And ours

When you will not see again
The whale calves trying the light
Consider what you will find in the black garden
And its court
The sea cows the Great Auks the gorillas
The irreplaceable hosts ranged countless
And foreordaining as stars
Our sacrifices

Join your word to theirs
Tell him
That it is we who are important

Fox Sleep

On a road through the mountains with a friend many years ago
        I came to a curve on a slope where a clear stream
flowed down flashing across dark rocks through its own
        echoes that could neither be caught nor forgotten
it was the turning of autumn and already
        the mornings were cold with ragged clouds in the hollows
long after sunrise but the pasture sagging like a roof
        the glassy water and flickering yellow leaves
in the few poplars and knotted plum trees were held up
        in a handful of sunlight that made the slates on the silent
mill by the stream glisten white above their ruin
        and a few relics of the life before had been arranged
in front of the open mill house to wait
        pale in the daylight out on the open mountain
after whatever they had been made for was over
        the dew was drying on them and there were few who took that road
who might buy one of them and take it away somewhere
        to be unusual to be the only one
to become unknown a wooden bed stood there on rocks
        a cradle the color of dust a cracked oil jar iron pots
wooden wheels iron wheels stone wheels the tall box of a clock
        and among them a ring of white stone the size of an
embrace set into another of the same size
        an iron spike rising from the ring where the wooden
handle had fitted that turned it in its days as a hand mill
        you could see if you looked closely that the top ring

that turned in the other had been carved long before in the form
      of a fox lying nose in tail seeming to be
asleep the features worn almost away where it
      had gone around and around grinding grain and salt
to go into the dark and to go on and remember

. . .

What I thought I had left I kept finding again
      but when I went looking for what I thought I remembered
as anyone could have foretold it was not there
      when I went away looking for what I had to do
I found that I was living where I was a stranger
      but when I retraced my steps the familiar vision
turned opaque and all surface and in the wrong places
      and the places where I had been a stranger appeared to me
to be where I had been at home called by name and answering
      getting ready to go away and going away

. . .

Every time they assembled and he spoke to them
      about waking there was an old man who stood listening
and left before the others until one day the old man stayed
      and Who are you he asked the old man
and the old man answered I am not a man
      many lives ago I stood where you are standing
and they assembled in front of me and I spoke to them
      about waking until one day one of them asked me
When someone has wakened to what is really there
      is that person free of the chain of consequences
and I answered yes and with that I turned into a fox
      and I have been a fox for five hundred lives
and now I have come to ask you to say what will
      free me from the body of a fox please tell me

when someone has wakened to what is really there
     is that person free of the chain of consequences
and this time the answer was That person sees it as it is
     then the old man said Thank you for waking me
you have set me free of the body of the fox
     which you will find on the other side of the mountain
I ask you to bury it please as one of your own
     that evening he announced a funeral service
for one of them but they said nobody has died
     then he led them to the other side of the mountain
and a cave where they found a fox's body
     and he told them the story and they buried the fox
as one of them but later one of them asked
     what if he had given the right answer every time

. . .

Once again I was there and once again I was leaving
     and again it seemed as though nothing had changed
even while it was all changing but this time
     was a time of ending this time the long marriage was over
the orbits were flying apart it was autumn again
     sunlight tawny in the fields where the shadows
each day grew longer and the still afternoons
     ripened the distance until the sun went down
across the valley and the full moon rose out of the trees
     it was the time of year when I was born and that evening
I went to see friends for the last time and I came back
     after midnight along the road white with the moon
I was crossing the bars of shadow and seeing ahead of me
     the wide silent valley full of silver light
and there just at the corner of the land that I had
     come back to so many times and now was leaving
at the foot of the wall built of pale stone I saw the body
     stretched in the grass and it was a fox a vixen

just dead with no sign of how it had come to happen
  no blood the long fur warm in the dewy grass
nothing broken or lost or torn or unfinished
  I carried her home to bury her in the garden
in the morning of the clear autumn that she had left
  and to stand afterward in the turning daylight

. . .

There are the yellow beads of the stonecrops and the twisted flags
  of dried irises knuckled into the hollows
of moss and rubbly limestone on the waves of the low wall
  the ivy has climbed along them where the weasel ran
the light has kindled to gold the late leaves of the cherry tree
  over the lane by the house chimney there is the roof
and the window looking out over the garden
  summer and winter there is the field below the house
there is the broad valley far below them all with the curves
  of the river a strand of sky threaded through it
and the notes of bells rising out of it faint as smoke
  and there beyond the valley above the rim of the wall
the line of mountains I recognize like a line of writing
  that has come back when I had thought it was forgotten

Before the Flood

Why did he promise me
that we would build ourselves
an ark all by ourselves
out in back of the house
on New York Avenue
in Union City New Jersey
to the singing of the streetcars

after the story
of Noah whom nobody
believed about the waters
that would rise over everything
when I told my father
I wanted us to build
an ark of our own there
in the backyard under
the kitchen could we do that
he told me that we could
I want to I said and will we
he promised me that we would
why did he promise that
I wanted us to start then
nobody will believe us
I said that we are building
an ark because the rains
are coming and that was true
nobody ever believed
we would build an ark there
nobody would believe
that the waters were coming

Good People

From the kindness of my parents
I suppose it was that I held
that belief about suffering

imagining that if only
it could come to the attention
of any person with normal

feelings certainly anyone
literate who might have gone

to college they would comprehend
pain when it went on before them
and would do something about it
whenever they saw it happen
in the time of pain the present
they would try to stop the bleeding
for example with their hands

but it escapes their attention
or there may be reasons for it
the victims under the blankets
the meat counters the maimed children
the animals the animals
staring from the end of the world

To the Consolations of Philosophy

Thank you but
not just at the moment

I know you will say
I have said that before
I know you have been
there all along somewhere
in another time zone

I studied once
those beautiful instructions
when I was young and
far from here

they seemed distant then
they seem distant now
from everything I remember

I hope they stayed with you
when the noose started to tighten
and you could say no more
and after wisdom
and the days in iron
the eyes started from your head

I know the words
must have been set down
partly for yourself
unjustly condemned after
a good life

I know the design
of the world is beyond
our comprehension
thank you
but grief is selfish and in
the present when
the stars do not seem to move
I was not listening

I know it is not
sensible to expect
fortune to grant her
gifts forever
I know

Good Night

Sleep softly my old love
my beauty in the dark
night is a dream we have
as you know as you know

night is a dream you know
an old love in the dark
around you as you go
without end as you know

in the night where you go
sleep softly my old love
without end in the dark
in the love that you know

Rain Light

All day the stars watch from long ago
my mother said I am going now
when you are alone you will be all right
whether or not you know you will know
look at the old house in the dawn rain
all the flowers are forms of water
the sun reminds them through a white cloud
touches the patchwork spread on the hill
the washed colors of the afterlife
that lived there long before you were born
see how they wake without a question
even though the whole world is burning

Alba

Climbing in the mist I came to a terrace wall
and saw above it a small field of broad beans in flower
their white fragrance was flowing through the first light
of morning there a little way up the mountain
where I had made my way through the olive groves
and under the blossoming boughs of the almonds
above the old hut of the charcoal burner
where suddenly the scent of the bean flowers found me
and as I took the next step I heard
the creak of the harness and the mule's shod hooves
striking stones in the furrow and then the low voice
of the man talking softly praising the mule
as he walked behind through the cloud in his white shirt
along the row and between his own words
he was singing under his breath a few phrases
at a time of the same song singing it
to his mule it seemed as I listened
watching their breaths and not understanding a word

Forgotten Fountain

Water dripping year after year
from the green mossed crevice in the east cliff
through my absences and through winter
through the shadows after midday
as they deepened to nightfall
the clear drops arriving through the stone
with no color of their own as they
appear one by one on the threshold
of the world in its full color
and each one pauses for a moment

before starting on its way down
to itself as it has been doing
ever since the cliff rose
from the seafloor and then the bees found it
the badgers the foxes the birds
until the day came with voices
from the village to clear the slope
singing as the tools rose and fell
turning the stiff yellow soil to plant
vineyards and peaches and I stood
by the clear source once listening
to their last singing together
with the mattocks keeping time and I
thought of Édouard and the village
as it had been when he was young
and his name was called with the others
to the colors as they put it
in the language of elsewhere and of
what it felt like in those last days
to be leaving for Verdun with no words
in a moment with no color of its own

KAY RYAN

(1945-)

Poet Laureate Consultant in Poetry (2007-2010)

It's poetry's uselessness that excites me. . . . Prose is practical language. Conversation is practical language. Let them handle the usefulness jobs. But of course, poetry has its balms. It makes us feel less lonely by one. It makes us have more room inside ourselves. But it's paralyzing to think of usefulness and poetry in the same breath.

Chief among the pleasures found in Kay Ryan's poetry is her unorthodox use of rhyme: slant rhymes form small light bridges throughout her slim poems, connecting a mid-line here with a final word there. It's a technique she calls "recombinant rhyme" and likens to adding "a snip of the jellyfish's glow-in-the-dark gene to bunnies [to] make them glow green. By snipping up pieces of sound and redistributing them throughout a poem I found I could get the poem to go a little bit luminescent."

Hers is a poetics of play: "There's always a smidgen of laughter in it, however sad it might be, however lonely or lost. If you feel worse after you've read it, then I have failed." Ryan, who was born in 1945 in San Jose, grew up in the San Joaquin Valley and has lived in California for most of her life. She first sensed her poetic calling when she was reading a novel (she thinks it was Proust), and suddenly the entire page began to recombine in rhyme. For more than thirty years, Ryan has limited her professional responsibilities to the part-time teaching of remedial English, thus leaving much of her life free for "a lot of mountain bike riding plus the idle maunderings poets feed upon." She has never taken a creative writing class. In an interview she outlined her life's aims: "I have tried to live very quietly, so I could be happy. . . . It seems like many people think that if you drive yourself crazy, then you can write. I wanted to see what a fortunate life would produce. What writing would come out of this mind that didn't try to torment itself." Most days begin with writing in pajamas in bed ("I've always liked the uniform of the poet"), then biking, chatting with strangers about fruit in supermarkets ("I love superficial relationships with people. They satisfy me"). She steadfastly refuses to carry a notebook and often finds herself thinking in clichés, which she teases apart and refreshes in poems that resemble Emily Dickinson's riddle poems.

Most of Ryan's career has been spent on the outskirts of the literary establishment. She self-published her first book and for decades had trouble placing her work in periodicals. But she never stopped writing and, when the literary world came to embrace her work, had an abundance of material and has published her eight award-winning volumes of poetry in quick succession.

Things Shouldn't Be So Hard

A life should leave
deep tracks:
ruts where she
went out and back
to get the mail
or move the hose
around the yard;
where she used to
stand before the sink,
a worn-out place;
beneath her hand
the china knobs
rubbed down to
white pastilles;
the switch she
used to feel for
in the dark
almost erased.
Her things should
keep her marks.
The passage
of a life should show;
it should abrade.
And when life stops,
a certain space—
however small—
should be left scarred
by the grand and

damaging parade.
Things shouldn't
be so hard.

This Life

It's a pickle, this life.
Even shut down to a trickle
it carries every kind of particle
that causes strife on a grander scale:
to be miniature is to be swallowed
by a miniature whale. Zeno knew
the law that we know: no matter
how carefully diminished, a race
can only be *half* finished with success;
then comes the endless halving of the rest—
the ribbon's stalled approach, the helpless
red-faced urgings of the coach.

Flamingo Watching

Wherever the flamingo goes,
she brings a city's worth
of furbelows. She seems
unnatural by nature—
too vivid and peculiar
a structure to be pretty,
and flexible to the point

of oddity. Perched on
those legs, anything she does
seems like an act. Descending
on her egg or draping her head
along her back, she's
too exact and sinuous
to convince an audience
she's serious. The natural elect,
they think, would be less pink,
less able to relax their necks,
less flamboyant in general.
They privately expect that it's some
poorly jointed bland grey animal
with mitts for hands
whom God protects.

Force

Nothing forced works.
The Gordian knot just worsens
if it's jerked at by a person.
One of the main stations
of the cross is patience.
Another, of course, is impatience.
There is such a thing as
too much tolerance
for unpleasant situations,
a time when the gentle
teasing out of threads
ceases to be pleasing
to a woman born for conquest.
Instead she must assault
the knot or alp or everest

with something sharp,
and take upon herself
the moral warp of sudden progress.

Paired Things

Who, who had only seen wings,
could extrapolate the
skinny sticks of things
birds use for land,
the backward way they bend,
the silly way they stand?
And who, only studying
birdtracks in the sand,
could think those little forks
had decamped on the wind?
So many paired things seem odd.
Who ever would have dreamed
the broad winged raven of despair
would quit the air and go
bandylegged upon the ground,
a common crow?

Doubt

A chick has just so much time
to chip its way out, just so much
egg energy to apply to the weakest spot
or whatever spot it started at.
It can't afford doubt. Who can?

Doubt uses albumen
at twice the rate of work.
One backward look by any of us
can cost what it cost Orpheus.
Neither may you answer
the stranger's knock;
you know it is the Person from Porlock
who eats dreams for dinner,
his napkin stained the most delicate colors.

Mirage Oases

First among places
susceptible to trespass
are mirage oases

whose graduated pools
and shaded grasses, palms
and speckled fishes give
before the lightest pressure
and are wrecked.

For they live
only in the kingdom
of suspended wishes,

thrive only at our pleasure
checked.

That Vase of Lilacs

Not just lilacs
are like that;
other purples also
leave us vacant
portals, susceptible
to vagrant spirits.
But take that vase
of lilacs: who goes
near it is erased.
In spite of Proust,
the senses don't
attach us to a place
or time: we're *used*
by sweetness—
taken, defenseless,
invaded by a line
of Saracens,
Picts, Angles,
double rows of
fragrance-loving
ancients—people
matched casually
by nose in an
impersonal and
intermittent immortality
of purple.

Turtle

Who would be a turtle who could help it?
A barely mobile hard roll, a four-oared helmet,
she can ill afford the chances she must take
in rowing toward the grasses that she eats.
Her track is graceless, like dragging
a packing-case places, and almost any slope
defeats her modest hopes. Even being practical,
she's often stuck up to the axle on her way
to something edible. With everything optimal,
she skirts the ditch which would convert
her shell into a serving dish. She lives
below luck-level, never imagining some lottery
will change her load of pottery to wings.
Her only levity is patience,
the sport of truly chastened things.

Relief

We know it is close
to something lofty.
Simply getting over being sick
or finding lost property
has in it the leap,
the purge, the quick humility
of witnessing a birth—
how love seeps up
and retakes the earth.
There is a dreamy
wading feeling to your walk
inside the current

of restored riches,
clocks set back,
disasters averted.

A Plain Ordinary Steel Needle Can Float on Pure Water

—Ripley's *Believe It or Not!*

Who hasn't seen
a plain ordinary
steel needle float serene
on water as if lying on a pillow?
The water cuddles up like Jell-O.
It's a treat to see water
so rubbery, a needle
so peaceful, the point encased
in the tenderest dimple.
It seems so *simple*
when things or people
have modified each other's qualities
somewhat;
we almost forget the oddity
of that.

A Hundred Bolts of Satin

All you
have to lose
is one
connection

and the mind
uncouples
all the way back.
It seems
to have been
a train.
There seems
to have been
a track.
The things
that you
unpack
from the
abandoned cars
cannot sustain
life: a crate of
tractor axles,
for example,
a dozen dozen
clasp knives,
a hundred
bolts of satin—
perhaps you
specialized
more than
you imagined.

Crown

Too much rain
loosens trees.
In the hills giant oaks
fall upon their knees.

You can touch parts
you have no right to—
places only birds
should fly to.

Home to Roost

The chickens
are circling and
blotting out the
day. The sun is
bright, but the
chickens are in
the way. Yes,
the sky is dark
with chickens,
dense with them.
They turn and
then they turn
again. These
are the chickens
you let loose
one at a time
and small—
various breeds.
Now they have
come home
to roost—all
the same kind
at the same speed.

Sharks' Teeth

Everything contains some
silence. Noise gets
its zest from the
small shark's-tooth-
shaped fragments
of rest angled
in it. An hour
of city holds maybe
a minute of these
remnants of a time
when silence reigned,
compact and dangerous
as a shark. Sometimes
a bit of a tail
or fin can still
be sensed in parks.

Hide and Seek

It's hard not
to jump out
instead of
waiting to be
found. It's
hard to be
alone so long
and then hear
someone come
around. It's

like some form
of skin's developed
in the air
that, rather
than have torn,
you tear.

Odd Blocks

Every Swiss-village
calendar instructs
as to how stone
gathers the landscape
around it, how
glacier-scattered
thousand-ton
monuments to
randomness become
fixed points in
finding home.
Order is always
starting over.
And why not
also in the self,
the odd blocks,
all lost and left,
become first facts
toward which later
a little town
looks back?

CHARLES SIMIC

(1938-)

Poet Laureate Consultant in Poetry (2007-2008)

I remember once—I was teaching in the schools in El Paso, Texas. And a student had asked . . . me what poetry was good for. And I was stunned, because it's such a serious question. It's a difficult question. And suddenly a hand went up. It was a young woman. So I said . . . "What do you think?" And she said, "To remind people of their own humanity." That struck me as so sensible, so moving, so poignant . . . . You know, I'm mortal, I exist, I have my own conscience, I have my own being, myself. Here I am with this universe. Maybe there's a God; maybe there's no God. This is my predicament, my human predicament. Poetry reminds readers of that.

U pon being appointed poet laureate, Charles Simic, the author of nineteen books of poems and nearly that many of both criticism and translation of works from Serbo-Croatian languages, said, "I am especially touched and honored to be selected because I am an immigrant boy who didn't speak English until I was fifteen." Simic was born in Yugoslavia, and his childhood was marked by the events of World War II. He moved to Paris with his mother, a music teacher, when he was fifteen. A year later, they joined his father, after a ten-year separation, in New York, and then all moved to a suburb of Chicago. With characteristic dark humor, Simic said of arriving in America, "My travel agents were Hitler and Stalin."

Simic attended the University of Chicago, working nights in an office at the *Chicago Sun-Times*, but was drafted into the U.S. Army in 1961 and served until 1963. He earned his bachelor's degree from New York University in 1966. Though he moved to New Hampshire in 1973 to take a teaching job, his sensibility is decidedly urban, full of images from the war-torn Belgrade of his youth and the seedy New York hotels in which he stayed up all night writing his first poems: "I am not rapturous about nature, although I live in nature. I don't have some sort of nature poem where I idealize a sunrise or climbing a mountain or being outdoors." The city glimpsed through the haze of memory ("My memory is so poor that everything appears poorly lit and full of shadows") is Simic's milieu, and even his more rural poems seem to speak from the voice of the city poet on the lam.

Simic's love of American art forms such as film noir, jazz, and the found-object collages of outsider artists like Joseph Cornell infiltrate his poetry. In this sense, he shows us what is best about American art. But he is also scathing about the self-centeredness he sees in much American writing: "For most poetry today history does not exist. One can read literally hundreds of pages of contemporary poetry without encountering any significant aspect of our common twentieth-century existence."

Few writers are as cheerfully articulate about winding up in the land of opportunity—and as pointedly critical about American culture, seen with the clear eyes of the outsider. Simic has said he probably would have wound up as a gangster, or in a low-grade manual labor job, had he managed to survive and grow up in postwar Belgrade, where he was a below-average student and a troublemaker. He recalls scavenging the rubble of Belgrade as a boy, looking for gunpowder to trade for a "particularly tasty can of American corned beef."

Simic believes it is the lyric poet's responsibility to bear witness, to record his or her reactions to a historical moment so that there is an alternative narrative to the often distorting propaganda written for or by politicians: "The poet like anyone else is part of history, but he or she ought to be the conscious part. That's the ideal. . . . If history, as it comes through the historian, retains, analyzes, and connects significant events, in contrast, what poets insist on is history of 'unimportant' events. In place of historian's 'distance,' I want to experience the vulnerability of those participating in tragic events."

My Weariness of Epic Proportions

I like it when
Achilles
Gets killed
And even his buddy Patroclus—
And that hothead Hector—
And the whole Greek and Trojan
Jeunesse dorée
Are more or less
Expertly slaughtered
So there's finally
Peace and quiet
(The gods having momentarily
Shut up)
One can hear
A bird sing
And a daughter ask her mother
Whether she can go to the well
And of course she can
By that lovely little path
That winds through
The olive orchard

from *The World Doesn't End*

My mother was a braid of black smoke.
She bore me swaddled over the burning cities.
The sky was a vast and windy place for a child to play.
We met many others who were just like us. They were trying to put on their overcoats with arms made of smoke.
The high heavens were full of little shrunken deaf ears instead of stars.

I was stolen by the gypsies. My parents stole me right back. Then the gypsies stole me again. This went on for some time. One minute I was in the caravan suckling the dark teat of my new mother, the next I sat at the long dining room table eating my breakfast with a silver spoon.

It was the first day of spring. One of my fathers was singing in the bathtub; the other one was painting a live sparrow the colors of a tropical bird.

My father loved the strange books of André Breton. He'd raise the wine glass and toast those far-off evenings "when butterflies formed a single uncut ribbon." Or we'd go out for a piss in the back alley and he'd say: "Here are some binoculars for blindfolded eyes." We lived in a run-down tenement that smelled of old people and their pets.

"Hovering on the edge of the abyss, permeated with the perfume of the forbidden," we'd take turns cutting the smoked sausage on the table. "I love America," he'd tell us. We were going to make a million dollars manufacturing objects we had seen in dreams that night.

Evening Talk

Everything you didn't understand
Made you what you are. Strangers
Whose eye you caught on the street
Studying you. Perhaps they were the all-seeing
Illuminati? They knew what you didn't,
And left you troubled like a strange dream.

Not even the light stayed the same.
Where did all that hard glare come from?
And the scent, as if mythical beings
Were being groomed and fed stalks of hay
On these roofs drifting among the evening clouds.

You didn't understand a thing!
You loved the crowds at the end of the day
That brought you so many mysteries.
There was always someone you were meant to meet
Who for some reason wasn't waiting.
Or perhaps they were? But not here, friend.

You should have crossed the street
And followed that obviously demented woman
With the long streak of blood-red hair
Which the sky took up like a distant cry.

In the Library

for Octavio

There's a book called
"A Dictionary of Angels."
No one has opened it in fifty years,
I know, because when I did,
The covers creaked, the pages
Crumbled. There I discovered

The angels were once as plentiful
As species of flies.
The sky at dusk
Used to be thick with them.
You had to wave both arms
Just to keep them away.

Now the sun is shining
Through the tall windows.
The library is a quiet place.
Angels and gods huddled
In dark unopened books.
The great secret lies
On some shelf Miss Jones
Passes every day on her rounds.

She's very tall, so she keeps
Her head tipped as if listening.
The books are whispering.
I hear nothing, but she does.

Cameo Appearance

I had a small, nonspeaking part
In a bloody epic. I was one of the
Bombed and fleeing humanity.
In the distance our great leader
Crowed like a rooster from a balcony.
Or was it a great actor
Impersonating our great leader?

That's me there, I said to the kiddies.
I'm squeezed between the man
With two bandaged hands raised
And the old woman with her mouth open
As if she were showing us a tooth

That hurts badly. The hundred times
I rewound the tape, not once
Could they catch sight of me
In that huge gray crowd.
That was like any other gray crowd.

Trot off to bed, I said finally.
I know I was there. One take
Is all they had time for.
We ran, and the planes grazed our hair,
And then they were no more
As we stood dazed in the burning city,
But, of course, they didn't film that.

An Address with Exclamation Points

I accused History of gluttony;
Happiness of anorexia!

O History, cruel and mystical,
You ate Russia as if it were
A pot of white beans cooked with
Sausage, smoked ribs and ham hocks!

O Happiness, whose every miserly second
Is brimming with eternity!
You sat over a dish of vanilla custard
Without ever touching it!

The silent heavens were peeved!
They made the fair skies at sunset
Flash their teeth and burp from time to time,
Till our wedding picture slid off the wall.

The kitchen is closed, the waiters shouted!
No more vineyard snails in garlic butter!
No more ox tripe fried in onions!
We have only tears of happiness left!

Entertaining the Canary

Yellow feathers,
Is it true
You chirp to the cop
On the beat?

Desist. Turn your
Nervous gaze
At the open bathroom door
Where I'm soaping

My love's back
And putting my chin on her shoulder
So I can do the same for her
Breasts and crotch.

Sing. Flutter your wings
As if you were applauding,
Or I'll throw her black slip
Over your gilded cage.

Against Winter

The truth is dark under your eyelids.
What are you going to do about it?
The birds are silent; there's no one to ask.
All day long you'll squint at the gray sky.
When the wind blows you'll shiver like straw.

A meek little lamb, you grew your wool
Till they came after you with huge shears.
Flies hovered over your open mouth,
Then they, too, flew off like the leaves,
The bare branches reached after them in vain.

Winter coming. Like the last heroic soldier
Of a defeated army, you'll stay at your post,
Head bared to the first snowflake.
Till a neighbor comes to yell at you,
You're crazier than the weather, Charlie.

Empire of Dreams

On the first page of my dreambook
It's always evening
In an occupied country.
Hour before the curfew.
A small provincial city.
The houses all dark.
The storefronts gutted.

I am on a street corner
Where I shouldn't be.
Alone and coatless
I have gone out to look
For a black dog who answers to my whistle.
I have a kind of Halloween mask
Which I am afraid to put on.

My Beloved

after D. Khrams

In the fine print of her face
Her eyes are two loopholes.
No, let me start again.
Her eyes are flies in milk,
Her eyes are baby Draculas.

To hell with her eyes.
Let me tell you about her mouth.
Her mouth's the red cottage
Where the wolf ate grandma.

Ah, forget about her mouth,
Let me talk about her breasts.
I get a peek at them now and then
And even that's more than enough
To make me lose my head,
So I better tell you about her legs.

When she crosses them on the sofa
It's like the jailer unwrapping a parcel
And in that parcel is a Christmas cake
And in that cake a sweet little file
That gasps her name as it files my chains.

Prodigy

I grew up bent over
a chessboard.

I loved the word *endgame*.

All my cousins looked worried.

It was a small house
near a Roman graveyard.
Planes and tanks
shook its windowpanes.

A retired professor of astronomy
taught me how to play.

That must have been in 1944.

In the set we were using,
the paint had almost chipped off
the black pieces.

The white King was missing
and had to be substituted for.

I'm told but do not believe
that that summer I witnessed
men hung from telephone poles.

I remember my mother
blindfolding me a lot.
She had a way of tucking my head
suddenly under her overcoat.

In chess, too, the professor told me,
the masters play blindfolded,
the great ones on several boards
at the same time.

The Return of the Invisible Man

The invisible man, it turns out, had a daughter,
Equally ethereal.
He wants to know, have I bumped into her lately?
You bet, I says to him.
She's the one wearing me out
With her vanishing acts,
Her I'll-be-damned reappearances.

An apparition I'll cross the street for
Against the traffic,
The buses and honking cabs about to
Leave me legless, or worse.
Even so, day and night
I'm roaming the city, hearing the tap
Of her spiked heels at midnight.

Tell me, he says to that,
Is she still Daddy's little girl?
And how, I assure him, especially
When she's nothing but a figment
Wearing black lace panties,
Fluffing the fat pillows
And teasing the covers off our bed.

Love Poem

Feather duster.
Birdcage made of whispers.
Tail of a black cat.

I'm a child running
With open scissors.
My eyes are bandaged.

You are a heart pounding
In a dark forest.
The shriek from the Ferris wheel.

That's it, *bruja*
With arms akimbo
Stamping your foot.

Night at the fair.
Woodwind band.
Two blind pickpockets in the crowd.

Couple at Coney Island

It was early one Sunday morning,
So we put on our best rags
And went for a stroll along the boardwalk
Till we came to a kind of palace
With turrets and pennants flying.
It made me think of a wedding cake
In the window of a fancy bakery shop.

I was warm, so I took my jacket off
And put my arm round your waist
And drew you closer to me
While you leaned your head on my shoulder,
Anyone could see we'd made love
The night before and were still giddy on our feet.
We looked naked in our clothes

Staring at the red and white pennants
Whipped by the sea wind.
The rides and shooting galleries
With their ducks marching in line
Still boarded up and padlocked.
No one around yet to take our first dime.

Listen

Everything about you,
My life, is both
Make-believe and real.
We are a couple
Working the night shift
In a bomb factory.

"Come quietly," one says
To the other
As he takes her by the hand
And leads her
To a rooftop
Overlooking the city.

At this hour, if one listens
Long and hard,
One can hear a fire engine
In the distance,
But not the cries for help,

Just the silence
Growing deeper
At the sight of a small child
Leaping out of a window
With its nightclothes on fire.

DONALD HALL

(1928–)

Poet Laureate Consultant in Poetry (2006–2007)

Work, love, build a house, and die. But build a house.

When news hit that Donald Hall would be the next United States poet laureate, *New York Times* columnist Verlyn Klinkenborg wrote that he hoped Donald Hall would not be the kind of laureate who would speak tirelessly on behalf of poetry because "so much of his poetry has emerged from the rigor of his privacy—from what appears in his verse to be a deep, unsettling sense of what's possible in one's life." Physical remove, quiet, and routine have been the key elements in Hall's richly prolific writing life, which to date totals eighteen books of poetry, twenty-one books of prose, and twelve children's books.

Hall lives in a white clapboard farmhouse in New Hampshire that has been in his family for generations, one he retreated to with his wife, the poet Jane Kenyon, in the early seventies when the couple decided to leave Hall's life as a tenured professor at the University of Michigan. His mid-career poetry reflects his return to the family farm, exploring the continuity between generations in narrative reminiscences about the past, generations, and his marriage. Kenyon's death in 1995 deeply affected Hall's verse. His poems turned inward, away from the New England landscape, bringing to life one of literature's most direct, painstaking, inspiring, and heartbreaking portraits of marriage. Hall has called his marriage to Kenyon "the most important thing in my life. Period." He survived her death by working "every morning on letters and on earlier poems that I had begun about her illness. . . . So for about two hours every morning I could work on poems. Writing them over and over again. And those were the hours in the day I was happy."

Hall now leads an orderly, monastic life that most days begins at 5 a.m., when he heads to the shedlike study where he wrote his first poems as a boy visiting his grandmother. "Contentment," for Hall, "is work so engrossing that you do not know you are working." Ideally his long writing days wind up with watching a Red Sox game on TV in the company of his two cats. And though his subjects have ranged, he remains true to his Frostian roots as a plainspoken rural poet who favors concrete diction and imagery and declarative sentences, giving his poetry and prose a tone of sincere, understated authority.

White Apples

when my father had been dead a week
I woke
with his voice in my ear

                        I sat up in bed
and held my breath
and stared at the pale closed door

white apples and the taste of stone

if he called again
I would put on my coat and galoshes

Gold

Pale gold of the walls, gold
of the centers of daisies, yellow roses
pressing from a clear bowl. All day
we lay on the bed, my hand
stroking the deep
gold of your thighs and your back.
We slept and woke
entering the golden room together,
lay down in it breathing
quickly, then

slowly again,
caressing and dozing, your hand sleepily
touching my hair now.

We made in those days
tiny identical rooms inside our bodies
which the men who uncover our graves
will find in a thousand years,
shining and whole.

To a Waterfowl

Women with hats like the rear ends of pink ducks
applauded you, my poems.
These are the women whose husbands I meet on airplanes,
who close their briefcases and ask, "What are *you* in?"
I look in their eyes, I tell them I am in poetry,

and their eyes fill with anxiety, and with little tears.
"Oh, yeah?" they say, developing an interest in clouds.
"My wife, she likes that sort of thing? Hah-hah?
I guess maybe I'd better watch my grammar, huh?"
I leave them in airports, watching their grammar,

and take a limousine to the Women's Goodness Club
where I drink Harvey's Bristol Cream with their wives,
and eat chicken salad with capers, with little tomato wedges,
and I read them "The Erotic Crocodile," and "Eating You."
Ah, when I have concluded the disbursement of sonorities,

crooning, "High on thy thigh I cry, Hi!"—and so forth—
they spank their wide hands, they smile like Jell-O,
and they say, "Hah-hah? My goodness, Mr. Hall,
but you certainly do have an imagination, huh?"
"Thank you, indeed," I say; "it brings in the bacon."

But now, my poems, now I have returned to the motel,
returned to *l'éternel retour* of the Holiday Inn,
naked, lying on the bed, watching *Godzilla Sucks Mount Fuji*,
addressing my poems, feeling superior, and drinking bourbon
from a flask disguised to look like a transistor radio.

And what about you? You, laughing? You, in the bluejeans,
laughing at your mother who wears hats, and at your father
who rides airplanes with a briefcase watching his grammar?
Will you ever be old and dumb, like your creepy parents?
Not you, not you, not you, not you, not you, not you.

Maple Syrup

August, goldenrod blowing. We walk
into the graveyard, to find
my grandfather's grave. Ten years ago
I came here last, bringing
marigolds from the round garden
outside the kitchen.
I didn't know you then.
               We walk
among carved names that go with photographs
on top of the piano at the farm:
Keneston, Wells, Fowler, Batchelder, Buck.
We pause at the new grave
of Grace Fenton, my grandfather's

sister. Last summer
we called on her at the nursing home,
eighty-seven, and nodding
in a blue housedress. We cannot find
my grandfather's grave.
                    Back at the house
where no one lives, we potter
and explore the back chamber
where everything comes to rest: spinning wheels,
pretty boxes, quilts,
bottles, books, albums of postcards.
Then with a flashlight we descend
frail steps to the root cellar—black,
cobwebby, huge,
with dirt floors and fieldstone walls,
and above the walls, holding the hewn
sills of the house, enormous
granite foundation stones.
Past the empty bins
for squash, apples, carrots, and potatoes,
we discover the shelves for canning, a few
pale pints
of tomato left, and—what
is this?—syrup, maple syrup
in a quart jar, syrup
my grandfather made twenty-five
years ago
for the last time.
                    I remember
coming to the farm in March
in sugaring time, as a small boy.
He carried the pails of sap, sixteen-quart
buckets, dangling from each end
of a wooden yoke
that lay across his shoulders, and emptied them
into a vat in the saphouse

where fire burned day and night
for a week.
     Now the saphouse
tilts, nearly to the ground,
like someone exhausted
to the point of death, and next winter
when snow piles three feet thick
on the roofs of the cold farm,
the saphouse will shudder and slide
with the snow to the ground.
       Today
we take my grandfather's last
quart of syrup
upstairs, holding it gingerly,
and we wash off twenty-five years
of dirt, and we pull
and pry the lid up, cutting the stiff,
dried rubber gasket, and dip our fingers
in, you and I both, and taste
the sweetness, you for the first time,
the sweetness preserved, of a dead man
in the kitchen he left
when his body slid
like anyone's into the ground.

Names of Horses

All winter your brute shoulders strained against collars, padding
and steerhide over the ash hames, to haul
sledges of cordwood for drying through spring and summer,
for the Glenwood stove next winter, and for the simmering range.

In April you pulled cartloads of manure to spread on the fields,
dark manure of Holsteins, and knobs of your own clustered with oats.
All summer you mowed the grass in meadow and hayfield, the
      mowing machine
clacketing beside you, while the sun walked high in the morning;

and after noon's heat, you pulled a clawed rake through the same acres,
gathering stacks, and dragged the wagon from stack to stack,
and the built hayrack back, up hill to the chaffy barn,
three loads of hay a day, hanging wide from the hayrack.

Sundays you trotted the two miles to church with the light load
of a leather quartertop buggy, and grazed in the sound of hymns.
Generation on generation, your neck rubbed the window sill
of the stall, smoothing the wood as the sea smooths glass.

When you were old and lame, when your shoulders hurt bending to
      graze,
one October the man who fed you and kept you, and harnessed you
      every morning,
led you through corn stubble to sandy ground above Eagle Pond,
and dug a hole beside you where you stood shuddering in your skin,

and laid the shotgun's muzzle in the boneless hollow behind your ear,
and fired the slug into your brain, and felled you into your grave,
shoveling sand to cover you, setting goldenrod upright above you,
where by next summer a dent in the ground made your monument.

For a hundred and fifty years, in the pasture of dead horses,
roots of pine trees pushed through the pale curves of your ribs,
yellow blossoms flourished above you in autumn, and in winter
frost heaved your bones in the ground—old toilers, soil makers:

O Roger, Mackerel, Riley, Ned, Nellie, Chester, Lady Ghost.

The Ship Pounding

Each morning I made my way
among gangways, elevators,
and nurses' pods to Jane's room
to interrogate the grave helpers
who tended her through the night
while the ship's massive engines
kept its propellers turning.
Week after week, I sat by her bed
with black coffee and the *Globe*.
The passengers on this voyage
wore masks or cannulae
or dangled devices that dripped
chemicals into their wrists.
I believed that the ship
traveled to a harbor
of breakfast, work, and love.
I wrote: "When the infusions
are infused entirely, bone
marrow restored and lymphoblasts
remitted, I will take my wife,
bald as Michael Jordan,
back to our dog and day." Today,
months later at home, these
words turned up on my desk
as I listened in case Jane called
for help, or spoke in delirium,
ready to make the agitated
drive to Emergency again
for readmission to the huge
vessel that heaves water month
after month, without leaving
port, without moving a knot,
without arrival or destination,
its great engines pounding.

Her Garden

I let her garden go.
      let it go, let it go
How can I watch the hummingbird
      Hover to sip
      With its beak's tip
The purple bee balm—whirring as we heard
      It years ago?

The weeds rise rank and thick
      let it go, let it go
Where annuals grew and burdock grows,
      Where standing she
      At once could see
The peony, the lily, and the rose
      Rise over brick

She'd laid in patterns. Moss
      let it go, let it go
Turns the bricks green, softening them
      By the gray rocks
      Where hollyhocks
That lofted while she lived, stem by tall stem,
      Blossom with loss.

Ardor

Nursing her I felt alive
in the animal moment,
scenting the predator.
Her death was the worst thing
that could happen,
and caring for her was best.

After she died I screamed,
upsetting the depressed dog.
Now I no longer
address the wall covered
with many photographs,
nor call her "you"
in a poem. She recedes
into the granite museum
of JANE KENYON 1947–1995.

I long for the absent
woman of different faces
who makes metaphors
and chops onion, drinking
a glass of Chardonnay,
oiling the wok, humming
to herself, maybe thinking
how to conclude a poem.
When I make love now,
something is awry.
Last autumn a woman said,
"I mistrust your ardor."

This winter in Florida
I loathed the old couples
my age who promenaded
in their slack flesh

holding hands. I gazed
at young women with outrage
and desire—unable to love
or to work, or to die.

Hours are slow and weeks
rapid in their vacancy.
Each day lapses as I recite
my complaints. Lust is grief
that has turned over in bed
to look the other way.

Kill the Day

Work, love, build a house, and die.
—The One Day

When she died it was as if his car accelerated
off the pier's end and zoomed upward over death water
for a year without gaining or losing altitude,
then plunged to the bottom of the sea where his corpse
lay twisted in a honeycomb of steel, still dreaming
awake, as dead as she was but conscious still.
There is nothing so selfish as misery nor so boring,
and depression is devoted only to its own practice.
Mourning resembles melancholia precisely except
that melancholy adds a self-loathing to stuporous sorrow

and turns away from the dead its exclusive attention.
Mania is melancholy reversed. Bereavement, loss,
and guilt provide excitement for conversion
to dysphoria, murderous rage, and unsleeping joy.
When he rose from the painted bed, he alternated or cycled

from dedicated hatred through gaiety and inflation
to the vacancy of breathing in-and-out, in-and-out.
He awakened daily to the prospect of nothingness
in the day's house that like all houses was mortuary.
He slept on the fornicating bed of the last breath.

He closed her eyes in the noon of her middle life;
he no longer cut and pruned for her admiration;
he worked for the praise of women and they died.
For months after her chest went still, he nightmared
that she had left him for another man. Everything
became its opposite and returned to itself.
As the second summer of her death approached him,
goldfinches flew at her feeder like daffodils
with wings and he could no longer tell her so.
Her absence could no longer be written to.

He emptied her shelves, dressers, and closets,
stacking rings and bracelets, pendants and necklaces.
He bundled sweaters and jeans, brassieres and blouses,
scarves and nightgowns and suits and summer dresses
and mailed them to Rosie's Place for indigent women.
For decades a man and a woman living together
learned each other for pleasure, giving and taking,
studying every other day predictable ecstasy
secure without secrecy or adventure, without romance,
without anxiety or jealousy, without content

except for the immaculate sexual content of sex.
The toad sat still for the toad's astounding moment,
but the day wasted whatever lived for the day
and the only useful desire obliterates desire.
Now the one day extended into multiple encounters
with loneliness that could not endure a visitor.
Machinery corroded in the barn no longer entered,
and no smoke rose from the two opposite chimneys.

It is naïve to complain over death and abandonment,
and the language of houses praised only itself.

Bone's Orchard bragged of breakfast and work, church
with neighbors on Sunday, gardening, the pond, and love
in the afternoon. The day ignored that it undertook
mere interruption on the trudge to fathomless loss.
"The days you work," said O'Keeffe, "are the best days."
Work without love is idle, idleness doing its job
for the velvet approbation of kings and presidents
without art's purpose to excite a lover's pleasure.
He turned into the ash heap damp in the Glenwood,
the burnt shape and constitution of wretchedness

in his ludicrous rage that things are as they are.
When she died, at first the outline of absence defined
a presence that disappeared. He wept for the body
he could no longer reach to touch in bed on waking.
He wept for her silver thimble. He wept when the dog
brought him a slipper that smelled of her still.
In another summer, her pheromones diminished.
The negative space of her body dwindled as she receded
deeper into the ground, smaller and fainter each day,
dried out, shrunken, separated from the news of the day.

When the coffee cup broke, when her yellow bathrobe
departed the bathroom door, when the address book
in her hand altered itself into scratchings-out,
he dreaded an adventure of self-hatred accomplished
by the finger or toe of an old man alone without
an onion to eat between slices of store-bought bread.
There was nothing to do, and nothing required doing.
Her vanishing constructed a blue synagogue
in a universe without solace or a task for doing.
He imagined that on shelves at his workroom's end

lay stacked two hundred and sixty-seven tiny
corpses, bodies of her body, porcelain mannequins.
In this dream or story he had neglected to bury them;
it was something still to do, something to be done.
In the second year, into the third and fourth years,
she died again and again, she died by receding
while he recited each day the stanzas of her dying:
He watched her chest go still; he closed her eyes.
Without birthdays, she remained her age at death.
The figurine broke that clutched its fists

as she did dying. In the pantry there were cans
and boxes and jars she bought in the supermarket
seven years ago. He walked through the vacancies,
burying her again. He had imagined an old man
alone in this white house, looking in the mirror.
Looking in the mirror now, he was old and alone.
He felt solitude's relief and intolerably lonely.
He envied whatever felt nothing: He envied oak
sills and the green hill rising and the boulder
by the side of the road and his dead love rotting

in her best white dress inside Vermont hardwood.
It was useful to set his name on her black granite,
but imminent or eventual cellular junction provided
the comfort of stone: to keep her safe beside him.
Visions of pleasure departed when she departed.
The condition of contentment or satisfaction
remains unattainable because of affect's agreement:
Whatever the measure of joy in the day's day,
no pleasure carries with it one part in ten million
of agony's vastation in loss and abandonment.

Therefore the condition of being alive is intolerable,
with no reason for endurance except that DNA

continues itself in order to continue itself.
Agreeing to love each other, they perfected a system:
Love is the exchange of a double narcissism,
agreement of twin surrender, the weapons laid by,
the treaty enforced by habitual daily negotiation.
What would he do if he could do what he wanted?
The day prevented him from doing what he wanted.
Now he woke each morning wretched with morning's

regret that he woke. He woke looking forward
to a nap, to a cigarette, to supper, to port measured,
to sleep blessed sleep on the permanent painted bed
of death: Sleep, rage, kill the day, and die.
When she died, he died also. For the first year
his immediate grief confused him into feeling alive.
He endured the grief of a two-month love affair.
When women angry and free generously visited
the frenzy of his erotic grief, melancholia
became ecstasy, then sank under successful dirt.

Without prospect or purpose, who dares to love meat
that will putrefy? He rejoiced that he was meat.
How many times will he die in his own lifetime?
When TWA 800 blew out of the sky, his heart ascended
and exploded in gratitude, finding itself embodied
and broken as fragments scattering into water.
Then little green testicles dropped from the oaks
on New Canada Road again, another August of death,
and autumn McIntoshes rotted on the dwarf trees
already pecked by the loathsome birds of July.

Each day identified itself as a passage to elsewhere,
which was a passage to elsewhere and to elsewhere.
What did she look like now? Dried and slackening maybe.
Do the worms eat her? He supposed that they ate her.
Now he dreamed again of her thick and lavish hair,

of her lush body wetting and loosening beside him.
He remembered ordinary fucking that shone like the sun
in their household solar system, brighter than Jesus,
than poetry, than their orchard under the mountain—
the crossing place of bodies that regarded each other

with more devotion the more they approached her death
until they were singular, gazing speechless together
while she vanished into open eyes staring all night.
In the day's crush and tangle of melted nails,
collapsed foundation stones, and adze-trimmed beams,
the widower alone glimpsed the beekeeper's mask
in high summer as it approached the day they built,
now fallen apart with bark still on its beams,
nine layers of wallpaper over the dry laths—
always ending, no other ending, in dead eyes open.

Affirmation

To grow old is to lose everything.
Aging, everybody knows it.
Even when we are young,
we glimpse it sometimes, and nod our heads
when a grandfather dies.
Then we row for years on the midsummer
pond, ignorant and content. But a marriage,
that began without harm, scatters
into debris on the shore,
and a friend from school drops
cold on a rocky strand.
If a new love carries us
past middle age, our wife will die

at her strongest and most beautiful.
New women come and go. All go.
The pretty lover who announces
that she is temporary
is temporary. The bold woman,
middle-aged against our old age,
sinks under an anxiety she cannot withstand.
Another friend of decades estranges himself
in words that pollute thirty years.
Let us stifle under mud at the pond's edge
and affirm that it is fitting
and delicious to lose everything.

Safe Sex

If he and she do not know each other, and feel confident
they will not meet again; if he avoids affectionate words;

if she has grown insensible skin under skin; if they desire
only the tribute of another's cry; if they employ each other

as revenge on old lovers or families of entitlement and steel—
then there will be no betrayals, no letters returned unread,

no frenzy, no hurled words of permanent humiliation,
no trembling days, no vomit at midnight, no repeated

apparition of a body floating face-down at the pond's edge.

Nymph and Shepherd

She died a dozen times before I died,
And kept on dying, nymph of fatality.
I could not die but once although I tried.

I envied her. She whooped, she laughed, she cried
As she contrived each fresh mortality,
Numberless lethal times before I died.

I plunged, I plugged, I twisted, and I sighed
While she achieved death's Paradise routinely.
I lagged however zealously I tried.

She writhed, she bucked, she rested, and, astride,
She posted, cantering on top of me
At least a hundred miles until I died.

I'd never blame you if you thought I lied
About her deadly prodigality.
She died a dozen times before I died
Who could not die so frequently. I tried.

After Love

When love empties itself out,
it fills our bodies full.

For an hour we lie braiding
pulse and skin together,

like infants who sigh
and doze, dreamy with milk.

TED KOOSER

(1939–)

Poet Laureate Consultant in Poetry 2004–2006

I detest elitism of any kind. There's been this assumption along with mod-
ernism that the reader should come halfway to the work. I frankly don't
believe readers should be expected to make an effort to learn something
in order to understand a poem. I've never met readers like that, although
I'm sure there are some, particularly on campuses. I'm not saying it's not all
right to write challenging poetry. But the reader I'm interested in is the aver-
age person on the street.

The Nebraskan poet Ted Kooser was the first laureate from the Great Plains and held the position for two years. During his tenure he wrote a regular newspaper column and created a Web site called "American Life in Poetry," launched "to convince people who don't read poetry that there are things in it for them." For the site he selected poems that "an average newspaper reader could pick up and understand." Newspapers had free access to the column, which appeared weekly in 150 to 200 papers. The Web site has received over 100 million hits. As poet laureate, Kooser made some two hundred appearances and gave a hundred interviews. During his first year in the post he won the Pulitzer Prize for *Delights and Shadows*, his eleventh volume of poetry.

Kooser strives for clarity and accessibility in his poems, which are seldom more than twenty lines and full of readily available imagery from rural life in Nebraska. But Kooser has maintained that he is not a "regionalist" writer. His verse, while grounded in commonplace images—such as a beer bottle, the glow of lights on a highway, a jar of buttons—nearly always employs surprising metaphors, imbuing even his shortest poems with a visionary quality. For most of his writing life, Kooser worked as an executive at an insurance company where his secretary was often the first reader of his poems. If she didn't understand them, he would revise: "You can tweak a poem just slightly and broaden the audience." In a recent interview he said he is "still interested in acknowledging that the people who read books have other priorities, and I want to consider those. I want to write books of poems interesting enough that they can compete with the need to get a raincoat cleaned."

Kooser is currently a professor of English at the University of Nebraska at Lincoln. In addition to his numerous collections of poetry, he recently wrote a how-to book for beginning poets, *The Poetry Home Repair Manual*. He lives on an acreage near Garland, Nebraska, with his wife and their two dogs.

So This Is Nebraska

The gravel road rides with a slow gallop
over the fields, the telephone lines
streaming behind, its billow of dust
full of the sparks of redwing blackbirds.

On either side, those dear old ladies,
the loosening barns, their little windows
dulled by cataracts of hay and cobwebs
hide broken tractors under their skirts.

So this is Nebraska. A Sunday
afternoon; July. Driving along
with your hand out squeezing the air,
a meadowlark waiting on every post.

Behind a shelterbelt of cedars,
top-deep in hollyhocks, pollen and bees,
a pickup kicks its fenders off
and settles back to read the clouds.

You feel like that; you feel like letting
your tires go flat, like letting the mice
build a nest in your muffler, like being
no more than a truck in the weeds,

clucking with chickens or sticky with honey
or holding a skinny old man in your lap
while he watches the road, waiting
for someone to wave to. You feel like

waving. You feel like stopping the car
and dancing around on the road. You wave
instead and leave your hand out gliding
larklike over the wheat, over the houses.

Selecting a Reader

First, I would have her be beautiful,
and walking carefully up on my poetry
at the loneliest moment of an afternoon,
her hair still damp at the neck
from washing it. She should be wearing
a raincoat, an old one, dirty
from not having money enough for the cleaners.
She will take out her glasses, and there
in the bookstore, she will thumb
over my poems, then put the book back
up on its shelf. She will say to herself,
"For that kind of money, I can get
my raincoat cleaned." And she will.

Carrie

"There's never an end to dust
and dusting," my aunt would say
as her rag, like a thunderhead,
scudded across the yellow oak
of her little house. There she lived

seventy years with a ball
of compulsion closed in her fist,
and an elbow that creaked and popped
like a branch in a storm. Now dust
is her hands and dust her heart.
There's never an end to it.

My Grandfather Dying

I could see bruises or shadows
deep under his skin, like the shapes
skaters find frozen in rivers—
leaves caught in flight,
or maybe the hand of a man reaching up
out of the darkness for help.

I was helpless as flowers
there at his bedside. I watched
his legs jerk in the sheets.
He answered doors,
he kicked loose stones from his fields.
I leaned down to call out my name
and he called it back. His breath
was as sour as an orchard
after the first frost.

Highway 30

At two in the morning, when the moon
has driven away,
leaving the faint taillight of one star
at the horizon, a light
like moonlight leaks
from broken crates that lie fallen
along the highway, becoming
motels, all-night cafes, and bus stations
with greenhouse windows,
where lone women sit like overturned flowerpots,
crushing the soft, gray petals of old coats.

Flying at Night

Above us, stars. Beneath us, constellations.
Five billion miles away, a galaxy dies
like a snowflake falling on water. Below us,
some farmer, feeling the chill of that distant death,
snaps on his yard light, drawing his sheds and barn
back into the little system of his care.
All night, the cities, like shimmering novas,
tug with bright streets at lonely lights like his.

The Fan in the Window

It is September, and a cool breeze
from somewhere ahead is turning the blades;
night, and the slow flash of the fan

the last light between us and the darkness.
Dust has begun to collect on the blades,
haymaker's dust from distant fields,
dust riding to town on the night-black wings
of the crows, a thin frost of dust
which clings to the fan in just the way
we cling to the earth as it spins.
The fan has brought us through,
its shiny blades like the screw of a ship
that has pushed its way through summer—
cut flowers awash in its wake,
the stagnant Sargasso Sea of July
far behind us. For the moment, we rest,
we lie in the dark hull of the house,
we rock in the troughs off the shore
of October, the engine cooling,
the fan blades so lazily turning, but turning.

december 15

Clear and thirty-four at 6 a.m.

An old moon, lying akilter
among a few pale stars,
and so quiet on the road
I can hear every bone in my body
hefting some part of me
over its shoulder. Behind me,
my shadow stifles a cough
as it tries to keep up,
for I have set out fast and hard

against this silence,
filling my lungs with hope
on this, my granddaughter's
birthday, her first, and the day
of my quarterly cancer tests.

february 10

Cloudy, cool and very still.

Sometimes at night, my old dog Hattie
will lift her head to bark at nothing,
as if that nothing were silently
crossing the yard in the darkness,
and then she'll listen hard and bark again
until it steals away. This morning
I woke at three o'clock, and nothing
was standing there, silently watching me,
holding its breath at the foot of the bed.
I must have made some little noise
because my wife turned toward me and asked,
"What's wrong?" "Nothing," I answered,
and suddenly nothing was gone
and from below us Hattie barked and barked.

february 21

Sunny and clear.

Fate, here I stand, hat in hand,
in my fifty-ninth year,
a man of able body and a merry spirit.
I'll take whatever work you have.

Tattoo

What once was meant to be a statement—
a dripping dagger held in the fist
of a shuddering heart—is now just a bruise
on a bony old shoulder, the spot
where vanity once punched him hard
and the ache lingered on. He looks like
someone you had to reckon with,
strong as a stallion, fast and ornery,
but on this chilly morning, as he walks
between the tables at a yard sale
with the sleeves of his tight black T-shirt
rolled up to show us who he was,
he is only another old man, picking up
broken tools and putting them back,
his heart gone soft and blue with stories.

At the Cancer Clinic

She is being helped toward the open door
that leads to the examining rooms
by two young women I take to be her sisters.
Each bends to the weight of an arm
and steps with the straight, tough bearing
of courage. At what must seem to be
a great distance, a nurse holds the door,
smiling and calling encouragement.
How patient she is in the crisp white sails
of her clothes. The sick woman
peers from under her funny knit cap
to watch each foot swing scuffing forward
and take its turn under her weight.
There is no restlessness or impatience
or anger anywhere in sight. Grace
fills the clean mold of this moment
and all the shuffling magazines grow still.

A Jar of Buttons

This is a core sample
from the floor of the Sea of Mending,

a cylinder packed with shells
that over many years

sank through fathoms of shirts—
pearl buttons, blue buttons—

and settled together
beneath waves of perseverance,

an ocean upon which
generations of women set forth,

under the sails of gingham curtains,
and, seated side by side

on decks sometimes salted by tears,
made small but important repairs.

Grasshoppers

This year they are exactly the size
of the pencil stub my grandfather kept
to mark off the days since rain,

and precisely the color of dust, of the roads
leading back across the dying fields
into the '30s. Walking the cracked lane

past the empty barn, the empty silo,
you hear them tinkering with irony,
slapping the grass like drops of rain.

LOUISE GLÜCK

(1943-)

Poet Laureate Consultant in Poetry (2003-2004)
Special Bicentennial Consultant in Poetry (1999-2000),
with Rita Dove and W. S. Merwin

It seems to me that the desire to make art produces an ongoing experience of longing, a restlessness sometimes, but not inevitably, played out romantically, or sexually. Always there seems something ahead, the next poem or story, visible, at least, apprehensible, but unreachable. To perceive it at all is to be haunted by it; some sound, some tone, becomes a torment—the poem embodying that sound seems to exist somewhere already finished. It's like a lighthouse, except that, as one swims toward it, it backs away.

ouise Glück has said she has "no concern with widening audience," preferring her readership "small, intense, passionate." She was very clear with the Library of Congress, before accepting the poet laureate's job, about her refusal to sit for interviews, promote poetry on television and radio, or travel the country giving interviews. She dislikes media attention not because she is an especially private person, but because she likes to control her words. She is the only laureate who has said that the year in and out of Washington had little impact on her writing life. She continued to teach. She continued to write poetry, and in doing so reinforced the antinomian role of the American poet which goes back to Emily Dickinson—the poet set against and apart from social, professional, and political expectations, maintaining critical distance, and protecting her inner life as the wellspring of lyric poety. Billy Collins, Glück's predecessor in the post, said of her appointment, "Some of us have chosen to spend a lot of time running round the country lighting poetry bonfires," but, he added, "the job can be tailored to each individual's personality."

Louise Glück's eleven books of poetry have won every major poetry award, including the Pulitzer Prize and the National Book Critics Circle Award. Her collection of essays *Proofs and Theories: Essays on Poetry* (1994) won the PEN/Martha Albrand Award for Nonfiction. She has taught at a number of schools, including Williams College and Yale University, and is known as a nurturer of student writers. Since 2003 she has been the judge of the Yale Series of Younger Poets. Her favorite responsibility as poet laureate was bestowing $10,000 grants to young poets.

Glück's early chiseled lyrics plumb romantic and familial disappointment. In an essay on her education she refers to her seven years of psychoanalytic treatment for a life-threatening case of anorexia nervosa as a crucial stepping-stone to writing: "The discipline gave me a place to use my mind, because my emotional condition, my extreme rigidity and frantic dependence on ritual, made other forms of education impossible. . . . At eighteen instead of going to college as I had always assumed I would, I enrolled in Léonie Adams' poetry workshop." Her mid-career poems retool classical myths and fairy tales with fierce, modern bluntness and intensity: "Persephone is having sex in hell. / Unlike the rest of us, / she doesn't know / what winter is, only that / she is what causes it." Her recent work has been in longer narrative poems that explore, among other themes, divorce, childhood memory, and enduring friendship. She continues to write in colloquial diction, which goes back to her childhood preference for what she calls "simple language," suited to liberating, "through subtleties of timing, of pacing, [a] word's full and surprising range of meaning."

Mock Orange

It is not the moon, I tell you.
It is these flowers
lighting the yard.

I hate them.
I hate them as I hate sex,
the man's mouth
sealing my mouth, the man's
paralyzing body—

and the cry that always escapes,
the low, humiliating
premise of union—

In my mind tonight
I hear the question and pursuing answer
fused in one sound
that mounts and mounts and then
is split into the old selves,
the tired antagonisms. Do you see?
We were made fools of.
And the scent of mock orange
drifts through the window.

How can I rest?
How can I be content
when there is still
that odor in the world?

The Drowned Children

You see, they have no judgment.
So it is natural that they should drown,
first the ice taking them in
and then, all winter, their wool scarves
floating behind them as they sink
until at last they are quiet.
And the pond lifts them in its manifold dark arms.

But death must come to them differently,
so close to the beginning.
As though they had always been
blind and weightless. Therefore
the rest is dreamed, the lamp,
the good white cloth that covered the table,
their bodies.

And yet they hear the names they used
like lures slipping over the pond:
What are you waiting for
come home, come home, lost
in the waters, blue and permanent.

A Novel

No one could write a novel about this family:
too many similar characters. Besides, they're all women;
there was only one hero.

Now the hero's dead. Like echoes, the women last longer;
they're all too tough for their own good.

From this point on, nothing changes:
there's no plot without a hero.
In this house, when you say *plot* what you mean is *love story*.

The women can't get moving.
Oh, they get dressed, they eat, they keep up appearances.
But there's no action, no development of character.

They're all determined to suppress
criticism of the hero. The problem is
he's weak; his scenes specify
his function but not his nature.

Maybe that explains why his death wasn't moving.
First he's sitting at the head of the table,
where the figurehead is most needed.
Then he's dying, a few feet away, his wife holding a mirror under his
    mouth.

Amazing, how they keep busy, these women, the wife and two
    daughters.
Setting the table, clearing the dishes away.
Each heart pierced through with a sword.

Celestial Music

I have a friend who still believes in heaven.
Not a stupid person, yet with all she knows, she literally talks to god,
she thinks someone listens in heaven.
On earth, she's unusually competent.
Brave, too, able to face unpleasantness.

We found a caterpillar dying in the dirt, greedy ants crawling over it.
I'm always moved by weakness, by disaster, always eager to oppose vitality.
But timid, also, quick to shut my eyes.
Whereas my friend was able to watch, to let events play out
according to nature. For my sake, she intervened,
brushing a few ants off the torn thing, and set it down across the road.

My friend says I shut my eyes to god, that nothing else explains
my aversion to reality. She says I'm like the child who buries her head in
    the pillow
so as not to see, the child who tells herself
that light causes sadness—
My friend is like the mother. Patient, urging me
to wake up an adult like herself, a courageous person—

In my dreams, my friend reproaches me. We're walking
on the same road, except it's winter now;
she's telling me that when you love the world you hear celestial music:
look up, she says. When I look up, nothing.
Only clouds, snow, a white business in the trees
like brides leaping to a great height—
Then I'm afraid for her; I see her
caught in a net deliberately cast over the earth—

In reality, we sit by the side of the road, watching the sun set;
from time to time, the silence pierced by a birdcall.
It's this moment we're both trying to explain, the fact
that we're at ease with death, with solitude.
My friend draws a circle in the dirt; inside, the caterpillar doesn't move.
She's always trying to make something whole, something beautiful, an image
capable of life apart from her.
We're very quiet. It's peaceful sitting here, not speaking, the composition
fixed, the road turning suddenly dark, the air
going cool, here and there the rocks shining and glittering—
it's this stillness that we both love.
The love of form is a love of endings.

First Memory

Long ago, I was wounded. I lived
to revenge myself
against my father, not
for what he was—
for what I was: from the beginning of time,
in childhood, I thought
that pain meant
I was not loved.
It meant I loved.

Penelope's Song

Little soul, little perpetually undressed one,
do now as I bid you, climb
the shelf-like branches of the spruce tree;
wait at the top, attentive, like
a sentry or look-out. He will be home soon;
it behooves you to be
generous. You have not been completely
perfect either; with your troublesome body
you have done things you shouldn't
discuss in poems. Therefore
call out to him over the open water, over the bright water
with your dark song, with your grasping,
unnatural song—passionate,
like Maria Callas. Who
wouldn't want you? Whose most demonic appetite
could you possibly fail to answer? Soon
he will return from wherever he goes in the meantime,
suntanned from his time away, wanting
his grilled chicken. Ah, you must greet him,

you must shake the boughs of the tree
to get his attention,
but carefully, carefully, lest
his beautiful face be marred
by too many falling needles.

Telemachus' Detachment

When I was a child looking
at my parents' lives, you know
what I thought? I thought
heartbreaking. Now I think
heartbreaking, but also
insane. Also
very funny.

Telemachus' Guilt

Patience of the sort my mother
practised on my father
(which in his self-
absorption he mistook
for tribute though it was in fact
a species of rage—didn't he
ever wonder why he was
so blocked in expressing
his native abandon?): it infected
my childhood. Patiently
she fed me; patiently
she supervised the kindly

slaves who attended me, regardless
of my behavior, an assumption
I tested with increasing
violence. It seemed clear to me
that from her perspective
I didn't exist, since
my actions had
no power to disturb her: I was
the envy of my playmates.
In the decades that followed
I was proud of my father
for staying away
even if he stayed away for
the wrong reasons;
I used to smile
when my mother wept.
I hope now she could
forgive that cruelty; I hope
she understood how like
her own coldness it was,
a means of remaining
separate from what
one loves deeply.

Telemachus' Fantasy

Sometimes I wonder about my father's
years on those islands: why
was he so attractive
to women? He was in straits then, I suppose
desperate. I believe
women like to see a man
still whole, still standing, but

about to go to pieces: such
disintegration reminds them
of passion. I think of them as living
their whole lives
completely undressed. It must have
dazzled him, I think, women
so much younger than he was
evidently wild for him, ready
to do anything he wished. Is it
fortunate to encounter circumstances
so responsive to one's own will, to live
so many years
unquestioned, unthwarted? One
would have to believe oneself
entirely good or worthy. I
suppose in time either
one becomes a monster or
the beloved sees what one is. I never
wish for my father's life
nor have I any idea
what he sacrificed
to survive that moment. Less dangerous
to believe he was drawn to them
and so stayed
to see who they were. I think, though,
as an imaginative man
to some extent he
became who they were.

Nest

A bird was making its nest.
In the dream, I watched it closely:
in my life, I was trying to be
a witness not a theorist.

The place you begin doesn't determine
the place you end: the bird

took what it found in the yard,
its base materials, nervously
scanning the bare yard in early spring;
in debris by the south wall pushing
a few twigs with its beak.

Image
of loneliness: the small creature
coming up with nothing. Then
dry twigs. Carrying, one by one,
the twigs to the hideout.
Which is all it was then.

It took what there was:
the available material. Spirit
wasn't enough.

And then it wove like the first Penelope
but toward a different end.
How did it weave? It weaved,
carefully but hopelessly, the few twigs

with any suppleness, any flexibility,
choosing these over the brittle, the recalcitrant.

Early spring, late desolation.
The bird circled the bare yard making
efforts to survive
on what remained to it.

It had its task:
to imagine the future. Steadily flying around,
patiently bearing small twigs to the solitude
of the exposed tree in the steady coldness
of the outside world.

I had nothing to build with.
It was winter: I couldn't imagine
anything but the past. I couldn't even
imagine the past, if it came to that.

And I didn't know how I came here.
Everyone else much farther along.
I was back at the beginning
at a time in life we can't remember beginnings.

The bird
collected twigs in the apple tree, relating
each addition to existing mass.
But when was there suddenly *mass?*

It took what it found after the others
were finished.
The same materials—why should it matter
to be finished last? The same materials, the same
limited good. Brown twigs,
broken and fallen. And in one,
a length of yellow wool.

Then it was spring and I was inexplicably happy.
I knew where I was: on Broadway with my bag of groceries.
Spring fruit in the stores: first
cherries at Formaggio. Forsythia
beginning.

First I was at peace.
Then I was contented, satisfied.
And then flashes of joy.
And the season changed—for all of us,
of course.

And as I peered out my mind grew sharper.
And I remember accurately
the sequence of my responses,
my eyes fixing on each thing
from the shelter of the hidden self:

first, *I love it.*
Then, *I can use it.*

Eros

I had drawn my chair to the hotel window, to watch the rain.

I was in a kind of dream or trance—
in love, and yet
I wanted nothing.

It seemed unnecessary to touch you, to see you again.
I wanted only this:
the room, the chair, the sound of the rain falling,
hour after hour, in the warmth of the spring night.

I needed nothing more; I was utterly sated.
My heart had become small; it took very little to fill it.
I watched the rain falling in heavy sheets over the darkened city—

You were not concerned; I could let you
live as you needed to live.

At dawn the rain abated. I did the things
one does in daylight, I acquitted myself,
but I moved like a sleepwalker.

It was enough and it no longer involved you.
A few days in a strange city.
A conversation, the touch of a hand.
And afterward, I took off my wedding ring.

That was what I wanted: to be naked.

Time

There was too much, always, then too little.
Childhood: sickness.
By the side of the bed I had a little bell—
at the other end of the bell, my mother.

Sickness, gray rain. The dogs slept through it. They slept on the bed,
at the end of it, and it seemed to me they understood
about childhood: best to remain unconscious.

The rain made gray slats on the windows.
I sat with my book, the little bell beside me.
Without hearing a voice, I apprenticed myself to a voice.
Without seeing any sign of the spirit, I determined
to live in the spirit.

The rain faded in and out.
Month after month, in the space of a day.
Things became dreams; dreams became things.

Then I was well; the bell went back to the cupboard.
The rain ended. The dogs stood at the door,
panting to go outside.

I was well, then I was an adult.
And time went on—it was like the rain,
so much, so much, as though it was a weight that couldn't be moved.

I was a child, half sleeping.
I was sick; I was protected.
And I lived in the world of the spirit,
the world of the gray rain,
the lost, the remembered.

Then suddenly the sun was shining.
And time went on, even when there was almost none left.
And the perceived became the remembered,
the remembered, the perceived.

Memoir

I was born cautious, under the sign of Taurus.
I grew up on an island, prosperous,
in the second half of the twentieth century;
the shadow of the Holocaust
hardly touched us.

I had a philosophy of love, a philosophy
of religion, both based on
early experience within a family.

And if when I wrote I used only a few words
it was because time always seemed to me short
as though it could be stripped away
at any moment.

And my story, in any case, wasn't unique
though, like everyone else, I had a story,
a point of view.

A few words were all I needed:
nourish, sustain, attack.

October

I.

Is it winter again, is it cold again,
didn't Frank just slip on the ice,
didn't he heal, weren't the spring seeds planted

didn't the night end,
didn't the melting ice
flood the narrow gutters

wasn't my body
rescued, wasn't it safe

didn't the scar form, invisible
above the injury

terror and cold,
didn't they just end, wasn't the back garden
harrowed and planted—

I remember how the earth felt, red and dense,
in stiff rows, weren't the seeds planted,
didn't vines climb the south wall

I can't hear your voice
for the wind's cries, whistling over the bare ground

I no longer care
what sound it makes

when was I silenced, when did it first seem
pointless to describe that sound

what it sounds like can't change what it is—

didn't the night end, wasn't the earth
safe when it was planted

didn't we plant the seeds,
weren't we necessary to the earth,

the vines, were they harvested?

II.

Summer after summer has ended,
balm after violence:
it does me no good
to be good to me now;
violence has changed me.

Daybreak. The low hills shine
ochre and fire, even the fields shine.
I know what I see: sun that could be
the August sun, returning
everything that was taken away—

You hear this voice? This is my mind's voice;
you can't touch my body now.
It has changed once, it has hardened,
don't ask it to respond again.

A day like a day in summer.
Exceptionally still. The long shadows of the maples
nearly mauve on the gravel paths.
And in the evening, warmth. Night like a night in summer.

It does me no good; violence has changed me.
My body has grown cold like the stripped fields;
now there is only my mind, cautious and wary,
with the sense it is being tested.

Once more, the sun rises as it rose in summer;
bounty, balm after violence.
Balm after the leaves have changed, after the fields
have been harvested and turned.

Tell me this is the future,
I won't believe you.
Tell me I'm living,
I won't believe you.

III.

Snow had fallen. I remember
music from an open window.

Come to me, said the world.
This is not to say
it spoke in exact sentences
but that I perceived beauty in this manner.

Sunrise. A film of moisture
on each living thing. Pools of cold light
formed in the gutters.

I stood
at the doorway,
ridiculous as it now seems.

What others found in art,
I found in nature. What others found
in human love, I found in nature.
Very simple. But there was no voice there.

Winter was over. In the thawed dirt,
bits of green were showing.

Come to me, said the world. I was standing
in my wool coat at a kind of bright portal—
I can finally say
long ago; it gives me considerable pleasure. Beauty

the healer, the teacher—

death cannot harm me
more than you have harmed me,
my beloved life.

IV.

The light has changed;
middle C is tuned darker now.
And the songs of morning sound over-rehearsed.

This is the light of autumn, not the light of spring.
The light of autumn: *you will not be spared.*

The songs have changed; the unspeakable
has entered them.

This is the light of autumn, not the light that says
I am reborn.

Not the spring dawn: *I strained, I suffered, I was delivered.*
This is the present, an allegory of waste.

So much has changed. And still, you are fortunate:
the ideal burns in you like a fever.
Or not like a fever, like a second heart.

The songs have changed, but really they are still quite beautiful.
They have been concentrated in a smaller space, the space of the mind.
They are dark, now, with desolation and anguish.

And yet the notes recur. They hover oddly
in anticipation of silence.
The ear gets used to them.
The eye gets used to disappearances.

You will not be spared, nor will what you love be spared.

A wind has come and gone, taking apart the mind;
it has left in its wake a strange lucidity.

How privileged you are, to be still passionately
clinging to what you love;
the forfeit of hope has not destroyed you.

Maestoso, doloroso:

This is the light of autumn; it has turned on us.
Surely it is a privilege to approach the end
still believing in something.

V.

It is true there is not enough beauty in the world.
It is also true that I am not competent to restore it.
Neither is there candor, and here I may be of some use.

I am
at work, though I am silent.

The bland

misery of the world
bounds us on either side, an alley

lined with trees; we are

companions here, not speaking,
each with his own thoughts;

behind the trees, iron
gates of the private houses,
the shuttered rooms

somehow deserted, abandoned,

as though it were the artist's
duty to create
hope, but out of what? what?

the word itself
false, a device to refute
perception—At the intersection,

ornamental lights of the season.

I was young here. Riding
the subway with my small book
as though to defend myself against

this same world:

you are not alone,
the poem said,
in the dark tunnel.

VI.

The brightness of the day becomes
the brightness of the night;
the fire becomes the mirror.

My friend the earth is bitter; I think
sunlight has failed her.
Bitter or weary, it is hard to say.

Between herself and the sun,
something has ended.
She wants, now, to be left alone;
I think we must give up
turning to her for affirmation.

Above the fields,
above the roofs of the village houses,
the brilliance that made all life possible
becomes the cold stars.

Lie still and watch:
they give nothing but ask nothing.

From within the earth's
bitter disgrace, coldness and barrenness

my friend the moon rises:
she is beautiful tonight, but when is she not beautiful?

At the River

One night that summer my mother decided it was time to tell me about
what she referred to as *pleasure,* though you could see she felt
some sort of unease about this ceremony, which she tried to cover up
by first taking my hand, as though somebody in the family had just
    died—
she went on holding my hand as she made her speech
which was more like a speech about mechanical engineering
than a conversation about pleasure. In her other hand
she had a book from which, apparently, she'd taken the main facts.
She did the same thing with the others, my two brothers and sister,
and the book was always the same book, dark blue,
though we each got our own copy.

There was a line drawing on the cover
showing a man and woman holding hands
but standing fairly far apart, like people on two sides of a dirt road.

Obviously, she and my father did not have a language for what they did
which, from what I could judge, wasn't pleasure.
At the same time, whatever holds human beings together
could hardly resemble those cool black-and-white diagrams, which
    suggested,
among other things, that you could only achieve pleasure
with a person of the opposite sex,
so you didn't get two sockets, say, and no plug.

School wasn't in session.
I went back to my room and shut the door
and my mother went into the kitchen
where my father was pouring glasses of wine for himself and his
    invisible guest

who—surprise—doesn't appear.
No, it's just my father and his friend the Holy Ghost
partying the night away until the bottle runs out,
after which my father continues sitting at the table
with an open book in front of him.

Tactfully, so as not to embarrass the Spirit,
my father handled all the glasses,
first his own, then the other, back and forth like every other night.

By then, I was out of the house.
It was summer; my friends used to meet at the river.
The whole thing seemed a grave embarrassment
although the truth was that, except for the boys, maybe we didn't
    understand mechanics.
The boys had the key right in front of them, in their hands if they
    wanted,
and many of them said they'd already used it,
though once one boy said this, the others said it too,
and of course people had older brothers and sisters.

We sat at the edge of the river discussing parents in general
and sex in particular. And a lot of information got shared,
and of course the subject was unfailingly interesting.
I showed people my book, *Ideal Marriage*—we all had a good laugh
    over it.
One night a boy brought a bottle of wine and we passed it around for
    a while.

More and more that summer we understood
that something was going to happen to us
that would change us.
And the group, all of us who used to meet this way,
the group would shatter, like a shell that falls away
so the bird can emerge.
Only of course it would be two birds emerging, pairs of birds.

We sat in the reeds at the edge of the river
throwing small stones. When the stones hit,
you could see the stars multiply for a second, little explosions of light
flashing and going out. There was a boy I was beginning to like,
not to speak to but to watch.
I liked to sit behind him to study the back of his neck.

And after a while we'd all get up together and walk back through the dark
to the village. Above the field, the sky was clear,
stars everywhere, like in the river, though these were the real stars,
even the dead ones were real.

But the ones in the river—
they were like having some idea that explodes suddenly into a thousand ideas,
not real, maybe, but somehow more lifelike.

When I got home, my mother was asleep, my father was still at the table,
reading his book. And I said, Did your friend go away?
And he looked at me intently for a while,
then he said, Your mother and I used to drink a glass of wine together
after dinner.

BILLY COLLINS

(1941-)

Poet Laureate Consultant in Poetry (2001-2003)

Time is not just money—sorry, Ben Franklin—time is a way of telling us if we are moving at the right pace through the life that has been given us. One of the most basic pleasures of poetry is the way it slows us down. The intentionality of its language gives us pause. Its formal arrangement checks our haste.

B illy Collins, a master of the art of engagement, writes poems that seem to speak only to you, the one-in-a-million reader. At his standing-room-only readings, alert audiences are by turns rapt, amused, wide-eyed, laughing out loud. Like a great athlete, Collins makes an extraordinarily difficult literary feat—capturing a reader's attention—appear easy. This isn't because he avoids difficult or even arcane topics. Collins, a professor at the City University of New York since 1968, is as learned as anyone writing today, and his poems are as likely to allude to figures from the history of art, literature, and political and historical events as to mugs of tea, suburban lawns, loaves of bread, and childrens' voices in swimming pools. However comfortable or reassuring his poems initially feel, they often turn on surprise—the quietest domestic scene opens up, without warning, to wonder or foreboding. Nearly every one of Collins's eight volumes of poems (the last of which, *Ballistics*, reportedly sold 65,000 copies) has one or two poems specifically addressed to his shapeshifting "Dear Reader," a figure, say, with a bowl of cereal just across the kitchen table or "the man I held the door for this / this morning at the bank or post office" or "the face behind the wheel of an oncoming car."

Collins believes that poetry should be a part of our daily lives. One of his major initiatives as poet laureate was Poetry 180, an online anthology of poems for high school and elementary school teachers "designed to make it easy for students to hear or read a poem on each of the 180 days of the school year." The poems he selects "are intended to be listened to. . . . A great time for the readings would be following the end of daily announcements over the public address system." His only stipulation: no analysis of the poems. The program was named for both the 180 days of the school year and the 180-degree turn Collins wants high school students to make in appreciating poetry by listening rather than dissecting. Collins's parodies his own relaxed activism for making the appreciation of poetry more intuitive in his well-known poem "Introduction to Poetry": "I ask them to take a poem and hold it up to the light / like a color slide. . . . / But all they want to do / is tie the poem to a chair with a rope / and torture a confession out of it. / They begin beating it with a hose / to find out what it really means."

Litany

You are the bread and the knife,
The crystal goblet and the wine.
—Jacques Crickillon

You are the bread and the knife,
the crystal goblet and the wine.
You are the dew on the morning grass,
and the burning wheel of the sun.
You are the white apron of the baker
and the marsh birds suddenly in flight.

However, you are not the wind in the orchard,
the plums on the counter,
or the house of cards.
And you are certainly not the pine-scented air.
There is no way you are the pine-scented air.

It is possible that you are the fish under the bridge,
maybe even the pigeon on the general's head,
but you are not even close
to being the field of cornflowers at dusk.

And a quick look in the mirror will show
that you are neither the boots in the corner
nor the boat asleep in its boathouse.

It might interest you to know,
speaking of the plentiful imagery of the world,
that I am the sound of rain on the roof.

I also happen to be the shooting star,
the evening paper blowing down an alley,
and the basket of chestnuts on the kitchen table.

I am also the moon in the trees
and the blind woman's teacup.
But don't worry, I am not the bread and the knife.
You are still the bread and the knife.
You will always be the bread and the knife,
not to mention the crystal goblet and—somehow—the wine.

Advice to Writers

Even if it keeps you up all night,
wash down the walls and scrub the floor
of your study before composing a syllable.

Clean the place as if the Pope were on his way.
Spotlessness is the niece of inspiration.

The more you clean, the more brilliant
your writing will be, so do not hesitate to take
to the open fields to scour the undersides
of rocks or swab in the dark forest
upper branches, nests full of eggs.

When you find your way back home
and stow the sponges and brushes under the sink,
you will behold in the light of dawn
the immaculate altar of your desk,
a clean surface in the middle of a clean world.

From a small vase, sparkling blue, lift
a yellow pencil, the sharpest of the bouquet,
and cover pages with tiny sentences
like long rows of devoted ants
that followed you in from the woods.

Introduction to Poetry

I ask them to take a poem
and hold it up to the light
like a color slide

or press an ear against its hive.

I say drop a mouse into a poem
and watch him probe his way out,

or walk inside the poem's room
and feel the walls for a light switch.

I want them to waterski
across the surface of a poem
waving at the author's name on the shore.

But all they want to do
is tie the poem to a chair with rope
and torture a confession out of it.

They begin beating it with a hose
to find out what it really means.

Pinup

The murkiness of the local garage is not so dense
that you cannot make out the calendar of pinup
drawings on the wall above a bench of tools.
Your ears are ringing with the sound of
the mechanic hammering on your exhaust pipe,
and as you look closer you notice that this month's
is not the one pushing the lawn mower, wearing
a straw hat and very short blue shorts,
her shirt tied in a knot just below her breasts.
Nor is it the one in the admiral's cap, bending
forward, resting her hands on a wharf piling,
glancing over the tiny anchors on her shoulders.
No, this is March, the month of great winds,
so appropriately it is the one walking her dog
along a city sidewalk on a very blustery day.
One hand is busy keeping her hat down on her head
and the other is grasping the little dog's leash,
so of course there is no hand left to push down
her dress which is billowing up around her waist
exposing her long stockinged legs and yes the secret
apparatus of her garter belt. Needless to say,
in the confusion of wind and excited dog
the leash has wrapped itself around her ankles
several times giving her a rather bridled
and helpless appearance which is added to
by the impossibly high heels she is teetering on.
You would like to come to her rescue,
gather up the little dog in your arms,
untangle the leash, lead her to safety,
and receive her bottomless gratitude, but

the mechanic is calling you over to look
at something under your car. It seems that he has
run into a problem and the job is going
to cost more than he had said and take
much longer than he had thought.
Well, it can't be helped, you hear yourself say
as you return to your place by the workbench,
knowing that as soon as the hammering resumes
you will slowly lift the bottom of the calendar
just enough to reveal a glimpse of what
the future holds in store: ah,
the red polka dot umbrella of April and her
upturned palm extended coyly into the rain.

Man in Space

All you have to do is listen to the way a man
sometimes talks to his wife at a table of people
and notice how intent he is on making his point
even though her lower lip is beginning to quiver,

and you will know why the women in science
fiction movies who inhabit a planet of their own
are not pictured making a salad or reading a magazine
when the men from earth arrive in their rocket,

why they are always standing in a semicircle
with their arms folded, their bare legs set apart,
their breasts protected by hard metal disks.

A Portrait of the Reader with a Bowl of Cereal

> *A poet . . . never speaks directly,*
> *as to someone at the breakfast table.*
> —Yeats

Every morning I sit across from you
at the same small table,
the sun all over the breakfast things—
curve of a blue-and-white pitcher,
a dish of berries—
me in a sweatshirt or robe,
you invisible.

Most days, we are suspended
over a deep pool of silence.
I stare straight through you
or look out the window at the garden,
the powerful sky,
a cloud passing behind a tree.

There is no need to pass the toast,
the pot of jam,
or pour you a cup of tea,
and I can hide behind the paper,
rotate in its drum of calamitous news.

But some days I may notice
a little door swinging open
in the morning air,
and maybe the tea leaves
of some dream will be stuck
to the china slope of the hour—

then I will lean forward,
elbows on the table,
with something to tell you,
and you will look up, as always,
your spoon dripping milk, ready to listen.

Picnic, Lightning

> *My very photogenic mother died in a freak accident (picnic, lightning)*
> *when I was three.*
> —*Lolita*

It is possible to be struck by a meteor
or a single-engine plane
while reading in a chair at home.
Safes drop from rooftops
and flatten the odd pedestrian
mostly within the panels of the comics,
but still, we know it is possible,
as well as the flash of summer lightning,
the thermos toppling over,
spilling out on the grass.

And we know the message
can be delivered from within.
The heart, no valentine,
decides to quit after lunch,
the power shut off like a switch,
or a tiny dark ship is unmoored
into the flow of the body's rivers,
the brain a monastery,
defenseless on the shore.

This is what I think about
when I shovel compost
into a wheelbarrow,
and when I fill the long flower boxes,
then press into rows
the limp roots of red impatiens—
the instant hand of Death
always ready to burst forth
from the sleeve of his voluminous cloak.

Then the soil is full of marvels,
bits of leaflike flakes off a fresco,
red-brown pine needles, a beetle quick
to burrow back under the loam.
Then the wheelbarrow is a wilder blue,
the clouds a brighter white,

and all I hear is the rasp of the steel edge
against a round stone,
the small plants singing
with lifted faces, and the click
of the sundial
as one hour sweeps into the next.

Forgetfulness

The name of the author is the first to go
followed obediently by the title, the plot,
the heartbreaking conclusion, the entire novel
which suddenly becomes one you have never read, never even heard of,

as if, one by one, the memories you used to harbor
decided to retire to the southern hemisphere of the brain,
to a little fishing village where there are no phones.

Long ago you kissed the names of the nine Muses goodbye
and watched the quadratic equation pack its bag,
and even now as you memorize the order of the planets,

something else is slipping away, a state flower perhaps,
the address of an uncle, the capital of Paraguay.

Whatever it is you are struggling to remember
it is not poised on the tip of your tongue,
not even lurking in some obscure corner of your spleen.

It has floated away down a dark mythological river
whose name begins with an *L* as far as you can recall,

well on your own way to oblivion where you will join those
who have even forgotten how to swim and how to ride a bicycle.

No wonder you rise in the middle of the night
to look up the date of a famous battle in a book on war.
No wonder the moon in the window seems to have drifted
out of a love poem that you used to know by heart.

Sonnet

All we need is fourteen lines, well, thirteen now,
and after this one just a dozen
to launch a little ship on love's storm-tossed seas,
then only ten more left like rows of beans.
How easily it goes unless you get Elizabethan

and insist the iambic bongos must be played
and rhymes positioned at the ends of lines,
one for every station of the cross.
But hang on here while we make the turn
into the final six where all will be resolved,
where longing and heartache will find an end,
where Laura will tell Petrarch to put down his pen,
take off those crazy medieval tights,
blow out the lights, and come at last to bed.

Another Reason Why I Don't Keep a Gun in the House

The neighbors' dog will not stop barking.
He is barking the same high, rhythmic bark
that he barks every time they leave the house.
They must switch him on on their way out.

The neighbors' dog will not stop barking.
I close all the windows in the house
and put on a Beethoven symphony full blast
but I can still hear him muffled under the music,
barking, barking, barking,

and now I can see him sitting in the orchestra,
his head raised confidently as if Beethoven
had included a part for barking dog.

When the record finally ends he is still barking,
sitting there in the oboe section barking,
his eyes fixed on the conductor who is
entreating him with his baton

while the other musicians listen in respectful
silence to the famous barking dog solo,
that endless coda that first established
Beethoven as an innovative genius.

The Names

Yesterday, I lay awake in the palm of the night.
A fine rain stole in, unhelped by any breeze,
And when I saw the silver glaze on the windows,
I started with A, with Ackerman, as it happened,
Then Baxter and Calabro,
Davis and Eberling, names falling into place
As droplets fell through the dark.
Names printed on the ceiling of the night.
Names slipping around a watery bend.
Twenty-six willows on the banks of a stream.
In the morning, I walked out barefoot
Among thousands of flowers
Heavy with dew like the eyes of tears,
And each had a name?
Fiori inscribed on a yellow petal
Then Gonzalez and Han, Ishikawa and Jenkins.
Names written in the air
And stitched into the cloth of the day.
A name under a photograph taped to a mailbox.
Monogram on a torn shirt,
I see you spelled out on storefront windows
And on the bright unfurled awnings of this city.
I say the syllables as I turn a corner?
Kelly and Lee,

Medina, Nardella, and O'Connor.
When I peer into the woods,
I see a thick tangle where letters are hidden
As in a puzzle concocted for children.
Parker and Quigley in the twigs of an ash,
Rizzo, Schubert, Torres, and Upton,
Secrets in the boughs of an ancient maple.
Names written in the pale sky.
Names rising in the updraft amid buildings.
Names silent in stone
Or cried out behind a door.
Names blown over the earth and out to sea.
In the evening? weakening light, the last swallows.
A boy on a lake lifts his oars.
A woman by a window puts a match to a candle,
And the names are outlined on the rose clouds?
Vanacore and Wallace,
(let X stand, if it can, for the ones unfound)
Then Young and Ziminsky, the final jolt of Z.
Names etched on the head of a pin.
One name spanning a bridge, another undergoing a tunnel.
A blue name needled into the skin.
Names of citizens, workers, mothers and fathers,
The bright-eyed daughter, the quick son.
Alphabet of names in green rows in a field.
Names in the small tracks of birds.
Names lifted from a hat
Or balanced on the tip of the tongue.
Names wheeled into the dim warehouse of memory.
So many names, there is barely room on the walls of the heart.

The Breather

Just as in the horror movies
when someone discovers that the phone calls
are coming from inside the house

so, too, I realized
that our tender overlapping
has been taking place only inside me.

All that sweetness, the love and desire—
it's just been me dialing myself
then following the ringing to another room

to find no one on the line,
well, sometimes a little breathing
but more often than not, nothing.

To think that all this time—
which would include the boat rides,
the airport embraces, and all the drinks—

it's been only me and the two telephones,
the one on the wall in the kitchen
and the extension in the darkened guestroom upstairs.

Searching

I recall someone once admitting
that all he remembered of *Anna Karenina*
was something about a picnic basket,

and now, after consuming a book
devoted to the subject of Barcelona—
its people, its history, its complex architecture—

all I remember is the mention
of an albino gorilla, the inhabitant of a park
where the Citadel of the Bourbons once stood.

The sheer paleness of him looms over
all the notable names and dates
as the evening strollers stop before him

and point to show their children.
These locals called him Snowflake,
and here he has been mentioned again in print

in the hope of keeping his pallid flame alive
and helping him, despite his name, to endure
in this poem where he has found another cage.

Oh, Snowflake,
I had no interest in the capital of Catalonia—
its people, its history, its complex architecture—

no, you were the reason
I kept my light on late into the night
turning all those pages, searching for you everywhere.

Pornography

In this sentimental painting of rustic life,
a rosy-cheeked fellow
in a broad hat and ballooning green pants

is twirling a peasant girl in a red frock
while a boy is playing a squeeze-box
near a turned-over barrel

upon which rest a knife, a jug, and a small drinking glass.
Two men in rough jackets
are playing cards at a wooden table.

And in the background a woman in a bonnet
stands behind the half-open Dutch door
talking to a merchant or a beggar who is leaning on a cane.

This is all I need to inject me with desire,
to fill me with the urge to lie down with you,
or someone very much like you,

on a cool marble floor or any fairly flat surface
as clouds go flying by
and the rustle of tall leafy trees

mixes with the notes of birdsong—
so clearly does the work speak of vanishing time,
obsolete musical instruments,

passing fancies, and the corpse
of the largely forgotten painter moldering
somewhere beneath the surface of present-day France.

STANLEY KUNITZ

(1905–2006)

Poet Laureate Consultant in Poetry (2000–2001)
Consultant in Poetry (1974–1976)

If we want to know what it felt like to be alive at any given moment in the long odyssey of the race, it is to poetry we must turn. The moment is dear to us, precisely because it is so fugitive, and it is somewhat of a paradox that poets should spend a lifetime hunting for the magic that will make the moment stay. Art is that chalice into which we pour the wine of transcendence. What is imagination but a reflection of our yearning to belong to eternity as well as to time?

Throughout his long and distinguished career, which spanned nearly eight decades, Stanley Kunitz maintained that poetry was the last form of uncorrupted art because it has no market value. He became the tenth poet laureate of the United States when he was ninety-five, having held the consultant's chair thirty years earlier. Born and raised in Worcester, Massachusetts, Kunitz published his first book in 1930, while supporting himself by restoring and living in old farmhouses in Connecticut and Bucks County. He then settled in Greenwich Village and Provincetown, Massachusetts. He helped found Poets House, an extensive poetry library and reading room in New York City, and the Fine Arts Work Center in Provincetown, taught writing at Bennington College and Columbia University, edited the Yale Series of Younger Poets for thirty-five years, and was mentor to many poets, including laureate Louise Glück.

Kunitz's second book, *Passport to the War: A Selection of Poems*, was published after he had been drafted into the army. A pacifist, Kunitz agreed to serve on the condition that he would not bear arms—he was assigned to latrine and KP duty but was permitted to start a camp newspaper in his free time, which received an award as the best camp publication in the Army. His early work reflected his admiration for the ornate poetic conceits of English metaphysical poets like John Donne and George Herbert. "In my youth, as might be expected, I had little knowledge of the world to draw on. . . . But I had fallen in love with language and was excited by ideas, including the idea of being a poet. Early poetry is much more likely to be abstract because of the poverty of experience." Kunitz urged young poets to put off academic careers for as long as possible, to live as free agents. He balked at the thought of being a poet laureate, saying it was "a vestige from a monarchic age which doesn't fit in with the adversary" spirit of the poet. In the end, he chose to use his various government posts (he was also poet laureate of New York State) as bully pulpits from which to praise and defend "the solitary conscience as opposed to the great power structure of the superstate."

Kunitz's Pulitzer Prize–winning *Selected Poems, 1928–1958* ended what he thought of as the more intellectual and remote poems of the first stage of his career. His later poems became more autobiographical, in some cases recounting the suicide of his father before his birth. Robert Lowell praised this shift in Kunitz's work, saying, "I don't know of another in prose or verse that gives in a few pages the impression of a large autobiography." Discussing his turn toward self-revelatory poetry, Kunitz said, "By its nature poetry is an intimate medium. . . . Perhaps that's why it is so dangerously seductive to the creative spirit. The transformation of individual experience—the transpersonalization of the persona, if you will—is work that the imagination has to do, its obligatory task. One of the problems with so much of what was called, in the sixties, confessional poetry was that it relied excessively on the exploitation of self, on the shock effect of raw experience. My conviction is that poetry is a legendary, not an anecdotal, art."

Halley's Comet

Miss Murphy in first grade
wrote its name in chalk
across the board and told us
it was roaring down the stormtracks
of the Milky Way at frightful speed
and if it wandered off its course
and smashed into the earth
there'd be no school tomorrow.
A red-bearded preacher from the hills
with a wild look in his eyes
stood in the public square
at the playground's edge
proclaiming he was sent by God
to save every one of us,
even the little children.
"Repent, ye sinners!" he shouted,
waving his hand-lettered sign.
At supper I felt sad to think
that it was probably
the last meal I'd share
with my mother and my sisters;
but I felt excited too
and scarcely touched my plate.
So mother scolded me
and sent me early to my room.
The whole family's asleep
except for me. They never heard me steal
into the stairwell hall and climb
the ladder to the fresh night air.
Look for me, Father, on the roof

of the red brick building
at the foot of Green Street—
that's where we live, you know, on the top floor.
I'm the boy in the white flannel gown
sprawled on this coarse gravel bed
searching the starry sky,
waiting for the world to end.

I Dreamed That I Was Old

I dreamed that I was old: in stale declension
Fallen from my prime, when company
Was mine, cat-nimbleness, and green invention,
Before time took my leafy hours away.

My wisdom, ripe with body's ruin, found
Itself tart recompense for what was lost
In false exchange: since wisdom in the ground
Has no apocalypse or pentecost.

I wept for my youth, sweet passionate young thought,
And cozy women dead that by my side
Once lay: I wept with bitter longing, not
Remembering how in my youth I cried.

The Waltzer in the House

A sweet, a delicate white mouse,
A little blossom of a beast,
Is waltzing in the house
Among the crackers and the yeast.

O the swaying of his legs!
O the bobbing of his head!
The lady, beautiful and kind,
The blue-eyed mistress, lately wed,
Has almost laughed away her wits
To see the pretty mouse that sits
On his tiny pink behind
And swaying, bobbing, begs.

She feeds him tarts and curds,
Seed packaged for the birds,
And figs, and nuts, and cheese;
Polite as Pompadour to please
The dainty waltzer of her house,
The sweet, the delicate, the innocent white mouse.

As in a dream, as in a trance,
She loves his rhythmic elegance,
She laughs to see his bobbing dance.

The War Against the Trees

The man who sold his lawn to standard oil
Joked with his neighbors come to watch the show
While the bulldozers, drunk with gasoline,
Tested the virtue of the soil
Under the branchy sky
By overthrowing first the privet-row.

Forsythia-forays and hydrangea-raids
Were but preliminaries to a war
Against the great-grandfathers of the town,
So freshly lopped and maimed.
They struck and struck again,
And with each elm a century went down.

All day the hireling engines charged the trees,
Subverting them by hacking underground
In grub-dominions, where dark summer's mole
Rampages through his halls,
Till a northern seizure shook
Those crowns, forcing the giants to their knees.

I saw the ghosts of children at their games
Racing beyond their childhood in the shade,
And while the green world turned its death-foxed page
And a red wagon wheeled,
I watched them disappear
Into the suburbs of their grievous age.

Ripped from the craters much too big for hearts
The club-roots bared their amputated coils,
Raw gorgons matted blind, whose pocks and scars
Cried Moon! on a corner lot
One witness-moment, caught
In the rear-view mirrors of the passing cars.

An Old Cracked Tune

My name is Solomon Levi,
the desert is my home,
my mother's breast was thorny,
and father I had none.

The sands whispered, *Be separate*,
the stones taught me, *Be hard*.
I dance, for the joy of surviving,
on the edge of the road.

The Portrait

My mother never forgave my father
for killing himself,
especially at such an awkward time
and in a public park,
that spring
when I was waiting to be born.
She locked his name
in her deepest cabinet
and would not let him out,
though I could hear him thumping.
When I came down from the attic
with the pastel portrait in my hand
of a long-lipped stranger
with a brave moustache
and deep brown level eyes,
she ripped it into shreds

without a single word
and slapped me hard.
In my sixty-fourth year
I can feel my cheek
still burning.

King of the River

If the water were clear enough,
if the water were still,
but the water is not clear,
the water is not still,
you would see yourself,
slipped out of your skin,
nosing upstream,
slapping, thrashing,
tumbling
over the rocks
till you paint them
with your belly's blood:
Finned Ego,
yard of muscle that coils,
uncoils.

If the knowledge were given you,
but it is not given,
for the membrane is clouded
with self-deceptions
and the iridescent image swims
through a mirror that flows,
you would surprise yourself

in that other flesh
heavy with milt,
bruised, battering toward the dam
that lips the orgiastic pool.

Come. Bathe in these waters.
Increase and die.

If the power were granted you
to break out of your cells,
but the imagination fails
and the doors of the senses close
on the child within,
you would dare to be changed,
as you are changing now,
into the shape you dread
beyond the merely human.
A dry fire eats you.
Fat drips from your bones.
The flutes of your gills discolor.
You have become a ship for parasites.
The great clock of your life
is slowing down,
and the small clocks run wild.
For this you were born.
You have cried to the wind
and heard the wind's reply:
"I did not choose the way,
the way chose me."
You have tasted the fire on your tongue
till it is swollen black
with a prophetic joy:
"Burn with me!
The only music is time,
the only dance is love."

If the heart were pure enough,
but it is not pure,
you would admit
that nothing compels you
any more, nothing
at all abides,
but nostalgia and desire;
the two-way ladder
between heaven and hell.
On the threshold
of the last mystery,
at the brute absolute hour,
you have looked into the eyes
of your creature self,
which are glazed with madness,
and you say
he is not broken but endures,
limber and firm
in the state of his shining,
forever inheriting his salt kingdom,
from which he is banished
forever.

The Knot

I've tried to seal it in,
that cross-grained knot
on the opposite wall,
scored in the lintel of my door,
but it keeps bleeding through
into the world we share.
Mornings when I wake,

curled in my web,
I hear it come
with a rush of resin
out of the trauma
of its lopping-off.
Obstinate bud,
sticky with life,
mad for the rain again,
it racks itself with shoots
that crackle overhead,
dividing as they grow.
Let be! Let be!
I shake my wings
and fly into its boughs.

Passing Through

—on my seventy-ninth birthday

Nobody in the widow's household
ever celebrated anniversaries.
In the secrecy of my room
I would not admit I cared
that my friends were given parties.
Before I left town for school
my birthday went up in smoke
in a fire at City Hall that gutted
the Department of Vital Statistics.
If it weren't for a census report
of a five-year-old White Male

sharing my mother's address
at the Green Street tenement in Worcester
I'd have no documentary proof
that I exist. You are the first,
my dear, to bully me
into these festive occasions.

Sometimes, you say, I wear
an abstracted look that drives you
up the wall, as though it signified
distress or disaffection.
Don't take it so to heart.
Maybe I enjoy not-being as much
as being who I am. Maybe
it's time for me to practice
growing old. The way I look
at it, I'm passing through a phase:
gradually I'm changing to a word.
Whatever you choose to claim
of me is always yours;
nothing is truly mine
except my name. I only
borrowed this dust.

My Mother's Pears

Plump, green-gold, Worcester's pride,
        transported through autumn skies
                in a box marked HANDLE WITH CARE

sleep eighteen Bartlett pears,
        hand-picked and polished and packed
                for deposit at my door,

each in its crinkled nest
        with a stub of stem attached
                and a single bright leaf like a flag.

A smaller than usual crop,
        but still enough to share with me,
                as always at harvest time.

Those strangers are my friends
        whose kindness blesses the house
                my mother built at the edge of town

beyond the last trolley-stop
        when the century was young, and she
                proposed, for her children's sake,

to marry again, not knowing how soon
        the windows would grow dark
                and the velvet drapes come down.

Rubble accumulates in the yard,
        workmen are hammering on the roof,
                I am standing knee-deep in dirt

with a shovel in my hand.
        Mother has wrapped a kerchief round her head,
                her glasses glint in the sun.

When my sisters appear on the scene,
        gangly and softly tittering,
                she waves them back into the house

to fetch us pails of water,
        and they skip out of our sight
                in their matching middy blouses.

I summon up all my strength
    to set the pear tree in the ground,
        unwinding its burlap shroud.

It is taller than I. "Make room
    for the roots!" my mother cries,
        "Dig the hole deeper."

Touch Me

Summer is late, my heart.
Words plucked out of the air
some forty years ago
when I was wild with love
and torn almost in two
scatter like leaves this night
of whistling wind and rain.
It is my heart that's late,
it is my song that's flown.
Outdoors all afternoon
under a gunmetal sky
staking my garden down,
I kneeled to the crickets trilling
underfoot as if about
to burst from their crusty shells;
and like a child again
marveled to hear so clear
and brave a music pour
from such a small machine.
What makes the engine go?
Desire, desire, desire.
The longing for the dance

stirs in the buried life.
One season only,

              and it's done.
So let the battered old willow
thrash against the windowpanes
and the house timbers creak.
Darling, do you remember
the man you married? Touch me,
remind me who I am.

Promise Me

Only, when I am sudden loss
Of consequence for mind and stair,
Picking my dogged way from us
To whom, recessive in some where
Of recollection, with the cross
Fallen, the breast in disrepair:

Only, when loosening clothes, you lean
Out of your window sleepily,
And with luxurious, lidded mien
Sniff at the bitter dark—dear she,
Think somewhat gently of, between
Love ended and beginning, me.

The System

That pack of scoundrels
tumbling through the gate
emerges
as the Order of the State.

Three Floors

Mother was a crack of light
and a gray eye peeping;
I made believe by breathing hard
that I was sleeping.

Sister's doughboy on last leave
had robbed me of her hand;
downstairs at intervals she played
Warum on the baby grand.

Under the roof a wardrobe trunk
whose lock a boy could pick
contained a red Masonic hat
and a walking stick.

Bolt upright in my bed that night
I saw my father flying;
the wind was walking on my neck,
the windowpanes were crying.

The Wellfleet Whale

*A few summers ago, on Cape Cod, a whale foundered on the beach, a
sixty-three-foot finback whale. When the tide went out, I approached him.
He was lying there, in monstrous desolation, making the most terrifying
noises—rumbling—groaning. I put my hands on his flanks and I could feel
the life inside him. And while I was standing there, suddenly he opened his
eye. It was a big, red, cold eye, and it was staring directly at me. A shudder of
recognition passed between us. Then the eye closed forever. I've been thinking
about whales ever since.*

—Journal entry

1

You have your language too,
      an eerie medley of clicks
           and hoots and trills,
location-notes and love calls,
      whistles and grunts. Occasionally,
          it's like furniture being smashed,
or the creaking of a mossy door,
      sounds that all melt into a liquid
          song with endless variations,
as if to compensate
      for the vast loneliness of the sea.
          Sometimes a disembodied voice
breaks in as if from distant reefs,
      and it's as much as one can bear
          to listen to its long mournful cry,
a sorrow without name, both more
      and less than human. It drags
          across the ear like a record
running down.

2

No wind. No waves. No clouds.
    Only the whisper of the tide,
        as it withdrew, stroking the shore,
a lazy drift of gulls overhead,
    and tiny points of light
        bubbling in the channel.
It was the tag-end of summer.
    From the harbor's mouth
        you coasted into sight,
flashing news of your advent,
    the crescent of your dorsal fin
        clipping the diamonded surface.
We cheered at the sign of your greatness
    when the black barrel of your head
        erupted, ramming the water,
and you flowered for us
    in the jet of your spouting.

3

All afternoon you swam
    tirelessly round the bay,
        with such an easy motion,
the slightest downbeat of your tail,
    an almost imperceptible
        undulation of your flippers,
you seemed like something poured,
    not driven; you seemed
        to marry grace with power.
And when you bounded into air,
    slapping your flukes,
        we thrilled to look upon

pure energy incarnate
          as nobility of form.
                    You seemed to ask of us
not sympathy, or love,
          or understanding,
                    but awe and wonder.

That night we watched you
          swimming in the moon.
                    Your back was molten silver.
We guessed your silent passage
          by the phosphorescence in your wake.
                    At dawn we found you stranded on the rocks.

4

There came a boy and a man
          and yet other men running, and two
                    schoolgirls in yellow halters
and a housewife bedecked
          with curlers, and whole families in beach
                    buggies with assorted yelping dogs.
The tide was almost out.
          We could walk around you,
                    as you heaved deeper into the shoal,
crushed by your own weight,
          collapsing into yourself,
                    your flippers and your flukes
quivering, your blowhole
          spasmodically bubbling, roaring.
                    In the pit of your gaping mouth
you bared your fringework of baleen,
          a thicket of horned bristles.
                    When the Curator of Mammals

arrived from Boston
     to take samples of your blood
         you were already oozing from below.
Somebody had carved his initials
     in your flank. Hunters of souvenirs
         had peeled off strips of your skin,
a membrane thin as paper.
     You were blistered and cracked by the sun.
         The gulls had been pecking at you.
The sound you made was a hoarse and fitful bleating.

What drew us, like a magnet, to your dying?
     You made a bond between us,
         the keepers of the nightfall watch,
who gathered in a ring around you,
     boozing in the bonfire light.
         Toward dawn we shared with you
your hour of desolation,
     the huge lingering passion
         of your unearthly outcry,
as you swung your blind head
     toward us and laboriously opened
         a bloodshot, glistening eye,
in which we swam with terror and recognition.

5

Voyager, chief of the pelagic world,
     you brought with you the myth
         of another country, dimly remembered,
where flying reptiles
     lumbered over the steaming marshes
         and trumpeting thunder lizards

wallowed in the reeds.
   While empires rose and fell on land,
     your nation breasted the open main,
rocked in the consoling rhythm
   of the tides. Which ancestor first plunged
     head-down through zones of colored twilight
to scour the bottom of the dark?
   You ranged the North Atlantic track
     from Port-of-Spain to Baffin Bay,
edging between the ice-floes
   through the fat of summer,
     lob-tailing, breaching, sounding,
grazing in the pastures of the sea
   on krill-rich orange plankton
     crackling with life.
You prowled down the continental shelf,
   guided by the sun and stars
     and the taste of alluvial silt
on your way southward
   to the warm lagoons,
     the tropic of desire,
where the lovers lie belly to belly
   in the rub and nuzzle of their sporting;
     and you turned, like a god in exile,
out of your wide primeval element,
   delivered to the mercy of time.

     Master of the whale-roads,
let the white wings of the gulls
   spread out their cover.
     You have become like us,
disgraced and mortal.

ROBERT PINSKY

(1940-)

Poet Laureate Consultant in Poetry (1997-2000)

The craving for [poetry] is even stronger in reaction to how powerful and brilliantly organized mass art has become. Mass art is being designed by talented experts, and being distributed and rapidly duplicated. The copy is the medium. The ultimate medium of the poem, even if the person reads the poem from a book that has been printed from 50,000 copies—the ultimate medium is one person's voice. Poetry is a vocal art. The medium of popular music is an album. It's an easily duplicable CD. In poetry, the mass distribution of the written word is only the means to an end.

During each of his record three terms as poet laureate, Robert Pinsky was the most visible laureate to hold the position. He often gave as many as three readings a day, all over the United States. "I think poetry is a vital part of our intelligence, our ability to learn, our ability to remember, the relationship between our bodies and minds," he told the *Christian Science Monitor* while in office. Pinsky deployed his new-media knowledge (he is the only laureate to have published a cybernovel and is currently poetry editor of the Internet magazine *Slate*) to distribute poetry more widely. In his first term he devised the Favorite Poem Project to publicize the universal presence of poetry in American life. The project began with a one-year open call for submissions. Ordinary Americans were invited to name their favorite poems—and some entrants were asked to read for a permanent audio archive at the Library of Congress. Eighteen thousand Americans wrote in volunteering to share their favorite poems, ranging from ages five to ninety-seven, from every state, with diverse occupations, levels of education, and backgrounds. Pinsky initially set a goal of recording one hundred people, but he was inundated with letters and e-mails, and the project took off of its own accord. In 1999 he coedited *Americans' Favorite Poems: The Favorite Poem Project Anthology*. The Web site for the Favorite Poem Project is now both an archive of Americans reciting favorite poems and a resource for elementary and high school teachers, with lesson plans culled from summer seminars at Boston University, where poets teach master classes on many of the favorite poems.

Born in New Jersey, Pinsky is the author, editor, or translator of nearly twenty acclaimed books. He received his B.A. from Rutgers and his Ph.D. in philosophy from Stanford, where he was a Stegner Fellow in creative writing and studied under the poet and critic Yvor Winters. Pinsky's first collection, *Sadness and Happiness*, was compared to the work of Rainer Maria Rilke, James Wright, and Robert Lowell. His book-length poem *An Explanation of America* links modern America and the ancient Roman Empire of Augustus and Horace. Pinsky has continued his exploration of history and connections between personal and national memory.

The power of memory as a wellspring to a meaningful collective American identity has been the subject of many of Pinsky's lectures and essays. In a *New York Times Book Review* essay, Pinsky wrote: "Poetry is, among other things, a technology for remembering. But this fact may touch our lives far more profoundly than jingles for remembering how many days there are in June. The buried conduits among memory and emotion and the physical sounds of language may touch our inner life every day.... Poetry, a form of language far older than prose, is under our skins." But this sense of memory is one Pinsky sees in a constant state of play with that other great American drive for "making it up as we go along." Pinsky, a devoted fan of jazz, believes that improvisation is America's greatest contribution to world culture. In a 1999 essay for *The Atlantic*, he observes: "Our greatness consists precisely in the fact that we are making it up as we go along—that we are perpetually in the process of devising ourselves as a people. An improvised, eclectic, synthesizing quality pervades our cultural products. This quality seems unmistakable in both the most glorious and the stupidest of our cultural manifestations— in the transcendent music of Charlie Parker and in the embarrassing dumbness of Super Bowl halftime shows. The improvisational, provisional spirit is in the poems of Wallace Stevens and in the denim pants of Levi Strauss."

Samurai Song

When I had no roof I made
Audacity my roof. When I had
No supper my eyes dined.

When I had no eyes I listened.
When I had no ears I thought.
When I had no thought I waited.

When I had no father I made
Care my father. When I had
No mother I embraced order.

When I had no friend I made
Quiet my friend. When I had no
Enemy I opposed my body.

When I had no temple I made
My voice my temple. I have
No priest, my tongue is my choir.

When I have no means fortune
Is my means. When I have
Nothing, death will be my fortune.

Need is my tactic, detachment
Is my strategy. When I had
No lover I courted my sleep.

Doctor Frolic

Felicity the healer isn't young
And you don't look him up unless you need him.
Clown's eyes, Pope's nose, a mouth for dirty stories,
He made his bundle in the Great Depression

And now, a jovial immigrant success
In baggy pinstripes, he winks and wheezes gossip,
Village stories that could lift your hair
Or lance a boil; the small town dirt, the dope,

The fishy deals and incestuous combinations,
The husband and the wife of his wife's brother,
The hospital contract, the certificate . . .
A realist and hardy omnivore,

He strolls the jetties when the month is right
With a knife and lemons in his pocket, after
Live mussels from among the smelly rocks,
Preventative of impotence and goitre.

And as though the sight of tissue healing crooked
Pleased him, like the ocean's vaginal taste,
He'll stitch your thumb up so it shows for life.
And where he once was the only quack in town

We all have heard his half-lame joke, the one
About the operation that succeeded,
The tangy line that keeps that clever eye
So merry in the punchinello face.

Ralegh's Prizes

And Summer turns her head with its dark tangle
All the way toward us; and the trees are heavy,
With little sprays of limp green maple and linden
Adhering after a rainstorm to the sidewalk
Where yellow pollen dries in pools and runnels.

Along the oceanfront, pink neon at dusk:
The long, late dusk, a light wind from the water
Lifting a girl's hair forward against her cheek
And swaying a chain of bulbs.
                                        In luminous booths,
The bright, traditional wheel is on its ratchet,
And ticking gaily at its little pawl;
And the surf revolves; and passing cars and people,
Their brilliant colors—all strange and hopeful as Ralegh's
Trophies: the balsam, the prizes of untried virtue,
Bananas and armadillos that a Captain
Carries his Monarch from another world.

Shirt

The back, the yoke, the yardage. Lapped seams,
The nearly invisible stitches along the collar
Turned in a sweatshop by Koreans or Malaysians

Gossiping over tea and noodles on their break
Or talking money or politics while one fitted
This armpiece with its overseam to the band

Of cuff I button at my wrist. The presser, the cutter,
The wringer, the mangle. The needle, the union,
The treadle, the bobbin. The code. The infamous blaze

At the Triangle Factory in nineteen-eleven.
One hundred and forty-six died in the flames
On the ninth floor, no hydrants, no fire escapes—

The witness in a building across the street
Who watched how a young man helped a girl to step
up to the windowsill, then held her out

Away from the masonry wall and let her drop.
And then another. As if he were helping them up
To enter a streetcar, and not eternity.

A third before he dropped her put her arms
Around his neck and kissed him. Then he held
Her into space, and dropped her. Almost at once

He stepped to the sill himself, his jacket flared
And fluttered up from his shirt as he came down,
Air filling up the legs of his gray trousers—

Like Hart Crane's Bedlamite, "shrill shirt ballooning."
Wonderful how the pattern matches perfectly
Across the placket and over the twin bar-tacked

Corners of both pockets, like a strict rhyme
Or a major chord. Prints, plaids, checks,
Houndstooth, Tattersall, Madras. The clan tartans

Invented by mill-owners inspired by the hoax of Ossian,
To control their savage Scottish workers, tamed
By a fabricated heraldry: MacGregor,

Bailey, MacMartin. The kilt, devised for workers
To wear among the dusty clattering looms.
Weavers, carders, spinners. The loader,

The docker, the navvy. The planter, the picker, the sorter
Sweating at her machine in a litter of cotton
As slaves in calico headrags sweated in fields:

George Herbert, your descendant is a Black
Lady in South Carolina, her name is Irma
And she inspected my shirt. Its color and fit

And feel and its clean smell have satisfied
Both her and me. We have culled its cost and quality
Down to the buttons of simulated bone,

The buttonholes, the sizing, the facing, the characters
Printed in black on neckband and tail. The shape,
The label, the labor, the color, the shade. The shirt.

ABC

Any body can die, evidently. Few
Go happily, irradiating joy,

Knowledge, love. Many
Need oblivion, painkillers,
Quickest respite.

Sweet time unafflicted,
Various world:

X = your zenith.

To Television

Not a "window on the world"
But as we call you,
A box a tube

Terrarium of dreams and wonders.
Coffer of shades, ordained
Cotillion of phosphors
Or liquid crystal

Homey miracle, tub
Of acquiescence, vein of defiance.
Your patron in the pantheon would be Hermes

Raster dance,
Quick one, little thief, escort
Of the dying and comfort of the sick,

In a blue glow my father and little sister sat
Snuggled in one chair watching you
Their wife and mother was sick in the head
I scorned you and them as I scorned so much

Now I like you best in a hotel room,
Maybe minutes
Before I have to face an audience: behind
The doors of the armoire, box
Within a box—Tom & Jerry, or also brilliant
And reassuring, Oprah Winfrey.

Thank you, for I watched, I watched
Sid Caesar speaking French and Japanese not
Through knowledge but imagination,
His quickness, and Thank you, I watched live
Jackie Robinson stealing

Home, the image—O strung shell—enduring
Fleeter than light like these words we
Remember in: they too are winged
At the helmet and ankles.

Jersey Rain

Now near the end of the middle stretch of road
What have I learned? Some earthly wiles. An art.
That often I cannot tell good fortune from bad,
That once had seemed so easy to tell apart.

The source of art and woe aslant in wind
Dissolves or nourishes everything it touches.
What roadbank gullies and ruts it doesn't mend
It carves the deeper, boiling tawny in ditches.

It spends itself regardless into the ocean.
It stains and scours and makes things dark or bright:
Sweat of the moon, a shroud of benediction,
The chilly liquefaction of day to night,

The Jersey rain, my rain, soaks all as one:
It smites Metuchen, Rahway, Saddle River,
Fair Haven, Newark, Little Silver, Bayonne.
I feel it churning even in fair weather

To craze distinction, dry the same as wet.
In ripples of heat the August drought still feeds
Vapors in the sky that swell to drench my state—
The Jersey rain, my rain, in streams and beads

Of indissoluble grudge and aspiration:
Original milk, replenisher of grief,
Descending destroyer, arrowed source of passion,
Silver and black, executioner, source of life.

Poem of Disconnected Parts

At Robben Island the political prisoners studied.
They coined the motto *Each one Teach one.*

In Argentina the torturers demanded the prisoners
Address them always as *"Profesor."*

Many of my friends are moved by guilt, but I
Am a creature of shame, I am ashamed to say.

Culture the lock, culture the key. Imagination
That calls the boiled sheep heads in the market "Smileys."

The first year at Guantánamo, Abdul Rahim Dost
Incised his Pashto poems into styrofoam cups.

*"The Sangomo says in our Zulu culture we do not
Worship our ancestors: we consult them."*

Becky is abandoned in 1902 and Rose dies giving
Birth in 1924 and Sylvia falls in 1951.

Still falling still dying still abandoned in 2006
Still nothing finished among the descendants.

I support the War, says the comic, it's just the Troops
I'm against: can't stand those Young People.

Proud of the fallen, proud of her son the bomber.
Ashamed of the government. Skeptical.

After the Klansman was found Not Guilty one juror
Said she just couldn't vote to convict a pastor.

Who do you write for? I write for dead people:
For Emily Dickinson, for my grandfather.

"The Ancestors say the problem with your Knees
Began in your Feet. It could move up your Back."

But later the Americans gave Dost not only paper
And pen but books. Hemingway, Dickens.

Old Aegyptius said, Whoever has called this Assembly,
For whatever reason—that is a good in itself.

O thirsty shades who regard the offering, O stained earth.
There are many fake Sangomos. This one is real.

Coloured prisoners got different meals and could wear
Long pants and underwear, Blacks got only shorts.

No he says he cannot regret the three years in prison:
Otherwise he would not have written those poems.

I have a small-town mind. Like the Greeks and Trojans.
Shame. Pride. Importance of looking bad or good.

Did he see anything like the prisoner on a leash? Yes,
In Afghanistan. In Guantánamo he was isolated.

Our enemies "disassemble" says the President.
Not that anyone at all couldn't mis-speak.

The *profesores* created nicknames for torture devices:
The Airplane. The Frog. Burping the Baby.

Not that those who behead the helpless in the name
Of God or tradition don't also write poetry.

Guilts, metaphors, traditions. Hunger strikes.
Culture the penalty. Culture the escape.

What could your children boast about you? What
Will your father say, down among the shades?

The Sangomo told Marvin, *"You are crushed by some
Weight. Only your own Ancestors can help you."*

The Forgetting

The forgetting I notice most as I get older is really a form of memory:
The undergrowth of things unknown to you young, that I have forgotten.

Memory of so much crap, jumbled with so much that seems to matter.
Lieutenant Calley. Captain Easy. Mayling Soong. Sibby Sisti.

And all the forgettings that preceded my own: Baghdad, Egypt, Greece,
The Plains, centuries of lootings of antiquities. Obscure atrocities.

Imagine!—a big tent filled with mostly kids, yelling for poetry. In fact
It happened, I was there in New Jersey at the famous poetry show.

I used to wonder, what if the Baseball Hall of Fame overflowed
With too many thousands of greats all in time unremembered?

Hardly anybody can name all eight of their great-grandparents.
Can you? Will your children's grandchildren remember your name?

You'll see, you little young jerks: your favorite music and your political
Furors, too, will need to get sorted in dusty electronic corridors.

In 1972, Chou En-lai was asked the lasting effects of the French
Revolution: "Too soon to tell." Remember?—or was it Mao Tse-tung?

Poetry made of air strains to reach back to Begats and suspiring
Forward into air, grunting to beget the hungry or overfed Future.

Ezra Pound praises the Emperor who appointed a committee of scholars
To pick the best 450 Noh plays and destroy all the rest, the fascist.

The stand-up master Steven Wright says he thinks he suffers from
Both amnesia and déjà vu: "I feel like I have forgotten this before."

Who remembers the arguments when jurors gave Pound the only prize
For poetry awarded by the United States Government? Until then.

I was in the big tent when the guy read his poem about how the Jews
Were warned to get out of the Twin Towers before the planes hit.

The crowd was applauding and screaming, they were happy—it isn't
That they were anti-Semitic, or anything. They just weren't listening. Or

No, they were listening, but that certain way. In it comes, you hear it, and
That selfsame second you swallow it or expel it: an ecstasy of forgetting.

Stupid Meditation on Peace

He does not come to coo.
—Gerard Manley Hopkins

Insomniac monkey-mind ponders the Dove,
Symbol not only of Peace but sexual
Love, the couple nestled and brooding.

After coupling, the human animal needs
The woman safe for nine months and more.
But the man after his turbulent minute or two

Is expendable. Usefully rash, reckless
For defense, in his void of redundancy
Willing to death and destruction.

Monkey-mind envies the male Dove
Who equally with the female secretes
Pigeon-milk for the young from his throat.

For peace, send all human males between
Fourteen and twenty-five to school
On the Moon, or better yet Mars.

But women too are capable of Unpeace,
Yes, and we older men too, venom-throats.
Here's a great comic who says on our journey

We choose one of two tributaries: the River
Of Peace, or the River of Productivity.
The current of Art he says runs not between

Banks with birdsong in the fragrant shadows—
No, an artist must follow the stinks and rapids
Of the branch that drives millstones and dynamos.

Is peace merely a vacuum, the negative
Of creation, or the absence of war?
The teaching says Peace is a positive energy:

Still something in me resists that sweet milk,
My mind resembles my restless, inferior cousin
Who fires his shit in handfuls from his cage.

XYZ

The cross the fork the zigzag—a few straight lines
For pain, quandary and evasion, the last of signs.

First Things to Hand

In the skull kept on the desk.
In the spider-pod in the dust.

Or nowhere. In milkmaids, in loaves,
Or nowhere. And if Socrates leaves

His house in the morning,
When he returns in the evening

He will find Socrates waiting
On the doorstep. Buddha the stick

You use to clear the path,
And Buddha the dog-doo you flick

Away with it, nowhere or in each
Several thing you touch:

The dollar bill, the button
That works the television.

Even in the joke, the three
Words American men say

After making love. *Where's
The remote?* In the tears

In things, proximate, intimate.
In the wired stem with root

And leaf nowhere of this lamp:
Brass base, aura of illumination,

Enlightenment, shade of grief.
Odor of the lamp, brazen.

The mind waiting in the mind
As in the first thing to hand.

Last Robot Song

It was a little newborn god
That made the first instrument:
Sweet vibration of
Mind, mind, mind
Enclosed in its orbit.

He scooped out a turtle's shell
And strung it with a rabbit's guts.
O what a stroke to invent
Music from an empty case
Strung with bloody filaments—

The wiry rabbitflesh
Plucked or strummed,
Pulled taut across the gutted
Resonant hull of the turtle:
Music from strings that
Tremble over a hollow—
Sweet conception, sweet
Instrument of

Mind, mind, mind:
Itself a capable vibration
Thrumming from here to there
In the cloven brainflesh
Contained in its helmet of bone—
Like an electronic boxful
Of channels and filaments
Bundled inside its case,
A little musical robot

Dreamed up by the mind
Embedded in the brain
With its blood-warm channels
And its humming network
Of neurons, engendering

The newborn baby god—
As clever and violent
As his own instrument

Of sweet, all-consuming
Imagination, held
By its own vibration,

Mind, mind, mind pulled
Taut in its bony shell,
Dreaming up Heaven and Hell.

ROBERT HASS

(1941–)

Poet Laureate Consultant in Poetry (1995–1997)

I think the task of art is to over and over again make images of a livable common life.

Robert Hass was the first poet laureate from the West Coast. Born in San Francisco, he began writing at the height of the Beat movement and poets like Allen Ginsberg and Gary Snyder were his early models. Hass has an abiding interest in world literature and has translated Chinese and Japanese poetry and was a close friend and translator of Nobel Prize winner Czeslaw Milosz. One of his most popular books is a translation of haiku by Basho, Buson, and Issan, which made haiku into one of the best-known poetic forms. Hass's engaging critical voice has introduced many new readers to the emotional and intellectual pleasures of reading poetry. His first book of poetry was published in the Yale Series of Younger Poets in 1973. His second, *Praise*, won the William Carlos Williams Award in 1979 and is widely regarded as one of the most influential poetry volume of the seventies.

As poet laureate, Hass continued the work of his predecessor, Rita Dove, in making the post a very public position, one primarily focused on programs that increased literacy. He read throughout the country, wrote a syndicated newspaper column for the *Washington Post* introducing general readers to short lyric poems and continued his full-time teaching position at the University of California, Berkeley. He did not write any new poetry during his two years in and out of Washington. During his readings as laureate Hass asked audiences to take action against cuts in funding for the National Endowment for the Arts and for the national parks. He said in an interview that "the first time I went to Washington was to levitate the Pentagon as a way of protesting the war . . . I've gone from trying to levitate the Pentagon to trying to levitate the Pentagon, just in a different way."

Hass ardently believes that "values come from the imagination," that "poets have a moral responsibility to make and refresh images of justice and images of common life." He sees—and urges others to see—a direct relationship between the imagination and public policy: "American writing, including poetry, is urgently about what we care about in all kinds of ways. In some long run, new writing creates the values that are eventually going to seep into the larger culture. Romanticism passed through Wordsworth to Thoreau, Thoreau to John Muir, to Teddy Roosevelt, and then you've got national parks. But somebody had to see Yosemite and the Adirondacks that way before we understood that they had to be valued."

Meditation at Lagunitas

All the new thinking is about loss.
In this it resembles all the old thinking.
The idea, for example, that each particular erases
the luminous clarity of a general idea. That the clown-
faced woodpecker probing the dead sculpted trunk
of that black birch is, by his presence,
some tragic falling off from a first world
of undivided light. Or the other notion that,
because there is in this world no one thing
to which the bramble of *blackberry* corresponds,
a word is elegy to what it signifies.
We talked about it late last night and in the voice
of my friend, there was a thin wire of grief, a tone
almost querulous. After a while I understood that,
talking this way, everything dissolves: *justice,*
pine, hair, woman, you and *I*. There was a woman
I made love to and I remembered how, holding
her small shoulders in my hands sometimes,
I felt a violent wonder at her presence
like a thirst for salt, for my childhood river
with its island willows, silly music from the pleasure boat,
muddy places where we caught the little orange-silver fish
called *pumpkinseed*. It hardly had to do with her.
Longing, we say, because desire is full
of endless distances. I must have been the same to her.
But I remember so much, the way her hands dismantled bread,
the thing her father said that hurt her, what
she dreamed. There are moments when the body is as numinous

as words, days that are the good flesh continuing.
Such tenderness, those afternoons and evenings,
saying *blackberry, blackberry, blackberry.*

Measure

Recurrences.
Coppery light hesitates
again in the small-leaved

Japanese plum. Summer
and sunset, the peace
of the writing desk

and the habitual peace
of writing, these things
form an order I only

belong to in the idleness
of attention. Last light
rims the blue mountain

and I almost glimpse
what I was born to,
not so much in the sunlight

or the plum tree
as in the pulse
that forms these lines.

Winter Morning in Charlottesville

Lead skies
and gothic traceries of poplar.
In the sacrament of winter
Savonarola raged against the carnal word.

Inside the prism of that eloquence
even Botticelli renounced the bestial gods
and beauty.
                    Florentine vanity
gathers in the dogwood buds.
How sexual
this morning is the otherwise
quite plain
white-crowned sparrow's
plumed head!
                    By a natural
selection, the word
originates its species,
                    the blood flowers,
republics scrawl their hurried declarations
& small birds scavenge
            in the chaste late winter grass.

Child Naming Flowers

When old crones wandered in the woods,
I was the hero on the hill
in clear sunlight.

Death's hounds feared me.

Smell of wild fennel,
high loft of sweet fruit high in the branches
of the flowering plum.

Then I am cast down
into the terror of childhood,
into the mirror and the greasy knives,
the dark
woodpile under the fig trees
in the dark.
          It is only
the malice of voices, the old horror
that is nothing, parents
quarreling, somebody
drunk.

I don't know how we survive it.
On this sunny morning
in my life as an adult, I am looking
at one clear pure peach
in a painting by Georgia O'Keeffe.
It is all the fullness that there is
in light. A towhee scratches in the leaves
outside my open door.
He always does.

A moment ago I felt so sick
and so cold
I could hardly move.

Museum

On the morning of the Käthe Kollwitz exhibit, a young man and
woman come into the museum restaurant. She is carrying a baby; he
carries the air-freight edition of the Sunday *New York Times*. She sits in
a high-backed wicker chair, cradling the infant in her arms. He fills a
tray with fresh fruit, rolls, and coffee in white cups and brings it to the
table. His hair is tousled, her eyes are puffy. They look like they were
thrown down into sleep and then yanked out of it like divers coming
up for air. He holds the baby. She drinks coffee, scans the front page,
butters a roll and eats it in their little corner in the sun. After a while,
she holds the baby. He reads the *Book Review* and eats some fruit. Then
he holds the baby while she finds the section of the paper she wants
and eats fruit and smokes. They've hardly exchanged a look. Mean-
while, I have fallen in love with this equitable arrangement, and with
the baby who cooperates by sleeping. All around them are faces Käthe
Kollwitz carved in wood of people with no talent or capacity for suf-
fering who are suffering the numbest kinds of pain: hunger, helpless
terror. But this young couple is reading the Sunday paper in the sun,
the baby is sleeping, the green has begun to emerge from the rind of
the cantaloupe, and everything seems possible.

Misery and Splendor

Summoned by conscious recollection, she
would be smiling, they might be in a kitchen talking,
before or after dinner. But they are in this other room,
the window has many small panes, and they are on a couch
embracing. He holds her as tightly
as he can, she buries herself in his body.
Morning, maybe it is evening, light
is flowing through the room. Outside,
the day is slowly succeeded by night,

succeeded by day. The process wobbles wildly
and accelerates: weeks, months, years. The light in the room
does not change, so it is plain what is happening.
They are trying to become one creature,
and something will not have it. They are tender
with each other, afraid
their brief, sharp cries will reconcile them to the moment
when they fall away again. So they rub against each other,
their mouths dry, then wet, then dry.
They feel themselves at the center of a powerful
and baffled will. They feel
they are an almost animal,
washed up on the shore of a world—
or huddled against the gate of a garden—
to which they can't admit they can never be admitted.

Happiness

Because yesterday morning from the steamy window
we saw a pair of red foxes across the creek
eating the last windfall apples in the rain—
they looked up at us with their green eyes
long enough to symbolize the wakefulness of living things
and then went back to eating—

and because this morning
when she went into the gazebo with her black pen and yellow pad
to coax an inquisitive soul
from what she thinks of as the reluctance of matter,
I drove into town to drink tea in the cafe
and write notes in a journal—mist rose from the bay
like the luminous and indefinite aspect of intention,
and a small flock of tundra swans

for the second winter in a row was feeding on new grass
in the soaked fields; they symbolize mystery, I suppose,
they are also called whistling swans, are very white,
and their eyes are black—

and because the tea steamed in front of me,
and the notebook, turned to a new page,
was blank except for a faint blue idea of order,
I wrote: *happiness! it is December, very cold,*
we woke early this morning,
and lay in bed kissing,
our eyes squinched up like bats.

Dragonflies Mating

1.

The people who lived here before us
also loved these high mountain meadows on summer mornings.
They made their way up here in easy stages
when heat began to dry the valleys out,
following the berry harvest probably and the pine buds:
climbing and making camp and gathering,
then breaking camp and climbing and making camp and gathering.
A few miles a day. They sent out the children
to dig up bulbs of the mariposa lilies that they liked to roast
at night by the fire where they sat talking about how this year
was different from last year. Told stories,
knew where they were on earth from the names,
owl moon, bear moon, gooseberry moon.

2.

Jaime de Angulo (1934) was talking to a Channel Island Indian
in a Santa Barbara bar. You tell me how your people said
the world was made. Well, the guy said, Coyote was on the mountain
and he had to pee. Wait a minute, Jaime said,
I was talking to a Pomo the other day and he said
Red Fox made the world. They say Red Fox, the guy shrugged,
we say Coyote. So, he had to pee
and he didn't want to drown anybody, so he turned toward the place
where the ocean would be. Wait a minute, Jaime said,
if there were no people yet, how could he drown anybody?
The Channelleño got a funny look on his face. You know,
he said, when I was a kid, I wondered about that,
and I asked my father. We were living up toward Santa Ynez.
He was sitting on a bench in the yard shaving down fence posts
with an ax, and I said, how come Coyote was worried about people
when he had to pee and there were no people? The guy laughed.
And my old man looked up at me with this funny smile
and said, You know, when I was a kid, I wondered about that.

3.

Thinking about that story just now, early morning heat,
first day in the mountains, I remembered stories about sick Indians
and—in the same thought—standing on the free throw line.

St. Raphael's parish, where the northern-most of the missions
had been, was founded as a hospital, was named for the angel
in the scriptures who healed the blind man with a fish
he laid across his eyes.—I wouldn't mind being that age again,
hearing those stories, eyes turned upward toward the young nun
in her white, fresh-smelling, immaculately laundered robes.—

The Franciscan priests who brought their faith in God
across the Atlantic, brought with the baroque statues and metalwork
  crosses
and elaborately embroidered cloaks, influenza and syphilis and the
  coughing disease.

Which is why we settled an almost empty California.
There were drawings in the mission museum of the long, dark wards
full of small brown people, wasted, coughing into blankets,

the saintly Franciscan fathers moving patiently among them.
It would, Sister Marietta said, have broken your hearts to see it.
They meant so well, she said, and such a terrible thing

came here with their love. And I remembered how I hated it
after school—because I loved basketball practice more than anything
on earth—that I never knew if my mother was going to show up

well into one of those weeks of drinking she disappeared into,
and humiliate me in front of my classmates with her bright, confident
  eyes,
and slurred, though carefully pronounced words, and the appalling

impromptu sets of mismatched clothes she was given to
when she had the dim idea of making a good impression in that state.
Sometimes from the gym floor with its sweet, heady smell of varnish

I'd see her in the entryway looking for me, and I'd bounce
the ball two or three times, study the orange rim as if it were,
which it was, the true level of the world, the one sure thing

the power in my hands could summon. I'd bounce the ball
once more, feel the grain of the leather in my fingertips and shoot.
It was a perfect thing; it was almost like killing her.

4.

When we say "mother" in poems,
we usually mean some woman in her late twenties
or early thirties trying to raise a child.

We use this particular noun
to secure the pathos of the child's point of view
and to hold her responsible.

5.

If you're afraid now?
Fear is a teacher.
Sometimes you thought that
Nothing could reach her,
Nothing can reach you.
Wouldn't you rather
Sit by the river, sit
On the dead bank,
Deader than winter,
Where all the roots gape?

6.

This morning in the early sun,
steam rising from the pond the color of smoky topaz,
a pair of delicate, copper-red, needle-fine insects
are mating in the unopened crown of a Shasta daisy
just outside your door. The green flowerheads look like wombs
or the upright, supplicant bulbs of a vegetal pre-erection.
The insect lovers seem to be transferring the cosmos into each other
by attaching at the tail, holding utterly still, and quivering intently.

I think (on what evidence?) that they are different from us.
That they mate and are done with mating.
They don't carry all this half-mated longing up out of childhood
and then go looking for it everywhere.
And so, I think, they can't wound each other the way we do.
They don't go through life dizzy or groggy with their hunger,
kill with it, smear it on everything, though it is perhaps also true
that nothing happens to them quite like what happens to us
when the blue-backed swallow dips swiftly toward the green pond
and the pond's green-and-blue reflected swallow marries it a moment
in the reflected sky and the heart goes out to the end of the rope
it has been throwing into abyss after abyss, and a singing shimmers
from every color the morning has risen into.

My insect instructors have stilled, they are probably stuck together
in some bliss and minute pulse of after-longing
evolution worked out to suck the last juice of the world
into the receiver body. They can't separate probably
until it is done.

Sonnet

A man talking to his ex-wife on the phone.
He has loved her voice and listens with attention
to every modulation of its tone. Knowing
it intimately. Not knowing what he wants
from the sound of it, from the tendered civility.
He studies, out the window, the seed shapes
of the broken pods of ornamental trees.
The kind that grow in everyone's garden, that no one
but horticulturists can name. Four arched chambers
of pale green, tiny vegetal proscenium arches,
a pair of black tapering seeds bedded in each chamber.

A wish geometry, miniature, Indian or Persian,
lovers or gods in their apartments. Outside, white,
patient animals, and tangled vines, and rain.

A Supple Wreath of Myrtle

Poor Nietzsche in Turin, eating sausage his mother
Mails to him from Basel. A rented room,
A small square window framing August clouds
Above the mountain. Brooding on the form
Of things: the dangling spur
Of an Alpine columbine, winter-tortured trunks
Of cedar in the summer sun, the warp in the aspen's trunk
Where it torqued up through the snowpack.

"Everywhere the wasteland grows; woe
To him whose wasteland is within."

Dying of syphilis. Trimming a luxuriant mustache.
In love with the opera of Bizet.

Futures in Lilacs

"Tender little Buddha," she said
Of my least Buddha-like member.
She was probably quoting Allen Ginsberg,
Who was probably paraphrasing Walt Whitman.
After the Civil War, after the death of Lincoln,
That was a good time to own railroad stocks,
But Whitman was in the Library of Congress,

Researching alternative Americas,
Reading up on the curiosities of Hindoo philosophy,
Studying the etchings of stone carvings
Of strange couplings in a book.

She was taking off a blouse,
Almost transparent, the color of a silky tangerine.
From Capitol Hill Walt Whitman must have been able to see
Willows gathering the river haze
In the cooling and still-humid twilight.
He was in love with a trolley conductor
In the summer of—what was it?—1867? 1868?

Etymology

Her body by the fire
Mimicked the light-conferring midnights
Of philosophy.
Suppose they are dead now.
Isn't "dead now" an odd expression?
The sound of the owls outside
And the wind soughing in the trees
Catches in their ears, is sent out
In scouting parties of sensation down their spines.
If you say it became language or it was nothing,
Who touched whom?
In what hurtle of starlight?
Poor language, poor theory
Of language. The shards of skull
In the Egyptian museum looked like maps of the wind-eroded
Canyon labyrinths from which,
Standing on the verge
In the yellow of a dwindling fall, you hear

Echo and re-echo the cries of terns
Fishing the worked silver of a rapids.
And what to say of her wetness? The Anglo-Saxons
Had a name for it. They called it *silm*.
They were navigators. It was also
Their word for the look of moonlight on the sea.

Time and Materials

Gerhard Richter: *Abstrakt Bilden*

1.

To make layers,
As if they were a steadiness of days:

It snowed; I did errands at a desk;
A white flurry out the window thickening; my tongue
Tasted of the glue on envelopes.

On this day sunlight on red brick, bare trees,
Nothing stirring in the icy air.

On this day a blur of color moving at the gym
Where the heat from bodies
Meets the watery, cold surface of the glass.

Made love, made curry, talked on the phone
To friends, the one whose brother died
Was crying and thinking alternately,
Like someone falling down and getting up
And running and falling and getting up.

2.

The object of this poem is not to annihila

To not annih

The object of this poem is to report a theft,
    In progress, of everything

That is not these words
    And their disposition on the page.

The object o   f this poem is to report a theft,
    In progre   ss of everything that exists
That is not th   ese words
    And their d   isposition on the page.

The object of his poe is t epor a theft
        In rogres f ever hing at xists
Th   is no ese   w rds
        And their disp sit on o   the pag

3.

To score, to scar, to smear, to streak,
To smudge, to blur, to gouge, to scrape.

"Action painting," i.e.,
The painter gets to behave like time.

4.

The typo would be "paining."

(To abrade.)

5.

Or to render time and stand outside
The horizontal rush of it, for a moment
To have the sensation of standing outside
The greenish rush of it.

6.

Some vertical gesture then, the way that anger
Or desire can rip a life apart,

Some wound of color.

Then Time

In winter, in a small room, a man and a woman
Have been making love for hours. Exhausted,
Very busy wringing out each other's bodies,
They look at one another suddenly and laugh.
"What is this?" he says. "I can't get enough of you,"
She says, a woman who thinks of herself as not given
To cliché. She runs her fingers across his chest,
Tentative touches, as if she were testing her wonder.
He says, "Me too." And she, beginning to be herself
Again, "You mean you can't get enough of you either?"
"I mean," he takes her arms in his hands and shakes them,
"Where does this come from?" She cocks her head
And looks into his face. "Do you really want to know?"
"Yes," he says. "Self-hatred," she says, "longing for God."
Kisses him again. "It's not what it is," a wry shrug,
"It's where it comes from." Kisses his bruised mouth
A second time, a third. Years later, in another city,

They're having dinner in a quiet restaurant near a park.
Fall. Earlier that day, hard rain: leaves, brass-colored
And smoky crimson, flying everywhere. Twenty years older,
She is very beautiful. An astringent person. She'd become,
She said, an obsessive gardener, her daughters grown.
He's trying not to be overwhelmed by love or pity
Because he sees she has no hands. He thinks
She must have given them away. He imagines,
Very clearly, how she wakes some mornings
(He has a vivid memory of her younger self, stirred
From sleep, flushed, just opening her eyes)
To momentary horror because she can't remember
What she did with them, why they were gone,
And then remembers, and calms herself, so that the day
Takes on its customary sequence once again.
She asks him if he thinks about her. "Occasionally,"
He says, smiling. "And you?" "Not much," she says,
"I think it's because we never existed inside time."
He studies her long fingers, a pianist's hands,
Or a gardener's, strong, much-used, as she fiddles
With her wineglass and he understands, vaguely,
That it must be his hands that are gone. Then
He's describing a meeting that he'd sat in all day,
Chaired by someone they'd felt, many years before,
Mutually superior to. "You know the expression
'A perfect fool,' " she'd said, and he had liked her tone
Of voice so much. She begins a story of the company
In Maine she orders bulbs from, begun by a Polish refugee
Married to a French-Canadian separatist from Quebec.
It's a story with many surprising turns and a rare
Chocolate-black lily at the end. He's listening,
Studying her face, still turning over her remark.
He decides that she thinks more symbolically
Than he does and that it seemed to have saved her,
For all her fatalism, from certain kinds of pain.
She finds herself thinking what a literal man he is,

Notices, as if she were recalling it, his pleasure
In the menu, and the cooking, and the architecture of the room.
It moves her—in the way that earnest limitation
Can be moving, and she is moved by her attraction to him.
Also by what he was to her. She sees her own avidity
To live then, or not to not have lived might be more accurate,
From a distance, the way a driver might see from the road
A startled deer running across an open field in the rain.
Wild thing. Here and gone. Death made it poignant, or,
If not death exactly, which she'd come to think of
As creatures seething in a compost heap, then time.

Bush's War

I typed the brief phrase, "Bush's War,"
At the top of a sheet of white paper,
Having some dim intuition of a poem
Made luminous by reason that would,
Though I did not have them at hand,
Set the facts out in an orderly way.
Berlin is a northerly city. In May
At the end of the twentieth century
In the leafy precincts of Dahlem Dorf,
South of the Grunewald, near Krumme Lanke,
The northern spring begins before dawn
In a racket of birdsong, when the *amsels,*
Black European thrushes, shiver the sun up
As if they were shaking a great tangle
Of golden wire. There are two kinds
Of flowering chestnuts, red and white,
And the wet pavements are speckled
With petals from the incandescent spikes
Of their flowers; the shoes at U-Bahn stops

Are flecked with them. Green of holm oaks,
Birch tassels, the soft green of maples,
And the odor of lilacs is everywhere.
At Oskar-Helene-Heim station a farmer
Sells white asparagus from a heaped table.
In a month he'll be selling chanterelles;
In the month after that, strawberries
And small, rosy crawfish from the Spree.
The piles of stalks of the asparagus
Are startlingly phallic, phallic and tender
And deathly pale. Their seasonal appearance
Must be the remnant of some fertility ritual
Of the German tribes. Steamed, they are the color
Of old ivory. In May, in restaurants
They are served on heaped white platters
With boiled potatoes and parsley butter,
Or shavings of Parma ham and lemon juice
Or sprigs of sorrel and smoked salmon. And,
Walking home in the slant, widening,
Brilliant northern light that falls
On the new-leaved birches and the elms,
Nightingales singing at the first, subtlest,
Darkening of dusk, it is a trick of the mind
That the past seems just ahead of us,
As if we were being shunted there
In the surge of a rattling funicular.
Flash forward: firebombing of Hamburg,
Fifty thousand dead in a single night,
"The children's bodies the next day
Set in the street in rows like a market
In charred chicken." Flash forward:
Firebombing of Tokyo, a hundred thousand
In a night. Flash forward: forty-five
Thousand Polish officers slaughtered
By the Russian army in the Katyn Woods,
The work of half a day. Flash forward:

Two million Russian prisoners of war
Murdered by the German army all across
The eastern front, supplies low,
Winter of 1943. Flash: Hiroshima.
Flash: Auschwitz, Dachau, Thersienstadt,
The train lurching and the stomach woozy
Past the displays of falls of hair, the piles
Of monogrammed valises, spectacles. Flash:
The gulags, seven million in Byelorussia
And Ukraine. In innocent Europe on a night
In spring, among the light-struck birches,
Students holding hands. One of them
Is carrying a novel, the German translation
Of a slim book by Marguerite Duras
About a love affair in old Saigon. (Flash:
Two million Vietnamese, fifty-five thousand
Of the American young, whole races
Of tropical birds extinct from saturation bombing)
The kind of book the young love
To love, about love in time of war.
Forty-five million, all told, in World War II.
In Berlin, pretty Berlin, in the springtime,
You are never not wondering how
It happened, and these Germans, too,
Children then, or unborn, never not
Wondering. Is it that we like the kissing
And bombing together, in prospect
At least, girls in their flowery dresses?
Someone will always want to mobilize
Death on a massive scale for economic
Domination or revenge. And the task, taken
As a task, appeals to the imagination.
The military is an engineering profession.
Look at boys playing: they love
To figure out the ways to blow things up.
But the rest of us have to go along.

Why do we do it? Certainly there's a rage
To injure what's injured us. Wars
Are always pitched to us that way.
The well-paid news readers read the reasons
On the air. And the us who are injured,
Or have been convinced that we are injured,
Are always identified with virtue. It's
That—the rage to hurt mixed up
With self-righteousness—that's murderous.
The young Arab depiliated himself as an act
Of purification before he drove the plane
Into the office building. It's not just
The violence, it's a taste for power
That amounts to contempt for the body.
The rest of us have to act like we believe
The dead women in the rubble of Baghdad
Who did not cast a vote for their deaths
Or the raw white of the exposed bones
In the bodies of their men or their children
Are being given the gift of freedom
Which is the virtue of the injured us.
It's hard to say which is worse, the moral
Sloth of it or the intellectual disgrace.
And what good is indignation to the dead?
Or our mild forms of rational resistance?
And death the cleanser, Walt Whitman's
Sweet death, the scourer, the tender
Lover, shutter of eyelids, turns
The heaped bodies into summer fruit,
Magpies eating dark berries in the dusk
And birch pollen staining sidewalks
To the faintest gold. *Bald nur*—Goethe—no,
Warte nur, bald ruhest du auch. Just wait.
You will be quiet soon enough. In Dahlem,
Under the chestnuts, in the leafy spring.

RITA DOVE

(1952-)

Poet Laureate Consultant in Poetry (1993–1995)
Special Bicentennial Consultant in Poetry (1999–2000),
with Louise Glück and W. S. Merwin

A lot of what I've done these past two years has involved educating young
people in matters of poetry, and bringing real poetry into real life—and by
that I mean serious and difficult poetry. My experience has been that as
soon as people are relaxed, even very difficult poetry becomes accessible.
It's when someone is told: "This is great literature; you should appreciate it"
that they get uptight and don't do very well with the poem. So by helping
introduce people to poetry and widening the audience for poetry, I do think
my term has served a more serious purpose.

At Rita Dove's first press conference after being appointed U.S. poet laureate, she was asked how she felt about the post. "It'll ruin my life," she answered without missing a beat, "but I'd be crazy not to accept it." She recognized that the funding for programs in the arts, and for poetry in particular, was in grave jeopardy in Washington in the late eighties and early nineties, and she devoted herself to working steadfastly to come up with solutions. She was promptly dubbed the "New Generation laureate" because of her age (at forty, she was among the youngest incumbents to hold the job) and because she was a whirlwind of activity. Dove organized more programs for poetry than any of her predecessors. Much of her time was spent soliciting sponsorship for a range of initiatives: teleconferences allowing her to discuss poetry simultaneously with different schools around the country, readings at the library by Crow Indian schoolchildren from Montana, and an annual poetry and jazz series in Washington. She opted for a second term because she could not accomplish everything she wanted to in eight months.

Her activism as a laureate corresponds to the questions her poetry has long raised about the relationship between the private voice of the lyric and the public, historical voice of epic poetry. Her Pulitzer Prize–winning sequence *Thomas and Beulah* chronicles the lives of her maternal grandparents as they make their way from rural Tennessee to Akron, Ohio. The lyrics are strung together, as Dove put it, "like beads on a necklace," the necklace representing the history of African-American migration in the first sixty years of the twentieth century. In a later book, *Mother Love*, Dove interweaves narrative poems about a contemporary relationship between mother and daughter with poems about the greatest archetypal mother-daughter story in literary history, the myth of Demeter and Persephone. In a 1995 interview she said, about her first book: "I was working the lyric moment against the narrative impulse, so that they would counterpoint each other. In the States there has been such division between narrative poetry and lyric poetry;

frankly I've never felt that much of a difference. A good poem usually has both. A lyric may not have a traditional narrative line, but it all depends what you define as story. Even a leaf falling from a tree is a pretty dramatic story—to the leaf!"

Dove was born in Akron, Ohio, where her father was a chemist. After college, Dove traveled to Germany as a Fulbright fellow, where she met her future husband, the German writer and photographer Fred Viebahn. She has played the cello seriously all her life, is an amateur opera singer, and believes that "music and poetry have much in common." The second African-American poet to hold the poetry post at the library, she says that her "reluctance with being labeled an African-American poet comes from battling the assumption that this means writing in a racially programmatic way. As far as I'm concerned no programmatic poetry, no matter how well meant the ideology, can be truly free."

This Life

My grandmother told me there'd be good days
to counter the dark ones,
with blue skies in the heart as far
as the soul could see. She said
you could measure a life in as many ways
as there were to bake a pound cake,
but you still needed real butter and eggs
for a good one—pound cake, that is,
but I knew what she meant. She was always
talking around corners like that;
she knew words carried their treasures
like a grape clusters around its own juice.
She loved words; she thought a book
was a monument to the glory of creation
and a library . . . well, sometimes
just trying to describe Jubilation
will get you a bit tongue, so let's
leave it at that. But my grandmother
was nobody's fool, and she'd tell anybody
smart enough to listen. Don't let a little pain
stop you; try as hard as you can
every minute you're given or else
sit down and shut up—though in her opinion,
keeping quiet in noisy times was a sin
against everything God and democracy
intended us for. I know she'd like
where I'm standing right now. She'd say
a man who could measure his life in deeds
was larger inside than the vessel that carried him;
she'd say he was a cluster of grapes.

My grandmother was only four feet ten
but when she entered a room, even the books
came to attention. Giants come in all sizes:
Sometimes a moment is a monument;
sometimes an institution breathes—
like a library. Like this halcyon day.

Dusting

Every day a wilderness—no
shade in sight. Beulah
patient among knickknacks,
the solarium a rage
of light, a grainstorm
as her gray cloth brings
dark wood to life.

Under her hand scrolls
and crests gleam
darker still. What
was his name, that
silly boy at the fair with
the rifle booth? And his kiss and
the clear bowl with one bright
fish, rippling
wound!

Not Michael—
something finer. Each dust
stroke a deep breath and
the canary in bloom.

Wavery memory: home
from a dance, the front door
blown open and the parlor
in snow, she rushed
the bowl to the stove, watched
as the locket of ice
dissolved and he
swam free.

That was years before
Father gave her up
with her name, years before
her name grew to mean
Promise, then
Desert-in-Peace.
Long before the shadow and
sun's accomplice, the tree.

Maurice.

Weathering Out

She liked mornings the best—Thomas gone
to look for work, her coffee flushed with milk,

outside autumn trees blowsy and dripping.
Past the seventh month she couldn't see her feet

so she floated from room to room, houseshoes flapping,
navigating corners in wonder. When she leaned

against a door jamb to yawn, she disappeared entirely.

Last week they had taken a bus at dawn
to the new airdock. The hangar slid open in segments

and the zeppelin nosed forward in its silver envelope.
The man walked it out gingerly, like a poodle,

then tied it to a mast and went back inside.
Beulah felt just that large and placid, a lake;

she glistened from cocoa butter smoothed in
when Thomas returned every evening nearly

in tears. He'd lean an ear on her belly
and say: *Little fellow's really talking,*

though to her it was more the *pok-pok-pok*
of a fingernail tapping a thick cream lampshade.

Sometimes during the night she woke and found him
asleep there and the child sleeping, too.

The coffee was good but too little. Outside
everything shivered in tinfoil—only the clover

between the cobblestones hung stubbornly on,
green as an afterthought. . . .

Daystar

She wanted a little room for thinking:
but she saw diapers steaming on the line,
a doll slumped behind the door.

So she lugged a chair behind the garage
to sit out the children's naps.

Sometimes there were things to watch—
the pinched armor of a vanished cricket,
a floating maple leaf. Other days
she stared until she was assured
when she closed her eyes
she'd see only her own vivid blood.

She had an hour, at best, before Liza appeared
pouting from the top of the stairs.
And just *what* was mother doing
out back with the field mice? Why,

building a palace. Later
that night when Thomas rolled over and
lurched into her, she would open her eyes
and think of the place that was hers
for an hour—where
she was nothing,
pure nothing, in the middle of the day.

"Teach Us to Number Our Days"

In the old neighborhood, each funeral parlor
is more elaborate than the last.
The alleys smell of cops, pistols bumping their thighs,
each chamber steeled with a slim blue bullet.

Low-rent balconies stacked to the sky.
A boy plays tic-tac-toe on a moon
crossed by TV antennae, dreams

he has swallowed a blue bean.
It takes root in his gut, sprouts
and twines upward, the vines curling
around the sockets and locking them shut.

And this sky, knotting like a dark tie?
The patroller, disinterested, holds all the beans.

August. The mums nod past, each a prickly heart on a sleeve.

The House Slave

The first horn lifts its arm over the dew-lit grass
and in the slave quarters there is a rustling—
children are bundled into aprons, cornbread

and water gourds grabbed, a salt pork breakfast taken.
I watch them driven into the vague before-dawn
while their mistress sleeps like an ivory toothpick

and Massa dreams of asses, rum and slave-funk.
I cannot fall asleep again. At the second horn,
the whip curls across the backs of the laggards—

sometimes my sister's voice, unmistaken, among them.
"Oh! pray," she cries. "Oh! pray!" Those days
I lie on my cot, shivering in the early heat,

and as the fields unfold to whiteness,
and they spill like bees among the fat flowers,
I weep. It is not yet daylight.

My Mother Enters the Work Force

The path to ABC Business School
was paid for by a lucky sign:
ALTERATIONS, QUALIFIED SEAMSTRESS INQUIRE WITHIN.
Tested on sleeves, hers
never puckered—puffed or sleek,
leg-o'-mutton or raglan—
they barely needed the damp cloth
to steam them perfect.

Those were the afternoons. Evenings
she took in piecework, the treadle machine
with its locomotive whir
traveling the lit path of the needle
through quicksand taffeta
or velvet deep as a forest.
And now and now sang the treadle,
I know, I know. . . .

And then it was day again, all morning
at the office machines, their clack and chatter
another journey—rougher,
that would go on forever
until she could break a hundred words
with no errors—ah, and then

no more postponed groceries,
and that blue pair of shoes!

Canary

for Michael S. Harper

Billie Holiday's burned voice
had as many shadows as lights,
a mournful candelabra against a sleek piano,
the gardenia her signature under that ruined face.

(Now you're cooking, drummer to bass,
magic spoon, magic needle.
Take all day if you have to
with your mirror and your bracelet of song.)

Fact is, the invention of women under siege
has been to sharpen love in the service of myth.

If you can't be free, be a mystery.

Persephone, Falling

One narcissus among the ordinary beautiful
flowers, one unlike all the others! She pulled,
stooped to pull harder—
when, sprung out of the earth
on his glittering terrible
carriage, he claimed his due.
It is finished. No one heard her.
No one! She had strayed from the herd.

(Remember: go straight to school.
This is important, stop fooling around!
Don't answer to strangers. Stick
with your playmates. Keep your eyes down.)
This is how easily the pit
opens. This is how one foot sinks into the ground.

Golden Oldie

I made it home early, only to get
stalled in the driveway, swaying
at the wheel like a blind pianist caught in a tune
meant for more than two hands playing.

The words were easy, crooned
by a young girl dying to feel alive, to discover
a pain majestic enough
to live by. I turned the air-conditioning off,

leaned back to float on a film of sweat,
and listened to her sentiment:
Baby, where did our love go?—a lament
I greedily took in

without a clue who my lover
might be, or where to start looking.

Wiring Home

Lest the wolves loose their whistles
and shopkeepers inquire,

keep moving; though your knees flush
red as two chapped apples,

keep moving, head up,
past the beggar's cold cup,

past fires banked under chestnuts
and the trumpeting kiosk's

tales of odyssey and heartbreak
until, turning a corner, you stand

staring: ambushed
by a window of canaries

bright as a thousand
golden narcissi.

Ta Ta Cha Cha

One, two—no, five doves
scatter before a wingtip's
distracted tread.
Lost, lost, they coo, and
they're probably right:
It's Venice, I'm American,
besandaled and backpacked,
sunk in a bowl of sky
trimmed with marbled statuary
(slate, snow, ash)—
a dazed array, dipped
in the moon's cold palette.

Who, you? No. But here,
lost from a wing, drifts
one pale, italicized
answer. I pick it up
as the bold shoe
continues conversation
(*one two*) with its mate,
and the nearest scavenger
skips three times
to the side, bobs to pluck
his crackerjack prize, a child's
dropped gelato cone.

Tip, tap: early warning code
for afternoon rain. Gray
vagabond, buffoon messenger
for grounded lovers—where to?
Teach me this dance
you make, snatching a sweet
from the path of a man

who, because he knows
where he's headed, walks
without seeing, face hidden
by a dirty wingspan
of the daily news.

The Bridgetower

> *per il Mulatto Brischdauer*
> *gran pazzo e compositore mulattico*
> —Ludwig van Beethoven, 1803

If was at the Beginning. If
he had been older, if he hadn't been
dark, brown eyes ablaze
in that remarkable face;
if he had not been so gifted, so young
a genius with no time to grow up;
if he hadn't grown up, undistinguished,
to an obscure old age.
If the piece had actually been,
as Kreutzer exclaimed, unplayable—even after
our man had played it, and for years
no one else was able to follow—
so that the composer's fury would have raged
for naught, and wagging tongues
could keep alive the original dedication
from the title page he shredded.

Oh, if only Ludwig had been better-looking,
or cleaner, or a real aristocrat,
von instead of the unexceptional ***van***
from some Dutch farmer; if his ears

had not already begun to squeal and whistle;
if he hadn't drunk his wine from lead cups,
if he could have found True Love. Then
the story would have held: In 1803
George Polgreen Bridgetower,
son of Friedrich Augustus the African Prince
and Maria Anna Sovinki of Biala in Poland,
traveled from London to Vienna
where he met the Great Master
who would stop work on his Third Symphony
to write a sonata for his new friend
to premiere triumphantly on May 24,
whereupon the composer himself
leapt up from the piano to embrace
his "lunatic mulatto."

Who knows what would have followed?
They might have palled around some,
just a couple of wild and crazy guys
strutting the town like rock stars,
hitting the bars for a few beers, a few laughs . . .
instead of falling out over a girl
nobody remembers, nobody knows.

Then this bright-skinned papa's boy
could have sailed his fifteen-minute fame
straight into the record books—where
instead of a Regina Carter or Aaron Dworkin or Boyd Tinsley
sprinkled here and there, we would find
rafts of black kids scratching out scales
on their matchbox violins so that some day
they might play the impossible:
Beethoven's Sonata No. 9 in A Major, Op. 47,
also known as The Bridgetower.

Ach, Wien

The truly great cities are never self-conscious:
They have their own music; they go about business.
London surges, Rome bubbles, Paris promenades;
Dresden stands rigid, gazes skyward, afraid.

Vienna canters in a slowly tightening spiral.
Golden façades line the avenues, ring after ring
tracing a curve as tender and maddening
as a smile on the face of a beautiful rival.

You can't escape it; everywhere's a circle.
Feel your knees bend and straighten
as you focus each step. Hum along with it;
succumb to the sway, enter the trance.

Ah, sweet scandal: No one admits it,
but we all know this dance.

MONA VAN DUYN

(1921–2004)

Poet Laureate Consultant in Poetry (1992–1993)

It's a strange title. All the public knows is England's long, long tradition of having a poet laureate, with each staying in the post until he dies. Whereas we, in our weird American way, have a new laureate every year. I find it hard to explain to my nonliterary friends . . . [and] keep the super-honorable title far back in my mind, because it makes me feel top heavy!

Mona Van Duyn, born in Waterloo, Iowa, received a bachelor's degree from the University of Northern Iowa and a master's from the University of Iowa. There were six women consultants in poetry, but Van Duyn was the first woman poet laureate. In 1991 her volume, *Near Changes*, won the 1991 Pulitzer Prize. Other honors include the 1971 National Book Award for *To See, To Take*, and the 1971 Bollingen Prize.

In 1943 Van Duyn married the literary scholar Jarvis Thurston, her husband of sixty-one years. Long marriage is a subject of many of her best-known poems. She and Thurston held professorships at Washington University and jointly edited *Perspective: A Quarterly of Literature* between 1947 and 1967. Her views of love and marriage ranged from the scathing to the optimistic. In "What I Want to Say," she called love "the absolute narrowing of possibilities / and everyone, down to the last man / dreads it." But in "Late Loving," she wrote: "Love is finding the familiar dear." Van Duyn said in an interview, "I use domestic imagery and extend that imagery through the whole poem . . . but I'm not writing about that. It's simply used as a metaphor."

While much of her poetry was written during a period when many American poets wrote confessional poems in free verse, Van Duyn remained squarely outside this trend. She battled depression for much of her life and was treated several times in psychiatric hospitals, yet she deliberately chose not to make this part of her private life the subject of her verse: "I have not found the subjects for my poems in my illness. . . . It is the years of good health between depressions that I cherish, that seem to me most real." The poet laureateship was not for her. She served one year and said she would "run kicking and screaming in the opposite direction" were she asked to serve a second term.

Death by Aesthetics

Here is the doctor, an abstracted lover,
dressed as a virgin, coming to keep the tryst.
The patient was early; she is lovely; but yet
she is sick, his instruments will agree on this.

Is this the place, she wonders, and is he the one?
Yes, love is the healer, he will strip her bare,
and all his machinery of definition
tells her experience is costly here,

so she is reassured. The doctor approaches
and bends to her heart. But she sees him sprout like a tree
with metallic twigs on his fingers and blooms of chrome
at his eye and ear for the sterile ceremony.

Oh tight and tighter his rubber squeeze of her arm.
"Ahhh" she sighs at a chilly touch on her tongue.
Up the tubes her breath comes crying, as over her,
back and breast, he moves his silver thumb.

His fluoroscope hugs her. Soft the intemperate girl,
disordered. Willing she lies while he unfolds
her disease, but a stem of glass protects his fingertips
from her heat, nor will he catch her cold.

He peels her. Under the swaddling epiderm
her body is the same blue bush. Beautiful canals
course like a postcard scene that's sent him often.
He counts the *tiptup, tiptup* of her dutiful valves.

Pain hides like a sinner in her mesh of nerves.
But her symptoms constellate! Quickly he warms
to his consummation, while her fever flares
in its wick of vein, her wicked blood burns.

He hands her a paper. "Goodbye. Live quietly,
make some new friends. I've seen these stubborn cases
cured with time. My bill will arrive. Dear lady,
it's been a most enjoyable diagnosis."

She clings, but her fingers slip on his starchy dress.
"Don't leave me! Learn me! If this is all, you've swindled
my whole booty of meaning, where is my dearness?
Pore against pore, the delicate hairs commingled,

with cells and ligaments, tissue lapped on bone,
meet me, feel the way my body feels,
and in my bounty of dews, fluxes and seasons,
orifices, in my wastes and smells

see self. Self in the secret stones I chafed
to shape in my bladder. Out of a dream I fished
the ache that feeds in my stomach's weedy slough.
This tender swelling's the bud of my frosted wish.

Search out my mind's embroidery of scars.
My ichor runs to death so speedily,
spit up your text and taste my living texture.
Sweat to hunt me with love, and burn with me."

But he is gone. "Don't touch me" was all he answered.
"Separateness," says the paper. The world, we beg,
will keep her though she's caught its throbbing senses,
its bugs still swim in her breath, she's bright with its plague.

The Gentle Snorer

When summer came, we locked up our lives and fled
to the woods in Maine, and pulled up over our heads
a comforter filled with batts of piney dark,
tied with crickets' chirretings and the *bork*
of frogs; we hid in a sleep of strangeness from
the human humdrum.

A pleasant noise the unordered world makes wove
around us. Burrowed, we heard the scud of waves,
wrack of bending branch, or plop of a fish
on his heavy home; the little beasts rummaged the brush.
We dimmed to silence, slipped from the angry pull
of wishes and will.

And then we had a three-week cabin guest
who snored; he broke the wilderness of our rest.
As all night long he sipped the succulent air,
that rhythm we shared made visible to the ear
a rich refreshment of the blood. We fed in
unison with him.

A sound we dreamed and woke to, over the snuff
of wind, not loud enough to scare off the roof
the early morning chipmunks. Under our skins
we heard, as after disease, the bright, thin
tick of our time. Sleeping, he mentioned death
and celebrated breath.

He went back home. The water flapped the shore.
A thousand bugs drilled at the darkness. Over
the lake a loon howled. Nothing spoke up for us,
salvagers always of what we have always lost;
and we thought what the night needed was more of man,
he left us so partisan.

Sonnet for Minimalists

From a new peony,
my last anthem,
a squirrel in glee
broke the budded stem.
I thought, Where is joy
without fresh bloom,
that old hearts' ploy
to mask the tomb?

Then a volunteer
stalk sprung from sour
bird-drop this year
burst in frantic flower.

The world's perverse,
but it could be worse.

Late Loving

> What Christ was saying, what he meant [in the story of Mary and Martha]
> was that the pleasures of that hair, that ointment, must be taken. Because the
> accidents of death would deprive us soon enough. We must not deprive our-
> selves, our loved ones, of the luxury of our extravagant affections. We must not
> try to second-guess death by refusing to love the ones we loved. . . .
> —Mary Gordon, *Final Payments*

If in my mind I marry you every year
it is to calm an extravagance of love
with dousing custom, for it flames up fierce
and wild whenever I forget that we live
in double rooms whose temperature's controlled
by matrimony's turned-down thermostat.

I need the mnemonics, now that we are old,
of oath and law in rememorizing that.
Our dogs are dead, our child never came true,
I might use up, in my weak-mindedness,
the whole human supply of warmth on you
before I could think of others and digress.
"Love" is finding the familiar dear.
"In love" is to be taken by surprise.
Over, in the shifty face you wear,
and over, in the assessments of your eyes,
you change, and with new sweet or barbed word
find out new entrances to my inmost nerve.
When you stand at the stove it's I who am most stirred.
When you finish work I rest without reserve.
Daytimes, sometimes, our three-legged race seems slow.
Squabbling onward, we chafe from being so near.
But all night long we lie like crescents of Velcro,
turning together till we readhere.
Since you, with longer stride and better vision,
more clearly see the finish line, I stoke
my hurrying self, to keep it in condition,
with light and life-renouncing meals of smoke.
As when a collector scoops two Monarchs in
at once, whose fresh flights to and from each other
are netted down, so in vows I re-imagine
I re-invoke what keeps us stale together.
What you try to give is more than I want to receive,
yet each month when you pick up scissors for our appointment
and my cut hair falls and covers your feet I believe
that the house is filled again with the odor of ointment.

For William Clinton, President-Elect

I.

In a tiny museum in Florence, a great maker,
Michelangelo, has left his image of David.
Raised on a marble platform, his pure white,
naked, marble beauty glows in bright light.
He towers and shines before us, perfect in body,
fair of face—perfect in spirit too,
for we know who he is: the hero, young and alone,
who destroys a gigantic evil with one slung stone.
Time cannot smudge his form nor erase his story.
The caught breath at first sight of him, the tear
that his flawless being brings the uplifted eye
will last while men breathe and see. This cannot die.

II.

Some distance from "David," lit only by daylight,
is the master's other work in this museum.
Puzzled, one turns to it, a great, dull boulder
out of whose widest side, wedged shoulder to shoulder,
a group of people are surging out of the rock.
They seem to strain toward the "David" but are held,
part of their bodies still in the unshaped stone.
An unfinished work? Cast off? Its intentions unknown?
But wait. They are men and women like ourselves.
Their leaders are wedged among them, pressing strongly
toward freedom and light before them, but caught like the rest
in the hard mass, the mass of unshapeliness
that holds, no doubt, farther back, many thronging others
deeply hidden or with only an arm or hand
outstretched. It's the mass of necessity, mistakes,

accidents, defective love, mindquakes,
crippling of spirit, losses, terrible needs,
failure of empathy, loneliness, greed, envy,
starvation of body, of mind—the unremission,
the hard anti-art of the human condition.

III.

May our leaders hold in their hearts a tiny museum
which keeps for us all The Great Maker's double truth,
as we strain together, imperfect in act and plan,
toward freedom, toward light, toward the perfect idea of man.

The Burning of Yellowstone

Squaring their papers—tap, tap—the news team finds
one last feature to catch St. Louis ears
following days of rage and roar on the screen
as feather, fur, nest, cave, hide disappears.
"Don't miss the sunset tonight or tomorrow night!"
For two thousand miles, it appears, wind bore to the eye
smoke from unseen deaths and wounds to remind us
how beautiful, at the end, is the earth, the sky.
Driving west from the towers that block our view
we find a hillside pull-off. Every sense
confounded by the vision that wraps us round,
we feel to the bone its burning radiance.
Orange daylily uncurls its lips and presses
them urgently on the blue-veined brow of space.
Rose at its ripest spreads wide its fervent petals

to welcome the other hues. An intense trace
of crushed violet scent lies on the air.
Petunia tongues a pink both sweet and clear.
Fallout of deep red peony litters the treeline.
We take each other's hand, eyes wet, and hear
how gently the world informs its witnesses,
as jonquil yellow trumpets a floral boom,
of its debt to the artistry of their beholding,
of their culpability for its final bloom.

Falling in Love at Sixty-Five

It is like the first and last time I tried a Coleman
for reading in bed in Maine. Too early the camp
went dark for fossil habits, no longer could candleflame
convince my eyes, and I lit that scary lamp.
Instant outcry came from the savage white light
of the mantles, as if a star had been brought down
out of space and trapped by the unchinked logs of the bedroom,
roaring its threat to explode the walls and be gone,
or as if the lamp could tell time and knew that one tongue
was no longer enough to speak with, it must double its blare,
overwhelm two senses at once, that the jaded heart
might burst into ravished applause for its *son et lumière*.

Perched on a pile of books on the seat of a chair
drawn to the head of the bed, the lamp called out
the guilty years and shamed them for cracks and shrivels
that bent the patient, scabbed logs of the walls and ceiling.
Then I opened a book whose every radiant page
was illuminated in colors of lightning and thunder

by the quick-witted lamp in its artistry of rage.
The book and the lamp fused to one voice, whose sense
became mine, strokes of a slow, rhythmic broom
swept a dusty pith that seemed to lie still until
some other sense told me that there were wings in the room.

In one much earlier year I had fallen asleep
in the meadow, head near bright heights of fireweed, fireweed
strewn on my chest from a hand that let go its bouquet,
and had wakened at eyelash touches, the delicate need
of five blue butterflies that found me in bloom.
Now, striking my neck and cheeks, came the first
wave of this late invasion, three flying bugs
that hit me, lit, flew again, hit, an outburst
the lamp had called for through log-gaps and screenholes, then
more entered the air, winged in gray, brown, dun,
and more, as I tried to read on, in the muted shades
brushed on by sundown's dimming imagination.

Beetle-bodied or light as moths they came
and, big and small, bombed the lit skin of face,
arms, shoulders, rested, crawled, unfurled, and sent
the blind wanting that stuffed full each one's carapace
in a clicking crash at the lampglass, then crazily flew
back to me, the bared part of me becoming a plan
for plates of an insect book whose specimens
rearranged themselves fiercely over and over again.
For as long as the lantern lasted they would have kept coming
as if the grave darkness had smiled at that tiny dawn
and had hurled them in fistfuls straight at the speaking light
in answer to what was being insisted upon.

Earth Tremors Felt in Missouri

The quake last night was nothing personal,
you told me this morning. I think one always wonders,
unless, of course, something is visible: tremors
that take us, private and willy-nilly, are usual.

But the earth said last night that what I feel,
you feel; what secretly moves you, moves me.
One small, sensuous catastrophe
makes inklings letters, spelled in a worldly tremble.

The earth, with others on it, turns in its course
as we turn toward each other, less than ourselves, gross,
mindless, more than we were. Pebbles, we swell
to planets, nearing the universal roll,
in our conceit even comprehending the sun,
whose bright ordeal leaves cool men woebegone.

The Block

Childless, we bought the big brick house on the block,
just in case. We walked the dog. Mornings the women
looked up from their clipping and pruning and weeding
to greet us, at dusk the men stopped their mowing to chat.
The children were newly married or off to college,
and dogs they had left behind them barked from backyards
at our dog, first in warning, later in greeting.
On other blocks we walked in the zany blare
of adolescent records and stepped around skates
and tricycles left on the sidewalk, but our middle-aged block,
busy and quiet, settled us into its solace.

The years bloomed by. The old dogs were put to sleep.
We bought a scoop to walk our new pup on his leash
as the block turned newly cranky about its curbs.
A lucky few dragged a staggering grandchild on visit
up and down, shyly accepting praise.
The wife on the corner shovelled their snow. "They say
it's what kills the men. I won't take a chance with my husband."
Then bad news began to come, hushed voices passed it
across back fences, the job of collecting for plants
found its permanent volunteer on the block. Later
more flowers, and one left alone in some of the houses.
Salads and cakes and roasts criss-crossed the street.

Then the long, warm, secret descent began
and we slid along with it. "We need a last dog," I said,
"but I can't face it." My husband became the husband
of the widows on either side in his husbandly tasks
of lifting and drilling for pictures and fixing faucets,
and a kindly old handyman took over, house by house,
the outdoor chores of mowing and small repairs.
"What would we do without Andrew?" everyone said.
The graying children came oftener, checking on things.
One widower wanted to marry the widow next door,
but "I'm through with *that* business!" she told him. The lone lesbian
kept up her house, but nearly wrinkled away.
I turned my flower borders to beds of groundcover.

The end came before we knew it. All in one year
my husband retired and half of the houses emptied.
Cancer ate four, heart attacks toppled some others,
a nursinghome closed over one, the rest caned off
to apartments with elevators. For Sale signs loomed
like paper tombstones on the weedy lawns.
The gentle years turned vicious all of a sudden.
"I can't believe it," we said. "The block's gone.
No one buys houses now." Those of us left

drew close, exchanged keys "in case something happens."
The wealthy patriarch sat all day on his porch
across the street and watched the distant disaster.
"He's way in his nineties," our busybody reported.
"His day and night nurses keep leaving, he's so awful.
And he won't take his pills. He just says, 'What does it matter?' "

We left on a long vacation. Home to the block,
we saw For Sale signs gone, heard new dog voices.
Bedding plants sucked up color from the old soil.
"The block is filled with young families. Everything's changed,"
we heard right away. A flyer stuck in the door:
"Block Party Sunday. Street Blocked Off All Day.
Bring Something to Share. All Bikes and Trikes Are Welcome."
"Oh Lord, do we have to go to all that bedlam?"
my husband said. "Oh God, I think they eat
hot dogs or something like that," I said. Too late,
Time, in its merciless blindness, gave us children.

A Kind of Music

*When consciousness begins to add diversity to its intensity, its value is no
longer absolute and inexpressible. The felt variations in its tone are attached to
the observed movement of its objects; in these objects its values are embedded.
A world loaded with dramatic values may thus arise in imagination; terrible
and delightful presences may chase one another across the void; life will be a
kind of music made by all the senses together. Many animals probably have
this kind of experience.*

—Santayana

Irrelevance characterizes the behavior of our puppy.
In the middle of the night he decides that he wants to play,
runs off when he's called, when petted is liable to pee,
cowers at a twig and barks at his shadow or a tree,
grins at intruders and bites us in the leg suddenly.

No justification we humans have been able to see
applies to his actions. While we go by the time of day,
or the rules, or the notion of purpose or consistency,
he follows from moment to moment a sensuous medley
that keeps him both totally subject and totally free.

I'll have to admit, though, we've never been tempted to say
that he jumps up to greet us or puts his head on our knee
or licks us or lies at our feet irrelevantly.
When it comes to loving, we find ourselves forced to agree
all responses are reasons and no reason is necessary.

Notes from a Suburban Heart

> *Freud says that ideas are libidinal cathexes, that is to say, acts of love.*
> —Norman O. Brown

It's time to put fertilizer on the grass again.
The last time I bought it, the stuff was smelly and black,
and said "made from Philadelphia sewage" on the sack.
It's true that the grass shot up in a violent green,
but my grass-roots patriotism tells me to stick
to St. Louis sewage, and if the Mississippi isn't thick
enough to put in a bag and spread on a lawn,
I'll sprinkle 5-10-5 from nobody's home,
that is to say . . .

it's been a long winter. The new feeder scared off the birds
for the first month it was up. Those stupid starvelings,
puffed up like popcorn against the cold, thought the thing
was a death-trap. The seeds and suet on its boards

go down their gullets now, and come out song,
but scot-free bugs slit up the garden. It is spring.
I've "made bums out of the birdies," in my next-door neighbor's words,
that is to say . . .

your life is as much a mystery to me as ever.
The dog pretends to bite fleas out of sheer boredom,
and not even the daffodils know if it's safe to come
up for air in this crazy, hot-and-cold weather.
Recognitions are shy, the faintest tint of skin
that says we are opening up, is it the same
as it was last year? Who can remember that either?
That is to say,

I love you, in my dim-witted way.

Evening Stroll in the Suburbs

The night is uneasy, armed between streetlamps.
Gaslights watch, dusk-to-dawn, for the sneak.
A footfall brings raging dogs from their porches.
Thorned shrubs replace flowerbeds, and stumps
where walked dogs used to take a leak
are planted round with unkind cactus.
Murmur and rustle of lovers, sibilance
of a lone bike, jolly ker-slaps
of a jogger are stilled. Each front lawn,
which formerly proffered the elegance
of a poised rabbit, poisoned its slopes
with DDT. Fear is overgrown.
The corner drugstore's boarded, For Rent.

Somewhere out here the hater, the thief,
the hurter, the disturber of peace must be.
In this barbed neighborhood, oh I want
back the self that night-walked, safe
from screaming in the dark, It's only me.

JOSEPH BRODSKY

(1940-1996)

Poet Laureate Consultant in Poetry (1991-1992)

Language and, presumably, literature are things that are more ancient and inevitable, more durable than any form of social organization. The revulsion, irony, or indifference often expressed by literature towards the state is essentially a reaction of the permanent—better yet, the infinite—against the temporary, against the finite. To say the least, as long as the state permits itself to interfere with the affairs of literature, literature has the right to interfere with the affairs of the state.

Joseph Brodsky, the only American poet laureate to win the Nobel Prize in Literature, came to the United States in 1972, an involuntary exile from the Soviet Union. His earliest verse, published in Russia under the name Iosif Alexandrovich Brodsky, was sardonic and fiercely independent, and he was brought to trial on charges of "parasitism," "decadence," and "modernism." He was condemned to a Soviet mental institution, followed by five years in a Siberian labor camp. The following widely circulated transcript of his trial before a Soviet judge mobilized European and American intellectuals to secure his early release from the labor camp.

JUDGE: And what is your profession, in general?

BRODSKY: I am a poet and a literary translator.

JUDGE: Who recognizes you as a poet? Who enrolled you in the ranks of poets?

BRODSKY: No one. Who enrolled me in the ranks of humankind?

JUDGE: Did you study this?

BRODSKY: This?

JUDGE: How to become a poet. You did not even try to finish high school where they prepare, where they teach?

BRODSKY: I didn't think you could get this from school.

JUDGE: How then?

BRODSKY: I think that it . . . comes from God.

W. H. Auden helped Brodsky find a job at the University of Michigan upon his arrival in the United States. Brodsky became a prolific man of letters, publishing not only poetry but also essays and criticism in *The New Yorker* and the *New York Review of Books*. At first his poems were translated from Russian by American poets; most of the poems in his last two books were translated by Brodsky himself. He received one of the first MacArthur "genius" grants, and his first collection of essays won the National Book Critics Circle Award in 1986.

Brodsky embraced the public service spirit of the job of poet laureate: "I'm a government worker, as it were. So my concern here is not so much the well-being of poets themselves, my concern is with the well-being of the audience, the size of the audience. This next year looks like more reading and chatting than scribbling. For a year I can do that. For me it's in many ways to pay back what I've been given by this country." In his October 1991 address, "An Immodest Proposal," he called for publishers to print cheaper copies of poetry books that could be sold or even given away in public places such as supermarkets, hotel lobbies, and airports.

Brodsky described the exiled writer as one "who survives like a fish in the sand." He was nonetheless largely unmoved by the political changes that accompanied the fall of the Soviet Union. He told David Remnick, then of the *Washington Post,* that those changes were "devoid of autobiographical interest" for him. His allegiance was to his language: "I belong to the Russian culture. I feel part of it, its component, and no change of place can influence the final consequence of this. A language is a much more ancient and inevitable thing than a state. I belong to the Russian language."

To the President-elect

You've climbed the mountain. At its top,
the mountain and the climbing stop.
A peak is where the climber finds
his biggest step is not mankind's.

Proud of your stamina and craft
you stand there being photographed
transfixed between nowhere-to-go
and us who give you vertigo.

Well, strike your tent and have your lunch
before you stir an avalanche
of brand-new taxes whose each cent
will mark the speed of your descent.

Six Years Later

So long had life together been that now
the second of January fell again
on Tuesday, making her astonished brow
lift like a windshield wiper in the rain,
      so that her misty sadness cleared, and showed
      a cloudless distance waiting up the road.

So long had life together been that once
the snow began to fall, it seemed unending;
that, lest the flakes should make her eyelids wince,
I'd shield them with my hand, and they, pretending
     not to believe that cherishing of eyes,
     would beat against my palm like butterflies.

So alien had all novelty become
that sleep's entanglements would put to shame
whatever depths the analysts might plumb;
that when my lips blew out the candle flame,
     her lips, fluttering from my shoulder, sought
     to join my own, without another thought.

So long had life together been that all
that tattered brood of papered roses went,
and a whole birch grove grew upon the wall,
and we had money, by some accident,
     and tonguelike on the sea, for thirty days,
     the sunset threatened Turkey with its blaze.

So long had life together been without
books, chairs, utensils—only that ancient bed—
that the triangle, before it came about,
had been a perpendicular, the head
     of some acquaintance hovering above
     two points which had been coalesced by love.

So long had life together been that she
and I, with our joint shadows, had composed
a double door, a door which, even if we
were lost in work or sleep, was always closed:
     somehow its halves were split and we went right
     through them into the future, into night.

Anno Domini

The provinces are celebrating Christmas.
The Governor-general's mansion is bedecked
with mistletoe, torches smoke by the entrance.
In the lanes the people press and lark around.
A merry, idle, dirty, boisterous
throng crowds in the rear of the mansion.

The Governor-general is ill. He lies
on a couch, wrapped in a shawl from Alcazar,
where he once served, and his thoughts turn
on his wife and on his secretary
receiving guests downstairs in the hall.
He is not really jealous. At this moment

it's more important to him to retire
into his shell of illness, dreams, the deferment of
his transfer to the capital. And since
he knows that freedom is not needed
by the crowd at all to make a public holiday—
for this same reason he allows

even his wife to be unfaithful. What would
he think of if ennui attacks
did not plague him? If he loved?
A chilly tremor runs through his shoulders,
he chases these alarming thoughts away.
In the hall the merrymaking subsides

but does not end. Muddled with drink,
the leaders of the tribes stare glassily
into a distance now devoid of enemies.
Their teeth, expressive of their rage,
set in a smile that's like a wheel
held fast by brakes—and a servant

is loading them with food. In his sleep
a merchant cries out. Snatches of song are heard.
The Governor-general's wife and secretary
slip out into the garden. And on the wall
the imperial eagle, like a bat, stares down,
having gorged on the Governor-general's liver.

And I, a writer who has seen the world,
who has crossed the equator on an ass,
look out of the window at the hills asleep
and think about the identity of our woes:
the Emperor won't see him, I won't be
seen by my son and Cynthia . . . And we,

we here shall perish. Arrogance will not raise
our bitter fate to the level of proof
that we are made in the Creator's image.
The grave will render all alike.
So, if only in our lifetime, let us be various!
For what reason should we rush from the mansion,

we cannot judge our homeland. The sword of justice
will stick fast in our personal disgrace:
the heirs, the power, are in stronger hands . . .
How good that vessels are not sailing!
How good that the sea is freezing!
How good that the birds in the clouds

are too frail for such cumbrous frames!
For that, nobody is to blame.
But perhaps our weights will be
proportionate exactly to their voices.
Therefore, let them fly to our homeland.
Therefore, let them yell out to us.

My country . . . foreign gentlemen,
visiting Cynthia, are leaning
over the crib like latter-day magi.
The infant slumbers. A star glimmers
like a coal under a cold font.
And the visitors, not touching his head,

replace the halo by an aureole of lies,
and the Virgin Birth by gossip,
by the passing over of the father in silence . . .
The mansion empties. The lights on each floor die.
First one, then another. Finally, the last.
And only two windows in the whole palace

are alight: mine, where, with my back to the torchlight,
I watch the moon's disk glide
over the sparsely growing trees, and see
Cynthia, the snow; the Governor-general's, where
he struggles silently all night with his illness
and keeps the fire lit, to see his enemy.

The enemy withdraws. The faint light of day
barely breaking in the world's East,
creeps through the window, straining
to see what is happening within,
and, coming across the remnants of the feast,
falters. But continues on its way.

Autumn in Norenskaia

We return from the field. The wind
clangs buckets upturned,
unbraids the willow fringe,
whistles through boulder piles.
The horses, inflated casks
of ribs trapped between shafts,
snap at the rusted harrows
with gnashing profiles.

A gust combs frostbitten sorrel,
bloats kerchiefs and shawls, searches
up the skirts of old hags, scrolls them
tight up as cabbageheads.
Eyes lowered, hacking out phlegm,
the women scissor their way home,
like cutting along a dull hem,
lurch toward their wooden beds.

Between folds flash the thighs of scissors,
wet eyes blur with the vision
of crabbed little imps that dance on
the farm women's pupils as a shower flings
the semblance of faces against a bare
pane. The furrows fan out in braids
under the harrow. The wind breaks
a chain of crows into shrieking links.

These visions are the final sign
of an inner life that seizes on
any specter to which it feels kin
till the specter scares off for good
at the church bell of a creaking axle,

at the metal rattle of the world as it
lies reversed in a rut of water,
at a starling soaring into cloud.

The sky lowers. The shouldered rake
sees the damp roofs first, staked
out against the ridge of a dark
hill that's just a mound far off.
Three versts still to cover. Rain
lords it over this beaten plain,
and to the crusted boots cling brown
stubborn clods of the native earth.

—————————

For E.R.

A second Christmas by the shore
of Pontus, which remains unfrozen.
The Star of Kings above the sharp horizon
of harbor walls. And I can't say for sure
that I can't live without you. As
this paper proves, I do exist: I'm living
enough to gulp my beer, to soil the leaves, and
trample the grass.

Retreating south before winter's assault,
I sit in that café from which we two were
exploded soundlessly into the future
according to the unrelenting law
that happiness can't last. My finger tries
your face on poor man's marble. In the distance,
brocaded nymphs leap through their jerky dances,
flaunting their thighs.

Just what, you gods—if this dilating blot,
glimpsed through a murky window, symbolizes
your selves now—were you trying to advise us?
The future has arrived and it is not
unbearable. Things fall, the fiddler goes,
the music ebbs, and deepening creases
spread over the sea's surface and men's faces.
But no wind blows.

Someday the slowly rising breakers but,
alas, not we, will sweep across this railing,
crest overhead, crush helpless screams, and roll in
to find the spot where you drank wine, took cat-
naps, spreading to the sun your wet
thin blouse—to batter benches, splinter boardwalks,
and build for future molluscs
a silted bed.

from *A Part of Speech*

I was born and grew up in the Baltic marshland
by zinc-gray breakers that always marched on
in twos. Hence all rhymes, hence that wan flat voice
that ripples between them like hair still moist,
if it ripples at all. Propped on a pallid elbow,
the helix picks out of them no sea rumble
but a clap of canvas, of shutters, of hands, a kettle
on the burner, boiling—lastly, the seagull's metal
cry. What keeps hearts from falseness in this flat region
is that there is nowhere to hide and plenty of room for vision.
Only sound needs echo and dreads its lack.
A glance is accustomed to no glance back.

Törnfallet

There is a meadow in Sweden
where I lie smitten,
eyes stained with clouds'
white ins and outs.

And about that meadow
roams my widow
plaiting a clover
wreath for her lover.

I took her in marriage
in a granite parish.
The snow lent her whiteness,
a pine was a witness.

She'd swim in the oval
lake whose opal
mirror, framed by bracken,
felt happy broken.

And at night the stubborn
sun of her auburn
hair shone from my pillow
at post and pillar.

Now in the distance
I hear her descant.
She sings "Blue Swallow,"
but I can't follow.

The evening shadow
robs the meadow
of width and color.
It's getting colder.

As I lie dying
here, I'm eyeing
stars. Here's Venus;
no one between us.

Love Song

If you were drowning, I'd come to the rescue,
    wrap you in my blanket and pour hot tea.
If I were a sheriff, I'd arrest you
    and keep you in a cell under lock and key.

If you were a bird, I'd cut a record
    and listen all night long to your high-pitched trill.
If I were a sergeant, you'd be my recruit,
    and boy, I can assure you, you'd love the drill.

If you were Chinese, I'd learn the language,
    burn a lot of incense, wear funny clothes.
If you were a mirror, I'd storm the Ladies',
    give you my red lipstick, and puff your nose.

If you loved volcanoes, I'd be lava,
    relentlessly erupting from my hidden source.
And if you were my wife, I'd be your lover,
    because the Church is firmly against divorce.

Folk Tune

It's not that the Muse feels like clamming up,
it's more like high time for the lad's last nap.
And the scarf-waving lass who wished him the best
drives a steamroller across his chest.

And the words won't rise either like that rod
or like logs to rejoin their old grove's sweet rot,
and, like eggs in the frying pan, the face
spills its eyes all over the pillowcase.

Are you warm tonight under those six veils
in that basin of yours whose strung bottom wails;
where like fish that gasp at the foreign blue
my raw lip was catching what then meant you?

I would have hare's ears sewn to my bald head,
in thick woods for your sake I'd gulp drops of lead,
and from black gnarled snags in the oil-smooth pond
I'd bob up to your face as some *Tirpitz* won't.

But it's not on the cards or the waiter's tray,
and it pains to say where one's hair turns gray.
There are more blue veins than the blood to swell
their dried web, let alone some remote brain cell.

We are parting for good, little friend, that's that.
Draw an empty circle on your yellow pad.
This will be me: no insides in thrall.
Stare at it a while, then erase the scrawl.

Bosnia Tune

As you sip your brand of scotch,
crush a roach, or scratch your crotch,
as your hand adjusts your tie,
people die.

In the towns with funny names,
hit by bullets, caught in flames,
by and large not knowing why,
people die.

In small places you don't know
of, yet big for having no
chance to scream or say goodbye,
people die.

People die as you elect
brand-new dudes who preach neglect,
self-restraint, etc.—whereby
people die.

Too far off to practice love
for thy neighbor/brother Slav,
where your cherubs dread to fly,
people die.

While the statues disagree,
Cain's version, history
for its fuel tends to buy
those who die.

As you watch the athletes score,
check your latest statement, or
sing your child a lullaby,
people die.

Time, whose sharp bloodthirsty quill
parts the killed from those who kill,
will pronounce the latter band
as your brand.

Once More by the Potomac

Here is a Jolly Good Fellow,
he's painted the White House yellow.

Here are the Mighty Generals,
bemedaled for fighting memories.

Here are the Hallowed Offices,
groggy with foggy prophecies.

Here are the Strategic Centers,
filled with their caviar emptors.

Here is our Congress, scrupulous
in making their marbles the cupola's.

And here are We, the People;
each one a moral cripple

or athlete, well trained in frowning
on someone else's drowning.

MARK STRAND

(1934–)

Poet Laureate Consultant in Poetry (1990–1991)

Politicians are always looking for people to agree with them, but they tend to do the most disagreeable things. . . . Poets, on the other hand, tend to be cheerleaders for the universe. That's why it's dangerous for them to align themselves with political causes. People will say they've (the poets) been taken in. They should stick to the broad issues, and the broadest issues of our experience are life and death. That's the stuff of all great poems.

Mark Strand's childhood was characterized by great geographic moves. He was born of American parents on Prince Edward Island, Canada, and his father's job as a salesman took the family from Canada to New York, Cleveland, Philadelphia, Peru, and Mexico before Strand went off to Antioch College and then Yale, intent on becoming a painter. By the age of twenty he had begun to write poetry seriously and went to Italy on a Fulbright scholarship to study nineteenth-century Italian poetry.

In addition to his twelve acclaimed volumes of poetry, Strand has published translations from the Spanish and the Portuguese, fiction, children's books, and works of art criticism, including a monograph on Edward Hopper, whose paintings influenced Strand's early windswept brand of American surrealism. "When I was a child what I saw of the world I saw from the backseat of my parents' car," Strand writes of his kinship with Hopper. "It was a world beyond my immediate neighborhood glimpsed in passing. It was still. It had its own life and did not know or care that I happened by at a particular time. Like the world of Hopper paintings, it did not return my gaze."

The rootless speakers in Strand's first three volumes move through empty landscapes that are charged with erotic melancholy. But they often look out upon their bleak surroundings with humor, seeming to shrug at the world's indifference and unpredictability. In the seventies, his verse became more intimate and parents, wives, and children populated his poetry. He reflects on this period as being his most imitative: "Lots of poets I admired were writing about their childhoods, so I wanted to be a member of the childhood club. But I discovered I didn't have much gift for it. Nor could I sustain an interest in it." His laureate year followed a mid-career period of transition; his seventh book, *The Continuous Life,* had just been published following a decade-long period of poetic silence during which he wrote fiction and art criticism.

Strand's recent writing often praises the physical world: the sun on our faces, a lover undressing and slipping into bed, a woman's reflection in a gilt-framed mirror, the day's first cup of coffee, a well-cut sports coat worn with jeans. His mature poetry is suffused with subtle emotion: "I look to be moved, to have my view of the world in which I live somewhat changed, enlarged. I want both to belong more strongly to it or more emphatically to it, and yet, to be able to see it, to have—well, it's almost a paradox to say this—a more compassionate distance."

Keeping Things Whole

In a field
I am the absence
of field.
This is
always the case.
Wherever I am
I am what is missing.

When I walk
I part the air
and always
the air moves in
to fill the spaces
where my body's been.

We all have reasons
for moving.
I move
to keep things whole.

Eating Poetry

Ink runs from the corners of my mouth.
There is no happiness like mine.
I have been eating poetry.

The librarian does not believe what she sees.
Her eyes are sad
and she walks with her hands in her dress.

The poems are gone.
The light is dim.
The dogs are on the basement stairs and coming up.

Their eyeballs roll,
their blond legs burn like brush.
The poor librarian begins to stamp her feet and weep.

She does not understand.
When I get on my knees and lick her hand,
she screams.

I am a new man.
I snarl at her and bark.
I romp with joy in the bookish dark.

The Remains

I empty myself of the names of others. I empty my pockets.
I empty my shoes and leave them beside the road.
At night I turn back the clocks;
I open the family album and look at myself as a boy.

What good does it do? The hours have done their job.
I say my own name. I say goodbye.
The words follow each other downwind.
I love my wife but send her away.

My parents rise out of their thrones
into the milky rooms of clouds. How can I sing?
Time tells me what I am. I change and I am the same.
I empty myself of my life and my life remains.

Coming to This

We have done what we wanted.
We have discarded dreams, preferring the heavy industry
of each other, and we have welcomed grief
and called ruin the impossible habit to break.

And now we are here.
The dinner is ready and we cannot eat.
The meat sits in the white lake of its dish.
The wine waits.

Coming to this
has its rewards: nothing is promised, nothing is taken away.
We have no heart or saving grace,
no place to go, no reason to remain.

The Coming of Light

Even this late it happens:
the coming of love, the coming of light.
You wake and the candles are lit as if by themselves,
stars gather, dreams pour into your pillows,
sending up warm bouquets of air.
Even this late the bones of the body shine
and tomorrow's dust flares into breath.

Lines for Winter

for Ros Krauss

Tell yourself
as it gets cold and gray falls from the air
that you will go on
walking, hearing
the same tune no matter where
you find yourself—
inside the dome of dark
or under the cracking white
of the moon's gaze in a valley of snow.
Tonight as it gets cold
tell yourself
what you know which is nothing
but the tune your bones play
as you keep going. And you will be able
for once to lie down under the small fire
of winter stars.
And if it happens that you cannot
go on or turn back
and you find yourself
where you will be at the end,
tell yourself
in that final flowing of cold through your limbs
that you love what you are.

For Jessica, My Daughter

Tonight I walked,
close to the house,
and was afraid,
not of the winding course

that I have made of love and self
but of the dark and faraway.
I walked, hearing the wind
and feeling the cold,
but what I dwelled on
were the stars blazing
in the immense arc of sky.

Jessica, it is so much easier
to think of our lives,
as we move under the brief luster of leaves,
loving what we have,
than to think of how it is
such small beings as we
travel in the dark
with no visible way
or end in sight.

Yet there were times I remember
under the same sky
when the body's bones became light
and the wound of the skull
opened to receive
the cold rays of the cosmos,
and were, for an instant,
themselves the cosmos,
there were times when I could believe
we were the children of stars
and our words were made of the same
dust that flames in space,
times when I could feel in the lightness of breath
the weight of a whole day
come to rest.

But tonight
it is different.
Afraid of the dark
in which we drift or vanish altogether,
I imagine a light
that would not let us stray too far apart,
a secret moon or mirror,
a sheet of paper,
something you could carry
in the dark
when I am away.

Pot Roast

I gaze upon the roast,
that is sliced and laid out
on my plate,
and over it
I spoon the juices
of carrot and onion.
And for once I do not regret
the passage of time.

I sit by a window
that looks
on the soot-stained brick of buildings
and do not care that I see
no living thing—not a bird,
not a branch in bloom,
not a soul moving
in the rooms
behind the dark panes.
These days when there is little

to love or to praise
one could do worse
than yield
to the power of food.
So I bend

to inhale
the steam that rises
from my plate, and I think
of the first time
I tasted a roast
like this.
It was years ago
in Seabright,
Nova Scotia;
my mother leaned
over my dish and filled it
and when I finished
filled it again.
I remember the gravy,
its odor of garlic and celery,
and sopping it up
with pieces of bread.

And now
I taste it again.
The meat of memory.
The meat of no change.
I raise my fork
and I eat.

The Continuous Life

What of the neighborhood homes awash
In a silver light, of children hunched in the bushes,
Watching the grown-ups for signs of surrender,
Signs that the irregular pleasures of moving
From day to day, of being adrift on the swell of duty,
Have run their course? O parents, confess
To your little ones the night is a long way off
And your taste for the mundane grows; tell them
Your worship of household chores has barely begun;
Describe the beauty of shovels and rakes, brooms and mops;
Say there will always be cooking and cleaning to do,
That one thing leads to another, which leads to another;
Explain that you live between two great darks, the first
With an ending, the second without one, that the luckiest
Thing is having been born, that you live in a blur
Of hours and days, months and years, and believe
It has meaning, despite the occasional fear
You are slipping away with nothing completed, nothing
To prove you existed. Tell the children to come inside,
That your search goes on for something you lost—a name,
A family album that fell from its own small matter
Into another, a piece of the dark that might have been yours,
You don't really know. Say that each of you tries
To keep busy, learning to lean down close and hear
The careless breathing of earth and feel its available
Languor come over you, wave after wave, sending
Small tremors of love through your brief,
Undeniable selves, into your days, and beyond.

A Piece of the Storm

for Sharon Horvath

From the shadow of domes in the city of domes,
A snowflake, a blizzard of one, weightless, entered your room
And made its way to the arm of the chair where you, looking up
From your book, saw it the moment it landed. That's all
There was to it. No more than a solemn waking
To brevity, to the lifting and falling away of attention, swiftly,
A time between times, a flowerless funeral. No more than that
Except for the feeling that this piece of the storm,
Which turned into nothing before your eyes, would come back,
That someone years hence, sitting as you are now, might say:
It's time. The air is ready. The sky has an opening.

The Night, the Porch

To stare at nothing is to learn by heart
What all of us will be swept into, and baring oneself
To the wind is feeling the ungraspable somewhere close by.
Trees can sway or be still. Day or night can be what they wish.
What we desire, more than a season or weather, is the comfort
Of being strangers, at least to ourselves. This is the crux
Of the matter, which is why even now we seem to be waiting
For something whose appearance would be its vanishing—
The sound, say, of a few leaves falling, or just one leaf,
Or less. There is no end to what we can learn. The book out there
Tells us as much, and was never written with us in mind.

Our Masterpiece Is the Private Life

for Jules

I

Is there something down by the water keeping itself from us,
Some shy event, some secret of the light that falls upon the deep,
Some source of sorrow that does not wish to be discovered yet?

Why should we care? Doesn't desire cast its rainbows over the coarse
    porcelain
Of the world's skin and with its measures fill the air? Why look for
    more?

II

And now, while the advocates of awfulness and sorrow
Push their dripping barge up and down the beach, let's eat
Our brill, and sip this beautiful white Beaune.

True, the light is artificial, and we are not well-dressed.
So what. We like it here. We like the bullocks in the field next door,
We like the sound of wind passing over grass. The way you speak,

In that low voice, our late-night disclosures . . . why live
For anything else? Our masterpiece is the private life.

III

Standing on the quay between the *Roving Swan* and the *Star
    Immaculate*,
Breathing the night air as the moment of pleasure taken
In pleasure vanishing seems to grow, its self-soiling

Beauty, which can only be what it was, sustaining itself
A little longer in its going, I think of our own smooth passage
Through the graded partitions, the crises that bleed

Into the ordinary, leaving us a little more tired each time,
A little more distant from the experiences, which, in the old days,
Held us captive for hours. The drive along the winding road

Back to the house, the sea pounding against the cliffs,
The glass of whiskey on the table, the open book, the questions,
All the day's rewards waiting at the doors of sleep . . .

The View

for Derek Walcott

This is the place. The chairs are white. The table shines.
The person sitting there stares at the waxen glow.
The wind moves the air around, repeatedly,
As if to clear a space. "A space for me," he thinks.
He's always been drawn to the weather of leave-taking,
Arranging itself so that grief—even the most intimate—
Might be read from a distance. A long shelf of cloud
Hangs above the open sea with the sun, the sun
Of no distinction, sinking behind it—a mild version
Of the story that is told just once if true, and always too late.
The waitress brings his drink, which he holds
Against the waning light, but just for a moment.
Its red reflection tints his shirt. Slowly the sky becomes darker,
The wind relents, the view sublimes. The violet sweep of it
Seems, in this effortless nightfall, more than a reason
For being there, for seeing it, seems itself a kind
Of happiness, as if that plain fact were enough and would last.

Black Sea

One clear night while the others slept, I climbed
the stairs to the roof of the house and under a sky
strewn with stars I gazed at the sea, at the spread of it,
the rolling crests of it raked by the wind, becoming
like bits of lace tossed in the air. I stood in the long,
whispering night, waiting for something, a sign, the approach
of a distant light, and I imagined you coming closer,
the dark waves of your hair mingling with the sea,
and the dark became desire, and desire the arriving light.
The nearness, the momentary warmth of you as I stood
on that lonely height watching the slow swells of the sea
break on the shore and turn briefly into glass and disappear . . .
Why did I believe you would come out of nowhere? Why with all
that the world offers would you come only because I was here?

My Name

Once when the lawn was a golden green
and the marbled moonlit trees rose like fresh memorials
in the scented air, and the whole countryside pulsed
with the chirr and murmur of insects, I lay in the grass,
feeling the great distances open above me, and wondered
what I would become and where I would find myself,
and though I barely existed, I felt for an instant
that the vast star-clustered sky was mine, and I heard
my name as if for the first time, heard it the way
one hears the wind or the rain, but faint and far off
as though it belonged not to me but to the silence
from which it had come and to which it would go.

Mirror

A white room and a party going on
and I was standing with some friends
under a large gilt-framed mirror
that tilted slightly forward
over the fireplace.
We were drinking whiskey
and some of us, feeling no pain,
were trying to decide
what precise shade of yellow
the setting sun turned our drinks.
I closed my eyes briefly,
then looked up into the mirror:
a woman in a green dress leaned
against the far wall.
She seemed distracted,
the fingers of one hand
fidgeted with her necklace,
and she was staring into the mirror,
not at me, but past me, into a space
that might be filled by someone
yet to arrive, who at that moment
could be starting the journey
which would lead eventually to her.
Then, suddenly, my friends
said it was time to move on.
This was years ago,
and though I have forgotten
where we went and who we all were,
I still recall that moment of looking up
and seeing the woman stare past me
into a place I could only imagine,
and each time it is with a pang,

as if just then I were stepping
from the depths of the mirror
into that white room, breathless and eager,
only to discover too late
that she is not there.

HOWARD NEMEROV

(1920–1999)

Poet Laureate Consultant in Poetry (1988–1990)
Consultant in Poetry (1963–1964)

Oh, you want praise and recognition and above all money. But if that was your true motive, you would have done something else. All this fame and honor is a very nice thing, as long as you don't believe it.

oward Nemerov's first talk as poet laureate at the Library of Congress, "Poetry and Nonsense," began by praising the shrill, unconscious humor he had found in recent newspaper headlines, such as "Summit Reaches Its Peak" and "Tear Gas used on Mourners." That split moment between chuckle and puzzlement, during which a reader might wonder what the article was really about, animates many of Nemerov's most memorable poems. A stanza might take off with a volley of offhand amusements—"because reverence has never been america's thing . . . ," "Here is Joe Blow the poet . . ."—but the poem will turn at some point to question the source of its own humor, often revealing some uncomfortable existential truth. Or, if Nemerov maintains his wisecracking tone throughout a poem, he might clinch it at the end with a pat but self-parodying declaration of sententiousness. Price of admission: You can only laugh along with the poem if you can laugh at yourself.

The lure of games is everywhere in Nemerov's work, even in his haunting elegy to his sister, the photographer Diane Arbus, "To D——, Dead by Her Own Hand." Nemerov often toys with the confessional voice in his poetry. If his poem does speak in the first person, the perspective will broaden into an inclusive, omniscient point of view. The radicalization of the sixties focused his satiric intelligence in a number of poems that question and make fun of American zealousness, such as "The Statues in the Public Gardens," which declares, "Children, to be illustrious is sad." At the same time, Nemerov's increasingly topical poetry became more formal. His is the unusual poetic career that moved from free verse to more traditional meters, while maintaining its conversational tone, full of quips and contemporary idioms. He liked to think of poems as puzzles: "It's such a blessed relief to have some little formal problem to work out, so you don't have to think about the earthshaking importance of what you are going to say."

Nemerov was one of the finest of American poets to begin writing verse during World War II. Born in New York City, he served as a pilot in the Royal Canadian unit of the U.S. Army Air Corps over the North Sea. He was a versatile writer, producing novels, short stories, plays, and essays in addition to his many volumes of poetry. In 1978 his *Collected Poems* won both the National Book Award and the Pulitzer Prize. He served as Distinguished Poet in Residence at Washington University in St. Louis from 1969 until his death.

Money

an introductory lecture

This morning we shall spend a few minutes
Upon the study of symbolism, which is basic
To the nature of money. I show you this nickel.
Icons and cryptograms are written all over
The nickel: one side shows a hunchbacked bison
Bending his head and curling his tail to accommodate
The circular nature of money. Over him arches
UNITED STATES OF AMERICA, and, squinched in
Between that and his rump, E PLURIBUS UNUM,
A Roman reminiscence that appears to mean
An indeterminately large number of things
All of which are the same. Under the bison
A straight line giving him a ground to stand on
Reads FIVE CENTS. And on the other side of our nickel
There is the profile of a man with long hair
And a couple of feathers in the hair; we know
Somehow that he is an American Indian, and
He wears the number nineteen-thirty-six.
Right in front of his eyes the word LIBERTY, bent
To conform with the curve of the rim, appears
To be falling out of the sky Y first; the Indian
Keeps his eyes downcast and does not notice this;
To notice it, indeed, would be shortsighted of him.
So much for the iconography of one of our nickels,
Which is now becoming a rarity and something of
A collectors' item: for as a matter of fact
There is almost nothing you can buy with a nickel,
The representative American Indian was destroyed

A hundred years or so ago, and his descendants'
Relations with liberty are maintained with reservations,
Or primitive concentration camps; while the bison,
Except for a few examples kept in cages,
Is now extinct. Something like that, I think,
Is what Keats must have meant in his celebrated
Ode on a Grecian Urn.
                                Notice, in conclusion,
A number of circumstances sometimes overlooked
Even by experts: (a) Indian and bison,
Confined to obverse and reverse of the coin,
Can never see each other; (b) they are looking
In opposite directions, the bison past
The Indian's feathers, the Indian past
The bison's tail; (c) they are upside down
To one another; (d) the bison has a human face
Somewhat resembling that of Jupiter Ammon.
I hope that our studies today will have shown you
Something of the import of symbolism
With respect to the understanding of what is symbolized.

Storm Windows

People are putting up storm windows now,
Or were, this morning, until the heavy rain
Drove them indoors. So, coming home at noon,
I saw storm windows lying on the ground,
Frame-full of rain; through the water and glass
I saw the crushed grass, how it seemed to stream
Away in lines like seaweed on the tide
Or blades of wheat leaning under the wind.

The ripple and splash of rain on the blurred glass
Seemed that it briefly said, as I walked by,
Something I should have liked to say to you,
Something . . . the dry grass bent under the pane
Brimful of bouncing water . . . something of
A swaying clarity which blindly echoes
This lonely afternoon of memories
And missed desires, while the wintry rain
(Unspeakable, the distance in the mind!)
Runs on the standing windows and away.

The Blue Swallows

Across the millstream below the bridge
Seven blue swallows divide the air
In shapes invisible and evanescent,
Kaleidoscopic beyond the mind's
Or memory's power to keep them there.

"History is where tensions were,"
"Form is the diagram of forces."
Thus, helplessly, there on the bridge,
While gazing down upon those birds—
How strange, to be above the birds!—
Thus helplessly the mind in its brain
Weaves up relation's spindrift web,
Seeing the swallows' tails as nibs
Dipped in invisible ink, writing . . .

Poor mind, what would you have them write?
Some cabalistic history
Whose authorship you might ascribe
To God? to Nature? Ah, poor ghost,

You've capitalized your Self enough.
That villainous William of Occam
Cut out the feet from under that dream
Some seven centuries ago.
It's taken that long for the mind
To waken, yawn and stretch, to see
With opened eyes emptied of speech
The real world where the spelling mind
Imposes with its grammar book
Unreal relations on the blue
Swallows. Perhaps when you will have
Fully awakened, I shall show you
A new thing: even the water
Flowing away beneath those birds
Will fail to reflect their flying forms,
And the eyes that see become as stones
Whence never tears shall fall again.

O swallows, swallows, poems are not
The point. Finding again the world,
That is the point, where loveliness
Adorns intelligible things
Because the mind's eye lit the sun.

The Vacuum

The house is so quiet now
The vacuum cleaner sulks in the corner closet,
Its bag limp as a stopped lung, its mouth
Grinning into the floor, maybe at my
Slovenly life, my dog-dead youth.

I've lived this way long enough,
But when my old woman died her soul
Went into that vacuum cleaner, and I can't bear
To see the bag swell like a belly, eating the dust
And the woolen mice, and begin to howl

Because there is old filth everywhere
She used to crawl, in the corner and under the stair.
I know now how life is cheap as dirt,
And still the hungry, angry heart
Hangs on and howls, biting at air.

To D——, Dead by Her Own Hand

My dear, I wonder if before the end
You ever thought about a children's game—
I'm sure you must have played it too—in which
You ran along a narrow garden wall
Pretending it to be a mountain ledge
So steep a snowy darkness fell away
On either side to deeps invisible;
And when you felt your balance being lost
You jumped because you feared to fall, and thought
For only an instant: That was when I died.

That was a life ago. And now you've gone,
Who would no longer play the grown-ups' game
Where, balanced on the ledge above the dark,
You go on running and you don't look down,
Nor ever jump because you fear to fall.

I Only Am Escaped Alone to Tell Thee

I tell you that I see her still
At the dark entrance of the hall.
One gas lamp burning near her shoulder
Shone also from her other side
Where hung the long inaccurate glass
Whose pictures were as troubled water.
An immense shadow had its hand
Between us on the floor, and seemed
To hump the knuckles nervously,
A giant crab readying to walk,
Or a blanket moving in its sleep.

You will remember, with a smile
Instructed by movies to reminisce,
How strict her corsets must have been,
How the huge arrangements of her hair
Would certainly betray the least
Impassionate displacement there.
It was no rig for dallying,
And maybe only marriage could
Derange that queenly scaffolding—
As when a great ship, coming home,
Coasts in the harbor, dropping sail
And loosing all the tackle that had laced
Her in the long lanes. . . .
                              I know
We need not draw this figure out.
But all that whalebone came from whales.
And all the whales lived in the sea,
In calm beneath the troubled glass,
Until the needle drew their blood.

I see her standing in the hall,
Where the mirror's lashed to blood and foam,
And the black flukes of agony
Beat at the air till the light blows out.

The Goose Fish

On the long shore, lit by the moon
To show them properly alone,
Two lovers suddenly embraced
So that their shadows were as one.
The ordinary night was graced
For them by the swift tide of blood
That silently they took at flood,
And for a little time they prized
    Themselves emparadised.

Then, as if shaken by stage-fright
Beneath the hard moon's bony light,
They stood together on the sand
Embarrassed in each other's sight
But still conspiring hand in hand,
Until they saw, there underfoot,
As though the world had found them out,
The goose fish turning up, though dead,
    His hugely grinning head.

There in the china light he lay,
Most ancient and corrupt and grey.
They hesitated at his smile,
Wondering what it seemed to say
To lovers who a little while

Before had thought to understand,
By violence upon the sand,
The only way that could be known
    To make a world their own.

It was a wide and moony grin
Together peaceful and obscene;
They knew not what he would express,
So finished a comedian
He might mean failure or success,
But took it for an emblem of
Their sudden, new and guilty love
To be observed by, when they kissed,
    That rigid optimist.

So he became their patriarch,
Dreadfully mild in the half-dark.
His throat that the sand seemed to choke,
His picket teeth, these left their mark
But never did explain the joke
That so amused him, lying there
While the moon went down to disappear
Along the still and tilted track
    That bears the zodiac.

Style

Flaubert wanted to write a novel
About nothing. It was to have no subject
And be sustained upon style alone,
Like the Holy Ghost cruising above

The abyss, or like the little animals
In Disney cartoons who stand upon a branch
That breaks, but do not fall
Till they look down. He never wrote that novel,
And neither did he write another one
That would have been called *La Spirale*,
Wherein the hero's fortunes were to rise
In dreams, while his waking life disintegrated.

Even so, for these two books
We thank the master. They can be read,
With difficulty, in the spirit alone,
Are not so wholly lost as certain works
Burned at Alexandria, flooded at Florence,
And are never taught at universities.
Moreover, they are not deformed by style,
That fire that eats what it illuminates.

Boy with Book of Knowledge

He holds a volume open in his hands:
Sepia portraits of the hairy great,
The presidents and poets in their beards
Alike, simplified histories of the wars,
Conundrums, quizzes, riddles, games and poems,

"Immortal Poems"; at least he can't forget them,
Barbara Fritchie and the Battle Hymn,
And best of all America the Beautiful,
Whose platitudinous splendors ended with
"From sea to shining sea," and made him cry

And wish to be a poet, only to say such things,
From sea to shining sea. Could that have been
Where it began? the vast pudding of knowledge,
With poetry rare as raisins in the midst
Of those gold-lettered volumes black and green?

Mere piety to think so. But being now
As near his deathday as his birthday then,
He would acknowledge all he will not know,
The silent library brooding through the night
With all its lights continuing to burn

Insomniac, a luxury liner on what sea
Unfathomable of ignorance who could say?
And poetry, as steady, still, and rare
As the lighthouses now unmanned and obsolete
That used to mark America's dangerous shores.

On an Occasion of National Mourning

It is admittedly difficult for a whole
Nation to mourn and be seen to do so, but
It can be done, the silvery platitudes
Were waiting in their silos for just such
An emergent occasion, cards of sympathy
From heads of state were long ago prepared
For launching and are bounced around the world
From satellites at near the speed of light,
The divine services are telecast
From the home towns, children are interviewed
And say politely, gravely, how sorry they are.

And in a week or so the thing is done,
The sea gives up its bits and pieces and
The investigating board pinpoints the cause
By inspecting bits and pieces, nothing of the sort
Can ever happen again, the prescribed course
Of tragedy is run through omen to amen
As in a play, the nation rises again
Reborn of grief and ready to seek the stars;
Remembering the shuttle, forgetting the loom.

To the Congress of the United States, Entering Its Third Century

because reverence has never been america's thing,
    this verse in your honor will not begin "o thou."
but the great respect our country has to give
may you all continue to deserve, and have.

· · ·

here at the fulcrum of us all,
the feather of truth against the soul
is weighed, and had better be found to balance
lest our enterprise collapse in silence.

for here the million varying wills
get melted down, get hammered out
until the movie's reduced to stills
that tell us what the law's about.

conflict's endemic in the mind:
your job's to hear it in the wind
and compass it in opposites,
and bring the antagonists by your wits

to being one, and that the law
thenceforth, until you change your minds
against and with the shifting winds
that this and that way blow the straw.

so it's a republic, as Franklin said,
if you can keep it; and we did
thus far, and hope to keep our quarrel
funny and just, though with this moral:—

praise without end for the go-ahead zeal
of whoever it was invented the wheel;
but never a word for the poor soul's sake
that thought ahead, and invented the brake.

26 ii 89

The Makers

Who can remember back to the first poets,
The greatest ones, greater even than Orpheus?
No one has remembered that far back
Or now considers, among the artifacts
And bones and cantilevered inference
The past is made of, those first and greatest poets,
So lofty and disdainful of renown
They left us not a name to know them by.

They were the ones that in whatever tongue
Worded the world, that were the first to say
Star, water, stone, that said the visible
And made it bring invisibles to view
In wind and time and change, and in the mind
Itself that minded the hitherto idiot world
And spoke the speechless world and sang the towers
Of the city into the astonished sky.

They were the first great listeners, attuned
To interval, relationship, and scale,
The first to say above, beneath, beyond,
Conjurors with love, death, sleep, with bread and wine,
Who having uttered vanished from the world
Leaving no memory but the marvelous
Magical elements, the breathing shapes
And stops of breath we build our Babels of.

On Being Asked for a Peace Poem

Here is Joe Blow the poet
Sitting before the console of the giant instrument
That mediates his spirit to the world.
He flexes his fingers nervously,
He ripples off a few scale passages
(Shall I compare thee to a summer's day?)
And resolutely readies himself to begin
His poem about the War in Vietnam.

This poem, he figures, is
A sacred obligation: all by himself,
Applying the immense leverage of art,

He is about to stop this senseless war.
So Homer stopped that dreadful thing at Troy
By giving the troops the Iliad to read instead;
So Wordsworth stopped the Revolution when
He felt that Robespierre had gone too far;
So Yevtushenko was invited in the *Times*
To keep the Arabs out of Israel
By smiting once again his mighty lyre.*
Joe smiles. He sees the Nobel Prize
Already, and the reading of his poem
Before the General Assembly, followed by
His lecture to the Security Council
About the Creative Process; probably
Some bright producer would put it on TV.
Poetry might suddenly be the in thing.

Only trouble was, he didn't have
A good first line, though he thought that for so great
A theme it would be right to start with O,
Something he would not normally have done,

O

And follow on by making some demands
Of a strenuous sort upon the Muse
Polyhymnia of Sacred Song, that Lady
With the fierce gaze and implacable small smile.

---

*"An Open Letter to Yevgeny Yevtushenko, Poet Extraordinary of Humanity," advt.,
Charles Rubinstein, *New York Times,* November 3, 1966.

Elegy for a Nature Poet

It was in October, a favorite season,
He went for his last walk. The covered bridge,
Most natural of all the works of reason,
Received him, let him go. Along the hedge

He rattled his stick; observed the blackening bushes
In his familiar field; thought he espied
Late meadow larks; considered picking rushes
For a dry arrangement; returned home, and died

Of a catarrh caught in the autumn rains
And let go on uncared for. He was too rapt
In contemplation to recall that brains
Like his should not be kept too long uncapped

In the wet and cold weather. While we mourned,
We thought of his imprudence, and how Nature,
Whom he'd done so much for, had finally turned
Against her creature.

His gift was daily his delight, he peeled
The landscape back to show it was a story;
Any old bird or burning bush revealed
At his hands just another allegory.

Nothing too great, nothing too trivial
For him; from mountain range or humble vermin
He could extract the hidden parable—
If need be, crack the stone to get the sermon.

And now, poor man, he's gone. Without his name
The field reverts to wilderness again,
The rocks are silent, woods don't seem the same;
Demoralized small birds will fly insane.

Rude Nature, whom he loved to idealize
And would have wed, pretends she never heard
His voice at all, as, taken by surprise
At last, he goes to her without a word.

RICHARD WILBUR

(1921–)

Poet Laureate Consultant in Poetry (1987–1988)

If, in the process [of writing poetry], I also find out something about myself, I think it is indirectly done. It is the thing, and not myself, that I set out to explore. But then, having chosen my subject and explored it, and having seen what I can say, I suppose one result of the poem is that I know myself a little better.

R ichard Wilbur remains America's reigning master of poems in traditional forms, creating pitch-perfect, balanced couplets, sonnets, and sapphics, as well as his own original, intricately constructed stanzas. He has won nearly every award in American letters, and many of them (the Pulitzer, the Guggenheim, the PEN Translation Award) twice. Born in New York City, he grew up on a farm in New Jersey, the son of a painter and a prominent journalist. In a biographical essay on Wilbur, poet Dana Gioia writes, "In a nation famously composed of immigrants, Wilbur had unusually deep native roots—he was an eleventh-generation American descended from the original settlers of Massachusetts and Rhode Island. . . . His Nebraska-born father came to New York City at sixteen to study art and became a successful commercial artist, and his mother came from a family of newspaper journalists." Wilbur published his first poems at the age of eight. At Amherst College, he met Charlotte Ward, his wife of sixty-four years and his muse and critic. After college, Wilbur served in the U.S. Army, where he trained as a cryptographer but was transferred to the infantry and World War II, where he saw combat for three years. He began to write poetry during his downtime and sent his efforts to his wife, who was the daughter of a writer and literary editor. His first poem in the *Saturday Evening Post* was published while he was on active duty abroad. In an interview, Wilbur said his experience of war shaped his sense of avocation: "One does not use poetry for its major purposes, as a means to organize oneself and the world, until one's world somehow gets out of hand."

His third volume of poetry, *Things of This World,* won the 1957 Pulitzer Prize, which he won a second time in 1989 for his *New and Collected Poems.* He taught at Harvard and Wellesley College, and at Wesleyan University for twenty years, where he helped found the Wesleyan University Press. He translated Molière and wrote the libretto for Leonard Bernstein's musical version of *Candide.*

When asked in interviews about the abiding formal elements in his verse, Wilbur replied: "Limitation makes for power. . . . The strength of the genie comes of his being confined in a bottle." Wilbur's poetry has been noted for its religious qualities: "I feel that the universe is full of glorious energy. . . . the energy tends to take pattern and shape, and that the ultimate character of things is comely and good. I am perfectly aware that I say this in the teeth of all sorts of contrary evidence, and that I must be basing it partly on temperament and partly on faith, but that's my attitude."

Blackberries for Amelia

Fringing the woods, the stone walls, and the lanes,
Old thickets everywhere have come alive,
Their new leaves reaching out in fans of five
From tangles overarched by this year's canes.

They have their flowers too, it being June,
And here or there in brambled dark-and-light
Are small, five-petaled blooms of chalky white,
As random-clustered and as loosely strewn

As the far stars, of which we now are told
That ever faster do they bolt away,
And that a night may come in which, some say,
We shall have only blackness to behold.

I have no time for any change so great,
But I shall see the August weather spur
Berries to ripen where the flowers were—
Dark berries, savage-sweet and worth the wait—

And there will come the moment to be quick
And save some from the birds, and I shall need
Two pails, old clothes in which to stain and bleed,
And a grandchild to talk with while we pick.

The Sirens

I never knew the road
From which the whole earth didn't call away,
With wild birds rounding the hill crowns,
Haling out of the heart an old dismay,
Or the shore somewhere pounding its slow code,
Or low-lighted towns
Seeming to tell me, stay.

Lands I have never seen
And shall not see, loves I will not forget,
All I have missed, or slighted, or foregone
Call to me now. And weaken me. And yet
I would not walk a road without a scene.
I listen going on,
The richer for regret.

Clearness

There is a poignancy in all things clear,
In the stare of the deer, in the ring of a hammer in the morning.
Seeing a bucket of perfectly lucid water
We fall to imagining prodigious honesties.

And feel so when the snow for all its softness
Tumbles in adamant forms, turning and turning
Its perfect faces, littering on our sight
The heirs and types of timeless dynasties.

In pine-woods once that huge precision of leaves
Amazed my eyes and closed them down a dream.
I lost to mind the usual southern river,
Mud, mist, the plushy sound of the oar,

And pondering north through lifted veils of gulls,
Through sharpening calls, and blue clearings of steam,
I came and anchored by a fabulous town
Immaculate, high, and never found before.

This was the town of my mind's exacted vision
Where truths fell from the bells like a jackpot of dimes,
And the people's voices, carrying over the water,
Sang in the ear as clear and sweet as birds.

But this was Thulë of the mind's worst vanity;
Nor could I tell the burden of those clear chimes;
And the fog fell, and the stainless voices faded;
I had not understood their lovely words.

A Simile for Her Smile

Your smiling, or the hope, the thought of it,
Makes in my mind such pause and abrupt ease
As when the highway bridgegates fall,
Balking the hasty traffic, which must sit
On each side massed and staring, while
Deliberately the drawbridge starts to rise:

Then horns are hushed, the oilsmoke rarefies,
Above the idling motors one can tell
The packet's smooth approach, the slip,
Slip of the silken river past the sides,
The ringing of clear bells, the dip
And slow cascading of the paddle wheel.

A Grasshopper

But for a brief
Moment, a poised minute,
He paused on the chicory-leaf;
Yet within it

The sprung perch
Had time to absorb the shock,
Narrow its pitch and lurch,
Cease to rock.

A quiet spread
Over the neighbor ground;
No flower swayed its head
For yards around;

The wind shrank
Away with a swallowed hiss;
Caught in a widening, blank
Parenthesis,

Cry upon cry
Faltered and faded out;
Everything seemed to die.
Oh, without doubt

Peace like a plague
Had gone to the world's verge,
But that an aimless, vague
Grasshopper-urge

Leapt him aloft,
Giving the leaf a kick,
Starting the grasses' soft
Chafe and tick,

So that the sleeping
Crickets resumed their chimes,
And all things wakened, keeping
Their several times.

In gay release
The whole field did what it did,
Peaceful now that its peace
Lay busily hid.

Someone Talking to Himself

Even when first her face,
Younger than any spring,
Older than Pharaoh's grain
And fresh as Phoenix-ashes,
Shadowed under its lashes
Every earthly thing,
There was another place
I saw in a flash of pain:
Off in the fathomless dark
Beyond the verge of love
I saw blind fishes move,
And under a stone shelf
Rode the recusant shark—
Cold, waiting, himself.

Oh, even when we fell,
Clean as a mountain source
And barely able to tell
Such ecstasy from grace,
Into the primal bed
And current of our race,

We knew yet must deny
To what we gathered head:
That music growing harsh,
Trees blotting the sky
Above the roaring course
That in the summer's drought
Slowly would peter out
Into a dry marsh.

Love is the greatest mercy,
A volley of the sun
That lashes all with shade,
That the first day be mended;
And yet, so soon undone,
It is the lover's curse
Till time be comprehended
And the flawed heart unmade.
What can I do but move
From folly to defeat,
And call that sorrow sweet
That teaches us to see
The final face of love
In what we cannot be?

Love Calls Us to the Things of This World

　　　The eyes open to a cry of pulleys,
And spirited from sleep, the astounded soul
Hangs for a moment bodiless and simple
As false dawn.
　　　　　　Outside the open window
The morning air is all awash with angels.

Some are in bed-sheets, some are in blouses,
Some are in smocks: but truly there they are.
Now they are rising together in calm swells
Of halcyon feeling, filling whatever they wear
With the deep joy of their impersonal breathing;

    Now they are flying in place, conveying
The terrible speed of their omnipresence, moving
And staying like white water; and now of a sudden
They swoon down into so rapt a quiet
That nobody seems to be there.
                  The soul shrinks

    From all that it is about to remember,
From the punctual rape of every blessed day,
And cries,
       "Oh, let there be nothing on earth but laundry,
Nothing but rosy hands in the rising steam
And clear dances done in the sight of heaven."

    Yet, as the sun acknowledges
With a warm look the world's hunks and colors,
The soul descends once more in bitter love
To accept the waking body, saying now
In a changed voice as the man yawns and rises,
       "Bring them down from their ruddy gallows;
Let there be clean linen for the backs of thieves;
Let lovers go fresh and sweet to be undone,
And the heaviest nuns walk in a pure floating
Of dark habits,
          keeping their difficult balance."

Piazza di Spagna, Early Morning

              I can't forget
    How she stood at the top of that long marble stair
    Amazed, and then with a sleepy pirouette
Went dancing slowly down to the fountain-quieted square;

              Nothing upon her face
But some impersonal loneliness,—not then a girl,
    But as it were a reverie of the place,
        A called-for falling glide and whirl;

    As when a leaf, petal, or thin chip
Is drawn to the falls of a pool and, circling a moment above it,
        Rides on over the lip—
    Perfectly beautiful, perfectly ignorant of it.

The Beacon

Founded on rock and facing the night-fouled sea
A beacon blinks at its own brilliance,
Over and over with cutlass gaze
Solving the Gordian waters,

Making the sea-roads out, and the lounge of the weedy
Meadows, finding the blown hair
As it always has, and the buxom, lavish
Romp of the ocean-daughters.

Then in the flashes of darkness it is all gone,
The flung arms and the hips, meads
And meridians, all; and the dark of the eye
Dives for the black pearl

Of the sea-in-itself. Watching the blinded waves
Compounding their eclipse, we hear their
Booms, rumors and guttural sucks
Warn of the pitchy whirl

At the mind's end. All of the sense of the sea
Is veiled as voices nearly heard
In morning sleep; nor shall we wake
At the sea's heart. Rail

At the deaf unbeatable sea, my soul, and weep
Your Alexandrine tears, but look:
The beacon-blaze unsheathing turns
The face of darkness pale

And now with one grand chop gives clearance to
Our human visions, which assume
The waves again, fresh and the same.
Let us suppose that we

See most of darkness by our plainest light.
It is the Nereid's kick endears
The tossing spray; a sighted ship
Assembles all the sea.

Boy at the Window

Seeing the snowman standing all alone
In dusk and cold is more than he can bear.
The small boy weeps to hear the wind prepare
A night of gnashings and enormous moan.
His tearful sight can hardly reach to where

The pale-faced figure with bitumen eyes
Returns him such a god-forsaken stare
As outcast Adam gave to Paradise.

The man of snow is, nonetheless, content,
Having no wish to go inside and die.
Still, he is moved to see the youngster cry.
Though frozen water is his element,
He melts enough to drop from one soft eye
A trickle of the purest rain, a tear
For the child at the bright pane surrounded by
Such warmth, such light, such love, and so much fear.

All These Birds

Agreed that all these birds,
Hawk or heavenly lark or heard-of nightingale,
Perform upon the kitestrings of our sight
In a false distance, that the day and night
Are full of winged words
                                    gone rather stale,
That nothing is so worn
As Philomel's bosom-thorn,

That it is, in fact, the male
Nightingale which sings, and that all these creatures wear
Invisible armor such as Hébert beheld
His water-ousel through, as, wrapped or shelled
In a clear bellying veil
                                    or bubble of air,
It bucked the flood to feed
At the stream-bottom. Agreed

That the sky is a vast claire
In which the gull, despite appearances, is not
            Less claustral than the oyster in its beak
            And dives like nothing human; that we seek
            Vainly to know the heron
                                    (but can plot
                  What angle of the light
                  Provokes its northern flight.)

            Let them be polyglot
And wordless then, those boughs that spoke with Solomon
            In Hebrew canticles, and made him wise;
            And let a clear and bitter wind arise
            To storm into the hotbeds
                              of the sun,
                  And there, beyond a doubt,
                  Batter the Phoenix out.

            Let us, with glass or gun,
Watch (from our clever blinds) the monsters of the sky
            Dwindle to habit, habitat, and song,
            And tell the imagination it is wrong
            Till, lest it be undone,
                              it spin a lie
                  So fresh, so pure, so rare
                  As to possess the air.

            Why should it be more shy
Than chimney-nesting storks, or sparrows on a wall?
            Oh, let it climb wherever it can cling
            Like some great trumpet-vine, a natural thing
            To which all birds that fly
                                    come natural.
                  Come, stranger, sister, dove:
                  Put on the reins of love.

A Pasture Poem

This upstart thistle
Is young and touchy; it is
All barb and bristle,

Threatening to wield
Its green, jagged armament
Against the whole field.

Butterflies will dare
Nonetheless to lay their eggs
In that angle where

The leaf meets the stem,
So that ants or browsing cows
Cannot trouble them.

Summer will grow old
As will the thistle, letting
A clenched bloom unfold

To which the small hum
Of bee wings and the flash of
Goldfinch wings will come,

Till its purple crown
Blanches, and the breezes strew
The whole field with down.

A Measuring Worm

This yellow striped green
Caterpillar, climbing up
The steep window screen,

Constantly (for lack
Of a full set of legs) keeps
Humping up his back.

It's as if he sent
By a sort of semaphore
Dark omegas meant

To warn of Last Things.
Although he doesn't know it,
He will soon have wings,

And I, too, don't know
Toward what undreamt condition
Inch by inch I go.

Terza Rima

In this great form, as Dante proved in Hell,
There is no dreadful thing that can't be said
In passing. Here, for instance, one could tell

How our jeep skidded sideways toward the dead
Enemy soldier with the staring eyes,
Bumping a little as it struck his head,

And then flew on, as if toward Paradise.

ROBERT PENN WARREN

(1905–1989)

Poet Laureate Consultant in Poetry (1986–1987)
Consultant in Poetry (1944–1945)

In one way, of course, all writing that is any good is experimental; that is, it's a way of seeing what is possible—what poem, what novel is possible. Experiment—they define it as putting a question to nature, and that is true of writing undertaken with seriousness. You put the question to human nature—and especially your own nature—and see what comes out. It is unpredictable. If it is predictable—not experimental in that sense—then it will be worthless.

R obert Penn Warren is the only writer to win the Pulitzer Prize in both fiction and poetry, which he received twice, in 1957 and in 1979. He also served twice as the nation's representative poet: once as consultant in 1944–45, and then as the nation's first poet laureate consultant in poetry in 1986–87 (after Congress changed the name to increase the post's visibility). He set the tone for distancing the job from government. In an early press conference he said that he had no intention of acting as a "hired applauder" or of writing "odes on the death of the president cat."

His poetry work in Washington framed a long and distinguished literary career. Though he is best known for his novel *All the King's Men* (adapted into two Hollywood films, in 1949 and 2006), his increasingly lyrical poems were widely acclaimed in the late sixties. "Between the ages of sixty-one and eighty-one," Harold Bloom writes, he "enjoyed a poetic renascence fully comparable to the great final phases of Thomas Hardy, William Butler Yeats, and Wallace Stevens." His later poetry was more autobiographical, recalling his relationship with his father (who regretted that he himself did not become a poet), and an early accident in which he lost sight in one eye.

Warren was born in Guthrie, Kentucky, in 1905 and the American South loomed large in his imagination. As a boy, he spent summers on his family's remote tobacco farm, where his grandfather, who had fought on the Confederate side of the Civil War, told tales of the war and recited the poetry of Sir Walter Scott and Robert Burns. Warren attended Vanderbilt University in Nashville, Tennessee, where he met Cleanth Brooks, Allen Tate, and John Crowe Ransom, with whom he formed a small, fiercely Southern-minded literary group, the Fugitives. He later denounced many of his early political opinions in the 1950s and became active in the civil rights movement. With Brooks, Warren wrote *Understanding Poetry and Understanding Fiction,* two New Critical textbooks that defined the way a generation coming of age just after two world wars learned to read. He taught throughout the country, but spent the most time at Yale University, where he taught from 1950 until 1973.

Patriotic Tour and Postulate of Joy

Once, once, in Washington,
D.C., in June,
All night—I swear it—a single mockingbird
Sang,
Sang to the Presidential ear,
Wherein it poured
Such criticism and advice as that ear
Had rarely had the privilege to hear.

And sang to every senator
Available,
And some, as sources best informed affirm,
Rose,
Rose with a taste in the throat like bile,
To the bathroom fled
And spat, and faced the mirror there, and while
The bicarb fizzed, stared, feet cold on tile.

And sang to Edgar Hoover, too,
And as it preached
Subversion and all bright disaster, he
Woke;
Woke, then looked at Mom's photo, so heard
No more. But far,
Far off in Arlington, the heroes stirred
And meditated on the message of that bird.

And sang—oh, merciless!—to me,
Who to that place
And to that massive hour had moved, and now
Rose,
Rose naked, and shivered in moonlight, and cried
Out in my need
To know what postulate of joy men have tried
To live by, in sunlight and moonlight, until they died.

Bearded Oaks

The oaks, how subtle and marine,
Bearded, and all the layered light
Above them swims; and thus the scene,
Recessed, awaits the positive night.

So, waiting, we in the grass now lie
Beneath the languorous tread of light:
The grasses, kelp-like, satisfy
The nameless motions of the air.

Upon the floor of light, and time,
Unmurmuring, of polyp made,
We rest; we are, as light withdraws,
Twin atolls on a shelf of shade.

Ages to our construction went,
Dim architecture, hour by hour:
And violence, forgot now, lent
The present stillness all its power.

The storm of noon above us rolled,
Of light the fury, furious gold,
The long drag troubling us, the depth:
Dark is unrocking, unrippling, still.

Passion and slaughter, ruth, decay
Descend, minutely whispering down,
Silted down swaying streams, to lay
Foundation for our voicelessness.

All our debate is voiceless here,
As all our rage, the rage of stone;
If hope is hopeless, then fearless fear,
And history is thus undone.

Our feet once wrought the hollow street
With echo when the lamps were dead
At windows, once our headlight glare
Disturbed the doe that, leaping, fled.

I do not love you less that now
The caged heart makes iron stroke,
Or less that all that light once gave
The graduate dark should now revoke.

We live in time so little time
And we learn all so painfully,
That we may spare this hour's term
To practice for eternity.

Revelation

Because he had spoken harshly to his mother,
The day became astonishingly bright,
The enormity of distance crept to him like a dog now,
And earth's own luminescence seemed to repel the night.

Roof was rent like the loud paper tearing to admit
Sun-sulphurous splendor where had been before
But the submarine glimmer by kindly countenances lit,
As slow, phosphorescent dignities light the ocean floor.

By walls, by walks, chrysanthemum and aster,
All hairy, fat-petalled species, lean, confer,
And his ears, and heart, should burn at that insidious whisper
Which concerns him so, he knows; but he cannot make out the words.

The peacock screamed, and his feathered fury made
Legend shake, all day, while the sky ran pale as milk;
That night, all night, the buck rabbit stamped in the moonlit glade,
And the owl's brain glowed like a coal in the grove's combustible dark.

When Sulla smote and Rome was rent, Augustine
Recalled how Nature, shuddering, tore her gown,
And kind changed kind, and the blunt herbivorous tooth dripped blood;
At Duncan's death, at Dunsinane, chimneys blew down.

But, oh! his mother was kinder than ever Rome,
Dearer than Duncan—no wonder, then, Nature's frame
Thrilled in voluptuous hemispheres far off from his home;
But not in terror: only as the bride, as the bride.

In separateness only does love learn definition,
Though Brahma smiles beneath the dappled shade,
Though tears, that night, wet the pillow where the boy's head was laid
Dreamless of splendid antipodal agitation;

And though across what tide and tooth Time is,
He was to lean back toward that recalcitrant face,
He would think, than Sulla more fortunate, how once he had learned
Something important about love, and about love's grace.

Founding Fathers, Nineteenth-Century Style, Southeast U.S.A.

They were human, they suffered, wore long black coat and gold watch
    chain.
They stare from daguerreotype with severe reprehension,
Or from genuine oil, and you'd never guess any pain
In those merciless eyes that now remark our own time's sad
    declension.

Some composed declarations, remembering Jefferson's language.
Knew pose of the patriot, left hand in crook of the spine or
With finger to table, while right invokes the Lord's just rage.
There was always a grandpa, or cousin at least, who had been, of
    course, a real Signer.

Some were given to study, read Greek in the forest, and these
Longed for an epic to do their own deeds right honor:
Were Nestor by pigpen, in some tavern brawl played Achilles.
In the ring of Sam Houston they found, when he died, one word
    engraved: *Honor.*

Their children were broadcast, like millet seed flung in a wind-flare.
Wives died, were dropped like old shirts in some corner of country.
Said, "Mister," in bed, the child-bride; hadn't known what to find there;
Wept all the next morning for shame; took pleasure in silk; wore the
    keys to the pantry.

"Will die in these ditches if need be," wrote Bowie, at the Alamo.
And did, he whose left foot, soft-catting, came forward, and breath hissed:
Head back, gray eyes narrow, thumb flat along knife-blade, blade low.
"Great gentleman," said Henry Clay, "and a patriot." Portrait by
    Benjamin West.

Or take those, the nameless, of whom no portraits remain,
No locket or seal ring, though somewhere, broken and rusted,
In attic or earth, the long Decherd, stock rotten, has lain;
Or the mold-yellow Bible, God's Word, in which, in their strength,
    they had also trusted.

Some wrestled the angel, and took a fall by the corncrib.
Fought the brute, stomp-and-gouge, but knew they were doomed in
    that glory.
All night, in sweat, groaned; fell at last with spit red and a cracked rib.
How sweet were the tears! Thus gentled, they roved the dark land
    with their old story.

Some prospered, had black men and lands, and silver on table,
But remembered the owl call, the smell of burnt bear fat on dusk-air.
Loved family and friends, and stood it as long as able,
"But money and women, too much is ruination, am Arkansas-bound."
    So went there.

One of mine was a land shark, or so the book with scant praise
Denominates him, "a man large and shapeless,
Like a sack of potatoes set on a saddle," and says,
"Little learning but shrewd, not well trusted." Rides thus out of
    history, neck fat and napeless.

One saw Shiloh and such, got cranky, would fiddle all night.
The boys nagged for Texas. "God damn it, there's nothing, God damn it,
In Texas," but took wagons, went, and to prove he was right,
Stayed a year and a day, "hell, nothing in Texas," had proved it, came
    back to black vomit,

And died, and they died, and are dead, and now their voices
Come thin, like last cricket in frost-dark, in grass lost,
With nothing to tell us for our complexity of choices,
But beg us only one word to justify their own old life-cost.

So let us bend ear to them in this hour of lateness,
And what they are trying to say, try to understand,
And try to forgive them their defects, even their greatness,
For we are their children in the light of humanness, and under the
   shadow of God's closing hand.

Modification of Landscape

There will, indeed, be modification of landscape,
And in margin of natural disaster, substantial reduction.
There will be refinement of principle, and purified action,
And expansion, we trust, of the human heart-hope, and hand-scope.

But it is a meanness of spirit and indulgence of spite
To suggest that your fair time, and friends, will mirror our own
Somewhat, and ourselves, for flesh will yet grieve on the bone,
And the heart need compensation for its failure to study delight?

Some will take up religion, some discover the virtue of money.
Some will find liberal causes the mask for psychic disturbance.
Some will expiate ego with excessive kindness to servants,
And some make a cult of honor, having often quite little, if any.

Some, hating all humans, will cultivate love for cats,
And some from self-hate will give children a morbid devotion.
Some will glorify friendship, but watch for the slightest motion
Of eyelid, or lip-twitch, and the longed-for betrayal it indicates.

Success for the great will be heart-bread, and soul's only ease.
For some it will stink, like mackerel shining in moonlight.
At the mere thought of failure some will wet their sheets in the night,
Though some wear it proud as Kiwanis, or manhood's first social
  disease.

Yes, the new age will need the old lies, as our own once did;
For death is ten thousand nights—sure, it's only the process
Of accommodating flesh to idea, but there's natural distress
In learning to face Truth's glare-glory, from which our eyes are long hid.

Ways of Day

I have come all this way.
I am sitting in the shade.
Book on knee and mind on nothing,
I now fix my gaze
On my small son playing in the afternoon's blaze.

Convulsive and cantankerous,
Night heaved, and burning, the star
Fell. Oh, what do I remember?
I heard the swamp owl, night-long, call.
The far car's headlight swept the room wall.

I am the dark and tricky one.
I am watching from my shade.
Your tousled hair-tips prickle the sunlight.
I watch you at your sunlit play.
Teach me, my son, the ways of day.

The World Is a Parable

I must hurry, I must go somewhere
Where you are not, where you
Will never be, I
Must go somewhere where
Nothing is real, for only
Nothingness is real and is
A sea of light. The world
Is a parable and we are
The meaning. The traffic
Begins to move, and meaning
In my guts blooms like
A begonia, I dare not
Pronounce its name. —Oh, driver!
For God's sake catch that light, for

There comes a time for us all when we want to begin a new life.

All mythologies recognize that fact.

Evening Hawk

From plane of light to plane, wings dipping through
Geometries and orchids that the sunset builds,
Out of the peak's black angularity of shadow, riding
The last tumultuous avalanche of
Light above pines and the guttural gorge,
The hawk comes.

         His wing
Scythes down another day, his motion
Is that of the honed steel-edge, we hear
The crashless fall of stalks of Time.

The head of each stalk is heavy with the gold of our error.

Look! look! he is climbing the last light
Who knows neither Time nor error, and under
Whose eye, unforgiving, the world, unforgiven, swings
Into shadow.

        Long now,
The last thrush is still, the last bat
Now cruises in his sharp hieroglyphics. His wisdom
Is ancient, too, and immense. The star
Is steady, like Plato, over the mountain.

If there were no wind we might, we think, hear
The earth grind on its axis, or history
Drip in darkness like a leaking pipe in the cellar.

Unless

All will be in vain unless—unless what? Unless
You realize that what you think is Truth is only

A husk for something else. Which might,
Shall we say, be called energy, as good a word as any. As when

The rattlesnake, among desert rocks
And Freudian cactus tall in moonlight,

Scrapes off the old integument, and flows away,
Clean and lethal and gleaming like water over moon-bright sand,

Unhusked for its mission. Oh, *neo nato!* fanged, unforgiving,
We worship you. In the morning,

In the ferocity of daylight, the old skin
Will be translucent and abstract, like Truth. The mountains,

In distance, will glitter like diamonds, or salt.
They too will, in that light, seem abstract.

At night I have stood there, and the wide world
Was flat and circular under the storm of the

Geometry of stars. The mountains, in starlight, were black
And black-toothed to define the enormous circle

Of desert of which I was the center. This
Is one way to approach the question.

All is in vain unless you can, motionless, standing there,
Breathe with the rhythm of stars.

You cannot, of course, see your own face, but you know that it,
Lifted, is stripped to white bone by starlight. This is happening.

This is happiness.

Mortal Limit

I saw the hawk ride updraft in the sunset over Wyoming.
It rose from coniferous darkness, past gray jags
Of mercilessness, past whiteness, into the gloaming
Of dream-spectral light above the last purity of snow-snags.

There—west—were the Tetons. Snow-peaks would soon be
In dark profile to break constellations. Beyond what height
Hangs now the black speck? Beyond what range will gold eyes see
New ranges rise to mark a last scrawl of light?

Or, having tasted that atmosphere's thinness, does it
Hang motionless in dying vision before
It knows it will accept the mortal limit,
And swing into the great circular downwardness that will restore

The breath of earth? Of rock? Of rot? Of other such
Items, and the darkness of whatever dream we clutch?

Rumor at Twilight

Rumor at twilight of whisper, crepuscular
Agitation, from no quarter defined, or something
Like the enemy fleet below the horizon, in
Its radio blackout, unobserved. In a dark cave,
Dark fruit, bats hang. Droppings
Of generations, soft underfoot, would carpet the gravel—
That is, if you came there again. Have you ever felt,
Between thumb and forefinger, texture
Of the bat's wing? Their hour soon comes.

You stand in the dark, under the maples, digesting
Dinner. You have no particular
Financial worries, just nags. Your children
Seem to respect you. Your wife is kind. Fireflies
Punctuate the expensive blackness of shrubbery,
Their prickling glows—here, there—like the phosphorescent

Moments of memory when, in darkness, your head first
Dents the dark pillow, eyes wide, ceilingward.
Can you really reconstruct your mother's smile?

You stand in the dark, heart even now filling, and think of
A boy who, drunk with the perfume of elder blossoms
And the massiveness of moonrise, stood
In a lone lane, and cried out,
In a rage of joy, to seize, and squeeze, significance from,
What life is, whatever it is. Now
High above the maples the moon presides. The first bat
Mathematically zigzags the stars. You fling down
The cigarette butt. Set heel on it. It is time to go in.

Little Girl Wakes Early

Remember when you were the first one awake, the first
To stir in the dawn-curdled house, with little bare feet
Cold on boards, every door shut and accurst,
And behind shut doors no breath perhaps drew, no heart beat.

You held your breath and thought how all over town
Houses had doors shut, and no whisper of breath sleeping,
And that meant no swinging, nobody to pump up and down,
No hide-and-go-seek, no serious play at housekeeping.

So you ran outdoors, bare feet from the dew wet,
And climbed the fence to the house of your dearest friend,
And opened your lips and twisted your tongue, all set
To call her name—but the sound wouldn't come in the end,

For you thought how awful, if there was no breath there
For answer. Tears start, you run home, where now mother,
Over the stove, is humming some favorite air.
You seize her around the legs, but tears aren't over,

And won't get over, not even when she shakes you—
And shakes you hard—and more when you can't explain.
Your mother's long dead. And you've learned that when loneliness
    takes you
There's nobody ever to explain to—though you try again and again.

The Loose Shutter

All night the loose shutter bangs. This way it won't last
Till morning. Something now bangs in my head. The past
Bangs in my head, hinges rust, hasps rip, all
The slotted crosspieces split. In the morning I'll call

The outfit that used to specialize in such matters
But now always bungles a job, mad as hatters,
For few are expert in repairing old jobs these days,
And the past seems to get out of order a thousand new ways,

And who now plays the decrepit piano downstairs
While the frisky old skeletons scuffle at Musical Chairs,
With old silk and broadcloth in tatters, and sex a debate?
But the party's now over. The last cab horse stamps at the gate.

If that goddam shutter stopped banging, I'd undertake
At least some amateur readjustments, and make
The great banging stop inside my head, and set
Certain matters to rights that now perpetually get

All sequences tangled, wear false faces, deny
All that happened—how at the orgasmic shudder's choked cry
Once ecstasy named the wrong name. The shutter goes *bang.*
What voice? What name? By what thin thread does the past hang?

GWENDOLYN BROOKS

(1917–2000)

Consultant in Poetry (1985–1986)

I am interested in relations between the races, but it is always something personal and specific that will drive me to pen and paper. I am interested in the issue of abortion and I have a poem that so many people call the "abortion poem," which it is not. It is called "The Mother." I am interested in the problem of young people committing suicide and I have a poem called "To the Young Who Want to Die Today." I like to say that poetry is life distilled. Anything that happens is grist for my mill.

Gwendolyn Brooks chronicled the African-American experience and the civil rights movement in America for most of the twentieth century. Her poems give voice to the experience of inner-city blacks in lyric and epic sequences that make full use of modernist poetic innovation. Many of her shorter poems are written in the bare-bones style of the blues and swing from emotional directness to sly, dry wit, as illustrated in such minimalist masterpieces as her best-known poem, "We Real Cool." A signature musical quality pervades her verse, and her sense of syncopation and perfect ear for rhyme make many of her poems readily memorizable. Every phase of her poetic development reveals a mind attuned to the political realities of her time.

Brooks was born in Topeka, Kansas, and raised on the South Side of Chicago, where she spent most of her life. Her father was a janitor who had hoped to become a doctor; her mother was a schoolteacher and classically trained pianist. They revered education. In an interview, she recalled growing up "bookish and lonely." Brooks published her first poem in *American Childhood* magazine at thirteen. Her mother sent her earliest poems to Langston Hughes and James Weldon Johnson. Hughes wrote back: "You're talented, keep writing. You'll have a book published one day." Johnson encouraged her to read American modernist innovators such as Wallace Stevens, E. E. Cummings, and T. S. Eliot. By the age of sixteen, Brooks was a regular contributor to the *Chicago Defender* newspaper, where she published nearly a hundred poems in a weekly poetry column.

Brooks once described her own style as "folksy narrative," which she varied by writing in free verse, quatrains, sonnets, her own idiosyncratic, playful combinations, and a range of hybrid poetic forms. She succeeded Carl Sandburg as poet laureate of Illinois, and became the first African-American female consultant in poetry to the Library of Congress at the age of sixty-eight. Her long sequences on inner-city family life are among the greatest epic poetry in the English language, though there have been few poets of any era who are equally gifted at writ-

ing both short stand-alone lyrics and long narrative sequences. In the
1950s Brooks published her first and only novel, *Maud Martha*, which
details a black woman's life in short vignettes. The critic David Little-
john described it as "a powerful, beautiful dagger of a book, as generous
as it can possibly be. It teaches more, more quickly, more lastingly, than
a thousand pages of protest."

Her early poetry draws from her experience as a young wife and
mother on Chicago's South Side, which she named Bronzeville. In the
late sixties she began to write in a new lean, compressed style, prompted
by a change in her political outlook resulting from a conference of black
writers she attended at Fisk University in 1967. When she returned from
the conference, she started a workshop that included members of the
Chicago street gang the Blackstone Rangers and a number of younger
poets, such as Sonia Sanchez and Nikki Giovanni. Her poetry from this
period balances graphic details of urban squalor with themes of recon-
ciliation and redemption. When asked if this new direction in her work
made her a "protest poet," Brooks replied, "No matter what the theme
is, I still want the poem to be a poem, not just a piece of propaganda."

Brooks's activism and her interest in nurturing black literature led
her to leave a major publishing house for a series of fledgling black pub-
lishing companies. She wrote verse until her death at eighty-three, hav-
ing witnessed and chronicled the racial tumult of the twentieth century.
She was the first black woman elected to the National Institute of Arts
and Letters, received over fifty honorary degrees, a lifetime achieve-
ment award from the National Endowment for the Arts and from the
National Book Foundation, and a National Medal of Arts award. There
is a Gwendolyn Brooks Chair in Black Literature and Creative Writ-
ing at Chicago State University, a junior high school in Harvey, Illinois,
named for her, and a Gwendolyn Brooks Center for African-American
Literature at Western Illinois University.

Brooks was one of the most accessible consultants, particularly with
children. In her view, her most important duties were visits to local
schools and prisons, and she regularly invited students and local poets
to read informally in her office, after which she invited them back
to her poetry office for what she called her "brownbag" lunches. She
responded with warmth and encouragement to the many letters that

came her way. In one letter a young woman asked Brooks to "play" a Mr. James Weldon Johnson to her; Brooks responded: "Thank you for your funny note ... but the conditions are hardly similar! I was a sixteen-year-old (yes, I was once sixteen)—and James Weldon Johnson was this gr-r-eat, accomplished poet-supreme. Whereas, you and I are *colleagues!* Your poetry is exciting—it is nimble and *ready.* I *could* say to you what I say to myself: revise, revise, revise." In response to a request for a visit from a teacher at the Maryland Correctional House who had discussed Brooks's famous poem "We Real Cool" (the teacher had written: "I have never seen them 'go after' a poem in such a manner"), Brooks replied, "I'd love to come. I have a packed calendar, but your request is so important, I really want to honor it." She did visit, and also read and spoke at the Lorton Prison in Virginia at the Comprehensive Alcohol and Drug Abuse Center. Always noted for her extraordinary energy, Brooks also managed to finish up the second volume of her autobiography during her year as consultant.

We Real Cool

THE POOL PLAYERS.
SEVEN AT THE GOLDEN SHOVEL.

We real cool. We
Left school. We

Lurk late. We
Strike straight. We

Sing sin. We
Thin gin. We

Jazz June. We
Die soon.

kitchenette building

We are things of dry hours and the involuntary plan,
Grayed in, and gray. "Dream" makes a giddy sound, not strong
Like "rent," "feeding a wife," "satisfying a man."

But could a dream send up through onion fumes
Its white and violet, fight with fried potatoes
And yesterday's garbage ripening in the hall,
Flutter, or sing an aria down these rooms

Even if we were willing to let it in,
Had time to warm it, keep it very clean,
Anticipate a message, let it begin?

We wonder. But not well! not for a minute!
Since Number Five is out of the bathroom now,
We think of lukewarm water, hope to get in it.

a song in the front yard

I've stayed in the front yard all my life.
I want a peek at the back
Where it's rough and untended and hungry weed grows.
A girl gets sick of a rose.

I want to go in the back yard now
And maybe down the alley,
To where the charity children play.
I want a good time today.

They do some wonderful things.
They have some wonderful fun.
My mother sneers, but I say it's fine
How they don't have to go in at quarter to nine.
My mother, she tells me that Johnnie Mae
Will grow up to be a bad woman.
That George'll be taken to Jail soon or late
(On account of last winter he sold our back gate).

But I say it's fine. Honest, I do.
And I'd like to be a bad woman, too,
And wear the brave stockings of night-black lace
And strut down the streets with paint on my face.

Sadie and Maud

Maud went to college.
Sadie stayed at home.
Sadie scraped life
With a fine-tooth comb.

She didn't leave a tangle in.
Her comb found every strand.
Sadie was one of the livingest chits
In all the land.

Sadie bore two babies
Under her maiden name.
Maud and Ma and Papa
Nearly died of shame.

When Sadie said her last so-long
Her girls struck out from home.
(Sadie had left as heritage
Her fine-tooth comb.)

Maud, who went to college,
Is a thin brown mouse.
She is living all alone
In this old house.

The Last Quatrain of the Ballad of Emmett Till

After the Murder
After the Burial

Emmett's mother is a pretty-faced thing;
    the tint of pulled taffy.
She sits in a red room,
    drinking black coffee.
She kisses her killed boy.
    And she is sorry.
Chaos in windy grays
    through a red prairie.

The Ballad of Rudolph Reed

Rudolph Reed was oaken.
His wife was oaken too.
And his two good girls and his good little man
Oakened as they grew.

"I am not hungry for berries.
I am not hungry for bread.
But hungry hungry for a house
Where at night a man in bed

"May never hear the plaster
Stir as if in pain.
May never hear the roaches
Falling like fat rain.

"Where never wife and children need
Go blinking through the gloom.
Where every room of many rooms
Will be full of room.

"Oh my home may have its east or west
Or north or south behind it.
All I know is I shall know it,
And fight for it when I find it."

It was in a street of bitter white
That he made his application.
For Rudolph Reed was oakener
Than others in the nation.

The agent's steep and steady stare
Corroded to a grin.
Why, you black old, tough old hell of a man,
Move your family in!

Nary a grin grinned Rudolph Reed,
Nary a curse cursed he,
But moved in his House. With his dark little wife,
And his dark little children three.

A neighbor would *look*, with a yawning eye
That squeezed into a slit.
But the Rudolph Reeds and the children three
Were too joyous to notice it.

For were they not firm in a home of their own
With windows everywhere
And a beautiful banistered stair
And a front yard for flowers and a back yard for grass?

The first night, a rock, big as two fists.
The second, a rock big as three.
But nary a curse cursed Rudolph Reed.
(Though oaken as man could be.)

The third night, a silvery ring of glass.
Patience ached to endure.
But he looked, and lo! small Mabel's blood
Was staining her gaze so pure.

Then up did rise our Rudolph Reed
And pressed the hand of his wife,
And went to the door with a thirty-four
And a beastly butcher knife.

He ran like a mad thing into the night.
And the words in his mouth were stinking.
By the time he had hurt his first white man
He was no longer thinking.

By the time he had hurt his fourth white man
Rudolph Reed was dead.
His neighbors gathered and kicked his corpse.
"Nigger—" his neighbors said.

Small Mabel whimpered all night long,
For calling herself the cause.
Her oak-eyed mother did no thing
But change the bloody gauze.

when you have forgotten Sunday: the love story

——And when you have forgotten the bright bedclothes on a
     Wednesday and a Saturday,
And most especially when you have forgotten Sunday—
When you have forgotten Sunday halves in bed,
Or me sitting on the front-room radiator in the limping afternoon
Looking off down the long street
To nowhere,
Hugged by my plain old wrapper of no-expectation
And nothing-I-have-to-do and I'm-happy-why?
And if-Monday-never-had-to-come—
When you have forgotten that, I say,
And how you swore, if somebody beeped the bell,
And how my heart played hopscotch if the telephone rang;
And how we finally went in to Sunday dinner,
That is to say, went across the front room floor to the ink-spotted table
     in the southwest corner
To Sunday dinner, which was always chicken and noodles
Or chicken and rice
And salad and rye bread and tea
And chocolate chip cookies—
I say, when you have forgotten that,
When you have forgotten my little presentiment
That the war would be over before they got to you;
And how we finally undressed and whipped out the light and flowed
     into bed,
And lay loose-limbed for a moment in the week-end
Bright bedclothes,
Then gently folded into each other—
When you have, I say, forgotten all that,
Then you may tell,
Then I may believe
You have forgotten me well.

Boy Breaking Glass

To Marc Crawford
from whom the commission

Whose broken window is a cry of art
(success, that winks aware
as elegance, as a treasonable faith)
is raw: is sonic: is old-eyed première.
Our beautiful flaw and terrible ornament.
Our barbarous and metal little man.

"I shall create! If not a note, a hole.
If not an overture, a desecration."

Full of pepper and light
and Salt and night and cargoes.

"Don't go down the plank
if you see there's no extension.
Each to his grief, each to
his loneliness and fidgety revenge.
Nobody knew where I was and now I am no longer there."

The only sanity is a cup of tea.
The music is in minors.

Each one other
is having different weather.

"It was you, it was you who threw away my name!
And this is everything I have for me."

Who has not Congress, lobster, love, luau,
the Regency Room, the Statue of Liberty,
runs. A sloppy amalgamation.

A mistake.
A cliff.
A hymn, a snare, and an exceeding sun.

The Second Sermon on the Warpland

For Walter Bradford

1.

This is the urgency: Live!
and have your blooming in the noise of the whirlwind.

2.

Salve salvage in the spin.
Endorse the splendor splashes;
stylize the flawed utility;
prop a malign or failing light—
but know the whirlwind is our commonwealth.
Not the easy man, who rides above them all,
not the jumbo brigand,
not the pet bird of poets, that sweetest sonnet,
shall straddle the whirlwind.
Nevertheless, live.

3.

All about are the cold places,
all about are the pushmen and jeopardy, theft—
all about are the stormers and scramblers but

what must our Season be, which starts from Fear?
Live and go out.
Define and
medicate the whirlwind.

4.

The time
cracks into furious flower. Lifts its face
all unashamed. And sways in wicked grace.
Whose half-black hands assemble oranges
is tom-tom hearted
(goes in bearing oranges and boom).
And there are bells for orphans—
and red and shriek and sheen.
A garbageman is dignified
as any diplomat.
Big Bessie's feet hurt like nobody's business,
but she stands—bigly—under the unruly scrutiny, stands in the wild
    weed.

In the wild weed
she is a citizen,
and is a moment of highest quality; admirable.

It is lonesome, yes. For we are the last of the loud.
Nevertheless, live.

Conduct your blooming in the noise and whip of the whirlwind.

The Crazy Woman

I shall not sing a May song.
A May song should be gay.
I'll wait until November
And sing a song of gray.

I'll wait until November.
That is the time for me.
I'll go out in the frosty dark
And sing most terribly.

And all the little people
Will stare at me and say,
"That is the Crazy Woman
Who would not sing in May."

A Lovely Love

Lillian's

Let it be alleys. Let it be a hall
Whose janitor javelins epithet and thought
To cheapen hyacinth darkness that we sought
And played we found, rot, make the petals fall.
Let it be stairways, and a splintery box
Where you have thrown me, scraped me with your kiss,
Have honed me, have released me after this
Cavern kindness, smiled away our shocks.
That is the birthright of our lovely love

In swaddling clothes. Not like that Other one.
Not lit by any fondling star above.
Not found by any wise men, either. Run.
People are coming. They must not catch us here
Definitionless in this strict atmosphere.

Of Robert Frost

There is a little lightning in his eyes.
Iron at the mouth.
His brows ride neither too far up nor down.

He is splendid. With a place to stand.

Some glowing in the common blood.
Some specialness within.

Langston Hughes

        is merry glory.
Is saltatory.
Yet grips his right of twisting free.

Has a long reach,
Strong speech,
Remedial fears.
Muscular tears.

Holds horticulture
In the eye of the vulture
Infirm profession.
In the Compression—
In mud and blood and sudden death—
In the breath
Of the holocaust he
Is helmsman, hatchet, headlight.
See
One restless in the exotic time! and ever,
Till the air is cured of its fever.

Medgar Evers

        For Charles Evers

The man whose height his fear improved he
arranged to fear no further. The raw
intoxicated time was time for better birth or
a final death.

Old styles, old tempos, all the engagement of
the day—the sedate, the regulated fray—
the antique light, the Moral rose, old gusts,
tight whistlings from the past, the mothballs
in the Love at last our man forswore.

Medgar Evers annoyed confetti and assorted
brands of businessmen's eyes.

The shows came down: to maxims and surprise.
And palsy.

Roaring no rapt arise-ye to the dead, he
leaned across tomorrow. People said that
he was holding clean globes in his hands.

ROBERT FITZGERALD

(1910–1985)

Consultant in Poetry (1984–1985)

Our lifetimes have seen the opening of abysses before which the mind quails. But it seems to me there are few things everyone can humbly try to hold onto: love and mercy (and humor) in everyday living; the quest for exact truth in language and affairs of the intellect; self-recollection or prayer; and the peace, the composed energy of art.

R obert Fitzgerald served as consultant in poetry in a health-limited capacity. He arranged several programs, but did not come to work in Washington. Fitzgerald grew up in Springfield, Illinois, and received a bachelor's degree from Harvard in 1933. He is best known as a translator of ancient Greek and Latin, though he also worked as a journalist and taught literature all over the world.

Fitzgerald's versions of Sophocles' Oedipus plays, Homer's *Iliad* and *Odyssey*, and Virgil's *Aeneid* are still used in many schools throughout the world to introduce students to the foundations of Western thought. Because he was a poet, his translations are known for their musicality and their vivid imagery, rather than for being scrupulously faithful to the original text. In 1961 he won the Bollingen Prize for his rendering of *The Odyssey*. Fitzgerald published four books of his own poetry; a book of his selected poems, *Spring Shade*, was published in 1972.

Born in Geneva, New York, he grew up in Springfield, Illinois, and attended Harvard to study the classics. His first group of poems was published in *Poetry* magazine while he was an undergraduate. Fitzgerald moved to New York City in the early thirties and worked as a reporter for the *New York Herald Tribune* and *Time* magazine, and during this period he began translating plays by Sophocles with his friend and former teacher Dudley Fitts. What began as an exercise in maintaining his language skills became a vocation once their version of Euripedes' *Alcestis* came out in 1936, to critical acclaim. Together Fitzgerald and Fitts went on to publish translations of each of Sophocles' Oedipus plays between 1939 and 1949. During World War II, he served in the navy at Guam and Pearl Harbor. Fitzgerald became a professor at Sarah Lawrence in 1946, and continued to teach at colleges and universities around the country almost until the end of his life. He returned to Harvard in 1965 as Boylston Professor of Rhetoric, a position he held until 1981.

July in Indiana

The wispy cuttings lie in rows
      where mowers passed in the heat.
A parching scent enters the nostrils.

Morning barely breathed before
      noon mounted on tiers of maples,
fiery and still. The eye smarts.

Moisture starts on the back of the hand.

Gloss and chrome on burning cars fan out
cobwebby lightning over children
      damp and flushed in the shade.

Over all the back yards, locusts
buzz like little sawmills in the trees,
      or is the song ecstatic?—rising
rising until it gets tired and dies away.

Grass baking, prickling sweat, great blazing tree,
magical shadow and cicada song
      recall
those heroes that in ancient days, reclining
on roots and hummocks, tossing pen-knives,
      delved in earth's cool underworld
and lightly squeezed the black clot from the blade.

Evening came, will come with lucid stillness
        printed by the distinct cricket
and, far off, by the freight cars' coupling clank.

        A warm full moon will rise
out of the mothering dust, out of the dry corn land.

Song After Campion

Ravished lute, sing to her virgin ears,
Soft notes thy strings repeating;
Plucked harp, whose amorous song she hears,
Tell her the time is fleeting;
Night-tide and my distress of love
O speak, sweet numbers,
That pity her heart may move
Before she slumbers.

Pale moth, that from the moon doth fly,
Fickle enchantments weaving,
Night faery, come my lady nigh
When the rich masques are leaving;
Tell her who lieth still alone
Love is a treasure
Fair as the frail lute's tone
And perished measure.

Song for September

Respect the dreams of old men, said the cricket,
Summer behind the song, the streams falling
Ledge to ledge in the mountains where clouds come.
Attend the old men who wander
Daylight and evening in the air grown cold,
Time thins, leaving their will to wind and whispers;
The bells are swallowed gently under ground.

Because in time the birds will leave this country,
Waning south, not to return again;
Because we walk in gardens among grasses,
Touching the garments of the wind that passes,
Dimming our eyes—

Give benches to the old men, said the cricket,
Listening by cool ways to the world that dies
Fainter than seas drawn off from mist and stone.
The rain that speaks at night is the prayer's answer.
What are dry phantoms to the old men
Lying at night alone?

They are not here whose gestures we have known,
Their hands in the dusk, their frail hair in the sun.

Horae

I. It pales. As if a look,
Invisible, came in the east.

In some far vale a rooster
Expels his cry of life.

Now dark but not formless
On the grey meads the trees
Lean and are looming soft.

In those towers of night
Ruffling things awake
Their declaration and chuckle.

Starpoint fades from the dew.

To every mile that sleeps
The cock's barbaric cry
And the wind comes cool.

Shiver of day break.

II. Now air, gentle pillager
In the citadels of summer,
Lifts a leaf here and there.
Sun holds the cornfield still
In his dream of the real.

From a wavering of bees
One droning steers away,
Elated in his golden car.
A cow stumbles and streams,
Reaching the meadow.

Tiny brutality in the grass
Manipulates the foe
Sawing and champing. Oh, soundless.

What burning contemplation
Rests in these distances?
What is seen by the leaves
Mirrored as in fair water
Millionfold?—as the eye of man
Finds itself in myriads.

III. The limber shadow is longer.
Air moves now breathing
In the plumes of corn.

Gnats on their elastics
Are busy with evening.
Heavy with night, the owl
Floats through the forest.

Shadow takes all the grass.

Beyond indigo mountains
Golden sheaves are fastened
Lightly on the infinite
West. What joy or feast
Has these for ornament?
What reclining host?

They sink away in peace.

Cobb Would Have Caught It

In sunburnt parks where Sundays lie,
Or the wide wastes beyond the cities,
Teams in grey deploy through sunlight.

Talk it up, boys, a little practice.

Coming in stubby and fast, the baseman
Gathers a grounder in fat green grass,
Picks it stinging and clipped as wit
Into the leather: a swinging step
Wings it deadeye down to first.
Smack. Oh, attaboy, attyoldboy.

Catcher reverses his cap, pulls down
Sweaty casque, and squats in the dust:
Pitcher rubs new ball on his pants,
Chewing, puts a jet behind him;
Nods past batter, taking his time.
Batter settles, tugs at his cap:
A spinning ball: step and swing to it,
Caught like a cheek before it ducks
By shivery hickory: socko, baby:
Cleats dig into dust. Outfielder,
On his way, looking over shoulder,
Makes it a triple. A long peg home.

Innings and afternoons. Fly lost in sunset.
Throwing arm gone bad. There's your old ball game.
Cool reek of the field. Reek of companions.

Lightness in Autumn

The rake is like a wand or fan,
With bamboo springing in a span
To catch the leaves that I amass
In bushels on the evening grass.

I reckon how the wind behaves
And rake them lightly into waves
And rake the waves upon a pile,
Then stop my raking for a while.

The sun is down, the air is blue,
And soon the fingers will be, too,
But there are children to appease
With ducking in those leafy seas.

So loudly rummaging their bed
On the dry billows of the dead,
They are not warned at four and three
Of natural mortality.

Before their supper they require
A dragon field of yellow fire
To light and toast them in the gloom.
So much for old earth's ashen doom.

Aerial

Inaccurately from an old rocking chair
One saw the rivery lands and lifted snows.
Then the Wrights' fabrication and Bleriot's
Annexed the cumulus kingdom of the air.
Helmeted birdmen looped the loop at the Fair
And ranged in later squadrons to impose
On somber towns the tremor of their blows
Or lightning stitches, adding flare on flare.

So much of heaven gained, so much of hell,
Made way for transcendental craft ensuing,
Emissaries not to be disavowed;
But let us pause on thee, sweet Caravel,
Dauphin of jets, in azure halls reviewing
Tall *parfaits* and pudding of whipped cloud.

Metamorphosis

A body made of February rain,
Insipid deliquescence, flat and sane,
Non-alcoholic, chill, perfectly chaste,
Is that by which I feel my own replaced.

Patrum Propositum

for W.M.

Bewildered in our buying throng,
        What came of it too well we know,
Of Santa Fe and Oregon,
        Of Adams, Jefferson, Monroe.

The Fathers' influences abate;
        And yet they live in the mind's eye,
Their ancient quest and craft of state
        Essences above history,

Elated, practical, and proud—

As in high air to a small boy,
In August, wagon trains of cloud
Bear westward over Illinois.

Borges's Love's Priority

Neither the intimacy of your forehead, fair as
a feast-day,
Nor the favour of your body, still mysterious,
reserved and childlike,
Nor what comes to me of your life, settling in words
or silence,
Will be a grace so provocative of thoughts
As the sight of your sleep, enfolded
In the vigil of my covetous arms.
Virgin again, miraculously, by the absolving power
of Sleep,
Quiet and luminous like some happy thing recovered
by memory,
You will deed to me that shore of your life
that you yourself do not own.
Cast up into silence,
I shall discern that ultimate beach of your being
And see you for the first time as, perhaps,
God must see you,
The fiction of Time destroyed,
Free from love, from me.

ANTHONY HECHT

(1923–2004)

Consultant in Poetry (1982–1984)

Poetry has no distinctive social function, but it provides the impulse toward meditation.

nthony Hecht started writing poetry during his first year at
Bard College. As a child he was passionately interested in music
and was an ardent fan of Cole Porter in particular. His early
verse reads like song lyrics, and his nine volumes of poetry are enliv-
ened by his keen musicality. During a period when most poets turned
to free verse, Hecht remained an ardent formalist, always employ-
ing rhyme, meter, and stanzaic structure in his verse. He served in
the army during World War II and witnessed the liberation of the
Flossenbürg concentration camp, an event that affected him deeply.
His service interrupted his undergraduate studies, and for a period
upon returning he was unable to read or write. He worked through
the trauma of the war by writing poems about the war. While Hecht
wrote formal verse expressing dark observations of mankind, he also
wrote lyrical evocations of love, and in the 1950s, with the poet John
Hollander, invented a humorous poetic form similar to a limerick
called the double dactyl, composed of two four-line stanzas in dac-
tylic feet (one stressed syllable followed by two unstressed). *The Hard
Hours* won the Pulitzer Prize in 1968. He received the Bollingen Prize
in 1983, and taught at the University of Rochester and Georgetown
University.

During Hecht's first year as consultant he had a clear distaste for Wash-
ington: "The plain fact is that Washington does not yet furnish the sort
of loyal, enthusiastic, and informed audience that poetry can count on
in New York and on certain first-class university and college campuses."
During his second year, his attitude toward the post softened, as he took
solace in a Washington poetry audience he called "faithful and good . . .
well-educated and conscientious." He focused his work on the D.C.
area, talking in the schools, giving local readings, and receiving a steady
stream of visitors at the Poetry Office—and responding to the "mind-
boggling" quantities of verse submitted for evaluation, or, as he put it
in his annual report to the Library, "more accurately, for approval. . . . All
too often it comes from people terribly handicapped, and in conditions

of such pronounced despair that they are forced into the desperate hope that a straightforward account of their anguish will *ipso facto* be poetry." Throughout his career he supported young poets. During his tenure, he advised future consultants when reading the work of aspiring poets to "err on the side of patience, good will, and generosity."

A Hill

In Italy, where this sort of thing can occur,
I had a vision once—though you understand
It was nothing at all like Dante's, or the visions of saints,
And perhaps not a vision at all. I was with some friends,
Picking my way through a warm sunlit piazza
In the early morning. A clear fretwork of shadows
From huge umbrellas littered the pavement and made
A sort of lucent shallows in which was moored
A small navy of carts. Books, coins, old maps,
Cheap landscapes and ugly religious prints
Were all on sale. The colors and noise
Like the flying hands were gestures of exultation,
So that even the bargaining
Rose to the ear like a voluble godliness.
And then, when it happened, the noises suddenly stopped,
And it got darker; pushcarts and people dissolved
And even the great Farnese Palace itself
Was gone, for all its marble; in its place
Was a hill, mole-colored and bare. It was very cold,
Close to freezing, with a promise of snow.
The trees were like old ironwork gathered for scrap
Outside a factory wall. There was no wind,
And the only sound for a while was the little click
Of ice as it broke in the mud under my feet.
I saw a piece of ribbon snagged on a hedge,
But no other sign of life. And then I heard
What seemed the crack of a rifle. A hunter, I guessed;
At least I was not alone. But just after that
Came the soft and papery crash
Of a great branch somewhere unseen falling to earth.

And that was all, except for the cold and silence
That promised to last forever, like the hill.

Then prices came through, and fingers, and I was restored
To the sunlight and my friends. But for more than a week
I was scared by the plain bitterness of what I had seen.
All this happened about ten years ago,
And it hasn't troubled me since, but at last, today,
I remembered that hill; it lies just to the left
Of the road north of Poughkeepsie; and as a boy
I stood before it for hours in wintertime.

A Letter

I have been wondering
What you are thinking about, and by now suppose
It is certainly not me.
But the crocus is up, and the lark, and the blundering
Blood knows what it knows.
It talks to itself all night, like a sliding moonlit sea.

Of course, it is talking of you.
At dawn, where the ocean has netted its catch of lights,
The sun plants one lithe foot
On that spill of mirrors, but the blood goes worming through
Its warm Arabian nights,
Naming your pounding name again in the dark heart-root.

Who shall, of course, be nameless.
Anyway, I should want you to know I have done my best,
As I'm sure you have, too.

Others are bound to us, the gentle and blameless
Whose names are not confessed
In the ceaseless palaver. My dearest, the clear unquarried blue

Of those depths is all but blinding.
You may remember that once you brought my boys
Two little woolly birds.
Yesterday the older one asked for you upon finding
Your thrush among his toys.
And the tides welled about me, and I could find no words.

There is not much else to tell.
One tries one's best to continue as before,
Doing some little good.
But I would have you know that all is not well
With a man dead set to ignore
The endless repetitions of his own murmurous blood.

"The Darkness and the Light Are Both Alike to Thee"

Psalms 139:12

Like trailing silks, the light
Hangs in the olive trees
As the pale wine of day
Drains to its very lees:
Huge presences of gray
Rise up, and then it's night.

Distantly lights go on.
Scattered like fallen sparks
Bedded in peat, they seem

Set in the plushest darks
Until a timid gleam
Of matins turns them wan,

Like the elderly and frail
Who've lasted through the night,
Cold brows and silent lips,
For whom the rising light
Entails their own eclipse,
Brightening as they fail.

"It Out-Herods Herod. Pray You, Avoid It."

Tonight my children hunch
Toward their Western, and are glad
As, with a Sunday punch,
The Good casts out the Bad.

And in their fairy tales
The warty giant and witch
Get sealed in doorless jails
And the match-girl strikes it rich.

I've made myself a drink.
The giant and witch are set
To bust out of the clink
When my children have gone to bed.

All frequencies are loud
With signals of despair;
In flash and morse they crowd
The rondure of the air.

For the wicked have grown strong,
Their numbers mock at death,
Their cow brings forth its young,
Their bull engendereth.

Their very fund of strength,
Satan, bestrides the globe;
He stalks its breadth and length
And finds out even Job.

Yet by quite other laws
My children make their case;
Half God, half Santa Claus,
But with my voice and face,

A hero comes to save
The poorman, beggarman, thief,
And make the world behave
And put an end to grief.

And that their sleep be sound
I say this childermas
Who could not, at one time,
Have saved them from the gas.

"More Light! More Light!"

for Heinrich Blücher and Hannah Arendt

Composed in the Tower before his execution
These moving verses, and being brought at that time
Painfully to the stake, submitted, declaring thus:
"I implore my God to witness that I have made no crime."

Nor was he forsaken of courage, but the death was horrible,
The sack of gunpowder failing to ignite.
His legs were blistered sticks on which the black sap
Bubbled and burst as he howled for the Kindly Light.

And that was but one, and by no means one of the worst;
Permitted at least his pitiful dignity;
And such as were by made prayers in the name of Christ,
That shall judge all men, for his soul's tranquillity.

We move now to outside a German wood.
Three men are there commanded to dig a hole
In which the two Jews are ordered to lie down
And be buried alive by the third, who is a Pole.

Not light from the shrine at Weimar beyond the hill
Nor light from heaven appeared. But he did refuse.
A Lüger settled back deeply in its glove.
He was ordered to change places with the Jews.

Much casual death had drained away their souls.
The thick dirt mounted toward the quivering chin.
When only the head was exposed the order came
To dig him out again and to get back in.

No light, no light in the blue Polish eye.
When he finished a riding boot packed down the earth.
The Lüger hovered lightly in its glove.
He was shot in the belly and in three hours bled to death.

No prayers or incense rose up in those hours
Which grew to be years, and every day came mute
Ghosts from the ovens, sifting through crisp air,
And settled upon his eyes in a black soot.

An Overview

Here, god-like, in a 707,
As on an air-conditioned cloud,
One knows the frailties of the proud
And comprehends the Fall from Heaven.

The world, its highways, trees and ports,
Looks much as if it were designed
With nifty model trains in mind
By salesmen at F. A.O. Schwarz.

Such the enchantment distance lends.
The bridges, matchstick and minute,
Seem faultless, intricate and cute,
Contrived for slight, aesthetic ends.

No wonder the camaraderie
Of mission-happy Air Force boys
Above so vast a spread of toys,
Cruising the skies, lighthearted, free,

Or the engaging roguishness
With which a youthful bombardier
Unloads his eggs on what appear
The perfect patchwork squares of chess;

Nor that the brass hat general staff,
Tailored and polished to a fault,
Favor an undeclared assault
On what an aerial photograph

Shows as an unstrung ball of twine,
Or that the President insist
A nation colored amethyst
Should bow to his supreme design.

But in the toy store, right up close,
Chipped paint and mucilage represent
The wounded, orphaned, indigent,
The dying and the comatose.

Curriculum Vitae

As though it were reluctant to be day,
    Morning deploys a scale
    Of rarities in gray,
And winter settles down in its chain-mail,

Victorious over legions of gold and red.
    The smokey souls of stones,
    Blunt pencillings of lead,
Pare down the world to glintless monotones

Of graveyard weather, vapors of a fen
    We reckon through our pores.
    Save for the garbage men,
Our children are the first ones out of doors.

Book-bagged and padded out, at mouth and nose
    They manufacture ghosts,
    George Washington's and Poe's,
Banquo's, the Union and Confederate hosts',

And are themselves the ghosts, file cabinet gray,
    Of some departed us,
    Signing our lives away
On ferned and parslied windows of a bus.

The Book of Yolek

Wir haben ein Gesetz,
Und nach dem Gesetz soll er sterben.

The dowsed coals fume and hiss after your meal
Of grilled brook trout, and you saunter off for a walk
Down the fern trail, it doesn't matter where to,
Just so you're weeks and worlds away from home,
And among midsummer hills have set up camp
In the deep bronze glories of declining day.

You remember, peacefully, an earlier day
In childhood, remember a quite specific meal:
A corn roast and bonfire in summer camp.
That summer you got lost on a Nature Walk;
More than you dared admit, you thought of home;
No one else knows where the mind wanders to.

The fifth of August, 1942.
It was morning and very hot. It was the day
They came at dawn with rifles to The Home
For Jewish Children, cutting short the meal
Of bread and soup, lining them up to walk
In close formation off to a special camp.

How often you have thought about that camp,
As though in some strange way you were driven to,
And about the children, and how they were made to walk,
Yolek who had bad lungs, who wasn't a day
Over five years old, commanded to leave his meal
And shamble between armed guards to his long home.

We're approaching August again. It will drive home
The regulation torments of that camp
Yolek was sent to, his small, unfinished meal,
The electric fences, the numeral tattoo,
The quite extraordinary heat of the day
They all were forced to take that terrible walk.

Death the Painter

Snub-nosed, bone-fingered, deft with engraving tools,
    I have alone been given
The powers of Joshua, who stayed the sun
    In its traverse of heaven.
Here in this Gotham of unnumbered fools
I have sought out and arrested everyone.

Under my watchful eye all human creatures
    Convert to a *still life,*
As with unique precision I apply
    White lead and palette knife.
A model student of remodelled features,
The final barber, the last beautician, I.

You lordlings, what is Man, his blood and vitals,
    When all is said and done?
A poor forked animal, a nest of flies.
    Tell us, what is this one
Once shorn of all his dignities and titles,
Divested of his testicles and eyes?

A Certain Slant

Etched on the window were barbarous thistles of frost,
Edged everywhere in that tame winter sunlight
With pavé diamonds and fine prickles of ice
Through which a shaft of the late afternoon
Entered our room to entertain the sway
And float of motes, like tiny aqueous lives,
Then glanced off the silver teapot, raising stains
Of snailing gold upcast across the ceiling,
And bathed itself at last in the slop bucket
Where other aqueous lives, equally slow,
Turned in their sad, involuntary courses,
Swiveled in eel-green broth. Who could have known
Of any elsewhere? Even of out-of-doors,
Where the stacked firewood gleamed in drapes of glaze
And blinded the sun itself with jubilant theft,
The smooth cool plunder of celestial fire?

MAXINE KUMIN

(1925–)

Consultant in Poetry (1981–1982)

This is the one thing I feel truly evangelical about, spreading the word. . . .
I did a tremendous amount of outreach with high school English teachers.
And I always said to them, "As far as I'm concerned, you folks are on the
front line." I feel they are. The fate of poetry really rises and falls with them.
So that anything we practicing poets can do to reinforce the teacher's role—
as he or she for the first time faces a class of squirmy adolescents and has
to try to stimulate them to read a poem, with feeling—we need to do that.

M	axine Kumin, the twenty-fifth consultant in poetry, was the fifth woman in the chair in its forty-three years. As she later told an interviewer, she thought she must have appeared to be a "very safe, heterosexual, middle-class, middle-aged woman poet, the kind who wasn't going to disgrace anybody." When, at a meeting of the Council of Scholars, she found herself "among all those éminences grises, all of whom were male, I said I felt as if I had stumbled into a stag club and ought to leap out of a cake." As consultant, Kumin initiated a popular women's series of poetry workshops at the Library's Poetry and Literature Center.

Kumin was born and raised in Philadelphia, received a bachelor's degree in 1946 and a master's in 1948 from Radcliffe College, and settled into the life of a young mother in Cambridge, where she became close friends with Anne Sexton, another young poet-homemaker in her local poetry workshop. Kumin has written much about her long friendship with Sexton. During the years of trying to balance domestic responsibility and writing, the two women installed a special friendship "hotline" in their homes. Most mornings started, after their husbands had gone to the office, with a call to each other. They would greet each other, then put the receiver down on their desks and speak across the house or room during the course of the day, trying out a line, reading a just-finished poem, venting about the length of their children's naps. She has described this friendship as crucial to overcoming the isolation and depression many young creative mothers feel. Kumin and Sexton collaborated on four children's books. Deeply affected by Sexton's suicide, Kumin has written many luminous elegies in honor of Sexton's life, work, and their friendship. She won the Pulitzer Prize in 1973 for *Up Country: Poems of New England*, published eleven books of poetry, taught for several years at Tufts, and served as poet in residence at many colleges and universities. The abiding themes in her work include family relationships, rural life in New England, and the inner lives of women.

She and her husband now raise horses and grow vegetables on their farm in New Hampshire. Kumin is often referred to as a regional pastoral poet since her verse is deeply rooted in her native New England: "I have been twitted with the epithet 'Roberta Frost,' which is not a bad thing to be."

Credo

I believe in magic. I believe in the rights
of animals to leap out of our skins
as recorded in the Kiowa legend:
Directly there was a bear where the boy had been

as I believe in the resurrected wake-robin,
first wet knob of trillium to knock
in April at the underside of earth's door
in central New Hampshire where bears are

though still denned up at that early greening.
I believe in living on grateful terms
with the earth, with the black crumbles
of ancient manure that sift through my fingers

when I topdress the garden for winter. I believe
in the wet strings of earth worms aroused out of season
and in the bear, asleep now in the rock cave
where my outermost pasture abuts the forest.

I cede him a swale of chokecherries in August.
I give the sow and her cub as much yardage
as they desire when our paths intersect
as does my horse shifting under me

respectful but not cowed by our encounter.
I believe in the gift of the horse, which is magic,
their deep fear-snorts in play when the wind comes up,
the ballet of nip and jostle, plunge and crow hop.

I trust them to run from me, necks arched in a full
swan's S, tails cocked up over their backs
like plumes on a Cavalier's hat. I trust them
to gallop back, skid to a stop, their nostrils

level with my mouth, asking for my human breath
that they may test its intent, taste the smell of it.
I believe in myself as their sanctuary
and the earth with its summer plumes of carrots,

its clamber of peas, beans, masses of tendrils
as mine. I believe in the acrobatics of boy
into bear, the grace of animals
in my keeping, the thrust to go on.

Poem for My Son

Where water laps my hips
it licks your chin. You stand
on tiptoe looking up
and swivel on my hands.
We play at this and laugh,
but understand you weigh
now almost less than life
and little more than sea.
So fine a line exists
between buoyance and stone
that, catching at my wrists,
I feel love notch the bone
to think you might have gone.

To think they smacked and pumped
to squall you into being
when you swam down, lungs limp
as a new balloon, and dying.
Six years today they bent
a black tube through your chest.
The tank hissed in the tent.
I leaned against the mast
outside that sterile nest.

And now inside the sea
you bump along my arm,
learning the narrow way
you've come from that red worm.
I tell you, save your air
and let the least swell ease you.
Put down, you flail for shore.
I cannot bribe nor teach you
to know the wet will keep you.

And cannot tell myself
unfasten from the boy.
On the Atlantic shelf
I see you wash away
to war or love or luck,
prodigious king, a stranger.
Times I stepped on a crack
my mother was in danger,
and time will find the chinks
to work the same in me.
You bobbled in my flanks.
They cut you from my sea.
Now you must mind your way.

Once, after a long swim
come overhand and wheezy
across the dappled seam
of lake, I foundered, dizzy,
uncertain which was better:
to fall there and unwind
in thirty feet of water
or fight back for the land.
Life would not let me lose it.
It yanked me by the nose.
Blackfaced and thick with vomit
it thrashed me to my knees.
We only think we choose.

But say we choose. Pretend it.
My pulse knit in your wrist
expands. Go now and spend it.
The sea will take our kiss.
Now, boy, swim off for this.

Spree

My father paces the upstairs hall
a large confined animal
neither wild nor yet domesticated.
About him hangs the smell of righteous wrath.
My mother is meekly seated
at the escritoire. Rosy from my bath
age eight–nine–ten by now I understand
his right to roar, hers to defy

the bill from Wanamaker's in his hand
the bill from Strawbridge's held high
the bill from Bonwit Teller
and the all plum-colored Blum Store.

His anger smells like dinner parties
like trays of frothy daiquiris.
Against the pre-World-War-Two prime
standing ribs his carving knife
flashes a little drunkenly. He charms
all the other Bonwit-bedecked wives
but something overripe malingers.
I wear his wide cigar bands on my fingers.

Oh God it is so noisy!
Under my bed a secret stair
a gold and purple escalator
takes me nightly down under the sea.
Such dancings, such carryings on
with the prince of this-or-that
with the duke of ne'er-do-well
I the plain one, a size too large to tell
grow tremulous at stickpin and cravat
I in toe shoes and tutu suddenly
see shopping is an art form
a kind of costume ball.

Papá, would we so humbly come
to the scene in the upstairs hall
on the first of every month, except
you chose the mice for footmen, clapped
to call up the coach and four?
You sent to Paris for the ermine muff
that says I'm rich. To think twelve poor
little things had their heads chopped off

to keep my hands unseemly warm!
When you went fishing down the well
for fox furs, hats with peacock plumes
velvet evening capes, what else befell?

You paid the bills, Papá. You cast the spell.

A Calling

Over my desk Georgia O'Keeffe says
I have no theories to offer and then
takes refuge in the disembodied
third person singular: *One works
I suppose because it is the most
interesting thing one knows to do.*
O Georgia! Sashaying between
first base and shortstop as it were
drawing up a list of all the things
*one imagines one has to do . . .
You get the garden planted. You
take the dog to the vet. You
certainly have to do the shopping.*

Syntax, like sex, is intimate.
One doesn't lightly leap from person
to person. *The painting,* you said,
*is like a thread that runs
through all the reasons for all the other
things that make one's life.*
O awkward invisible third person,
come out, stand up, be heard!
Poetry is like farming. It's

a calling, it needs constancy,
the deep woods drumming of the grouse,
and long life, like Georgia's, who
is talking to one, talking to me,
talking to you.

Hay

Day One: Above the river I hear
the loud fields giving up their gold,
the giant scissors-clack of Ruddy and Ned's
antique machine laying the timothy
and brome in windrows to be tedded,
this fierce anthood that persists
in taking from and giving back to the land,
defying the chrome millennium
that has contempt for smallscale backbreak.

Three emeralds, these interlocked three fields
free-leased for the tending and brushing out,
tidied up every fall like a well-swept
thrifty kitchen, blackberry and sumac
held at bay, gray birch and popple
brought down, the wild cherry lopped,
and gloriously every March
the wide white satin stretch besmirched
with dripping cartloads of manure.

Day Two: Sun bakes the long lines dry.
Late afternoon clouds pile up to stir
the teased-up mass with a southerly breeze
and since the forecast's fair, Ruddy and Ned
relax, play-punch, kidding each other,

calling each other Shirley, a name neither
owns up to, although once Scots-common
enough in New England back when
their patched rig was a modern invention.

Their dogs, four littermates,
Nutmeg, Cinnamon, Allspice and Mace,
Chessies with gums as pink as rubber
erasers and pink-rimmed eyes,
flat irises you can't look into,
their dogs, companionable roughnecks
always riding in the backs of their pickups
or panting, lying under them for shade,
look benignly on their sweating labors.

Day Three: The old baler cobbled from
other parts, repaired last winter,
cussed at in the shed in finger-
splitting cold when rusted bolts
resisted naval jelly, Coca-Cola, and
had to be drilled out in gritty bits,
now thunking like a good eggbeater
kicks the four-foot cubes off
onto the stubble for the pickups

and aggie trucks—that's our three-quarter ton
Dodge '67, slant-six engine
on its third clutch, with a new tie rod,
absent one door handle and an
intermittent taillight—
we'll carry fifty-two bales at a time
if they're pitched up and set on right.
Grunters and haulers, all of us
in these late-August heroics.

Interlude: The summer I was eleven

I boarded on a dairy farm in Pennsylvania.
Mornings we rode the ponies bareback
up through eiderdowns of ground fog,
up through the strong-armed apple orchard
that snatched at us no matter how we ducked,
up to the cows' vasty pasture, hooting and calling
until they assembled in their secret order
and we escorted them down to the milking barn
where each one gravely entered her stanchion.
There was no pushing or shoving.
All was as solemn as a Quaker Meeting.

My four were: Lily, Martha, Grace and May.
May had only three tits. I learned to say *tit*
as it is written here. I learned to spend
twenty minutes per cow and five more stripping,
which you do by dipping your fingers in milk
and then flattening the aforementioned tit
again and again between forefinger and thumb
as you slide down it in a firm and soothing motion.
If they don't trust you they won't let down.
They'll get mastitis and their agony will be
forever on your conscience. To this day
I could close my eyes and strip a cow correctly.

I came to love my black and white ladies.
I loved pressing my cheek against each flank
as I milked. I almost came to love cowflops,
crisp at the edges, smelly pancakes.
I got pinkeye that summer, they say
I caught it from the cows, I almost lost the eye.
Meanwhile, we had squirt fights, cow to cow.
We squirted the waiting kittens full.
We drank milk warm from the pail,
thirsty and thoughtless of the mystery

we drank from the cow's dark body,
then filed in for breakfast.

They put up hay loose there, the old way,
forking it into the loft from the wagon rack
while the sweaty horses snorted and switched off flies
and the littlest kids were commanded to trample it flat
in between loads until the entire bay
was alight with its radiant sun-dried manna. . . .
It was paradise up there with dusty sun motes
you could write your name in as they skirled and drifted down.
There were ropes we swung on and dropped from and shinnied up
and the smell of the place was heaven, hurling me back
to some unknown plateau, tears standing up in my eyes
and an ancient hunger in my throat, a hunger. . . .

Perhaps in the last great turn of the wheel
I was some sort of grazing animal.
Perhaps—trundling hay in my own barn
tonight and salivating from the sweetness—
I will be again. . . . When I read Neruda's
we are approaching a great and common tenderness
my mind startles and connects to this
all but obsolete small scene above the river
where unspectacular people secure
their bulky loads and drive away at dusk.

Allegiance to the land is tenderness.
The luck of two good cuttings in this climate.
Now clean down to the alders in the swale,
the fields begin an autumn flush of growth,
the steady work of setting roots, and then
as in a long exhale, go dormant.

Fat Pets On

I am trying to make a palindrome
out of the stencil NO STEP AFT
as we sit on the tarmac in Geneva.
It says don't tread on me, at least
not on this tender lifting place
where ice glistens along the wing
like juice beading a slice of melon.
I toy with FAT PETS ON while the intercom
announces that takeoff is delayed.

Long ago, before plexiglass,
before terrorists, each time we parted
at the international gate we could
still touch fingers, talk across
the token lattice that divided
ARRIVAL from IN TRANSIT in
Boston, Brussels, Singapore.
Daughter, now at the boarding call
limbo sets in. One more farewell.

Eyes forward, we turn from each other
back the disciplined way we came.
You with your briefcase and U.N. pass,
I humbler than that, a visiting mother,
carried by moving steps to my plane
whose destination—after Zurich, where
I will transfer to a jumbo jet—
is to refuel in Abu Dhabi,
home of twenty refugees in orbit,
those intercepts whose costly black-market
papers are not in order. People who
cannot come in from place of origin
and steadfastly refuse to go back to.
Month after month they languish, locked inside

handsome airport hotels at Zaventem
in Brussels, Schipphol in Amsterdam,
in Belgrade, Copenhagen, Bucharest.
However deluxe, still it is house arrest.

They may dial room service, see
interminable movies in
a tongue they cannot comprehend,
roam the carpeted corridors
but keep to the assigned floor,
suffer a continuum of clean
sheets and nightmares in which, shackled,
they are returned to death squads
or twenty years in hardship prison.

Meanwhile, I ride the current
of time backward, FAT PETS ON,
suspended in a calm cocoon
with Nanny-brisk attendants
to pamper the paid-up overfed.
They bear hot towels, hard rolls, a ration
of double-rich Swiss chocolate
to all of us luck kissed and safely set
down at birth in a privileged nation.

Noah, at Six Months

While, this rainy summer of 1990
the swollen pond pushes past its spillway,
bean seeds rot in their rows and lilacs
bead up but drop their thousand
lavender nubs unopened,

one silvery baby named Noah
is almost sitting alone now.
He sucks his fingers like ten tarts.
Through drool and Bronx cheer
he crows, inventing speech.
A river of vowels starts,
broken here and there by the chance
rapids of new consonants.

We kindle a fire in the parlor stove.
The farmhouse steams with the smell
of damp wool recurling
its filaments, like family feeling.
Shall we say all this is Noah's marvelous work?
Today in the rain our world is cupped in his ark.

Déjà Vu

They met in a blackberry patch
before catapults, cannons or Spam.
Before longbows, the War of the Roses
and oh! it is true he was handsome.
He licked the blood from her scratches.
All too soon she went off with him
(the story is always the same)
to the kingdom of bitter surprises.

No thought of her parents, those furies,
once darkened their hedonic fancy.
No gendarmes, no CIA snooping.
The mosses they lay on were spongy.
All summer they dallied in briars,

fished brooks that gladdened them leaping.
He fed her on nine kinds of berries.
He fed her on salmon and honey.

By late fall when she married her bear
none could dispute her condition.
The winter cave they prepared
with its pallet of springy pine boughs
was cozy and amply proportioned.
They exchanged more tickles and vows
until he sank in a torpor
from which he could not be roused.

Denned up in that twilit world
she grew hairier, took to all fours.
When the baby was born (a girl)
she came to her senses. Of course
she still loved him! She loved the child!
But his smell was frankly distracting.
His grunts were driving her wild.
He said that the way she was acting

was bad for the cub. Soapy water
could not scour the birthmark of Ursus
from the breast of her darling daughter.
There were tears. Growls followed curses.
She left when the moon was a platter
of silver lighting the rises
and hollows that led, days later,
through thickets of furze and gorse

with the babe in her arms, to the castle
—six rooms, one full bath, one lav—
she had fled without suitcase or parcel,
a song on her lips, to her love.
Alas, it's the prick of the spindle

all over again. When this child
has grown to a toothsome bundle
with a heart that is ripe and wild,

in some woodland glade unseen
there are bound to be blackberries growing
beyond the strict reach of the queen
and a bear-prince will lurk there, all-knowing.
What will be already has been.

Our Ground Time Here Will Be Brief

Blue landing lights make
nail holes in the dark.
A fine snow falls. We sit
on the tarmac taking on
the mail, quick freight,
trays of laboratory mice,
coffee and Danish for
the passengers.

Wherever we're going
is Monday morning.
Wherever we're coming from
is Mother's lap.
On the cloud-pack above, strewn
as loosely as parsnip
or celery seeds, lie
the souls of the unborn:

my children's children's
children and their father.
We gather speed for the last run
and lift off into the weather.

Skinnydipping with William Wordsworth

I lie by the pond *in utter nakedness*
thinking of you, Will, your epiphanies
of woodcock, raven, rills, and craggy steeps,
the solace that seductive nature bore,
and how in my late teens I came to you
with other Radcliffe *pagans suckled in
a creed outworn*, declaiming whole swatches
of "Intimations" to each other.

Moist-eyed with reverence, lying about
the common room, rising to recite
Great God! I'd rather be . . . How else
redeem the first flush of experience?
How else create it again and again? *Not in
entire forgetfulness* I raise up my boyfriend,
a Harvard man who could outquote me
in his Groton elocutionary style.

Groping to unhook my bra he swore
poetry could change the world for the better.
The War was on. Was I to let him die
unfulfilled? Soon afterward we parted.
Years later, he a decorated vet,
I a part-time professor, signed the same
guest book in the Lake District. Stunned
by coincidence we gingerly shared a room.

Ah, Will, high summer now; how many more
of these? *Fair seed-time had my soul,*
you sang; what seed-times still to come?
How I mistrust them, cheaters that will flame,
gutter and go out, like the scarlet tanager
who lights in the apple tree but will not stay.

Here at the pond, your *meadow, grove, and stream*
lodged in my head as tight as lily buds,
sun slants through translucent minnows, dragonflies
in paintbox colors couple in midair.
The fickle tanager flies over the tasseled field.
I lay my "Prelude" down under the willow.
My old gnarled body prepares to swim
to the other side.
                    Come with me, Will.
Let us cross over sleek as otters,
each of us bobbing in the old-fashioned breaststroke,
each of us centered in our beloved Vales.

Fox on His Back

   homage to Theodore Roethke

On long nights shy of melt
implacable and clear
wind drilling the last leaf
the poet to play it safe
slept with a baby's quilt
pulled over his bald head.
O what's the winter for?
To remember love, he said.

Fox on his back in a hole
snake eyes in the wall asleep
grubs shellacked in their coils
sap locked tight to the pith
roots sucking a hollow tooth
a brown and pregnant bear
leaf-wrapped like an old cigar. . . .

O what's the winter for?
the quilted poet asked.
Doors slam overhead
as maple buffets ash.
To remember love, he said.

Seven Caveats in May

When the dog whines at 5 a.m., do not
make your first mistake and let him out.
When he starts to bark in a furious tom-tom rhythm
and you can just discern a shadowy feinting

taking place under the distant hemlocks
do not seize the small sledge from the worktable and fly
out there in your nightgown and unlaced high
tops preparing to whack this, the ninth of its kind

in the last ten weeks, over the head
before it can quill your canine.
But it's not a porcupine: it's a big, black, angry
bear. Now your dog has put him up a tree

and plans to keep him there, a perfect
piece of work by any hound. Do not
run back and grab the manure fork
thinking you can keep the prongs

between you and the elevated bear long
enough to dart in and corral your critter.
Isn't it true bears come down slower
than they go up? Half an hour later do not

give up, go in the house and call the cops.
The dispatcher regrets having to report
there's no patrol car at this time, the state
police are covering. No doubt the nearest

trooper, wearing his Smokey Bear Stetson
is forty miles up the highway.
When your closest neighbor, big burly Smitty
works his way into his jeans and roars up

your dirt road in his four-wheel diesel truck
strides over the slash pile and hauls your hound back
(by now, you've thrown something on
over your not-quite-diaphanous nightgown)

do not forget to thank him with a six-pack.
Do not fail to take your feeders in on April One
despite the arriving birds' insistent clamor
and do not put them out again

until the first of December.

Looking Back in My Eighty-first Year

> *How did we get to be old ladies—*
> *my grandmother's job—when we*
> *were the long-leggèd girls?*
> —Hilma Wolitzer

Instead of marrying the day after graduation,
in spite of freezing on my father's arm as
here comes the bride struck up,
saying, I'm not sure I want to do this,

I should have taken that fellowship
to the University of Grenoble to examine
the original manuscript
of Stendhal's unfinished *Lucien Leuwen*,

I, who had never been west of the Mississippi,
should have crossed the ocean
in third class on the Cunard White Star,
the war just over, the Second World War

when Kilroy was here, that innocent graffito,
two eyes and a nose draped over
a fence line. How could I go?
Passion had locked us together.

Sixty years my lover,
he says he would have waited.
He says he would have sat
where the steamship docked

till the last of the pursers
decamped, and I rushed back
littering the runway with carbon paper. . . .
Why didn't I go? It was fated.

Marriage dizzied us. Hand over hand,
flesh against flesh for the final haul,
we tugged our lifeline through limestone and sand,
lover and long-leggèd girl.

The Revisionist Dream

Well, she didn't kill herself that afternoon.
It was a mild day in October, we sat outside
over sandwiches. She said she had begun

to practice yoga, take piano lessons,
rewrite her drama rife with lust and pride
and so she didn't kill herself that afternoon,

hugged me, went home, cranked the garage doors open,
scuffed through the garish leaves, orange and red,
that brought on grief. She said she had begun

to translate Akhmatova, her handsome Russian
piano teacher rendering the word-for-word
so she didn't kill herself that afternoon.

She cooked for him, made quiche and coq au vin.
He stood the Czerny method on its head
while her fingers flew. She said she had begun

accelerandos, Julia Child, and some
expand-a-lung deep breaths to do in bed
so she didn't kill herself that afternoon.
We ate our sandwiches. The dream blew up at dawn.

WILLIAM MEREDITH

(1919–2007)

Consultant in Poetry (1978–1980)

It's the nature of the work that a poem is getting at something mysterious, which no amount of staring at straight-on has ever solved, something like death or love or treachery or beauty. And we keep doing this corner-of-the-eye thing. I remember when we were in training to be night fliers in the Navy, I learned, very strangely, that the rods of the eye perceive things at night in the corner of the eye that we can't see straight ahead. That's not a bad metaphor for the vision of art. You don't stare at the mystery, but you *can* see things out of the corner of your eye that you were supposed to see.

Few volumes of poetry are as movingly titled as William Meredith's final book, *Effort at Speech: New and Selected Poems.* Published in 1997, the book refers to Meredith's 1983 stroke, which left him with expressive aphasia. For the last two decades of his life he was unable to express himself precisely: "I know it," he said, "but I can't say the words." Speaking first in single words, then stringing several together, Meredith completed his last volume with the help of three friends; the book is both a triumph of working through his disability and the culmination of his richly varied career.

Meredith's early poetry reflects upon his five years of military service, most of it as a naval aviator in the Pacific Theater. In 1952 he reenlisted to fly missions in the Korean War. His experience of war imbues his poetry with a strange, nearly counterintuitive sense of optimism, which he calls "morale": "I see the need for keeping the morale of troops high. . . . My real concern is, in the first place, that we ought not to be solemn and, in the second place, the response to disaster, even cultural disaster, is an impersonal one and the personal obligation is to mental and spiritual health." His verse, while formally sophisticated, speaks mostly in plain diction. In several interviews he refers to himself as "a useful poet" who employs "common" language and writes for "ordinary people, not intellectuals." His poems are mostly praise songs, poems that ponder and revel in the full range of human emotion. At the same time, Meredith's writing is attuned to human fragility. Grand insights are few and far between. Even before his stroke, he wrote only six to eight poems a year. When an interviewer asked him "Why so few?" his response was, "Why so many? . . . Astonishing experience doesn't happen very often." He sought to capture "astonishment of insight" in his poems rather than "astonishment of reality."

Meredith was an active and creative consultant. At the outset, he compiled an informal anthology of poems for inner-city schoolteachers, which he thought would be effective for teaching poetry. He wrote a letter to President Jimmy Carter condemning his arrest of nuclear disarmament protesters at the White House. He added prodigiously to the Library's recording series—and accomplished all of this while continuing to teach at Princeton. During the latter half of his term he focused on Latin American and Eastern European poetry. Meredith also strongly supported Allen Ginsberg's appointment as his successor (Ginsberg was interested in the post): "Looking back over the last thirteen appointments, since Robert Frost, I see a kind of establishment pattern, of which I am perhaps a good example. As visible as this position is, here and abroad, I think it should be *representative*."

A Mild-Spoken Citizen Finally Writes to the White House

Please read this letter when you are alone.
Don't be afraid to listen to what may change you,
I am urging on you only what I myself have done.

In the first place, I respect the office, although one night
last spring, when you had committed (in my eyes)
criminal folly, and there was a toast to you, I wouldn't rise.

A man's mistakes (if I may lecture you), his worst acts,
aren't out of character, as he'd like to think,
are not put on him by power or stress or too much to drink,

but are simply a worse self he consents to be. Thus
there is no mistaking you. I marvel that there's
so much disrespect for a man just being himself, being his errors.

"I never met a worse man than myself,"
Thoreau said. When we're our best selves, we can all
afford to say that. Self-respect is best when marginal.

And when the office of the presidency will again
accommodate that remark (Did you see? Fidel Castro
said almost that recently), it may be held by better men

than you or me. Meantime, I hear there is music in your house,
your women wear queens' wear, though winds howl outside,
and I say, that's all right, the man should have some ease,

but does anyone say to your face who you really are?
No, they say *Mr. President*, while any young person
feels free to call me *voter*, *believer*, even *causer*.

And if I were also a pray-er, a man given to praying,
(I'm often in fact careless about great things, like you)
and I wanted to pray for your office, as in fact I do,

the words that would come to me would more likely be
god change you than *god bless the presidency.*
I would pray, *God cause the President to change.*

As I myself have been changed, first my head, then my heart,
so that I no longer pretend that I don't swindle or kill
when there is swindling and killing on my nation's part.

Well. Go out into your upstairs hall tonight with this letter.
Generous ghosts must walk that house at night,
carrying draughts of the Republic like cold water

to a man parched after too much talk and wine and smoke.
Hear them. They are elected ghosts, though some will be radicals
and all may want to tell you things you will not like.

It will seem dark in the carpeted hall, despite the night-lights
in the dull sconces. Make the guard let you pass.
"If you are the President," a shade with a water-glass

will ask you (and this is all I ask), calling you by name,
himself perhaps a famous name, "If you are the President,
and things in the land have come to all this shame,

why don't you try doing something new? This building rose,
laborious as a dream, to house one character:
man trusting man anew. That's who each tenant is

—or an impostor, as some of us have been."

Airman's Virtue

> after Herbert

High plane for whom the winds incline,
    Who own but to your own recall,
There is a flaw in your design
    For you must fall.

High cloud whose proud and angry stuff
    Rose up in heat against earth's thrall,
The nodding law has time enough
    To wait your fall.

High sky, full of high shapes and vapors,
    Against whose vault nothing is tall,
It is written that your torch and tapers
    Headlong shall fall.

Only an outward-aching soul
    Can hold in high disdain these ties
And fixing on a farther pole
    Will sheerly rise.

Envoi

Go, little book. If anybody asks
Why I add poems to a time like this,
Tell how the comeliness I can't take in
Of ships and other figures of content
Compels me still until I give them names;
And how I give them names impatiently,

As who should pull up roses by the roots
That keep him turning on his empty bed,
The smell intolerable and thick with loss.

The Illiterate

Touching your goodness, I am like a man
Who turns a letter over in his hand
And you might think this was because the hand
Was unfamiliar but, truth is, the man
Has never had a letter from anyone;
And now he is both afraid of what it means
And ashamed because he has no other means
To find out what it says than to ask someone.

His uncle could have left the farm to him,
Or his parents died before he sent them word,
Or the dark girl changed and want him for beloved.
Afraid and letter-proud, he keeps it with him.
What would you call his feeling for the words
That keep him rich and orphaned and beloved?

A Major Work

Poems are hard to read
Pictures are hard to see
Music is hard to hear
And people are hard to love

But whether from brute need
Or divine energy
At last mind eye and ear
And the great sloth heart will move.

An Assent to Wildflowers

> *"Ay" and "no" too was no good divinity.*
> *—King Lear*

Plucked from their sockets like eyes that gave offense,
Dozens of black-eyed susans gaze
Into the room—a composite lens
Like a fly's, staring out of a bronze vase.

Gloucestered out of the meadow by the hands
I love, they ask me do I know
What they mean by this bold flower-glance?
Do I know who made the room glow?

And the answer of course is love, but before I can say
Love, I see the other question they raise,
Like anything blind that gapes at you that way.
A man may see how this world goes with no eyes.

The luster of the room goes blear for a minute,
Then, like Gloucester, I begin to guess.
I imagine the world, I imagine the world and you in it:
There's flowering, there's a dark question answered yes.

The Wreck of the Thresher

(Lost at sea, April 10, 1963)

I stand on the ledge where rock runs into the river
As the night turns brackish with morning, and mourn the drowned.
Here the sea is diluted with river; I watch it slaver
Like a dog curing of rabies. Its ravening over,
Lickspittle ocean nuzzles the dry ground.
(But the dream that woke me was worse than the sea's gray
Slip-slap; there are no such sounds by day.)

This crushing of people is something we live with.
Daily, by unaccountable whim
Or caught up in some harebrained scheme of death,
Tangled in cars, dropped from the sky, in flame,
Men and women break the pledge of breath:
And now under water, gone all jetsam and small
In the pressure of oceans collected, a squad of brave men in a hull.

(Why can't our dreams be content with the terrible facts?
The only animal cursed with responsible sleep,
We trace disaster always to our own acts.
I met a monstrous self trapped in the black deep:
All these years, he smiled, *I've drilled at sea*
For this crush of water. Then he saved only me.)

Winter Verse for His Sister

Moonlight washes the west side of the house
As clean as bone, it carpets like a lawn
The stubbled field tilting eastward
Where there is no sign yet of dawn.
The moon is an angel with a bright light sent
To surprise me once before I die
With the real aspect of things.
It holds the light steady and makes no comment.

Practicing for death I have lately gone
To that other house
Where our parents did most of their dying,
Embracing and not embracing their conditions.
Our father built bookcases and little by little stopped reading,
Our mother cooked proud meals for common mouths.
Kindly, they raised two children. We raked their leaves
And cut their grass, we ate and drank with them.
Reconciliation was our long work, not all of it joyful.

Now outside my own house at a cold hour
I watch the noncommittal angel lower
The steady lantern that's worn these clapboards thin
In a wash of moonlight, while men slept within,
Accepting and not accepting their conditions,
And the fingers of trees plied a deep carpet of decay
On the gravel web underneath the field,
And the field tilting always toward day.

Accidents of Birth

> *Je vois les effroyables espaces de l'Univers qui m'enferment, et je me trouve*
> *attaché à un coin de cette vaste étendue, sans savoir pourquoi je suis plutôt*
> *en ce lieu qu'en un autre, ni pourquoi ce peu de temps qui m'est donné à*
> *vivre m'est assigné à ce point plutôt qu'à un autre de toute l'éternité qui m'a*
> *précédé, et de toute qui me suit.*
>
> —Pascal, *Pensées sur la religion*

> *The approach of a man's life out of the past is history, and the approach of time*
> *out of the future is mystery. Their meeting is the present, and it is consciousness,*
> *the only time life is alive. The endless wonder of this meeting is what causes the*
> *mind, in its inward liberty of a frozen morning, to turn back and question and*
> *remember. The world is full of places. Why is it that I am here?*
>
> —Wendell Berry, *The Long-Legged House*

Spared by a car or airplane crash or
cured of malignancy, people look
around with new eyes at a newly
praiseworthy world, blinking eyes like these.

For I've been brought back again from the
fine silt, the mud where our atoms lie
down for long naps. And I've also been
pardoned miraculously for years
by the lava of chance which runs down
the world's gullies, silting us back.
Here I am, brought back, set up, not yet
happened away.

        But it's not this random
life only, throwing its sensual
astonishments upside down on
the bloody membranes behind my eyeballs,
not just me being here again, old
needer, looking for someone to need,
but you, up from the clay yourself,

as luck would have it, and inching
over the same little segment of earth-
ball, in the same little eon, to
meet in a room, alive in our skins,
and the whole galaxy gaping there
and the centuries whining like gnats—
you, to teach me to see it, to see
it with you, and to offer somebody
uncomprehending, impudent thanks.

Poem About Morning

Whether it's sunny or not, it's sure
To be enormously complex—
Trees or streets outdoors, indoors whoever you share,
And yourself, thirsty, hungry, washing,
An attitude towards sex.
No wonder half of you wants to stay
With your head dark and wishing
Rather than take it all on again:
Weren't you duped yesterday?
Things are not orderly here, no matter what they say.

But the clock goes off, if you have a dog
It wags, if you get up now you'll be less
Late. Life is some kind of loathsome hag
Who is forever threatening to turn beautiful.
Now she gives you a quick toothpaste kiss
And puts a glass of cold cranberry juice,
Like a big fake garnet, in your hand.
Cranberry juice! You're lucky, on the whole,
But there is a great deal about it you don't understand.

In Memory of Robert Frost

Everyone had to know something, and what they said
About that, the thing they'd learned by curious heart,
They said well.
           That was what he wanted to hear,
Something you had done too exactly for words,
Maybe, but too exactly to lie about either.
Compared to such talk, most conversation
Is inadvertent, low-keyed lying.

If he walked in fear of anything, later on
(Except death, which he died with a healthy fear of)
It was that he would misspeak himself. Even his smile
He administered with some care, accurately.
You could not put words in his mouth
And when you quoted him in his presence
There was no chance that he would not contradict you.

Then there were apparent samenesses he would not
Be deceived by. The presidents of things,
Or teachers, braggarts, poets
Might offer themselves in stereotype
But he would insist on paying attention
Until you at least told him an interesting lie.
(That was perhaps your field of special knowledge?)
The only reason to lie, he said, was for a purpose:
To get something you wanted that bad.

I told him a couple—to amuse him,
To get something I wanted, his attention?
More likely, respite from that blinding attention,
More likely, a friendship
I felt I could only get by stealing.
('All that I value was come by
By theft,' I wrote in a poem once. Explanation
Is a gift, like natural honesty.)

What little I'd learned about flying
Must have sweated my language lean. *I'd respect you*
For that if for nothing else, he said not smiling
The time I told him, thirty-two night landings
On a carrier, or thirty-two night catapult shots—
Whatever it was, true, something I knew.

For Two Lovers in the Year 2075 in the Canadian Woods

If you have lips and forests,
you creatures years from now,
here are some lines to tell you
that we were among your trees
in extraordinary flesh
and ecstasy now gone,
and our tongues looked for each other
and after that for words.

If you have August moonrise
and bodies to undress,
here are some words we've left you
when we had had our say.
Put them beside your cummings,
if you still carry books,
not as sweet as Landor,
not as quick as Donne,
wrap them in still-warm clothing
beside your sleeping-bag
for when you want to speak.

These trees are stirred by ghosting,
not only ours but others.
Enjoy the feathery presences,
no sadder than your own,
they gather from the past—
last August's moan and whisper,
Indian brave and his maiden,
a French girl and her man—
the leaves renew the weavings
and lacings of the flesh.
Here is the sound of ours.

What I Remember the Writers Telling Me
When I Was Young

(for Muriel Rukeyser)

Look hard at the world, they said—
generously, if you can
manage that, but hard. To see
the extraordinary data, you
have to distance yourself a
little, utterly. Learn the
right words for the umpteen kinds
of trouble that you'll see,
avoiding elevated
generics like *misery*,
wretchedness. And find yourself
a like spectrum of exact
terms for joy, some of them
archaic, but all useful.

Sometimes when they spoke to me I
could feel their own purposes
gathering. Language, the dark-
haired woman said once, is like
water-color, it blots easily,
you've got to know what you're
after, and get it on quickly.
Everything gets watered
sooner or later with tears,
she said, your own or other
people's. The contrasts want to
run together and must not be
allowed to. They're what you
see with. Keep your word-hoard dry.

ROBERT HAYDEN

(1913–1980)

Consultant in Poetry (1976–1978)

There's a tendency today—more than a tendency. it's almost a conspiracy—
to delimit poets, to restrict them to the political. . . . I can't imagine any poet
worth his salt today not being aware of social evils. . . . But I feel I have the
right to deal with these matters in my own way. . . . I know who I am, and
pretty much what I want to say.

The nation's first African-American poetry consultant, Robert Hayden was born and raised in "Paradise Valley," Detroit, also known as the St. Antoine ghetto. He suffered from poor eyesight as a child, and as an adult he was legally blind. He wrote his first poems in grade school and, despite his eye troubles, read voraciously. His foster parents divorced shortly after his birth in August 1913, and he was relocated to a new family, whose surname he adopted. His new foster parents were often abusive and this environment had a lasting emotional impact, which Hayden called "my dark nights of the soul." Reading, poetry, and the world of literature and art were from the first an escape from the harsh circumstances of his upbringing.

After college in Detroit, Hayden researched local black history and folklore for the Federal Writers Project. He then earned a master's degree at the University of Michigan, where he studied with W. H. Auden, who strongly influenced the formal elegance of Hayden's first book of poems, *Heart-Shape in the Dust*. He taught for several years at Michigan and for twenty-three years at Fisk University, in Nashville, then returned to Michigan in 1968, where he taught until he retired.

His mature work was grounded in his extensive knowledge of American and black history. In the early forties, Hayden studied Stephen Vincent Benét, particularly Benét's long poem "John Brown's Body," which describes the black reaction to General Sherman's march through Georgia during the Civil War. This inspired Hayden to write a cycle of lyrics on slavery and the Civil War that won a Hopwood Award in 1942.

While Hayden did grapple with racial issues in his work, he repeatedly stressed that he did not subscribe to any aesthetic of black poetry. This stance earned Hayden harsh criticism from other African-American writers and intellectuals during the polarized 1960s. He was accused of abandoning his racial heritage to conform to the standards of a white, European literary establishment. "In the 1960s," fellow laureate William Meredith wrote in his foreword to Hayden's *Collected Poems*, "Hayden declared himself, at considerable cost in popularity, an American poet rather than a black poet, when for a time there was posited an unreconcilable difference between the two roles. . . . He would not relinquish the title of American writer for any narrower identity." Poet Michael Harper has called Hayden's work "a real testament to craft, to vision, to complexity and historical consciousness, and to love and transcendence."

An intensely private man, Hayden was shocked by the amount of publicity his appointment at the Library of Congress generated: "As the first African-American to become Consultant . . . I was a news item (however minor) in the United States, Europe, and Africa. I suddenly became 'public.' . . . I began to feel more and more alarmed as the notoriety swirled around me. I did not want any of this, for it had little to do with me as an artist and far too much to do with me as a member of an ethnic minority. I felt trapped in sociology and politics. I am, of course, enough of a realist to know that, given the racial dilemmas in our country, the situation hardly could have been otherwise. Cold comfort indeed."

Those Winter Sundays

Sundays too my father got up early
and put his clothes on in the blueblack cold,
then with cracked hands that ached
from labor in the weekday weather made
banked fires blaze. No one ever thanked him.

I'd wake and hear the cold splintering, breaking.
When the rooms were warm, he'd call,
and slowly I would rise and dress,
fearing the chronic angers of that house,

Speaking indifferently to him,
who had driven out the cold
and polished my good shoes as well.
What did I know, what did I know
of love's austere and lonely offices?

The Diver

Sank through easeful
azure. Flower
creatures flashed and
shimmered there—
lost images
fadingly remembered.

Swiftly descended
into canyon of cold
nightgreen emptiness.
Freefalling, weightless
as in dreams of
wingless flight,
plunged through infra–
space and came to
the dead ship,
carcass that swarmed with
voracious life.
Angelfish, their
lively blue and
yellow prised from
darkness by the
flashlight's beam,
thronged her portholes.
Moss of bryozoans
blurred, obscured her
metal. Snappers,
gold groupers explored her,
fearless of bubbling
manfish. I entered
the wreck, awed by her silence,
feeling more keenly
the iron cold.
With flashlight probing
fogs of water
saw the sad slow
dance of gilded
chairs, the ectoplasmic
swirl of garments,
drowned instruments
of buoyancy,
drunken shoes. Then
livid gesturings,

eldritch hide and
seek of laughing
faces. I yearned to
find those hidden
ones, to fling aside
the mask and call to them,
yield to rapturous
whisperings, have
done with self and
every dinning
vain complexity.
Yet in languid
frenzy strove, as
one freezing fights off
sleep desiring sleep;
strove against the
cancelling arms that
suddenly surrounded
me, fled the numbing
kisses that I craved.
Reflex of life-wish?
Respirator's brittle
belling? Swam from
the ship somehow;
somehow began the
measured rise.

Homage to the Empress of the Blues

Because there was a man somewhere in a candystripe silk shirt,
gracile and dangerous as a jaguar and because a woman moaned
for him in sixty-watt gloom and mourned him Faithless Love
Twotiming Love Oh Love Oh Careless Aggravating Love,

She came out on the stage in yards of pearls, emerging like
a favorite scenic view, flashed her golden smile and sang.

Because grey laths began somewhere to show from underneath
torn hurdy-gurdy lithographs of dollfaced heaven;
and because there were those who feared alarming fists of snow
on the door and those who feared the riot-squad of statistics,

  She came out on the stage in ostrich feathers, beaded satin,
  and shone that smile on us and sang.

The Whipping

The old woman across the way
  is whipping the boy again
and shouting to the neighborhood
  her goodness and his wrongs.

Wildly he crashes through elephant ears,
  pleads in dusty zinnias,
while she in spite of crippling fat
  pursues and corners him.

She strikes and strikes the shrilly circling
  boy till the stick breaks
in her hand. His tears are rainy weather
  to woundlike memories:

My head gripped in bony vise
  of knees, the writhing struggle
to wrench free, the blows, the fear
  worse than blows that hateful

Words could bring, the face that I
       no longer knew or loved . . . .
Well, it is over now, it is over,
       and the boy sobs in his room,

And the woman leans muttering against
       a tree, exhausted, purged—
avenged in part for lifelong hidings
       she has had to bear.

Middle Passage

I

Jesús, Estrella, Esperanza, Mercy:

      Sails flashing to the wind like weapons,
      sharks following the moans the fever and the dying;
      horror the corposant and compass rose.

Middle Passage:
        voyage through death
            to life upon these shores.

      "10 April 1800—
      Blacks rebellious. Crew uneasy. Our linguist says
      their moaning is a prayer for death,
      ours and their own. Some try to starve themselves.
      Lost three this morning leaped with crazy laughter
      to the waiting sharks, sang as they went under."

Desire, Adventure, Tartar, Ann:

>   Standing to America, bringing home
>   black gold, black ivory, black seed.

>> *Deep in the festering hold thy father lies,*
>> *of his bones New England pews are made,*
>> *those are altar lights that were his eyes.*

Jesus   Saviour   Pilot   Me
Over   Life's   Tempestuous   Sea

We pray that Thou wilt grant, O Lord,
safe passage to our vessels bringing
heathen souls unto Thy chastening.

Jesus   Saviour

>   "8 bells. I cannot sleep, for I am sick
>   with fear, but writing eases fear a little
>   since still my eyes can see these words take shape
>   upon the page & so I write, as one
>   would turn to exorcism. 4 days scudding,
>   but now the sea is calm again. Misfortune
>   follows in our wake like sharks (our grinning
>   tutelary gods). Which one of us
>   has killed an albatross? A plague among
>   our blacks—Ophthalmia: blindness—& we
>   have jettisoned the blind to no avail.
>   It spreads, the terrifying sickness spreads.
>   Its claws have scratched sight from the Capt.'s eyes
>   & there is blindness in the fo'c'sle
>   & we must sail 3 weeks before we come
>   to port."

What port awaits us, Davy Jones'
or home? I've heard of slavers drifting, drifting,
playthings of wind and storm and chance, their crews
gone blind, the jungle hatred
crawling up on deck.

Thou   Who   Walked   On   Galilee

"Deponent further sayeth *The Bella J*
left the Guinea Coast
with cargo of five hundred blacks and odd
for the barracoons of Florida:

"That there was hardly room 'tween-decks for half
the sweltering cattle stowed spoon-fashion there;
that some went mad of thirst and tore their flesh
and sucked the blood:

"That Crew and Captain lusted with the comeliest
of the savage girls kept naked in the cabins;
that there was one they called The Guinea Rose
and they cast lots and fought to lie with her:

"That when the Bo's'n piped all hands, the flames
spreading from starboard already were beyond
control, the negroes howling and their chains
entangled with the flames:

"That the burning blacks could not be reached,
that the Crew abandoned ship,
leaving their shrieking negresses behind,
that the Captain perished drunken with the wenches:

"Further Deponent sayeth not."

Pilot   Oh   Pilot   Me

II

Aye, lad, and I have seen those factories,
Gambia, Rio Pongo, Calabar;
have watched the artful mongos baiting traps
of war wherein the victor and the vanquished

Were caught as prizes for our barracoons.
Have seen the nigger kings whose vanity
and greed turned wild black hides of Fellatah,
Mandingo, Ibo, Kru to gold for us.

And there was one—King Anthracite we named him—
fetish face beneath French parasols
of brass and orange velvet, impudent mouth
whose cups were carven skulls of enemies:

He'd honor us with drum and feast and conjo
and palm-oil-glistening wenches deft in love,
and for tin crowns that shone with paste,
red calico and German-silver trinkets

Would have the drums talk war and send
his warriors to burn the sleeping villages
and kill the sick and old and lead the young
in coffles to our factories.

Twenty years a trader, twenty years,
for there was wealth aplenty to be harvested
from those black fields, and I'd be trading still
but for the fevers melting down my bones.

III

Shuttles in the rocking loom of history,
the dark ships move, the dark ships move,
their bright ironical names

like jests of kindness on a murderer's mouth;
plough through thrashing glister toward
fata morgana's lucent melting shore,
weave toward New World littorals that are
mirage and myth and actual shore.

Voyage through death,
                    voyage whose chartings are unlove.

A charnel stench, effluvium of living death
spreads outward from the hold,
where the living and the dead, the horribly dying,
lie interlocked, lie foul with blood and excrement.

> *Deep in the festering hold thy father lies,*
> *the corpse of mercy rots with him,*
> *rats eat love's rotten gelid eyes.*
>
> *But, oh, the living look at you*
> *with human eyes whose suffering accuses you,*
> *whose hatred reaches through the swill of dark*
> *to strike you like a leper's claw.*
>
> *You cannot stare that hatred down*
> *or chain the fear that stalks the watches*
> *and breathes on you its fetid scorching breath;*
> *cannot kill the deep immortal human wish,*
> *the timeless will.*

> > "But for the storm that flung up barriers
> > of wind and wave, *The Amistad,* señores,
> > would have reached the port of Príncipe in two,
> > three days at most; but for the storm we should
> > have been prepared for what befell.
> > Swift as the puma's leap it came. There was
> > that interval of moonless calm filled only

with the water's and the rigging's usual sounds,
then sudden movement, blows and snarling cries
and they had fallen on us with machete
and marlinspike. It was as though the very
air, the night itself were striking us.
Exhausted by the rigors of the storm,
we were no match for them. Our men went down
before the murderous Africans. Our loyal
Celestino ran from below with gun
and lantern and I saw, before the cane-
knife's wounding flash, Cinquez,
that surly brute who calls himself a prince,
directing, urging on the ghastly work.
He hacked the poor mulatto down, and then
he turned on me. The decks were slippery
when daylight finally came. It sickens me
to think of what I saw, of how these apes
threw overboard the butchered bodies of
our men, true Christians all, like so much jetsam.
Enough, enough. The rest is quickly told:
Cinquez was forced to spare the two of us
you see to steer the ship to Africa,
and we like phantoms doomed to rove the sea
voyaged east by day and west by night,
deceiving them, hoping for rescue,
prisoners on our own vessel, till
at length we drifted to the shores of this
your land, America, where we were freed
from our unspeakable misery. Now we
demand, good sirs, the extradition of
Cinquez and his accomplices to La
Havana. And it distresses us to know
there are so many here who seem inclined
to justify the mutiny of these blacks.
We find it paradoxical indeed
that you whose wealth, whose tree of liberty

are rooted in the labor of your slaves
should suffer the august John Quincy Adams
to speak with so much passion of the right
of chattel slaves to kill their lawful masters
and with his Roman rhetoric weave a hero's
garland for Cinquez. I tell you that
we are determined to return to Cuba
with our slaves and there see justice done. Cinquez—
or let us say 'the Prince'—Cinquez shall die."

The deep immortal human wish,
the timeless will:
   Cinquez its deathless primaveral image,
   life that transfigures many lives.

Voyage through death
       to life upon these shores.

Frederick Douglass

When it is finally ours, this freedom, this liberty, this beautiful
and terrible thing, needful to man as air,
usable as earth; when it belongs at last to all,
when it is truly instinct, brain matter, diastole, systole,
reflex action; when it is finally won; when it is more
than the gaudy mumbo jumbo of politicians:
this man, this Douglass, this former slave, this Negro
beaten to his knees, exiled, visioning a world
where none is lonely, none hunted, alien,
this man, superb in love and logic, this man
shall be remembered. Oh, not with statues' rhetoric,

not with legends and poems and wreaths of bronze alone,
but with the lives grown out of his life, the lives
fleshing his dream of the beautiful, needful thing.

"'Mystery Boy' Looks for Kin in Nashville"

Puzzle faces in the dying elms
promise him treats if he will stay.
Sometimes they hiss and spit at him
like varmints caught
in a thicket of butterflies.

A black doll,
one disremembered time,
came floating down to him
through mimosa's fancywork leaves and blooms
to be his hidden bride.

From the road beyond the creepered walls
they call to him now and then,
and he'll take off in spite of the angry trees,
hearing like the loudening of his heart
the name he never can he never can repeat.

And when he gets to where the voices were—
Don't cry, his dollbaby wife implores;
I know where they are, don't cry.
We'll go and find them, we'll go
and ask them for your name again.

Words in the Mourning Time

I

For King, for Robert Kennedy,
destroyed by those they could not save,
for King for Kennedy I mourn.
And for America, self-destructive, self-betrayed.

I grieve. Yet know the vanity
of grief—through power of
The Blessed Exile's
transilluminating word

aware of how these deaths, how all
the agonies of our deathbed childbed age
are process, major means whereby,
oh dreadfully, our humanness must be achieved.

II

Killing people to save, to free them?
With napalm lighting routes to the future?

A Plague of Starlings

(Fisk Campus)

Evenings I hear
the workmen fire
into the stiff
magnolia leaves,

routing the starlings
gathered noisy and
befouling there.

Their scissoring
terror like glass
coins spilling breaking
the birds explode
into mica sky
raggedly fall
to ground rigid
in clench of cold.

The spared return,
when the guns are through,
to the spoiled trees
like choiceless poor
to a dangerous
dwelling place,
chitter and quarrel
in the piercing dark
above the killed.

A Letter from Phillis Wheatley

London, 1773

Dear Obour
                Our crossing was without
event. I could not help, at times,
reflecting on that first—my Destined—
voyage long ago (I yet
have some remembrance of its Horrors)

and marvelling at God's Ways.

      Last evening, her Ladyship presented me
to her illustrious Friends.
I scarce could tell them anything
of Africa, though much of Boston
and my hope of Heaven. I read
my latest Elegies to them.
"O Sable Muse!" the Countess cried,
embracing me, when I had done.
I held back tears, as is my wont,
and there were tears in Dear
Nathaniel's eyes.

      At supper—I dined apart
like captive Royalty—
the Countess and her Guests promised
signatures affirming me
True Poetess, albeit once a slave.
Indeed, they were most kind, and spoke,
moreover, of presenting me
at Court (I thought of Pocahontas)—
an Honor, to be sure, but one,
I should, no doubt, as Patriot decline.

      My health is much improved;
I feel I may, if God so Wills,
entirely recover here.
Idyllic England! Alas, there is
no Eden without its Serpent. Under
the chiming Complaisance I hear him Hiss;
I see his flickering tongue
when foppish would-be Wits
murmur of the Yankee Pedlar
and his Cannibal Mockingbird.

      Sister, forgive th'intrusion of
my Sombreness—Nocturnal Mood
I would not share with any save
your trusted Self. Let me disperse,

in closing, such unseemly Gloom
by mention of an Incident
you may, as I, consider Droll:
Today, a little Chimney Sweep,
his face and hands with soot quite Black,
staring hard at me, politely asked:
"Does you, M'lady, sweep chimneys too?"
I was amused, but dear Nathaniel
(ever Solicitous) was not.
      I pray the Blessings of our Lord
and Saviour Jesus Christ be yours
Abundantly. In His Name,

                    Phillis

Names

Once they were sticks and stones
I feared would break my bones:
Four Eyes. And worse.
Old Four Eyes fled
to safety in the danger zones
Tom Swift and Kubla Khan traversed.

When my fourth decade came,
I learned my name was not my name.
I felt deserted, mocked.
Why had the old ones lied?
No matter. They were dead.

And the name on the books was dead,
like the life my mother fled,
like the life I might have known.

You don't exist—at least
not legally, the lawyer said.
As ghost, double, alter ego then?

The Islands

(for Steve and Nancy, Allen and Magda)

Always this waking dream of palmtrees,
magic flowers—of sensual joys
like treasures brought up from the sea.

Always this longing, this nostalgia
for tropic islands we
have never known and yet recall.

We look for ease upon these islands named
to honor holiness; in their chromatic
torpor catch our breath.

Scorn greets us with promises of rum,
hostility welcomes us to bargain sales.
We make friends with Flamboyant trees.

Jamaican Cynthie, called alien by dese lazy
islanders—wo'k hahd, treated bad,
oh, mahn, I tellin you. She's full

of raucous anger. Nevertheless brings gifts of
scarlet hibiscus when she comes to clean,
white fragrant spider-lilies too sometimes.

The roofless walls, the tidy ruins
of a sugar mill. More than cane
was crushed. But I am tired today

of history, its patina'd cliches
of endless evil. Flame trees.
The intricate sheen of waters flowing into sun.

I wake and see
the morning like a god
in peacock-flower mantle dancing

on opalescent waves—
and can believe my furies have
abandoned for a time their long pursuit.

Bone-Flower Elegy

In the dream I enter the house
    wander vast rooms that are
        catacombs midnight subway
            cavernous ruined movie-palace
        where presences in vulture masks
           play scenes of erotic violence
                on a scaffold stage   I want
        to stay and watch but know somehow
I must not linger and come to the funeral
        chamber   in its icy nonlight see
           a naked corpse
                turning with sensual movements
                    on its coffin-bed

I have wept for you many times
I whisper but shrink from the arms
that would embrace me
and treading water reach
arched portals opening on a desert
groves of enormous nameless flowers
twist up from firegold sand
skull flowers flowers of sawtooth bone
their leaves and petals interlock
caging me for you beastangel
raging toward me
angelbeast shining come
to rend me and redeem

DANIEL HOFFMAN

(1923-)

Consultant in Poetry (1973-1974)

I work for poems as close as speech can come to seeming scooped from the living flow of feelings, poems that grow from joy, from love, from the great consolation of humor, no less than poems that suffer and poems that think. To the contradictions of such feelings I try to be true. The water from the rock renews us, not the staff that strikes it forth; so I make no dogmas about how my poems are written.

Much of Daniel Hoffman's early writing reads like a foreshadowing of our current ecological woes. His first collection, *An Armada of Thirty Whales* (1954), was chosen for the Yale Series of Younger Poets by W. H. Auden, who saw in it "a new direction for nature poetry in the post-Wordsworthian world." That direction concerned man's responsibility for maintaining the natural world, which was not there simply as backdrop and source for American inspiration. Hoffman's writing raises questions about the Emersonian dictum that "Nature always wears the colors of the spirit." If that is the case, as Hoffman writes in a series of aphorisms called "Clarifications" from 1967, then we must first attempt to understand what the American spirit looks for in nature at different stages in history: "As long as man was subject to Nature he was cowed by the threat of a superior force. Now that men think superior force to be in their hands, what can keep them from destroying the earth? The greatest force is still the secret of Nature—creation. . . . Human power conceives its actions in immediate time only, its self-expression, as though by instinct, in destruction."

Hoffman was born in New York City and served in the U.S. Army Air Force from 1943 to 1946. He was educated at Columbia, where as a graduate student he researched his first book on the legendary lumberjack Paul Bunyan, the foundation for his well-researched exploration of America's mythical connection to the wilderness. His eleven books of lyric poetry, often set in the landscapes of Pennsylvania and Maine, generally employ the cadence and diction of everyday speech captured in a range of forms and styles. During his consultancy, Hoffman made use of the Library's resources to outline and research his epic poem *Brotherly Love*, published in 1981, which sets William Penn's luminous vision of America against the intractable conflicts of our history—struggles over the land, keeping faith with the Indians, the uses and abuses of power—that threaten Penn's ideal.

Hoffman taught for ten years at Swarthmore College and then for twenty-seven at the University of Pennsylvania, where he was poet in residence and Felix E. Schelling Professor of English Emeritus. From 1988 to 1999, he served as poet in residence at the Cathedral Church of St. John the Divine in New York City and administered the Poet's Corner. His late wife was the poet and influential *Ladies' Home Journal* poetry editor Elizabeth McFarland.

The seals in Penobscot Bay

hadn't heard of the atom bomb,
so I shouted a warning to them.

Our destroyer (on trial run) slid by
the rocks where they gamboled and played;

they must have misunderstood,
or perhaps not one of them heard

me over the engines and tides.
As I watched them over our wake

I saw their sleek skins in the sun
ripple, light-flecked, on the rock,

plunge, bubbling, into the brine,
and couple & laugh in the troughs

between the waves' whitecaps and froth.
Then the males clambered clumsily up

and lustily crowed like seacocks,
sure that their prowess held thrall

all the sharks, other seals, and seagulls.
And daintily flipped the females,

seawenches with musical tails;
each looked at the Atlantic as

though it were her looking-glass.
If my warning had ever been heard

it was sound none would now ever heed.
And I, while I watched those far seals,

tasted honey that buzzed in my ears
and saw, out to windward, the sails

of an obsolete ship with banked oars
that swept like two combs through the spray

And I wished for a vacuum of wax
to ward away all those strange sounds,

yet I envied the sweet agony
of him who was tied to the mast,

when the boom, when the boom, when the boom
of guns punched dark holes in the sky.

In the Days of Rin-Tin-Tin

In the days of Rin-Tin-Tin
There was no such thing as sin,
No boymade mischief worth God's wrath
And the good dog dogged the badman's path.

In the nights, the deliquescent horn of Bix
Gave presentiments of the pleasures of sex;
In the Ostrich Walk we walked by twos—
Ja–da, jing-jing, what could we lose?

The Elders mastered The Market, Mah-jongg,
Readily admitted the Victorians wrong,
While Caligari hobbled with his stick and his ghoul
And overtook the Little Fellow on his way to school.

Power

"My life is a one-billionth part
of history. I wish I was dead."

He rips the page from his notebook.
Litter in a rented room.

The neighbors will barely remember
His silence when they said Hello.

They'll not forget his odd smile.
Nobody comes to see him.

When he thinks of his folks he smiles oddly.
"It was broken but was it a home?"

At night, the wet dream. Arising,
He is afraid of women.

In his notebook, "Power over people!"
His job, scouring pots in a hash-house.

At last he will pick up a girl.
She'll think, Does he ever need love—

But I don't like him at all.
Her Mom will hang up on his phone call.

One day he will fondle a snub-nosed
Pistol deep in his pants.

What is his aim? The TV,
Even bumper stickers remind him

Who has the face and the name
His name and smile will replace.

His trigger will make him bigger.
He will become his victim.

When he steps from his rented room
History is in his hand.

from *Brotherly Love*

34

Silence, more
eloquent than
speech: the un-
spoken word
wiser than our

earnest trials
to say, to find
in the mind's hoard
praise that reveals
perfections known

and not diminished
in the telling—
in the silences
between speech and halt
speech, beseech

a gift of tongues
that words bear
witness, true
to what we hear
chiefly in silence

before and after
speech now, as
these letters
whiten the space
surrounding them.

from *Brotherly Love*

61

. . . On City Hall, above our lights,
Penn's statue spreads indulgent arms,
still beckoning the Welsh, the Mennonites
toward his green outlying farms,

his head in the clouds, his mood
benign, though slum-blocks sprawl,
splotches of rot, across Penn's Wood.
Beyond, bulldozers snarl

as behind his back, high-rise
investments abruptly obtrude
on our only noble boulevard
proportioned to delight men's eyes.

We cram the days, put time to use—
no hour but is a rush hour, and where rushing?
Our history grows longer, longer.
It's life that's getting away from us

as the city changes, seethes with being.
Our Founder's feet are stuck
to the cranium of a clock
whose four faces gaze on us unseeing,

yet there's a spirit in this place
that sifts through hands that clasp
what only time can grasp
—Here possibilities of grace

like fragrance from rich compost cling
to leaves where our each deed
and misdeed fall. The Seed
stirs, even now is quickening.

Reasons

Because when our clothes hung from the slanting alders
And summer the color of stream on wavering sand
Poured from the clouds, you waded under
Light-flecked glades reflected in the water
And repealed our exile from the Garden; because,

Seeing you of a sudden in the crowd
On Chestnut Street, the heedless, thoughtless plod
Of my heart was seized, and stilled, suspended
In another life, until
The beat of blood and breath resumed; because
While you're asleep the rhythm of your breathing
Sifts the air with a dark-flowered enticement;
Because when I grope through lightless labyrinths of despair
The unbroken thread of your love guides me back;
Because I cannot think of life without you
But as a season of ice and pain, of hunger
Without end; because in the candle-mold
I gave you thirty years ago, you've placed
Bouquets of pearly everlasting.

from *Middens of the Tribe*

42

Father dead and buried, the old house sold—
he's free, now free of everything that dragged him down.
His depression, he came at last to understand,
was caused by his long failure
to honor his ancestors. Overcome
by this inescapable guilt when he thought of
his father's fathers, of his own
late father, of how they had quarreled and how
little he knew of either his father's feelings
or of his own past, he
booked flight for a return
to the homeland his forebears had fled from
and four generations never had seen. On arrival,
wherever he went, scenes strangely excited him: peasants

beneath a sodden sky digging rutabagas with clumsy hoes;
women, heads tied up in ragged shawls, bearing
meager parcels in bags of knotted string
as they trudge through mud toward leaky farmhouses; and men
in fur hats who step down form the rattletrap bus
that once a day runs through the village. Standing
before the one café, he sees
just such a man get off the bus—a man
exactly like the photo his father
once had shown him of his own great-
great-grandfather! The same
fur hat, the same round spectacles, same mouth
tightly clenched above an identical beard. A great
flood of emotion—impulsively he rushes
forward, flings his arms
around the stranger, burying his head
on the man's shoulder and cries
'Grandfather!
Forgive me!' Then, getting a grip on himself,
he backs away, smiling,
opens the door of his rented car and
drives off unembarrassed,
more secure now in his deepened knowledge
of his past.
                    As his car sped off
between rows of leafless trees,
glancing at his rearview mirror for one last look
at the double of his ancestor,
he sees two men in uniform crossing the square,
then the road turned and he lost
their tiny image as they said
'We always knew you are an enemy
of the Fatherland,' confronting
the bearded man in fur hat (a tailor
who had lived all his life in this village).
'Tell us: What did the foreign stranger say to you?' In vain

he protests, he doesn't know—he
understands no language but their own. 'We have
devices in the barracks basement that can restore
memory of other tongues. . . . There must
have been *some* reason why the foreign agent
arrives in this village, waits half the morning for the bus,
and then confides his message
to you and you alone.' Expressionless,
he walks across the square between them
like a man who knows exactly
where he is going and what
is the shape of the future.

Violence

After I'd read my poem about a brawl
between two sidewalk hustlers—one,
insulted, throws the other down and nearly
kills him—over coffee and cookies a grave

senior citizen reproved me: *How*
could you see such violence and you
didn't try to stop them?—Oh, I explained,
it wasn't like that, really—I saw

two guys in a shoving match and thought
I'd write about aggression, what
anger really feels like. . . . *Yes,*

and if the one got killed
it would be on your head.
You should've stopped them, he said.

Owed to Dejection

The way the one who O so narrowly
won the election
bestows dejection

upon the one who O so nearly
won, the election
leaves him as a suitor

about to elope is left
with reservations for a double
and no hope

in his new role
as unloved lover
with no other

career opening,
yet in dreams, determined,
ardent, still he woos her

though she turn her face
from his embrace
as adamant in rejection

as the crowd
that spurns the loser
of an election.

JOSEPHINE JACOBSEN

(1908–2003)

Consultant in Poetry (1971–1973)

There's something deadly dangerous about the conjunction of poetry and bureaucracy. The grave peril is that poetry, a very intransigent, frequently violent, and utterly incontrollable force, could get swamped by an enormous, prestigious, global sort of organization. This is the kind of thing that so far has been avoided. Where protocol, or politics, or bureaucracy, or prestige, or international recognition or *anything* impinges on poetry, poetry has got to come unarguably on top.

J osephine Jacobsen was born on the shore of Lake Ontario in Canada, and soon after moved with her parents to Baltimore, Maryland, where she lived for the rest of her life. Though she wrote short fiction and literary criticism, her first love was always poetry. One of the country's first literary feminists, Jacobsen wrote brilliant appreciations of Anne Bradstreet and Emily Dickinson, paving the way for understanding the great toll that domestic and social responsibilities can take on the female artist's creative life. It comes as no surprise, she wrote, that two of our greatest female poets, Dickinson and Marianne Moore, never married: "Each had a fine quiddity that went its own way, owing nothing to the current poetic fashion." Throughout her own career, Jacobsen would eschew poetic trends, preferring to write in her unadorned style, in which she used a variety of verse forms that cut into the white page and a reader's mind with spare, Romanesque solemnity.

Jacobsen was celebrated for writing about nature, animals, and human relationships. Her first acclaimed collection centered on fifteen love sonnets that were interwoven with longer metaphysical poems. And her next two, more personal collections were nominated for National Book Awards. She was inducted into the American Academy of Arts and Letters in 1994 and received the Robert Frost Medal for Lifetime Achievement in Poetry in 1997.

Jacobsen published her first poem at age eleven, and although her formal education ended before college, she was an active literary scholar. In her poetry, Jacobsen consciously avoided any contrived style or mannerism, writing in both traditional forms and free verse. Her poems often ponder the relationship between the physical and the spiritual.

During her two years as consultant, Jacobsen expanded the Library's reading series. At the outset of her tenure she expressed concern at how few young African-American poets came to the Library's events or were being published. In her second year, as a result of her outreach, she noted, "The atmosphere has totally changed. . . . Black poets living in Washington have invited the Consultant to their homes, and discussed black and white relations in the world of poetry and of the arts in general."

In her 1973 lecture at the Library of Congress, Jacobsen defined poetic inspiration as a form of energy transferred, via attentive reading, from poet to reader. "Often the poet brings back very little from the instant of knowing. Sometimes, rarely, he brings back something that combines two worlds: something germane to what Yeats called 'the artifice of eternity'—the made and the eternal. Such poetry may wear any mode: the august, the raucous, the witty, the tragic. Nothing could matter less. Poetry is energy, and it is poetic energy that is the source of that instant of knowing that the poet tries to name."

First Woman

Do animals expect spring?
Ground hard as rancor,
wind colder than malice.
Do they think that will change?

Sky no color and low;
grass is no color, and trees
jerk in the bitter gust.
In this air nothing flies.

Do they believe it will change,
grass be soft and lustrous,
rigid earth crack
from the push of petals,

sky retreat into blue,
the red wide rose breathe
summer, and the butterfly
err on sweet air?

First woman, Lucy, or another,
did you know it all waited
somewhere to come back?
On the first stripped, iron day

did you believe that?
On this merciless morning
I wake, first woman,
with what belief?

Lines to a Poet

Be careful what you say to us now.
The street-lamp is smashed, the window is jagged,
There is a man dead in his blood by the base of the fountain.
If you speak
You cannot be delicate or sad or clever.
Some other hour, in a moist April,
We will consider similes for the budding larches.
You can teach our wits and our fancy then;
By a green-lit midnight in your study
We will delve in your sparkling rock.
But now at dreadful high noon
You may speak only to our heart,
Our honor and our need:
Saying such things as, "See, she is alive . . ."
Or "Here is water," or "Look behind you!"

Landscape Finally with Human Figure

The sky stainless, flawed by one gull
And stretched across no sight, silk-tight;
salt noon stranded like a hull
in clearest light;

clarity of palms splits the sun
to strike and shiver on the blue blue view,
so perfection not ended nor begun
is perfectly true.

The hollow setting (while the jewel lags),
infinite, unsoiled, smiling, clear:
    Appear!
Sly, dirty, cruel, lost and in rags
the beloved is here.

Gentle Reader

Late in the night when I should be asleep
under the city stars in a small room
I read a poet. A poet: not
a versifier. Not a hot-shot
ethic-monger, laying about
him; not a diary of lying
about in cruel cruel beds, crying.
A poet, dangerous and steep.

O God, it peels me, juices me like a press;
this poetry drinks me, eats me, gut and marrow
until I exist in its jester's sorrow,
until my juices feed a savage sight
that runs along the lines, bright
as beasts' eyes. The rubble splays to dust:
city, book, bed, leaving my ear's lust
saying like Molly, yes, yes, yes O yes.

How We Learn

Plurality in death
fogs our mind.
One man tries to breathe
in a sealed mine:
this is how we learn.
Eye to eye.

Corporate guilt, plague,
tidal wave, we make our
sluggish guess.
But the dead child in the ditch.
O yes.

At the siege of Stalingrad
an old man starving
ate his pet cat.
Later in the hall
hanged himself, because

after that meal
he looked around to find
all in its place;
his cat no longer there.
And he still was.

Language as an Escape from the Discrete

I came upon two wasps
with intricate legs all occupied.
If it was news communicated,
or if they mated or fought,
it was difficult to say of that clasp.

And a cold fear because I did not know
struck me apart from them, who moved,
whose wasp-blood circulated,
who, loveless, mated, who moved;
who moved and were not loved.

When the cat puts its furred illiterate
paw on my page and makes a starfish,
the space between us drains my marrow
like a roof's edge. It drinks milk,
as I do; one of its breaths is final.

And even the young child, whose eyes
follow what it speaks, to see in yours
what it will mean, is running away
from what it sent its secret out to prove.
And the illiterate body says hush,

in love, says hush; says, whatever
word can serve, it is not here.
All the terrible silences listen always; and hear
between breaths a gulf we know is evil.
It is the silence that built the tower of Babel.

The Arrivals

My dead are shining like washed gold.
Like gold from what-you-will freed:
cobwebs, mold, rust, the anonymous mud—
and plunged in the icy waver of water
to flash at the hot sun.

They come shining happily inside a moment
translated only now so long after.
They arrive in the comfort of comrades and a
nimbus of silence.

Accurate and able they shine
in ordinary glory
cleared from the clock's confusion that held them
distant, aghast.

The Monosyllable

One day
she fell
in love with its
heft and speed.
Tough, lean,

fast as light
slow
as a cloud.
It took care
of rain, short

noon, long dark.
It had rough kin;
did not stall.
With it, she said,
I may,

if I can,
sleep; since I must,
die.
Some say,
rise.

Over Timberline

It was never the air
betrayed them:
cloud-field, cloud-tower
or turret, shining
their wings that glitter
as they tilt. Air
held them like a comet in its course.

Earth was their enemy,
mother turned fury
to her strayed children:
gravity's anger, to call
them home in a long scream.

So a red scrap of cloth
whipped in the peak's breath
which no breath answers,
flays fast; over stone

the ants go their bright cold
ways; clouds join and part,
stunted green darkens
and shines and darkens.

The Dogs

It is obvious that the three brown dogs, on the beach
each day, are siblings—color of coats,
shape of head, upturned mongrel tail.

They are gritty from rolling in sand to catch
the unreachable flea; they never bark.
They come, against discouragement, to lie

in a blunt triangle close to human feet.
Sometimes by stealth they move a fraction
closer, until repulsed. All morning

unless the humans walk away or go
into the bright sea, the three brown dogs
stay there, chained by a private need.

It is not the simple communal drives:
sex, hunger, sleep. Certainly not trust:
they flinch at a sharp move. It seems

to cast the humans in some curious role
they can neither play nor comprehend:
their magnet otherness, imposed

without consent, unarticulated.
Each day, silent on the pitted sand,
like ignorant disciples, the dogs come

silently, to lie in their rough triangle.
What the humans helplessly represent
stays undefined; but the dogs arrive.

The Blue-Eyed Exterminator

The exterminator has arrived. He has not intruded. He was summoned.
At the most fruitless spot, a regiment
of the tiniest of ants, obviously deluded,
have a jetty ferment of undisclosed intent.

The blue-eyed exterminator is friendly and fair;
one can tell he knows exactly what he is about.
He is young as the day that makes the buds puff out,
grass go rampant, big bees ride the air;

it seems the spring could drown him in its flood.
But though he appears modest as what he was summoned for,
he will prove himself more potent than grass or bud,
being a scion of the greatest emperor.

His success is total: no jet platoon on the wall.
At the door he calls good-bye and hitches his thumb.
For an invisible flick, grass halts, buds cramp, bees stall
in air. He has called, and what has been called has come.

Hourglass

"Flawless" is the word, no doubt, for this third of May
that has landed on the grounds of Mayfair,
the Retirement Community par excellence.

Right behind the wheels of the mower, grass
explodes again, the bare trees most tenderly
push out their chartreuse tips.

Bottle bees are back. Feckless, reckless,
stingless, they probably have a function.
Above the cardinal, scarlet on the rim

of the birdbath, twinning himself,
they hover, cruise the flowers, mate.
The tiny water catches the sky.

On the circular inner road, the lady
untangles the poodle's leash from her cane.
He is wild to chase the splendid smells.

The small man with the small smile,
rapidly steering his Amigo,
bowls past. She would wave, but can't.

All around, birds and sexual flowers
are intent on color, flight, fragrance.
The gardener sweeps his sweaty face

with a khaki sleeve. His tulips are shined
black at their centers. They have come along nicely.
He is young and will be gone before dark.

The man in the Amigo has in mind a May
a mirror of this, but unobtainable
as the touch of the woman in that glass.

The sun's force chills him. But the lady
with the curly poodle could melt her cane
in the very heat of her precious pleasure.

She perfectly understands the calendar
and the sun's passage. But she grips the leash
and leans on the air that is hers and here.

The Edge

The edge? The edge is:
lie by the breath you cannot
do without; while
the breather sleeps.

Precious, subtle, that air
comes, goes, comes.
The heart propels it.   It has
its thousands of hours, but

it will not last as long
as the sun, the moon's subservient
tides. It will stop, go back
to the great air's surround.

But now, subtle, precious,
regular as tide and sun
it moves in the warm body, lifts
the chest, says yes.

Listen to it, through the night.
If you wish to know the extent
to which you are vulnerable
only listen.

This is called the breath
of life.   But it continues
saving your life
through the dark,

since this engine that drives your joy
is unrenounceable.
Listen, listen.   Say, Love, love,
breathe so, breathe so.

WILLIAM STAFFORD

(1914-1993)

Consultant in Poetry (1970-1971)

I inhale and exhale. I experience, write poems, get now and then great feelings of being on the edge of writing something that reverberates through my own self and that's very interesting. But I don't have any big or sustained project or any ending revelation that I can tell you about.

William Stafford woke every morning, seven days a week, at 4 a.m., made himself a cup of instant coffee and a piece of dry toast, and stretched out on his family's living room couch. There, notebook on lap, he wrote until the sun came up. He wrote a poem a day, a process he describes in the short lyric "Just Thinking": "Got up on a cool morning. Leaned out a window. / No cloud, no wind. . . . Let the bucket of memory down into the well, / bring it up. Cool, cool minutes. No one / stirring. No plans. Just being there." Stafford was a late bloomer whose first major collection of poems, *Traveling Through the Dark,* was published when he was forty-eight. It won the National Book Award in 1963. He went on to publish more than sixty-five volumes of poetry and prose.

His profound and illuminating poems are, at first reading, deceptively simple, taking their subject matter and vocabulary from the Midwest, where he grew up, and rural Oregon, where he taught for over forty years at Lewis & Clark College and raised his family. He was born in mid-Kansas, of Native American ancestry on his father's side, and maintains throughout his work a reverence for and childlike wonder in the natural world. But in his own understated way, he was also a political poet. During World War II, as a pacifist, he spent four years in CO camps, fighting forest fires, building trails and roads, and terracing eroding land—an experience he wrote about in the prose memoir *Down My Heart* and touched upon in his poem "Objector."

Stafford was the first Midwestern native and the first West Coast resident to have the Library's chair in poetry. He did not want to take the job in Washington. He did not want to uproot his wife and four children or leave his beloved Lake Oswego, Oregon, for city life in the nation's capitol. But his family voted, and it turned out all but Stafford wanted to go. Some two-thirds of Stafford's office time at the Library was spent reading and answering mail. To a teacher from the South who had written to ask how she should advise her students who were interested in writing poetry but unsure about their abilities, Stafford wrote a two-and-a-half-page reply, which contains this insight into his method: "I've purposely rambled, for the issue in your letter is one that requires a human interchange, not a formula. The question each writer has about his own work will never be solved, even if he has 'success,' for who is to say when the awarding has been right? I believe each of us should try out our attempts in the environment near us and harmonize with our backgrounds and expectations. Then we can attempt to enter larger and larger contexts, as we feel confident. We should not feel competitive, but just right, near, congenial. When we feel right, near, congenial with the next circle outward, we should attempt to move there. . . . You make me brood about my own moments of anguish. I hope my brooding related to your inquiry."

Objector

In line at lunch I cross my fork and spoon
to ward off complicity—the ordered life
our leaders have offered us. Thin as a knife,
our chance to live depends on such a sign
while others talk and The Pentagon from the moon
is bouncing exact commands: "Forget your faith;
be ready for whatever it takes to win: we face
annihilation unless all citizens get in line."

I bow and cross my fork and spoon: somewhere
other citizens more fearfully bow
in a place terrorized by their kind of oppressive state.
Our signs both mean, "You hostages over there
will never be slaughtered by my act." Our vows
cross: never to kill and call it fate.

An Introduction to Some Poems

Look: no one ever promised for sure
that we would sing. We have decided
to moan. In a strange dance that
we don't understand till we do it, we
have to carry on.

Just as in sleep you have to dream
the exact dream to round out your life,
so we have to live that dream into stories
and hold them close at you, close at the
edge we share, to be right.

We find it an awful thing to meet people,
serious or not, who have turned into vacant
effective people, so far lost that they
won't believe their own feelings
enough to follow them out.

The authentic is a line from one thing
along to the next; it interests us.
Strangely, it relates to what works,
but is not quite the same. It never
swerves for revenge,

Or profit, or fame: it holds
together something more than the world,
this line. And we are your wavery
efforts at following it. Are you coming?
Good: now it is time.

Ask Me

Some time when the river is ice ask me
mistakes I have made. Ask me whether
what I have done is my life. Others
have come in their slow way into
my thought, and some have tried to help
or to hurt: ask me what difference
their strongest love or hate has made.

I will listen to what you say.
You and I can turn and look
at the silent river and wait. We know
the current is there, hidden; and there
are comings and goings from miles away
that hold the stillness exactly before us.
What the river says, that is what I say.

Level Light

Sometimes the light when evening fails
stains all haystacked country and hills,
runs the cornrows and clasps the barn
with that kind of color escaped from corn
that brings to autumn the winter word—
a level shaft that tells the world:

> *It is too late now for earlier ways;*
> *now there are only some other ways,*
> *and only one way to find them—fail.*

In one stride night then takes the hill.

A Ritual to Read to Each Other

If you don't know the kind of person I am
and I don't know the kind of person you are
a pattern that others made may prevail in the world
and following the wrong god home we may miss our star.

For there is many a small betrayal in the mind,
a shrug that lets the fragile sequence break
sending with shouts the horrible errors of childhood
storming out to play through the broken dyke.

And as elephants parade holding each elephant's tail,
but if one wanders the circus won't find the park,
I call it cruel and maybe the root of all cruelty
to know what occurs but not recognize the fact.

And so I appeal to a voice, to something shadowy,
a remote important region in all who talk:
though we could fool each other, we should consider—
lest the parade of our mutual life get lost in the dark.

For it is important that awake people be awake,
or a breaking line may discourage them back to sleep;
the signals we give—yes or no, or maybe—
should be clear: the darkness around us is deep.

Traveling Through the Dark

Traveling through the dark I found a deer
dead on the edge of the Wilson River road.
It is usually best to roll them into the canyon:
that road is narrow; to swerve might make more dead.

By glow of the tail-light I stumbled back of the car
and stood by the heap, a doe, a recent killing;
she had stiffened already, almost cold.
I dragged her off; she was large in the belly.

My fingers touching her side brought me the reason—
her side was warm; her fawn lay there waiting,
alive, still, never to be born.
Beside that mountain road I hesitated.

The car aimed ahead its lowered parking lights;
under the hood purred the steady engine.
I stood in the glare of the warm exhaust turning red;
around our group I could hear the wilderness listen.

I thought hard for us all—my only swerving—,
then pushed her over the edge into the river.

The Little Ways That Encourage Good Fortune

Wisdom is having things right in your life
and knowing why.
If you do not have things right in your life
you will be overwhelmed:
you may be heroic, but you will not be wise.
If you have things right in your life
but do not know why,
you are just lucky, and you will not move
in the little ways that encourage good fortune.

The saddest are those not right in their lives
who are acting to make things right for others:
they act only from the self—
and that self will never be right:
no luck, no help, no wisdom.

When I Met My Muse

I glanced at her and took my glasses
off—they were still singing. They buzzed
like a locust on the coffee table and then
ceased. Her voice belled forth, and the
sunlight bent. I felt the ceiling arch, and
knew that nails up there took a new grip
on whatever they touched. "I am your own
way of looking at things," she said. "When
you allow me to live with you, every
glance at the world around you will be
a sort of salvation." And I took her hand.

Security

Tomorrow will have an island. Before night
I always find it. Then on to the next island.
These places hidden in the day separate
and come forward if you beckon.
But you have to know they are there before they exist.

Some time there will be a tomorrow without any island.
So far, I haven't let that happen, but after
I'm gone others may become faithless and careless.
Before them will tumble the wide unbroken sea,
and without any hope they will stare at the horizon.

So to you, Friend, I confide my secret:
to be a discoverer you hold close whatever
you find, and after a while you decide
what it is. Then, secure in where you have been,
you turn to the open sea and let go.

For My Young Friends Who Are Afraid

There is a country to cross you will
find in the corner of your eye, in
the quick slip of your foot—air far
down, a snap that might have caught.
And maybe for you, for me, a high, passing
voice that finds its way by being
afraid. That country is there, for us,
carried as it is crossed. What you fear
will not go away: it will take you into
yourself and bless you and keep you.
That's the world, and we all live there.

Just Thinking

Got up on a cool morning. Leaned out a window.
No cloud, no wind. Air that flowers held
for awhile. Some dove somewhere.

Been on probation most of my life. And
the rest of my life been condemned. So these moments
count for a lot—peace, you know.

Let the bucket of memory down into the well,
bring it up. Cool, cool minutes. No one
stirring, no plans. Just being there.

This is what the whole thing is about.

WILLIAM JAY SMITH

(1918-)

Consultant in Poetry (1968-1970)

I believe that poetry should communicate: it is, by its very nature, com-
plex, but its complexity should not prevent its making an immediate impact
on the reader. Great poetry must have its own distinctive music; it must
resound with the music of the human psyche.

William Jay Smith is a rare master of both the short formal lyric and longer, looser, but always musically charged narrative free verse. He is the author of ten books of poetry, one of the country's most celebrated composers of poetry for children, and an award-winning translator. Smith was a poet in residence at Williams College from 1959 to 1967, the chairman of the Writing Division of the School of Arts at Columbia University from 1973 until 1975, and is currently a professor emeritus of English at Hollins University. He also served in the U.S. Navy during World War II and for two years as Democratic representative to the Vermont House of Representatives. He now lives half the year in Massachusetts and half in Paris.

Smith's coming-of-age memoir, *Army Brat*, recounts, in the poet and critic Dana Gioia's words, "one of the oddest childhoods ever lived by an American poet." He grew up on an army base outside St. Louis between the two world wars, the son of a hard-drinking, hard-gambling army trumpet player. Smith describes the toll of a life spent waiting for military action, providing a rare glimpse into an overlooked aspect of military service—not, as Gioia writes, "the hectic military of civilian draftees brought temporarily together to fight a common war," but rather "the routine world of professional soldiers, who have no real function in society except to keep ready and wait."

As consultant in poetry, Smith brought literature from a range of cultures to the Library. He worked with a local television station to film Robert Hayden, from Ann Arbor, and Derek Walcott, of Trinidad, reading and discussing their poetry, and he invited the African-American poet M. B. Olson to read in the Library's endowed reading series. Smith learned late in life that his mother had Choctaw relatives. This discovery of his own mixed origins inspired his moving epic *The Cherokee Lottery*, a sequence of narrative poems that Harold Bloom has called the poet's "master work." This volume gives voice to the forced removal of

the Southern Indian tribes east of the Mississippi when gold was dis-
covered on Cherokee land in northern Georgia; the Indian Removal
Act in 1830 forcibly relocated 18,000 Cherokees, along with Choctaws,
Chickasaws, and Creeks, to Oklahoma Territory, and thousands per-
ished of cold and starvation as they walked thousands of miles on "the
Trail of Tears."

The Pumpkin Field

An Army Lieutenant observes the Cherokees he guards on
their passage to the west, Arkansas 1838

What a grand lot they were,
        the Cherokees I first saw in June,
lined up in their Georgian camp
        to greet the chief on their departure,
elegant blankets hanging loose
        about their shoulders, ramrod-straight,
dark eyes darting from high-boned
        copper faces under bright turbans
and striped caps pulled down at an angle,
        some in long robes, some in tunics,
all with sashes or wondrous drapery,
        they stood, framed by bearded oaks,
Old Testament patriarchs
        pausing on their way to the Promised Land.

Then in October, where I'd been sent ahead
        to patrol their passage here in Arkansas,
they came from a cold and threadbare wood,
        thin pines bent and tipped with sleet,
eyes glazed and blank,
        half-naked, barefoot,
bones poking through
        their scarecrow shredded clothing,
and stumbled through layers of mist
        onto a scraggly open field

where in wet and tangled grass
        fat pumpkins lay in rows
like painted severed heads.

Oblivious to all around them,
        skeletal automatons,
the Cherokees plunged ahead
        until a farmer on the edge
bade them halt
        and, breaking off a pumpkin,
invited them to take
        whatever his poor field could offer.

Flies swarming to their target,
        they darted up and down the rows,
black hair flying,
        long-nailed tentacles
protruding, they ripped apart
        the pumpkin flesh
until their brown and vacant
        faces merged with jagged pulp,
seeds foaming from
        their hungry mouths, and all I could see,
as on some battlefield, was
        everywhere a wasted mass of orange flesh.

A light rain then began to fall
        as if the shredded pumpkin fiber
drifted down around us:
        I felt ill
and sensed that cholera
        had set in. The farmer guided
me inside his cabin
        and put me down in a dark corner
where between the logs
        I could empty my stomach.

All night long I lay there
      while wind roared
and rain beat down
      and through it I could hear the sloshing
of the weary feet,
      the creak and rattle of ox-carts,
the cursing of the drivers,
      cracking their long whips to urge the oxen on,
the whinnying of horses
      as they struggled through the mud.

"What have we done to these people?"
      I cried out . . . And then a silence fell;
across the dark I saw
      row after row of pumpkins carved and slit,
their crooked eyes
      and pointed teeth all candle-lit within,
not pumpkins but death's-heads they were
      with features of the vacant
hungry faces I had seen,
      stretching to infinity
and glowing in the dark—
      and glowing still when I awoke—

as they do now, and as they always will.

Now Touch the Air Softly

Now touch the air softly,
Step gently. One, two . . .
I'll love you till roses
Are robin's-egg blue;
I'll love you till gravel
Is eaten for bread,
And lemons are orange,
And lavender's red.

Now touch the air softly,
Swing gently the broom.
I'll love you till windows
Are all of a room;
And the table is laid,
And the table is bare,
And the ceiling reposes
On bottomless air.

I'll love you till Heaven
Rips the stars from his coat,
And the Moon rows away in
A glass-bottomed boat;
And Orion steps down
Like a diver below,
And Earth is ablaze,
And Ocean aglow.

So touch the air softly,
And swing the broom high.
We will dust the gray mountains,
And sweep the blue sky;
And I'll love you as long

As the furrow the plow,
As However is Ever,
And Ever is Now.

Persian Miniature

Ah, all the sands of the earth lead unto heaven.
I have seen them rise on the wind, a golden thread,
The sands of the earth which enter the eye of heaven,
Over the graves, the poor, white bones of the dead.
Over the buckling ice, the swollen rivers,
Over the ravened plains, and the dry creek-beds,
The sands are moving. I have seen them move,
And where the pines are bent, the orient
Grain awaits the passage of the wind.
Higher still the laden camels thread
Their way beyond the mountains, and the clouds
Are whiter than the ivory they bear
For Death's black eunuchs. Gold, silk, furs
Cut the blood-red morning. All is vain.
I have watched the caravans through the needle's eye
As they turn, on the threshing floor, the bones of the dead,
And green as a grasshopper's leg is the evening sky.

A Room in the Villa

What is the mirror saying with its O?
What secret does the still, untroubled surface lock?
What terror told by chair, by unmade bed and bedclothes?
Now the clock is speaking; hear the clock.

Hear it tensely ask: Is someone coming?
Did someone just then step into the hall below?
Is someone there upon the stairway, whistling, humming?
    The solemn mirror's mottled, mocking O,

Like some black lake, absorbs all things in silence.
A tattered curtain flaps; the coals within the grate
Are kindled to a brief and unremarked refulgence
    While, patient in the eaves, the shadows wait.

Morels

A wet gray day—rain falling slowly, mist over the
    valley, mountains dark circumflex smudges in the distance—

Apple blossoms just gone by, the branches feathery still
    as if fluttering with half-visible antennae—

A day in May like so many in these green mountains, and
    I went out just as I had last year

At the same time, and found them there under the big maples—
    by the bend in the road—right where they had stood

Last year and the year before that, risen from the dark duff
    of the woods, emerging at odd angles

From spores hidden by curled and matted leaves, a fringe of
    rain on the grass around them,

Beads of rain on the mounded leaves and mosses round them,

Not in a ring themselves but ringed by jack-in-the-pulpits
    with deep eggplant-colored stripes;

Not ringed but rare, not gilled but polyp-like, having
      sprung up overnight—

These mushrooms of the gods, resembling human organs
      uprooted, rooted only on the air,

Looking like lungs wrenched from the human body, lungs
      reversed, not breathing internally

But being the externalization of breath itself, these
      spicy, twisted cones,

These perforated brown-white asparagus tips—these morels,
      smelling of wet graham crackers mixed with maple leaves;

And, reaching down by the pale green fern shoots, I nipped
      their pulpy stems at the base

And dropped them into a paper bag—a damp brown bag (their
      color)—and carried

Them (weighing absolutely nothing) down the hill and into
      the house; you held them

Under cold bubbling water and sliced them with a surgeon's
      stroke clean through,

And sautéed them over a low flame, butter-brown; and we ate
      them then and there—

Tasting of the sweet damp woods and of the rain one inch
      above the meadow:

It was like feasting upon air.

Winter Morning

All night the wind swept over the house
And through our dream,
Swirling the snow up through the pines,
Ruffling the white, ice-capped clapboards,
Rattling the windows,
Rustling around and below our bed
So that we rode
Over wild water
In a white ship breasting the waves.
We rode through the night
On green, marbled
Water, and, half-waking, watched
The white, eroded peaks of icebergs
Sail past our windows;
Rode out the night in that north country,
And awoke, the house buried in snow,
Perched on a
Chill promontory, a
Giant's tooth
In the mouth of the cold valley,
Its white tongue looped frozen around us,
The trunks of tall birches
Revealing the rib cage of a whale
Stranded by a still stream;
And saw, through the motionless baleen of their branches,
As if through time,
Light that shone
On a landscape of ivory,
A harbor of bone.

The World below the Window

The geraniums I left last night on the windowsill,
To the best of my knowledge now, are out there still,
And will be there as long as I think they will.

And will be there as long as I think that I
Can throw the window open on the sky,
A touch of geranium pink in the tail of my eye;

As long as I think I see, past leaves green-growing,
Barges moving down a river, water flowing,
Fulfillment in the thought of thought outgoing,

Fulfillment in the sight of sight replying,
Of sound in the sound of small birds southward flying,
In life life-giving, and in death undying.

American Primitive

Look at him there in his stovepipe hat,
His high-top shoes, and his handsome collar;
Only my Daddy could look like that,
And I love my Daddy like he loves his Dollar.

The screen door bangs, and it sounds so funny—
There he is in a shower of gold;
His pockets are stuffed with folding money,
His lips are blue, and his hands feel cold.

He hangs in the hall by his black cravat,
The ladies faint, and the children holler:
Only my Daddy could look like that,
And I love my Daddy like he loves his Dollar.

The Atoll

An island is all one can ever know
        And all that can ever be
Though part of a vast archipelago
        Rooted in the sea.

It is all one feels, all one finds,
        All that the heart lays bare:
An atoll formed (the waking mind's)
        Open on endless air.

Invitation to Ground Zero

Into the smoldering ruin now go down:
and walk where once she walked and breathe the air
she breathed that final day on the burning stair
and follow her, beyond the fleeing crowds,
into the fire, and through the climbing clouds.

Into the smoldering ruin now go down:
and find, in ashes bright as hammered tin,
a buried bone-white naked mannequin
that flung from some shop window serves to bind
her body, and its beauty, to your mind.

JAMES DICKEY

(1923–1997)

Consultant in Poetry (1966–1968)

What I want to do in living as well as in writing, is a kind of animal-like response.... I was watching the birds today perched on telephone wires, and I never saw one remotely missing what he was trying to do, no matter how hard or which way the wind was blowing. They were always perfectly and instinctively masters of their situation. That kind of thing is what I aspire to do in writing—to make the thing seem so natural that the earth itself might have said it, and that's mighty hard to get.

James Dickey, born in Atlanta, Georgia, was a high school football star who flew combat missions in the Pacific during World War II and was a training officer in the Korean War. His two most famous volumes of verse are *Helmets* (1964) and *Buckdancer's Choice* (1965), which won the 1966 National Book Award. In 1970 he wrote the best-selling novel *Deliverance*, which was made into a major motion picture for which he cowrote the screenplay. He had a successful career as an advertising copywriter before his first book of poems was published in 1960.

Like Faulkner, Dickey made his Dixie roots the subject of much of his art, and one of his principal themes is the disjunction between civilization and the natural world. He was the son of a successful small-town lawyer who often took him hunting in the Appalachian Mountains. His violent imagery and subject matter and often deliberately rough poetic style produced a quality he described as "country surrealism."

Dickey was determined to shake things up at the Library of Congress when he accepted the job as consultant in poetry. He arrived at his first day at the job in a maroon Corvette Sting Ray. At his first press conference as poetry's national spokesman, he entertained a wide-eyed crowd of librarians and journalists with descriptions of his experiences with LSD (tried it but was disappointed) and his opinions on the work of Allen Ginsberg ("the most inept and ludicrous writer on the scene") and Theodore Roethke ("immensely superior to any poet we have had in this country"). In a private interview with the *Washington Post* after the press conference, Dickey said his goal for the year was "to get every guy to sit down and have a beer with his soul . . . the ex–college football star, the ex–ad man, ex–World War II bomber pilot."

In the Child's Night

On distant sides of the bed
We lie together in the winter house
Trying to go away.

Something thinks, "You must be made for it,
And tune your quiet body like a fish
To the stars of the Milky Way

To pass into the star-sea, into sleep,
By means of the heart of the current,
The holy secret of flowing."

Yet levels of depth are wrestling
And rising from us; we are still.
The quilt pattern—a child's pink whale—

Has surfaced through ice at midnight
And now is dancing upon
The dead cold and middle of the air

On my son's feet:
His short legs are trampling the bedclothes
Into the darkness above us

Where the chill of consciousness broods
Like a thing of absolute evil.
I rise to do freezing battle

With my bare hands.
I enter the faraway other
Side of the struggling bed

And turn him to face me.
The stitched beast falls, and we
Are sewn warmly into a sea-shroud

It begins to haul through the dark.
Holding my son's
Best kicking foot in my hand,

I begin to move with the moon
As it must have felt when it went
From the sea to dwell in the sky,

As we near the vast beginning,
The unborn stars of the wellhead,
The secret of the game.

The Sheep Child

Farm boys wild to couple
With anything   with soft-wooded trees
With mounds of earth   mounds
Of pinestraw   will keep themselves off
Animals by legends of their own:
In the hay-tunnel dark
And dung of barns, they will
Say   I have heard tell

That in a museum in Atlanta
Way back in a corner somewhere
There's this thing that's only half
Sheep   like a woolly baby
Pickled in alcohol   because
Those things can't live   his eyes
Are open   but you can't stand to look
I heard from somebody who . . .

But this is now almost all
Gone. The boys have taken
Their own true wives in the city,
The sheep are safe in the west hill
Pasture   but we who were born there
Still are not sure. Are we,
Because we remember, remembered
In the terrible dust of museums?

Merely with his eyes, the sheep-child may

Be saying   saying

> *I am here, in my father's house.*
> *I who am half of your world, came deeply*
> *To my mother in the long grass*
> *Of the west pasture, where she stood like moonlight*
> *Listening for foxes. It was something like love*
> *From another world that seized her*
> *From behind, and she gave, not lifting her head*
> *Out of dew, without ever looking, her best*
> *Self to that great need. Turned loose, she dipped her face*
> *Farther into the chill of the earth, and in a sound*
> *Of sobbing   of something stumbling*
> *Away, began, as she must do,*
> *To carry me. I woke, dying,*

In the summer sun of the hillside, with my eyes
Far more than human. I saw for a blazing moment
The great grassy world from both sides,
Man and beast in the round of their need,
And the hill wind stirred in my wool,
My hoof and my hand clasped each other,
I ate my one meal
Of milk, and died
Staring. From dark grass I came straight

To my father's house, whose dust
Whirls up in the halls for no reason
When no one comes   piling deep in a hellish mild corner,
And, through my immortal waters,
I meet the sun's grains eye
To eye, and they fail at my closet of glass.
Dead, I am most surely living
In the minds of farm boys: I am he who drives
Them like wolves from the hound bitch and calf
And from the chaste ewe in the wind.
They go into woods   into bean fields   they go
Deep into their known right hands. Dreaming of me,
They groan   they wait   they suffer
Themselves, they marry, they raise their kind.

Adultery

We have all been in rooms
We cannot die in, and they are odd places, and sad.
Often Indians are standing eagle-armed on hills

In the sunrise   open wide to the Great Spirit
Or gliding in canoes   or cattle are browsing on the walls
Far away   gazing down with the eyes of our children

Not far away   or there are men driving
The last railspike, which has turned
Gold in their hands. Gigantic forepleasure lives

Among such scenes, and we are alone with it
At last. There is always some weeping
Between us   and someone is always checking

A wrist watch by the bed to see how much
Longer we have left. Nothing can come
Of this   nothing can come

Of us: of me with my grim techniques
Or you who have sealed your womb
With a ring of convulsive rubber:

Although we come together,
Nothing will come of us. But we would not give
It up, for death is beaten

By praying Indians   by distant cows   historical
Hammers   by hazardous meetings that bridge
A continent. One could never die here

Never die   never die
While crying. My lover, my dear one
I will see you next week

When I'm in town. I will call you
If I can. Please get hold of   please don't
Oh God, Please don't any more I can't bear . . . Listen:

We have done it again   we are
Still living. Sit up and smile,
God bless you. Guilt is magical.

The Heaven of Animals

Here they are. The soft eyes open.
If they have lived in a wood
It is a wood.
If they have lived on plains
It is grass rolling
Under their feet forever.

Having no souls, they have come,
Anyway, beyond their knowing.
Their instincts wholly bloom
And they rise.
The soft eyes open.

To match them, the landscape flowers,
Outdoing, desperately
Outdoing what is required:
The richest wood,
The deepest field.

For some of these,
It could not be the place
It is, without blood.
These hunt, as they have done,
But with claws and teeth grown perfect,

More deadly than they can believe.
They stalk more silently,
And crouch on the limbs of trees,
And their descent
Upon the bright backs of their prey

May take years
In a sovereign floating of joy.
And those that are hunted
Know this as their life,
Their reward: to walk

Under such trees in full knowledge
Of what is in glory above them,
And to feel no fear,
But acceptance, compliance.
Fulfilling themselves without pain

At the cycle's center,
They tremble, they walk
Under the tree,
They fall, they are torn,
They rise, they walk again.

In the Tree House at Night

And now the green household is dark.
The half-moon completely is shining
On the earth-lighted tops of the trees.
To bed dead, a house must be still.
The floor and the walls wave me slowly;
I am deep in them over my head.
The needles and pine cones about me

Are full of small birds at their roundest,
Their fists without mercy gripping
Hard down through the tree to the roots
To sing back at light when they feel it.

We lie here like angels in bodies,
My brothers and I, one dead,
The other asleep from much living,

In mid-air huddled beside me.
Dark climbed to us here as we climbed
Up the nails I have hammered all day
Through the sprained, comic rungs of the ladder
Of broom handles, crate slats, and laths
Foot by foot up the trunk to the branches
Where we came out at last over lakes

Of leaves, of fields disencumbered of earth
That move with the moves of the spirit.
Each nail that sustains us I set here;
Each nail in the house is now steadied
By my dead brother's huge, freckled hand.
Through the years, he has pointed his hammer
Up into these limbs, and told us

That we must ascend, and all lie here.
Step after step he has brought me,
Embracing the trunk as his body,
Shaking its limbs with my heartbeat,
Till the pine cones danced without wind
And fell from the branches like apples.
In the arm-slender forks of our dwelling

I breathe my live brother's light hair.
The blanket around us becomes
As solid as stone, and it sways.
With all my heart, I close
The blue, timeless eye of mind.
Wind springs, as my dead brother smiles
And touches the tree at the root;

A shudder of joy runs up
The trunk; the needles tingle;
One bird uncontrollably cries.
The wind changes round, and I stir
Within another's life. Whose life?
Who is dead? Whose presence is living?
When may I fall strangely to earth,

Who am nailed to this branch by a spirit?
Can two bodies make up a third?
To sing, must I feel the world's light?
My green, graceful bones fill the air
With sleeping birds. Alone, alone
And with them I move gently.
I move at the heart of the world.

The Hospital Window

I have just come down from my father.
Higher and higher he lies
Above me in a blue light
Shed by a tinted window.
I drop through six white floors
And then step out onto pavement.

Still feeling my father ascend,
I start to cross the firm street,
My shoulder blades shining with all
The glass the huge building can raise.
Now I must turn round and face it,
And know his one pane from the others.

Each window possesses the sun
As though it burned there on a wick.
I wave, like a man catching fire.
All the deep-dyed windowpanes flash,
And, behind them, all the white rooms
They turn to the color of Heaven.

Ceremoniously, gravely, and weakly,
Dozens of pale hands are waving
Back, from inside their flames.
Yet one pure pane among these
Is the bright, erased blankness of nothing.
I know that my father is there,

In the shape of his death still living.
The traffic increases around me
Like a madness called down on my head.
The horns blast at me like shotguns,
And drivers lean out, driven crazy—
But now my propped-up father

Lifts his arm out of stillness at last.
The light from the window strikes me
And I turn as blue as a soul,
As the moment when I was born.
I am not afraid for my father—
Look! He is grinning; he is not

Afraid for my life, either,
As the wild engines stand at my knees
Shredding their gears and roaring,
And I hold each car in its place
For miles, inciting its horn
To blow down the walls of the world

That the dying may float without fear
In the bold blue gaze of my father.
Slowly I move to the sidewalk
With my pin-tingling hand half dead
At the end of my bloodless arm.
I carry it off in amazement,

High, still higher, still waving,
My recognized face fully mortal,
Yet not; not at all, in the pale,
Drained, otherworldly, stricken,
Created hue of stained glass.
I have just come down from my father.

Cherrylog Road

Off Highway 106
At Cherrylog Road I entered
The '34 Ford without wheels,
Smothered in kudzu,
With a seat pulled out to run
Corn whiskey down from the hills,

And then from the other side
Crept into an Essex
With a rumble seat of red leather
And then out again, aboard
A blue Chevrolet, releasing
The rust from its other color,

Reared up on three building blocks.
None had the same body heat;
I changed with them inward, toward
The weedy heart of the junkyard,
For I knew that Doris Holbrook
Would escape from her father at noon

And would come from the farm
To seek parts owned by the sun
Among the abandoned chassis,
Sitting in each in turn
As I did, leaning forward
As in a wild stock-car race

In the parking lot of the dead.
Time after time, I climbed in
And out the other side, like
An envoy or movie star
Met at the station by crickets.
A radiator cap raised its head,

Become a real toad or a kingsnake
As I neared the hub of the yard,
Passing through many states,
Many lives, to reach
Some grandmother's long Pierce-Arrow
Sending platters of blindness forth

From its nickel hubcaps
And spilling its tender upholstery
On sleepy roaches,
The glass panel in between
Lady and colored driver
Not all the way broken out,

The back-seat phone
Still on its hook.
I got in as though to exclaim,
"Let us go to the orphan asylum,
John; I have some old toys
For children who say their prayers."

I popped with sweat as I thought
I heard Doris Holbrook scrape
Like a mouse in the southern-state sun
That was eating the paint in blisters
From a hundred car tops and hoods.
She was tapping like code,

Loosening the screws,
Carrying off headlights,
Sparkplugs, bumpers,
Cracked mirrors and gear-knobs,
Getting ready, already,
To go back with something to show

Other than her lips' new trembling
I would hold to me soon, soon,
Where I sat in the ripped back seat
Talking over the interphone,
Praying for Doris Holbrook
To come from her father's farm

And to get back there
With no trace of me on her face
To be seen by her red-haired father
Who would change, in the squalling barn,
Her back's pale skin with a strop,
Then lay for me

In a bootlegger's roasting car
With a string-triggered 12-gauge shotgun
To blast the breath from the air.
Not cut by the jagged windshields,
Through the acres of wrecks she came
With a wrench in her hand,

Through dust where the blacksnake dies
Of boredom, and the beetle knows
The compost has no more life.
Someone outside would have seen
The oldest car's door inexplicably
Close from within:

I held her and held her and held her,
Conveyed at terrific speed
By the stalled, dreaming traffic around us,
So the blacksnake, stiff
With inaction, curved back
Into life, and hunted the mouse

With deadly overexcitement,
The beetles reclaimed their field
As we clung, glued together,
With the hooks of the seat springs
Working through to catch us red-handed
Amidst the gray, breathless batting

That burst from the seat at our backs.
We left by separate doors
Into the changed, other bodies
Of cars, she down Cherrylog Road
And I to my motorcycle
Parked like the soul of the junkyard

Restored, a bicycle fleshed
With power, and tore off
Up Highway 106, continually
Drunk on the wind in my mouth,
Wringing the handlebar for speed,
Wild to be wreckage forever.

Drinking from a Helmet

I

I climbed out, tired of waiting
For my foxhole to turn in the earth
On its side or its back for a grave,
And got in line
Somewhere in the roaring of dust.
Every tree on the island was nowhere,
Blasted away.

II

In the middle of combat, a graveyard
Was advancing after the troops
With laths and balls of string;
Grass already tinged it with order.
Between the new graves and the foxholes
A green water-truck stalled out.
I moved up on it, behind
The hill that cut off the firing.

III

My turn, and I shoved forward
A helmet I picked from the ground,
Not daring to take mine off
Where somebody else may have come
Loose from the steel of his head.

IV

Keeping the foxhole doubled
In my body and begging
For water, safety, and air,
I drew water out of the truckside
As if dreaming the helmet full.
In my hands, the sun
Came on in a feathery light.

V

In midair, water trimming
To my skinny dog-faced look
Showed my life's first all-out beard
Growing wildly, escaping from childhood,
Like the beards of the dead, all now
Underfoot beginning to grow.
Selected ripples wove through it,
Knocked loose with a touch from all sides
Of a brain killed early that morning,
Most likely, and now
In its absence holding
My sealed, sunny image from harm,
Weighing down my hands,
Shipping at the edges,
Too heavy on one side, then the other.

VI

I drank, with the timing of rust.
A vast military wedding
Somewhere advanced one step.

VII

All around, equipment drifting in light,
Men drinking like cattle and bushes,
Cans, leather, canvas and rifles,
Grass pouring down from the sun
And up from the ground.
Grass: and the summer advances
Invisibly into the tropics.
Wind, and the summer shivers
Through many men standing or lying
In the GI gardener's hand
Spreading and turning green
All over the hill.

VIII

At the middle of water
Bright circles dawned inward and outward
Like oak rings surviving the tree
As its soul, or like
The concentric gold spirit of time.
I kept trembling forward through something
Just born of me.

IX

My nearly dead power to pray
Like an army increased and assembled,
As when, in a harvest of sparks,
The helmet leapt from the furnace
And clamped itself
On the heads of a billion men.
Some words directed to Heaven
Went through all the strings of the graveyard
Like a message that someone sneaked in,
Tapping a telegraph key
At dead of night, then running
For his life.

X

I swayed, as if kissed in the brain.
Above the shelled palm-stumps I saw
How the tops of huge trees might be moved
In a place in my own country
I never had seen in my life.
In the closed dazzle of my mouth
I fought with a word in the water
To call on the dead to strain
Their muscles to get up and go there.
I felt the difference between
Sweat and tears when they rise,
Both trying to melt the brow down.

XI

On even the first day of death
The dead cannot rise up,
But their last thought hovers somewhere
For whoever finds it.
My uninjured face floated strangely
In the rings of a bodiless tree.
Among them, also, a final
Idea lived, waiting
As in Ariel's limbed, growing jail.

XII

I stood as though I possessed
A cool, trembling man
Exactly my size, swallowed whole.
Leather swung at his waist,
Web-cord, buckles, and metal,
Crouching over the dead
Where they waited for all their hands
To be connected like grass-roots.

XIII

In the brown half-life of my beard
The hair stood up
Like the awed hair lifting the back
Of a dog that has eaten a swan.
Now light like this
Staring into my face
Was the first thing around me at birth.
Be no more killed, it said.

XIV

The wind in the grass
Moved gently in secret flocks,
Then spread to be
Nothing, just where they were.
In delight's
Whole shining condition and risk,
I could see how my body might come
To be imagined by something
That thought of it only for joy.

XV

Fresh sweat and unbearable tears
Drawn up by my feet from the field
Between my eyebrows became
One thing at last,
And I could cry without hiding.
The world dissolved into gold;
I could have stepped up into air.
I drank and finished
Like tasting of Heaven,
Which is simply of,
At seventeen years,
Not dying wherever you are.

XVI

Enough
Shining, I picked up my carbine and said.
I threw my old helmet down
And put the wet one on.

Warmed water ran over my face.
My last thought changed, and I knew
I inherited one of the dead.

XVII

I saw tremendous trees
That would grow on the sun if they could,
Towering. I saw a fence
And two boys facing each other,
Quietly talking,
Looking in at the gigantic redwoods,
The rings in the trunks turning slowly
To raise up stupendous green.
They went away, one turning
The wheels of a blue bicycle,
The smaller one curled catercornered
In the handlebar basket.

XVIII

I would survive and go there,
Stepping off the train in a helmet
That held a man's last thought,
Which showed him his older brother
Showing him trees.
I would ride through all
California upon two wheels
Until I came to the white
Dirt road where they had been,
Hoping to meet his blond brother,
And to walk with him into the wood
Until we were lost,

Then take off the helmet
And tell him where I had stood,
What poured, what spilled, what swallowed:

XIX

And tell him I was the man.

STEPHEN SPENDER

(1909–1995)

Consultant in Poetry (1965–1966)

The conversation—as always at Washington parties—turned to the President, and all three said from their experience how different he was when he talked in private from when he used his public voice. In private he was full of ideas, pithy. He employed brilliant metaphors and many anecdotes. In public he failed to communicate.

ir Stephen Harold Spender was a member of the Oxford Generation poets, including W. H. Auden and Christopher Isherwood, who came of age during the years of the Spanish Civil War. Spender was the first English subject appointed consultant, and his appointment caused a mild stir, raising questions about the function of the Library as a bastion for American as opposed to English letters, Spender's early Communist sympathies, and his poetry, compared to that of more prominent English poets (namely Auden). Spender had spent much of his time in the early sixties teaching in the States and had earned a reputation as an engaging and sympathetic lecturer.

His poem "What I Expected" reflects upon his early idealistic belief in the poet as a revolutionary figure whose sense of self and civic responsibility could help rebuild a Europe shattered by economic depression, industrialization, and the events leading up to the Second World War. Ever self-scrutinizing, Spender later criticized this view in his memoir: "The idealist expects too much of himself and others. He is like an artist who cannot relate inspiration to form, because the shift from vision to the discipline of form involves him in conscious deliberation—for him, a kind of disillusioning. In politics, I wished for a social revolution which would achieve justice without introducing new injustices. . . . In poetry I wished to create a purely inspirational kind of writing which rejected the modern day-to-day living."

His later writing became increasingly autobiographical, and he published his last volume of poems alongside a selection of his journal writing from the same period. Spender viewed all his writing, regardless of form, as personal testimony: "I myself am, it is only too clear, an autobiographer. Autobiography provides the line of continuity in my work. I am not someone who can shed or disclaim his past." In Spender's case, focus on the self is often paradoxically deferential and questioning. Unlike his close friend Auden, whom Spender groups with those of his generation he called "truly great," Spender located himself on the edge of greatness; this, he reflected, permitted him to write from "the exposed nerve" that responds with sympathy to others. His poem "Matter of Identity" is a kind of manifesto for his sense of self as an *un*great antihero: "Who he was, remained an open question / He asked himself, looking at all those others— / The Strangers, roaring down the street."

What I Expected

What I expected was
Thunder, fighting,
Long struggles with men
And climbing.
After continual straining
I should grow strong;
Then the rocks would shake
And I should rest long.

What I had not foreseen
Was the gradual day
Weakening the will
Leaking the brightness away,
The lack of good to touch
The fading of body and soul
Like smoke before wind
Corrupt, unsubstantial.

The wearing of Time,
And the watching of cripples pass
With limbs shaped like questions
In their odd twist,
The pulverous grief
Melting the bones with pity,
The sick falling from earth—
These, I could not foresee.

For I had expected always
Some brightness to hold in trust,
Some final innocence

To save from dust;
That, hanging solid,
Would dangle through all
Like the created poem
Or the dazzling crystal.

I Think Continually of Those Who Were Truly Great

I think continually of those who were truly great.
Who, from the womb, remembered the soul's history
Through corridors of light where the hours are suns,
Endless and singing. Whose lovely ambition
Was that their lips, still touched with fire,
Should tell of the Spirit clothed from head to foot in song.
And who hoarded from the Spring branches
The desires falling across their bodies like blossoms.

What is precious is never to forget
The essential delight of the blood drawn from ageless springs
Breaking through rocks in worlds before our earth.
Never to deny its pleasure in the morning simple light
Nor its grave evening demand for love.
Never to allow gradually the traffic to smother
With noise and fog, the flowering of the spirit.

Near the snow, near the sun, in the highest fields
See how these names are fêted by the waving grass
And by the streamers of white cloud
And whispers of wind in the listening sky.

The names of those who in their lives fought for life,
Who wore at their hearts the fire's centre.
Born of the sun, they travelled a short while towards the sun,
And left the vivid air singed with their honour.

Not Palaces

Not palaces, an era's crown
Where the mind dwells, intrigues, rests;
The architectural gold-leaved flower
From people ordered like a single mind,
I build. This only what I tell:
It is too late for rare accumulation,
For family pride, for beauty's filtered dusts;
I say, stamping the words with emphasis,
Drink from here energy and only energy,
As from the electric charge of a battery,
To will this Time's change.
Eye, gazelle, delicate wanderer,
Drinker of horizon's fluid line;
Ear that suspends on a chord
The spirit drinking timelessness;
Touch, love, all senses;
Leave your gardens, your singing feasts,
Your dreams of suns circling before our sun,
Of heaven after our world.
Instead, watch images of flashing brass
That strike the outward sense, the polished will,
Flag of our purpose which the wind engraves.
No spirit seek here rest. But this: No man
Shall hunger: Man shall spend equally.
Our goal which we compel: Man shall be man.

—That programme of the antique Satan
Bristling with guns on the indented page,
With battleship towering from hilly waves:
For what? Drive of a ruining purpose
Destroying all but its age-long exploiters.
Our programme like this, yet opposite,
Death to the killers, bringing light to life.

Awaking

Ever the same, forever new!
The gravel path searching the Way;
The cobwebs beaded with the dew;
The empty waiting of new day.

So I remember each new morning
From childhood, when pebbles amaze.
Outside my window, the forewarning
Glitter of those days.

The sense felt behind darkened walls,
An amber-solid world, a lake
Of light, through which light falls.
It is this to which I wake.

Then the sun shifts the trees around
And overtops the sky, and throws
House, horse and rider to the ground
With knockout shadows.

The whole sky opens to an O,
The cobweb dries, the petals spread,
The clocks grow beards, the people go
Walking over their graves, the dead.

The world's a circle where all moves
Before after after before.
Such joy my new-awaking proves
Each day—until I start to care.

Word

The word bites like a fish.
Shall I throw it back free
Arrowing to that sea
Where thoughts lash tail and fin?
Or shall I pull it in
To rhyme upon a dish?

Empty House

Then, when the child was gone,
I was alone
In the house, suddenly grown huge. Each noise
Explained its cause away,
Animal, vegetable, mineral,
But mostly there was quiet of after battle
Where round the room still lay
The soldiers and the paintbox, all the toys.
        Then, when I went to tidy these away,

My hands refused to serve:
My body was the house,
And everything he'd touched, an exposed nerve.

An Elementary School Class Room in a Slum

Far far from gusty waves, these children's faces.
Like rootless weeds the torn hair round their paleness.
The tall girl with her weighed-down head. The paper-
seeming boy with rat's eyes. The stunted unlucky heir
Of twisted bones, reciting a father's gnarled disease,
His lesson from his desk. At back of the dim class,
One unnoted, sweet and young: his eyes live in a dream
Of squirrels' game, in tree room, other than this.

On sour cream walls, donations. Shakespeare's head
Cloudless at dawn, civilized dome riding all cities.
Belled, flowery, Tyrolese valley. Open-handed map
Awarding the world its world. And yet, for these
Children, these windows, not this world, are world,
Where all their future's painted with a fog,
A narrow street sealed in with a lead sky,
Far far from rivers, capes, and stars of words.

Surely Shakespeare is wicked, the map a bad example
With ships and sun and love tempting them to steal—
For lives that slyly turn in their cramped holes
From fog to endless night? On their slag heap, these children
Wear skins peeped through by bones and spectacles of steel
With mended glass, like bottle bits on stones.
All of their time and space are foggy slum
So blot their maps with slums as big as doom.

Unless, governor, teacher, inspector, visitor,
This map becomes their window and these windows
That open on their lives like crouching tombs
Break, O break open, till they break the town
And show the children to the fields and all their world
Azure on their sands, to let their tongues
Run naked into books, the white and green leaves open
The history theirs whose language is the sun.

One More New Botched Beginning

Their voices heard, I stumble suddenly
Choking in undergrowth. I'm torn
Mouth pressed against the thorns,

                                remembering
Ten years ago, here in Geneva
I walked with Merleau-Ponty by the lake.
Upon his face, I saw his intellect.
Energy of the sun-interweaving
Waves, electric, danced on him. His eyes
Smiled with their gay logic through
Black coins flung down from leaves.

                                He who
Was Merleau-Ponty that day is no more
Irrevocable than the I that day who was
Beside him—I'm still living!

    Also that summer
My son stayed up the valley in the mountains.
One day I went to see him and he stood
Not seeing me, watching some hens.
Doing so, he was absorbed
In their wire-netted world. He danced

On one leg. Leaning forward, he became
A bird-boy. I am there
Still seeing him. To him
That moment—unselfknowing even then
Is drowned in the oblivious earliness . . .

                              Such pasts
Are not diminished distances, perspective
Vanishing points, but doors
Burst open suddenly by gusts
That seek to blow the heart out . . .
                              Today I see
Three undergraduates standing talking in
A college quad. They show each other poems—
Louis MacNeice, Bernard Spencer, and I.
Louis caught cold in the rain, Bernard fell
From a train door.

Their lives are now those poems that were
Pointers to the poems to be their lives.
We read there in the college quad. Each poem
Is still a new beginning. If
They had been finished though they would have died
Before they died. Being alive
Is when each moment's a new start, with past
And future shuffled between fingers
For a new game.
                         I'm dealing out
My hand to them, one more new botched beginning,
Here, where we still stand talking in the quad.

REED WHITTEMORE

(1919–)

Consultant in Poetry (1964–1965 and 1984–1985)

Institutions, whether the newspaper, the university, the foundation, or the government, can only deaden or paralyze art. . . . No academy should ever be put in the position of having to arbitrate and establish the values of works of art. This great and glorious Library had its knuckles rapped many years ago when it started to give out poetry prizes. And a good thing too.

Reed Whittemore is the author of thirteen books of poetry, including *The Self-Made Man, The Mother's Breast and The Father's House,* and *The Past, the Future, the Present: Poems Selected and New.* In addition to serving as poetry consultant to the Library of Congress, he was the poet laureate of Maryland. A literary editor of the *New Republic* for many years, he taught literature at Carleton College and the University of Maryland, wrote an acclaimed biography of William Carlos Williams, and published a collection of essays on the craft of literary biography. He now lives in College Park, his perch just outside Washington, D.C., from which he watches the goings-on in our capital with a wry, satirical eye.

During World War II Whittemore served in the U.S. Air Force and rose to the rank of major. Upon his return to the United States, he enrolled at Princeton University but left shortly thereafter for a teaching position at Carleton College in Northfield, Minnesota, where he revived the literary journal *Furioso,* which he had started as a sophomore at Yale. *Furioso* published some of the most important works of American modernism, including poetry by Ezra Pound, William Carlos Williams, and E. E. Cummings deemed too experimental for the bigger literary magazines. As poetry consultant, Whittemore organized a symposium on the little magazine and contemporary literature, bringing together over a hundred editors from as far away as Pakistan and Alaska. He was instrumental in forming the Association of Literary Magazines of America, which continues to help with the funding and distribution of independent journals.

Whittemore has lived and worked near Washington, D.C., for over four decades. His poetry often parodies his autobiographical speakers for being middle-aged and academic: "The author, critic and cultural messenger (me) / Comes to the cultural conference with snap-on tie." This stance is often the bemused guise for his most critical poems on the banality and materialism of American culture. Whittemore generally had more interaction with governmental Washington than prior Consultants. Her wrote that "he set up a cultural storm" in Washington and went on to recommend that "all poetry consultants hereafter should do the same. I am, however, confident that should the next Consultant choose to live in splendid isolation in his third floor retreat, the kindly Library officials would smile as sweetly upon him as they have smiled upon me as a greenhorn bureaucrat."

Clamming

I go digging for clams once every two or three years
Just to keep my hand in (I usually cut it),
And I'm sure that whenever I do so I tell the same story
Of how, at the age of four, I was trapped by the tide
As I clammed a sandbar. It's no story at all,
But I tell it and tell it. It serves my small lust
To be thought of as someone who's lived.
I've a war too to fall back on, and some years of flying,
As well as a high quota of drunken parties,
A wife and children; but somehow the clamming thing
Gives me an image of me that soothes my psyche
Like none of the louder events: me helpless,
Alone with my sandpail,
As fate in the form of soupy Long Island Sound
Comes stalking me.

I've a son now at that age.
He's spoiled. He's been sickly.
He's handsome and bright, affectionate and demanding.
I think of the tides when I look at him.
I'd have him alone and sea-girt, poor little boy.

The self, what a brute it is. It wants, wants.
It will not let go of its even most fictional grandeur,
But must grope, grope down in the muck of its past
For some little squirting life and bring it up tenderly
To the lo and behold of death, that it may weep
And pass on the weeping, keep the thing going.

                    Son, when you clam,
Watch out for the tides and take care of yourself,
Yet no great care,
Lest you care too much and talk of the caring
And bore your best friends and inhibit your children and sicken
At last into opera on somebody's sandbar. Son, when you clam,
Clam.

Preface to an Unwritten Text

Words of thanks and caution: to the many
Teachers, students, authors, friends, and loves
Whose words and writings made me, and who led me
From the errors that my work disproves;

And to the academic centers of complexity,
Without whose constant services my premises,
For better or for worse, were never scholarly;
And to my mother and my father and my nemesis,

I am grateful.
But all these I disjoin
From all that here is hateful.
The text which does not follow is my own.

Spring, etc.

And now at last I come to it: spring,
Spring with his shoures sote,
Shoures of snowe stille in Minnesota
But spring all the same, starting all over
All of those worthy projects in grass and clover
That somehow got tabled last October.

Spring in the trees and gardens, spring in the mind,
Spring in the fields and rivers, spring in the blood,
Spring, spring, spring, and then again spring,
Wet, warm, bright, green, good.

So now at last I come to it,
Long long overdue,
Come to it late by bobsled and skate, but come
To it, by golly and gum!
To it! Tu-whit, tu-who!

The Radio Under the Bed

Why was a radio sinful? Lord knows. But it was.
So I had one,
Which I kept locked in a strongbox under my bed
And brought forth, turned on, tuned and fondled at night
When the sneaky housemaster slept and vice was all right.

The music played in my ear from the Steel Pier,
Nob Hill, the Astor and other housemasterless
Hebrides where (I heard) the loved lived it up.
I listened myself to sleep, the sweet saxes
Filtering into my future, filling my cup.

All prohibitions have vanished. Radios bore me,
As do the two-step debauches I used to crave.
But the songs still remain, the old vulgar songs, and will play me,
Tum-te-tum, tum-te-tum, tum-te-tum, into my grave.

The Cultural Conference

The author, critic and cultural messenger (me)
Comes to the cultural conference with snap-on tie,
Two shirts and a briefcase; and in between drinks
Holds forth for a week on the state of the state
Of letters—
               that is, takes stock.
He finds science doing its best and wishes that artists
Would pay some attention to thermodynamics.
He doubts that our age will go down in the books for its verse,
But hopes for the novel. He thinks there is room
For a new vital form of some sort—the novella?—
And wonders if any mass culture, even our own,
Can really sustain a high art, thinking that paperbacks
Help. Lastly he knows it is late and the room is stuffy,
But if anyone really wishes to, he would be more than.
    Thereupon,
Asked if he thinks that the modern poets are difficult,
Or that writers should be depressing, defeatist or dirty,
He smiles, looks at his watch, hunches over the lectern
And recites (for another half hour) (with lengthy asides)
Passages out of the Great Tradition from Chaucer
To (with suitably deprecatory sniffles) himself, *simply to show*
—Uh, would the lady repeat the question? Thereupon

She does and he firmly agrees and everyone breaks up
And the week goes insanely on and he leaves at the end of it
Alone on a plane for home where, arriving, he'll take

Another week, of a cultural silence profound,
Getting used to the hardship of having himself (me) around.

The Philadelphia Vireo

> ". . . anyone unable to tell a Vireo from a Warbler is hardly ready to recognize
> this species."
>
> —A Field Guide to the Birds, by Roger Tory Peterson

One can't do much in these woods without a bird book.
Right on my porch sits a busy, light-breasted thing I name
          phoebe, building a nest;
And the pines by the house are held by a reddish-brown
          thrush and his reddish-brown mate,
Along with the smallest bird on the place, some warbler or finch,
Who struts down below on the needles on match-stick legs.
Far out and high I hear what I think is mockingbird;
          then there are crows,
Robins, jays, a few pheasants, what-all. I march up and
          down with my bird book, scholarly,
Interested in the variety of sounds and shapes,
Amused by my own insufficiencies as stalker of wild life,
But otherwise little disposed to be moved: to commune,
          to identify.

Back at the house I page through an angry Tolstoi
          berating the Greeks
For beguiling the artless Christians with nasty
          pre-Christian nudes.

I close Tolstoi. He should have sniped at the birds too,
     While he was at it,
Little pagans, for putting so many poets in bushes
     with bird books.
It's a bad day and I feel like a fool out here with the birds,
And now I'm writing these lines, dissonant things, and
     thinking bird things,
Because I'm a bloody professional bird and must damn well sing.
So I sing: chrrrk, chrrrk.

But why should I run down the birds? They have energy;
     they are strange.
There is wonder in energy, strangeness. Art needs that;
     man needs that;
And I seem to be in these woods for that, though writing
     a man book.
So I say to my phoebe, the one on the porch, the busy one,
Who is flying in sticks to her nest like a drunken west
     wind: bird,
Man thinks, though he thinks too much for all he knows of
     thee, well of thee.

What Was It Like?

What was it like? I can tell you what it was like.
We were sitting and drinking, drinking.
We ticked off all the hatreds of our acquaintance.
We banished the sky from the heavens and it was like death.

And what was death like?
Death, I can tell you now, was like being.
Death was 45, alcoholic, rational,
With the smoke curling up from the fingers, the words from the mouth,

And the wife sitting prim in the corner watching the world end.
Death was all that crap in somebody's living room
On a Saturday night on the circuit with plates in the laps.

We put on our coats and stumbled out to the car
And made it home to the babies and paid the baby-sitter
And lay down at last and slept. It was like that.

Let It Blow

Let it blow, said the union of amalgamated winds,
And let it drip, said the cloud trust.
Where is there an end to it,
The self-interest?
—Whither my feet takest me I find lobbying,
Invented by Joseph Lobby,
Who wrote a nonpartisan editorial in behalf of his own candidacy for
    alderman in a tiny New England slum housing development in 1802.

Now each purple mountain majesty requires a private sunrise.
We pass individually unto grace, cutting each other on the thruway,
Singing the brotherhood of one.

Let it blow;
Let the assorted selves drop leaflets against litter,
Picket the morning.

Who will volunteer to park in a bus stop?
Foul the word supply?

—The right of the people to keep and bear arms shall not be
    infringed
Nor other rights of the righteous
So that the pharmaceutical firms may suck forever
On the inner heart of our headache.

How can a nation of smart cookies be so dumb?
Did Jefferson do it? Hamilton? Thoreau maybe?

—I look into the kindly eyes of my anarchist soul mate,
She (he) dreaming of a Greek isle with her (his) American Express
    card,
She (he) wanting 400 hp and a water bed
        (and a mountain, a guru, and an independent income).

Not an institution in this country is not betrayed by its souls in
    residence.

Who is left to pull the weeds from the Xerox machine?
Where will we find the manpower to carry this week's privateering to
    the town dump?

—Let it blow,
And let the associations for the preservation of the freedoms publish
    the unexpurgated results
At a profit.

LOUIS UNTERMEYER

(1885–1977)

Consultant in Poetry (1961–1963)

I was meant to act as a poetic radiator, radiating a love of poetry over as many miles as possible.

ouis Untermeyer may be the only poet selected by the Librarian of Congress to come for his good cheer and his tireless promotion of others' poetry. Though he had published more than a dozen volumes of his own work, he was better known as an editor and an anthologist of over sixty compilations anthologies and selections of poets ranging from Heine to Dickinson. An autodidact who left high school before graduating to help run his father's successful jewelry business, Untermeyer, poetry's great middleman, was celebrated for his brio, his vast knowledge of literature, and the informal, humorous way he lectured and spoke about poetry, drama, and music. A poet who loved satire and parody, he got ribbed from time to time for anthologizing his own work, as in E. E. Cummings's mock epitaph: "mr u will not be missed / who as an anthologist / sold the many on the few / not excluding mr u."

During the McCarthy period Untermeyer was blacklisted, and he lost, among other things, a job he loved as a regular contestant on the popular television program *What's My Line?* His abiding interest in workers' rights began at the end of the nineteenth century, when he invited the hundred and fifty employees of his family's jewelry company to unionize; Untermeyer would later boast that he established the first forty-four-hour week in the industry. He also helped run the Marxist journal *The Masses*, a mouthpiece for left-leaning opposition to World War I, which was shut down after the United States entered the war. After Untermeyer was named during the House Un-American Activities investigation into communist subversion, he did not leave his home for a full year. A decade later, when the announcement for the poetry consultancy was released, a congressman wrote to the Library protesting Untermeyer's Communist affiliations. In response to this and other questions about his patriotism, Untermeyer drafted a statement for the Library: "I have offered to state before any Congressional Committee which might want to question me [that] I have . . . been, and will continue to be, opposed to all forms of dictatorship, whether from the extreme left or the extreme right." The Library's public honor and its attendant readings and lectures helped repair Untermeyer's damaged reputation, but he never recovered his subversive charm. His acceptance letter to the Librarian sums up his determination to avoid political controversy: "I expect to enjoy myself hugely, but I won't derive any enjoyment from the position unless I am of service."

Infidelity

You have not conquered me; it is the surge
     Of love itself that beats against my will;
It is the sting of conflict, the old urge
       That calls me still.

It is not you I love, it is the form
     And shadow of all lovers who have died
That gives you all the freshness of a warm
       And unfamiliar bride.

It is your name I breathe, your hands I seek;
     It will be you when you are gone;
And yet the dream, the name I cannot speak
       Is that which lures me on.

It is the golden summons, the bright wave
     Of banners calling me anew;
It is all passion, perilous and grave—
       It is not you.

Jerusalem Delivered

King David Hotel, Jerusalem, offers Tea Dances Wednesday and Saturday,
Aperitif Concerts every Sunday, and Cocktail Parties in the Winter Garden.
—Adv. in the *Palestine News*

Miriam, strike your cymbal,
        Young David, add your voice;
Once more the tribes are nimble,
        Once more the Jews rejoice.

Beneath the flowering mango
        Where peace and perfume drip,
Solomon does the tango
        And Sheba shakes a hip.

Rebekah trots with Aaron,
        Deborah treads the earth,
Fresh as the Rose of Sharon
        With evening gowns by Worth.

Susannah meets the Elders
        With an increased regard;
Pounds, dollars, marks, and guilders
        Receive their due award.

Jerusalem the Golden,
        With milk and honey blest,
Revive the rapt and olden
        Ardor within each breast;

Add Gilead to Gomorrah;
        Fling torches through the dark;
Dancing before the Torah,
        With cocktails at the Ark!

Scarcely Spring

Nothing is real. The world has lost its edges;
The sky, uncovered, is the one thing clear.
The earth is little more than atmosphere
Where yesterday were rocks and naked ridges.
Nothing is fixed. Tentative rain dislodges
Green upon green or lifts a coral spear
That breaks in blossom, and the hills appear
Too frail to be the stony fruit of ages.

Nothing will keep. Even the heavens waver.
Young larks, whose first thought is to cry aloud,
Have spent their bubble notes. And here or there
A few slow-hearted boys and girls discover
A moon as insubstantial as a cloud
Painted by air on washed and watery air.

Six Epigrams

On a Politician   After Hearing the Whip-poor-will

Loud laureate of nought, go play
Thy steam-calliope to frogs and 'fright 'em,
Thou who hast never anything to say,
And sayest it with force, *ad infinitum.*

On a Poet

She counts her world well lost for whom
A wisecrack is the Crack of Doom.
She gags as neatly as she grieves,
And wears her heart out—on both sleeves.

On a Popularizer

Midwife to all the Muses, you grow rich
By making the immortal less divine.
With what finesse you trim, and cut, and stitch,
Feigning that every stitch—in time—serves Nine.

On a Supreme Court Judge

How well this figure represents the Law:
      This pose of neuter justice, sterile cant;
This Roman Emperor with an iron jaw,
      Wrapped in the black silk of a maiden aunt.

On a Feeble Whistler

> *"Seated by the roadside I shall wait for America to catch up."*
> —G. S. Viereck

What though the crowd, with laudable defection
Has gone in quite the opposite direction,
His feeble penny-whistle demonstrates
It serves him right who only sits and waits.

On a Self-made Philosopher

"Life was my university,"
      He boasts, and waits for approbation;
Revealing, to the nth degree,
      The sad results of education.

Summer Storm

We lay together in the sultry night.
A feeble light
From some invisible street-lamp crept
Into the corner where you slept,
Fingered your cheeks, flew softly round your hair,
Then dipped in the sweet valley of your breasts
And fluttered, like a bird between two nests,
Till it lay quiet there.
My eyes were closing and I may have dreamed—
At least it seemed
That you and I
Had ceased to be but were somehow
As earth and sky. . . .

The night grew closer still, and now
Heat-lightnings played between us, and warm thrills
Ran through the cool sides of the trembling hills.
Then darkness and a tension in the black
Hush like a breath held back;
A rippling through the ground, a windless breeze
That reached down to the sensitive roots of trees;
A tremor like the pulse of muffled knocks,
Or like the silent opening of locks.
There was a rising of unfettered seas
With great tides pulling at the stars and rocks
As though to draw them all together.
Then in a burst of blinding weather,
The lightnings flung
Long, passionate arms about the earth that clung
To her wild lover.
Suddenly above her
The whole sky tumbled in a sweeping blaze,
Gathering earth in one tight-locked embrace,
Drenching her in a flood of silver flame.

Hot thunders came;
And still the storm kept plunging, seeking ever
The furthest cranny, till the faraway
Streams felt each penetrating quiver
And the most hidden river
Rose and became released.

At last the stabbings ceased,
The thunders died.
But still they lay
Side by side,
While moonbeams crept
Into the heavenly corner where earth slept;
Dipping among her rosy hills, lighting above
Her curved and sloping hollows, till
She too was still.
Beloved and blest,
His cloudy head lay, seeking rest
In the sweet-smelling valley of her breast,
And each was huddled in each other's love—
Or so it seemed.
My eyes were closing and I may have dreamed.

Upon Washington Bridge

Wordsworth, thou should'st be living in this, our
Victory over reason, life, and laws;
Daily the air with strictly timed applause
Expands in rumors of increasing power.
Rhetoric blooms, the world's perennial flower;
Raising a road-hymn to the latest cause,
We feed on platitudes and build with straws
Something we dream may be an ivory tower.

It is a beauteous evening; calm and free
We wash our minds of thought. Serenely clear
The lights upon the Palisades appear
To say the time is seven fifty-three.
Once more at peace, we go back home and hear
The Voice of God on Station XYZ.

Words for a Jig

(To be danced on the grave of an enemy)

Thus I pay the visit
    Promised years ago.
Tell me, oh my friend, how is it
    There below?

Do these weeds and mullein
    Choke each angry mood,
Or increase your hard and sullen
    Torpitude?

You who sought distractions
    Howsoever base,
Have you learned to love inaction's
    Slower pace?

Here, at least, you've found that
    You belong to earth;
Dying on the careless ground that
    Gave you birth.

Do not let it fret you;
    Things are not so drear.
Though the heartless world forget you,
    I am here!

I have not forgotten
    How you loved the stir;
Black at heart and doubly rotten
    Though you are.

So I take my fiddle,
    And I roar a stave;
Dancing gaily on the middle
    Of your grave.

Such regard must cheer you
    In your misery,
Although I can scarcely hear you
    Thanking me.

But I ask no hands in
    Thanks or loud applause;
I am glad to sing and dance in
    Such a cause.

Thus I pay the visit
    Promised years ago.
Tell me, oh my friend, how is it
    There below?

RICHARD EBERHART

(1904–2005)

Consultant in Poetry (1959–1961)

Poems in a way are spells against death. They are milestones to see where you are now, to perpetuate your feelings, to establish them. If you have in any way touched the central heart of mankind's feelings, you'll survive.

"Looks as unlike Byron as one can get," one reporter quipped in response to Richard Eberhart's hardy, cheerful, can-do demeanor at the consultant's first press conference. By the time he arrived in Washington, Eberhart had seen more of the world and worked in more nonliterary professions than any of his contemporaries. Financial ruin and the tragic death of his mother darkened Eberhart's idyllic childhood in small-town Minnesota. He was an excellent student and a five-letter athlete reputed to have run the hundred-yard dash in ten seconds. The poet had just graduated from high school when his mother fell ill with lung cancer, and he stayed by her side during the course of her illness. He said the experience of watching her die, chronicled in his long poem "Orchard," made him a poet. His poems often turn upon the loss of childhood innocence, and they probe death with clear-eyed, almost scientific rigor, as illustrated in his best-known poem, "The Groundhog," where a speaker returns four times to the decaying animal's corpse, mapping the progression of decay and renewal.

Eberhart left Minnesota for Dartmouth, and his first poems appeared while he was an undergraduate in an anthology introduced by Robert Frost. After graduation he worked his way round the world on a tramp steamer. He stayed in Cambridge for two years of graduate work, where he completed his first book, a long philosophical and autobiographical poem, published simultaneously in England and America in 1930. He returned to the United States in the midst of the Great Depression and worked in a New York slaughterhouse, then as a tutor to the adopted children of the King of Siam. Tutoring led to his first full-time teaching job at the St. Mark's School, where he became a mentor to Robert Lowell.

World War II changed his course as a poet. Four years of steady work as a naval officer teaching aerial gunnery and the stability of a new marriage contributed to Eberhart's most prolific period of writing. He returned from armed service to work happily—while publishing voluminously—in his wife's family's company, the Butcher Polish

528

Company in Boston. The life of the businessman-poet suited him, and he remained on the company's board of directors after joining the ranks of tenured poet-professors, culminating in two decades of teaching at Dartmouth College. A visionary poet compared to William Blake and Hart Crane, Eberhart never departed completely from mundane, workaday concerns; childhood delights combine with the satisfaction of work done well; the life force, balanced by a clear-eyed sense of mortality.

21st Century Man

Finally, he decided there was too much pain,
The hurt of everything.
In youth it was not knowing,

In middle age it was knowing,
In age it was not knowing.
He couldn't figure it out.

Would 21st century man do better
Or 21st century woman do better either?
The tides were always going in or out,

But what was the meaning of the ocean?
People were either growing up or growing down.
He decided to live for sensual reality,

Pure feeling. After this failed
He decided to espouse pure intelligence.
This never told him why he had to die.

He then decided to go to the Church
But after the supreme fiction of Christ
He thought Buddha and Mohamet had something to say.

Neither sense, intellect, nor religion
Told him why he was born or had to die
So he began to pay attention to poetry.

Non-suicidal, he desired to make something.
He decided the greatest thing was a perfect poem.
If he could make it he would be glad to live.

The brutal fact, dear reader, as you
Might suspect, is that he did not make it.
Somebody else made his perfect poem imperfect.

The Groundhog

In June, amid the golden fields,
I saw a groundhog lying dead.
Dead lay he; my senses shook,
And mind outshot our naked frailty.
There lowly in the vigorous summer
His form began its senseless change,
And made my senses waver dim
Seeing nature ferocious in him.
Inspecting close his maggots' might
And seething cauldron of his being,
Half with loathing, half with a strange love,
I poked him with an angry stick.
The fever arose, became a flame
And Vigour circumscribed the skies,
Immense energy in the sun,
And through my frame a sunless trembling.
My stick had done nor good nor harm.
Then stood I silent in the day
Watching the object, as before;
And kept my reverence for knowledge
Trying for control, to be still,

To quell the passion of the blood;
Until I had bent down on my knees
Praying for joy in the sight of decay.
And so I left; and I returned
In Autumn strict of eye, to see
The sap gone out of the groundhog,
But the bony sodden hulk remained.
But the year had lost its meaning,
And in intellectual chains
I lost both love and loathing,
Mured up in the wall of wisdom.
Another summer took the fields again
Massive and burning, full of life,
But when I chanced upon the spot
There was only a little hair left,
And bones bleaching in the sunlight
Beautiful as architecture;
I watched them like a geometer,
And cut a walking stick from a birch.
It has been three years, now.
There is no sign of the groundhog.
I stood there in the whirling summer,
My hand capped a withered heart,
And thought of China and of Greece,
Of Alexander in his tent;
Of Montaigne in his tower,
Of Saint Theresa in her wild lament.

The Fury of Aerial Bombardment

You would think the fury of aerial bombardment
Would rouse God to relent; the infinite spaces
Are still silent. He looks on shock-pried faces.
History, even, does not know what is meant.

You would feel that after so many centuries
God would give man to repent; yet he can kill
As Cain could, but with multitudinous will,
No farther advanced than in his ancient furies.

Was man made stupid to see his own stupidity?
Is God by definition indifferent, beyond us all?
Is the eternal truth man's fighting soul
Wherein the Beast ravens in its own avidity?

Of Van Wettering I speak, and Averill,
Names on a list, whose faces I do not recall
But they are gone to early death, who late in school
Distinguished the belt feed lever from the belt holding pawl.

The Hard Structure of the World

Is made up of reservoirs,
Birds flying South, mailmen

Snow falling or rain falling,
Railmen, Howard Johnsons and airmen

Birds of Paradise
Silk lined caskets

Prize poems and guitars,
Beatitudes and bestiaries,

Children taught contemporary manners,
Time taking time away

With a haymaker or a sleigh,
Hope always belaboring despair.

Form is a jostle, a throstle,
Life a slice of sleight,

Indians are looking out from the
Cheekbones of Connecticut Yankees,

Poltergeists deploy northward
To tinderboxes in cupboards in Maine,

The last chock knocked, the vessel
Would not go down the Damariscotta

Until the sick captain's four-poster,
Moved to the window by four oldsters

Gave him a sight of her, and
He gave her a beautiful sign,

And there was the witch of Nobleboro
Who confounded the native farmers

Who, having lost the plow-bolt
Right at their feet, found it

Concealed in her apron: she laughed,
And made the earth fecund again.

The hard structure of the world,
The world structure of illusion.

From seeing too much of the world
We do not understand it.

The Swallows Return

For five years the swallows did not build
In the treehouse near the door facing the sea.
I felt their absence as furtive and wordless.
They were put out of mind because they had to be.

Then they came again, two males attending one female,
Skimming in the late afternoon gracefully, ardent
And free in quick glides and arcs, catching flies on the wing,
Feeding their young in the house safely pent.

It was mid-summer, the time of high July,
Their return as mysterious as their former leaving.
They presented the spectacle of orderly nature,
Their lives to some deep purpose cleaving?

At night there was clamor. When morning came
The ground under the house was littered with feathers.
None knows who was the predator, but death
Is available to birds as to man in all weathers.

As If You Had Never Been

When I see your picture in its frame,
A strait jacket, pity rises in me,
And stronger than pity, revulsion.
　　　It is as if you had never been.

Nobody in the world can know your love,
You are strapped to the nothingness of ages,
Nobody can will you into life,
　　　It is as if you had never been.

I cannot break your anonymity,
The absolute has imprisoned you,
Most sentient, most prescient, most near.
      It is as if you had never been.

Gnat on My Paper

He has two antennae,
They search back and forth,
Left and right, up and down.

He has four feet,
He is exploring what I write now.

This is a living being,
Is this a living poem?

His life is a quarter of an inch.
I could crack him any moment now.

Now I see he has two more feet,
Almost too delicate to examine.

He is still sitting on this paper,
An inch away from An.

Does he know who I am,
Does he know the importance of man?

He does not know or sense me,
His antennae are still sensing.

I wonder if he knows it is June,
The world in its sensual height?

How absurd to think
That he never thought of Plato.

He is satisfied to sit on this paper,
For some reason he has not flown away.

Small creature, gnat on my paper,
Too slight to be given a thought,

I salute you as the evanescent,
I play with you in my depth.

What, still here? Still evanescent?
You are my truth, that vanishes.

Now I put down this paper,
He has flown into the infinite.
He could not say it.

Man's Type

When he considered his linguistic fallacy
He was thrown back to the primitive subhuman,
In consternation at the rise of man,
English not lasting millennially.

Something attractive in that slight figure
In the Rift valley millions of years ago,
Slinging his weight, craft outwitting his prey.
The crudest action would be long to stay.

Deft we are still to maim and kill,
We have the big means, the lack of sensitivity,
The annihilating energy.
Of redeeming grace who shall say?

Long Term Suffering

There will be no examination in Long Term Suffering,
The course will come to an end as planned,
I have found that examinations are useless,
We have altogether too short a time to spend.

Time, ladies and gentlemen, is the great examiner.
I have discovered that this is true.
It is what you write as you go through the course
Is the only determinant and determinator of you.

Long Term Suffering is for those of all ages
In our tussling University, our bulging classroom.
It may be that I will profess near madness,
It may be that you will write out your doom.

All that you will have at the end of the course
Is writings you indite, or poems you make,
If you make them. Words, words in a sea flow;
At any rate, a lot of heartbreak.

Save your papers. It may be that years later,
Forty, maybe, you would like to look back
At your course in Long Term Suffering,
And note how strangely you had to act.

You Think They Are Permanent but They Pass

You think they are permanent but they pass
And only contemplation serves to save their memory.
You are in the Pan-World building with the leaders.
They all seem real, they all seem permanent

But soon you are in the Pan-World building with the past.
How closely and with what immediacy
You scrutinize the features of each noted face,
President, old poet, Supreme Court chief justice,

Secretary to the United Nations,
How lively their speech, lively their looks,
As all together in one banquet place
You would think there would be no end to this.

Who in the reality of his high days
Thinks of the destitutions of the night?
You think they are permanent but they pass
To feed ravens of the ravenous past.

Coast of Maine

The flags are up again along the coast,
Gulls drop clams from a height onto the rocks,
The seas tend to be calm in July,
A swallow nests under our areaway,
It is high summer, the greatest days of the year,
Heat burgeoning the flowers, stones heating the tides,

This is peace, the indifference of nature, another year
Seeming the same as the year before,
The static ability of the world to endure.

There is Eagle Island twelve miles down the bay,
A mole has just dared to march over our garden,
The far islands seem changeless through decades.

Yet, think of the drama! Here am I,
One year older into inevitability,
The country torn in honor's toss-out,
What does nature care about the nature of man?
Three hundred years ago along this coast
The Europeans came to confront the Indians,

Yet the Ice Age shaped these shores millions
Of years ago, unimaginable upon our senses,
What do I say to the beneficent sun
Descending over the pine trees, the sun of our planet?
What does it care for the nature of man,
Its virile essence unassimilable?

Here come the hummingbirds, messengers
Of fragility, instantaneous as imagination,
How could they be so iridescent-evanescent,
Quick-darters, lovers of color, drinkers of nectar?
Do they remind us of a more spirited world
When everything was lithe, and quick, and visionary?

ROBERT FROST

(1874–1963)

Consultant in Poetry (1958–1959)

This year I have quarreled with the title of my position, "Consultant in Poetry." As I have said before, I think it should be Poetry Consultant and this would mean consultant in everything—poetry, politics, religion, and the arts. The Poetry Consultant should certainly not be concerned only with poetry, for then he would become just like a reader of theme papers. He should not take up his time with poems sent in for him to read. These should be treated slightly, because you cannot correct people into poets. . . . Poetry can become too special, isolated and separate a thing. The connection should be closer between Government and the arts.

When Robert Frost began work as the poetry consultant at the age of eighty-four, he was a national hero. He was determined to expand the job's responsibilities and influence far beyond anything the Library of Congress had dreamed. Within months the Library created a new post for Frost, a special three-year term as "Honorary Consultant in the Humanities." Less than a year later he would make headlines around the nation by declaring at a packed press conference "Somebody said to me that New England's in decay . . . but I said the next President is going to be from Boston." When pressed for a name, Frost replied, "Can't you figure it out? It's a Puritan named Kennedy." Kennedy asked Frost to read his famous poem "The Gift Outright," with a slightly altered last line, at his inauguration ceremony.

A poet of traditional forms who poked fun at literary trends and experimentation—he liked to say that he would as soon play tennis without a net as write free verse—Frost is anything but the quaintly regional or even a primarily pastoral New England bard he is so often reputed to be. His brutally frank and often dark meditations on universal themes use the vocabulary and inflections of everyday spoken language to create portraits of psychological complexity and depth. He lived and taught for many years in Massachusetts and Vermont, and died on January 29, 1963, in Boston, but he also spent significant portions of his life elsewhere. He was born in San Francisco and lived in California until he was eleven. When he was thirty-eight, he moved his family to England, where he lived for three years and published his first two volumes of poetry. In 1924 he received a Pulitzer Prize in poetry for *New Hampshire* (1923), a prize he would win three more times, for *Collected Poems* (1930), *A Further Range* (1936), and *A Witness Tree* (1942).

Frost famously described poetry as "a momentary stay against confusion," which, when read carefully, is not the optimistic statement it first seems to be. The stay is "momentary"; the "confusion," overriding and constant. For most of his life, Frost was regarded as the Grandma Moses of American poetry—as the cheerful voice of rural America and its simple-but-good people. At Frost's eighty-fifth birthday party, the young critic Lionel Trilling shocked a full house by saying, "I have to say that my Frost . . . is not the Frost who reassures us by his affirmations of old virtues, simplicities, pieties, and ways of feeling: anything but . . . I think of Robert Frost as a terrifying poet. . . . Read the poem 'Design' and see if you sleep the better for it." Frost welcomed Trilling's assessment: "You made my birthday party a surprise party. I should like nothing better than to do a thing like that myself—to depart from the Rotarian norm in a Rotarian situation. You weren't there to sing 'Happy Birthday, dear Robert,' and I don't mind being made controversial. No sweeter music can come to my ears than the clash of arms over my dead body when I am down."

The Gift Outright

The land was ours before we were the land's.
She was our land more than a hundred years
Before we were her people. She was ours
In Massachusetts, in Virginia,
But we were England's, still colonials,
Possessing what we still were unpossessed by,
Possessed by what we now no more possessed.
Something we were withholding made us weak
Until we found out that it was ourselves
We were withholding from our land of living,
And forthwith found salvation in surrender.
Such as we were we gave ourselves outright
(The deed of gift was many deeds of war)
To the land vaguely realizing westward,
But still unstoried, artless, unenhanced,
Such as she was, such as she would become.

The Pasture

I'm going out to clean the pasture spring;
I'll only stop to rake the leaves away
(And wait to watch the water clear, I may):
I shan't be gone long.—You come too.

I'm going out to fetch the little calf
That's standing by the mother. It's so young
It totters when she licks it with her tongue.
I shan't be gone long.—You come too.

Mending Wall

Something there is that doesn't love a wall,
That sends the frozen-ground-swell under it
And spills the upper boulders in the sun,
And makes gaps even two can pass abreast.
The work of hunters is another thing:
I have come after them and made repair
Where they have left not one stone on a stone,
But they would have the rabbit out of hiding,
To please the yelping dogs. The gaps I mean,
No one has seen them made or heard them made,
But at spring mending-time we find them there.
I let my neighbor know beyond the hill;
And on a day we meet to walk the line
And set the wall between us once again.
We keep the wall between us as we go.
To each the boulders that have fallen to each.
And some are loaves and some so nearly balls
We have to use a spell to make them balance:
"Stay where you are until our backs are turned!"
We wear our fingers rough with handling them.
Oh, just another kind of outdoor game,
One on a side. It comes to little more:
There where it is we do not need the wall:
He is all pine and I am apple orchard.
My apple trees will never get across
And eat the cones under his pines, I tell him.

He only says, "Good fences make good neighbors."
Spring is the mischief in me, and I wonder
If I could put a notion in his head:
"*Why* do they make good neighbors? Isn't it
Where there are cows? But here there are no cows.
Before I built a wall I'd ask to know
What I was walling in or walling out,
And to whom I was like to give offense.
Something there is that doesn't love a wall,
That wants it down." I could say "Elves" to him,
But it's not elves exactly, and I'd rather
He said it for himself. I see him there,
Bringing a stone grasped firmly by the top
In each hand, like an old-stone savage armed.
He moves in darkness as it seems to me,
Not of woods only and the shade of trees.
He will not go behind his father's saying,
And he likes having thought of it so well
He says again, "Good fences make good neighbors."

The Road Not Taken

Two roads diverged in a yellow wood,
And sorry I could not travel both
And be one traveler, long I stood
And looked down one as far as I could
To where it bent in the undergrowth;

Then took the other, as just as fair,
And having perhaps the better claim,
Because it was grassy and wanted wear;
Though as for that, the passing there
Had worn them really about the same,

And both that morning equally lay
In leaves no step had trodden black.
Oh, I kept the first for another day!
Yet knowing how way leads on to way,
I doubted if I should ever come back.

I shall be telling this with a sigh
Somewhere ages and ages hence:
Two roads diverged in a wood, and I—
I took the one less traveled by,
And that has made all the difference.

The Oven Bird

There is a singer everyone has heard,
Loud, a mid-summer and a mid-wood bird,
Who makes the solid tree trunks sound again.
He says that leaves are old and that for flowers
Mid-summer is to spring as one to ten.
He says the early petal-fall is past,
When pear and cherry bloom went down in showers.
On sunny days a moment overcast;
And comes that other fall we name the fall.
He says the highway dust is over all.
The bird would cease and be as other birds
But that he knows in singing not to sing.
The question that he frames in all but words
Is what to make of a diminished thing.

Birches

When I see birches bend to left and right
Across the lines of straighter darker trees,
I like to think some boy's been swinging them.
But swinging doesn't bend them down to stay
As ice storms do. Often you must have seen them
Loaded with ice a sunny winter morning
After a rain. They click upon themselves
As the breeze rises, and turn many-colored
As the stir cracks and crazes their enamel.
Soon the sun's warmth makes them shed crystal shells
Shattering and avalanching on the snow crust—
Such heaps of broken glass to sweep away
You'd think the inner dome of heaven had fallen.
They are dragged to the withered bracken by the load,
And they seem not to break; though once they are bowed
So low for long, they never right themselves:
You may see their trunks arching in the woods
Years afterwards, trailing their leaves on the ground
Like girls on hands and knees that throw their hair
Before them over their heads to dry in the sun.
But I was going to say when Truth broke in
With all her matter of fact about the ice storm,
I should prefer to have some boy bend them
As he went out and in to fetch the cows—
Some boy too far from town to learn baseball,
Whose only play was what he found himself,
Summer or winter, and could play alone.
One by one he subdued his father's trees
By riding them down over and over again
Until he took the stiffness out of them,
And not one but hung limp, not one was left
For him to conquer. He learned all there was
To learn about not launching out too soon

And so not carrying the tree away
Clear to the ground. He always kept his poise
To the top branches, climbing carefully
With the same pains you use to fill a cup
Up to the brim, and even above the brim.
Then he flung outward, feet first, with a swish,
Kicking his way down through the air to the ground.
So was I once myself a swinger of birches.
And so I dream of going back to be.
It's when I'm weary of considerations,
And life is too much like a pathless wood
Where your face burns and tickles with the cobwebs
Broken across it, and one eye is weeping
From a twig's having lashed across it open.
I'd like to get away from earth awhile
And then come back to it and begin over.
May no fate willfully misunderstand me
And half grant what I wish and snatch me away
Not to return. Earth's the right place for love:
I don't know where it's likely to go better.
I'd like to go by climbing a birch tree,
And climb black branches up a snow-white trunk
Toward heaven, till the tree could bear no more,
But dipped its top and set me down again.
That would be good both going and coming back.
One could do worse than be a swinger of birches.

Fire and Ice

Some say the world will end in fire,
Some say in ice.
From what I've tasted of desire
I hold with those who favor fire.

But if it had to perish twice,
I think I know enough of hate
To say that for destruction ice
Is also great
And would suffice.

Dust of Snow

The way a crow
Shook down on me
The dust of snow
From a hemlock tree

Has given my heart
A change of mood
And saved some part
Of a day I had rued.

Nothing Gold Can Stay

Nature's first green is gold,
Her hardest hue to hold.
Her early leaf's a flower;
But only so an hour.
Then leaf subsides to leaf.
So Eden sank to grief,
So dawn goes down to day.
Nothing gold can stay.

Stopping by Woods on a Snowy Evening

Whose woods these are I think I know.
His house is in the village, though;
He will not see me stopping here
To watch his woods fill up with snow.

My little horse must think it queer
To stop without a farmhouse near
Between the woods and frozen lake
The darkest evening of the year.

He gives his harness bells a shake
To ask if there is some mistake.
The only other sound's the sweep
Of easy wind and downy flake.

The woods are lovely, dark, and deep,
But I have promises to keep,
And miles to go before I sleep,
And miles to go before I sleep.

Design

I found a dimpled spider, fat and white,
On a white heal-all, holding up a moth
Like a white piece of rigid satin cloth—
Assorted characters of death and blight
Mixed ready to begin the morning right,
Like the ingredients of a witches' broth—
A snow-drop spider, a flower like a froth,
And dead wings carried like a paper kite.

What had that flower to do with being white,
The wayside blue and innocent heal-all?
What brought the kindred spider to that height,
Then steered the white moth thither in the night?
What but design of darkness to appall?—
If design govern in a thing so small.

The Silken Tent

She is as in a field a silken tent
At midday when a sunny summer breeze
Has dried the dew and all its ropes relent,
So that in guys it gently sways at ease,
And its supporting central cedar pole,
That is its pinnacle to heavenward
And signifies the sureness of the soul,
Seems to owe naught to any single cord,
But strictly held by none, is loosely bound
By countless silken ties of love and thought
To everything on earth the compass round,
And only by one's going slightly taut
In the capriciousness of summer air
Is of the slightest bondage made aware.

Never Again Would Birds' Song Be the Same

He would declare and could himself believe
That the birds there in all the garden round
From having heard the daylong voice of Eve
Had added to their own an oversound,

Her tone of meaning but without the words.
Admittedly an eloquence so soft
Could only have had an influence on birds
When call or laughter carried it aloft.
Be that as may be, she was in their song.
Moreover her voice upon their voices crossed
Had now persisted in the woods so long
That probably it never would be lost.
Never again would birds' song be the same.
And to do that to birds was why she came.

RANDALL JARRELL

(1914–1965)

Consultant in Poetry (1956–1958)

If there were only some mechanism (like Seurat's proposed system of paint-ing, or the projected Universal Algebra that Gödel believes Leibnitz to have perfected and mislaid) for reasonably and systematically converting into poetry what we see and feel and are! When one reads the verse of people who cannot write poems—people who sometimes have more intelligence, sensibility, and moral discrimination than most of the poets—it is hard not to regard the Muse as a sort of fairy godmother who says to the poet, after her colleagues have showered on him the most disconcerting and ambiguous gifts, "Well, never mind. You're still the only one that can write poetry."

Randall Jarrell took up the consultancy in the wake of William Carlos Williams's appointment, which was derailed by spurious Communist allegations. Jarrell committed to stay for a two-year appointment, and to do his best to get the office back on its feet. His opening lecture humorously decried the current rift he saw between the common reader and the poet: "The public has an unusual relationship to the poet: it doesn't even know that he is there." He went on to urge his audience to read a poet's work "with a certain willingness and interest; read him imaginatively and perceptively," and to eschew the intervention of critics: "Art is long, and critics are the insects of the day."

Interesting reading advice from the man who holds the mantle of most well-regarded critic of the twentieth century. But Jarrell had a particular kind of academic in mind, those who rely on other critics, who "have spent their life in card-indexes, or if they have not, no one can tell." One of the earliest accounts of Jarrell is from his teacher Robert Penn Warren, who let Jarrell, then an underclassman, into his advanced literature survey course because he had already read everything on the syllabus. Warren helped Jarrell transfer to Kenyon College, where he joined a group of young intellectuals that included three future consultant/laureates: Warren (who now taught there), Allen Tate (also a professor), and Robert Lowell (a student). Lowell, as Mary Jarrell remembers in her memoir about her husband, wrote to his prep school teacher Richard Eberhart about Jarrell's upsetting brilliance, saying he knew everything. Jarrell saw early promise in his fellow student's poetry and began a lifelong campaign to have Lowell recognized as one of the leading poets of his generation.

Jarrell found his voice as a poet during the Second World War, which left a dark psychological imprint on his imagination. Jarrell, too old to fly planes in combat, served as a pilot instructor. The war poems shaped his second and third volumes of poems, *Little Friend, Little Friend* (1945) and *Losses* (1948), which concentrate on the indifferent mechanisms of war and the fragile lives of the men caught up in service. After the war, Jarrell taught at Sarah Lawrence College, served as an editor at *The Nation*, and began to make a name for himself as America's most trusted—and feared—literary critic. As Lowell said, he "had a deadly hand for killing what he despised." But Jarrell was enthralling about the poets he loved and instrumental in establishing Robert Lowell, Elizabeth Bishop, and William Carlos Williams as the most significant American poets since Robert Frost, Marianne Moore, and Wallace Stevens. He was torn between his roles as poet and critic, and legend has it that he used to call to his second wife, Mary Jarrell, for help, shouting, "A wicked fairy has turned me into a prose writer!"

Jarrell accepted the post at the Library in September 1956 and held it for two years during which he wrote only four poems and translated a number of poems by Rilke and Goethe into English. One of the poems written during his tenure, "The Woman at the Washington Zoo," would become his most famous poem and the title of the volume that won the 1961 National Book Award. In a marvelous letter to Elizabeth Bishop just after he completed the zoo poem, he describes going to the zoo to see the animals and feeling a bit like a caged poet himself in his various roles as poetry consultant: "We've been going to the zoo here a lot and taking pieces of kidney to the lynx and two wolves; they come right up to the edge of the cage and almost eat from your hand. They're so beautiful, and look at you with such life and intensity; the wolves are tremendous white ones." And then, in a juxtaposition that Bishop, just six years clear of the job herself, surely appreciated, the next paragraph starts: "I've had to do lots of newspaper and radio things and, worst, a television program; they came to the house and took seven hours to make six or seven minutes of film—they had an incredibly arduous complicated technical procedure and not the tiniest bit of imaginative or dramatic knowledge; as they tried to make up an interview they were like children trying to improvise a play. And all this was supposed to produce five natural, unrehearsed, spontaneous minutes."

1945: The Death of the Gods

In peace tomorrow, when your slack hands weigh
Upon the causes; when the ores are rust
And the oil laked under the mandates
Has puffed from the turbines; when the ash of life
Is earth that has forgotten the first human sun
Your wisdom found: O bringers of the fire,
When you have shipped our bones home from the bases
To those who think of us, not as we were
(Defiled, annihilated—the forgotten vessels
Of the wrath that formed us; of the murderous
Dull will that worked out its commandment, death
For the disobedient and for us, obedient)—
When you have seen grief wither, death forgotten,
And dread and love, the witnesses of men,
Swallowed up in victory: you who determine
Men's last obedience, yourselves determined
In the first unjudged obedience of greed
And senseless power: you eternal States
Beneath whose shadows men have found the stars
And graves of men: O warring Deities,
Tomorrow when the rockets rise like stars
And earth is blazing with a thousand suns
That set up there within your realms a realm
Whose laws are ecumenical, whose life
Exacts from men a prior obedience—
Must you learn from your makers how to die?

A Girl in a Library

An object among dreams, you sit here with your shoes off
And curl your legs up under you; your eyes
Close for a moment, your face moves toward sleep . . .
You are very human.
                            But my mind, gone out in tenderness,
Shrinks from its object with a thoughtful sigh.
This is a waist the spirit breaks its arm on.
The gods themselves, against you, struggle in vain.
This broad low strong-boned brow; these heavy eyes;
These calves, grown muscular with certainties;
This nose, three medium-sized pink strawberries
—But I exaggerate. In a little you will leave:
I'll hear, half squeal, half shriek, your laugh of greeting—
Then, *decrescendo,* bars of that strange speech
In which each sound sets out to seek each other,
Murders its own father, marries its own mother,
And ends as one grand transcendental vowel.

(Yet for all I know, the Egyptian Helen spoke so.)
As I look, the world contracts around you:
I see Brünnhilde had brown braids and glasses
She used for studying; Salome straight brown bangs,
A calf's brown eyes, and sturdy light-brown limbs
Dusted with cinnamon, an apple-dumpling's . . .
Many a beast has gnawn a leg off and got free,
Many a dolphin curved up from Necessity—
The trap has closed about you, and you sleep.
If someone questioned you, *What doest thou here?*
You'd knit your brows like an orangoutang
(But not so sadly; not so thoughtfully)
And answer with a pure heart, guilelessly:
I'm studying. . . .

If only you were not!
Assignments,
       recipes,
            the *Official Rulebook*
Of Basketball—ah, let them go; you needn't mind.
The soul has no assignments, neither cooks
Nor referees: it wastes its time.
                    It wastes its time.
Here in this enclave there are centuries
For you to waste: the short and narrow stream
Of Life meanders into a thousand valleys
Of all that was, or might have been, or is to be.
The books, just leafed through, whisper endlessly . . .
Yet it is hard. One sees in your blurred eyes
The "uneasy half-soul" Kipling saw in dogs'.
One sees it, in the glass, in one's own eyes.
In rooms alone, in galleries, in libraries,
In tears, in searchings of the heart, in staggering joys
We memorize once more our old creation,
Humanity: with what yawns the unwilling
Flesh puts on its spirit, O my sister!

So many dreams! And not one troubles
Your sleep of life? no self stares shadowily
From these worn hexahedrons, beckoning
With false smiles, tears? . . .
                    Meanwhile Tatyana
Larina (gray eyes nickel with the moonlight
That falls through the willows onto Lensky's tomb;
Now young and shy, now old and cold and sure)
Asks, smiling: "But what is she dreaming of, fat thing?"
I answer: She's not fat. She isn't dreaming.
She purrs or laps or runs, all in her sleep;
Believes, awake, that she is beautiful;

She never dreams.
                    Those sunrise-colored clouds
Around man's head—that inconceivable enchantment
From which, at sunset, we come back to life
To find our graves dug, families dead, selves dying:
Of all this, Tanya, she is innocent.
For nineteen years she's faced reality:
They look alike already.
                    They say, man wouldn't be
The best thing in this world—and isn't he?—
If he were not too good for it. But she
—She's good enough for it.
                    And yet sometimes
Her sturdy form, in its pink strapless formal,
Is as if bathed in moonlight—modulated
Into a form of joy, a Lydian mode;
This Wooden Mean's a kind, furred animal
That speaks, in the Wild of things, delighting riddles
To the soul that listens, trusting . . .
                    Poor senseless Life:
When, in the last light sleep of dawn, the messenger
Comes with his message, you will not awake.
He'll give his feathery whistle, shake you hard,
You'll look with wide eyes at the dewy yard
And dream, with calm slow factuality:
"Today's Commencement. My bachelor's degree
In Home Ec., my doctorate of philosophy
In Phys. Ed.
            [Tanya, they won't even *scan*]
Are waiting for me. . . ."
                    Oh, Tatyana,
The Angel comes: better to squawk like a chicken
Than to say with truth, "But I'm a *good* girl,"
And Meet his Challenge with a last firm strange

Uncomprehending smile; and—then, then!—see
The blind date that has stood you up: your life.
(For all this, if it isn't, perhaps, life,
Has yet, at least, a language of its own
Different from the books'; worse than the books'.)
And yet, the ways we miss our lives are life.
Yet . . . yet . . .

        to have one's life add up to *yet!*

You sigh a shuddering sigh. Tatyana murmurs,
"Don't cry, little peasant"; leaves us with a swift
"Good-bye, good-bye . . . Ah, don't think ill of me . . ."
Your eyes open: you sit here thoughtlessly.

I love you—and yet—and yet—I love you.

Don't cry, little peasant. Sit and dream.
One comes, a finger's width beneath your skin,
To the braided maidens singing as they spin;
There sound the shepherd's pipe, the watchman's rattle
Across the short dark distance of the years.
I am a thought of yours: and yet, you do not think . . .
The firelight of a long, blind, dreaming story
Lingers upon your lips; and I have seen
Firm, fixed forever in your closing eyes,
The Corn King beckoning to his Spring Queen.

Children Selecting Books in a Library

With beasts and gods, above, the wall is bright.
The child's head, bent to the book-colored shelves,
Is slow and sidelong and food-gathering,
Moving in blind grace . . . Yet from the mural, Care,
The grey-eyed one, fishing the morning mist,
Seizes the baby hero by the hair

And whispers, in the tongue of gods and children,
Words of a doom as ecumenical as dawn
But blanched, like dawn, with dew. The children's cries
Are to men the cries of crickets, dense with warmth
—But dip a finger into Fafnir, taste it,
And all their words are plain as chance and pain.

Their tales are full of sorcerers and ogres
Because their lives are: the capricious infinite
That, like parents, no one has yet escaped
Except by luck or magic; and since strength
And wit are useless, be kind or stupid, wait
Some power's gratitude, the tide of things.

Read meanwhile . . . hunt among the shelves, as dogs do, grasses,
And find one cure for Everychild's diseases
Beginning: *Once upon a time there was*
A wolf that fed, a mouse that warned, a bear that rode
A boy. Us men, alas! wolves, mice, bears bore.
And yet wolves, mice, bears, children, gods and men

In slow perambulation up and down the shelves
Of the universe are seeking . . . who knows except themselves?
What some escape to, some escape: if we find Swann's
Way better than our own, and trudge on at the back
Of the north wind to—to—somewhere east
Of the sun, west of the moon, it is because we live

By trading another's sorrow for our own; another's
Impossibilities, still unbelieved in, for our own . . .
"I am myself still"? For a little while, forget:
The world's selves cure that short disease, myself,
And we see bending to us, dewy-eyed, the great
CHANGE, dear to all things not to themselves endeared.

The Snow-Leopard

His pads furring the scarp's rime,
Weightless in greys and ecru, gliding
Invisibly, incuriously
As the crystals of the cirri wandering
A mile below his absent eyes,
The leopard gazes at the caravan.
The yaks groaning with tea, the burlaps
Lapping and lapping each stunned universe
That gasps like a kettle for its thinning life
Are pools in the interminable abyss
That ranges up through ice, through air, to night.
Raiders of the unminding element,
The last cold capillaries of their kind,
They move so slowly they are motionless
To any eye less stubborn than a man's. . . .
From the implacable jumble of the blocks
The grains dance icily, a scouring plume,
Into the breath, sustaining, unsustainable,
They trade to that last stillness for their death.
They sense with misunderstanding horror, with desire,
Behind the world their blood sets up in mist
The brute and geometrical necessity:
The leopard waving with a grating purr

His six-foot tail; the leopard, who looks sleepily—
Cold, fugitive, secure—at all that he knows,
At all that he is: the heart of heartlessness.

Eighth Air Force

If, in an odd angle of the hutment,
A puppy laps the water from a can
Of flowers, and the drunk sergeant shaving
Whistles *O Paradiso!*—shall I say that man
Is not as men have said: a wolf to man?

The other murderers troop in yawning;
Three of them play Pitch, one sleeps, and one
Lies counting missions, lies there sweating
Till even his heart beats: One; One; One.
O murderers! . . . Still, this is how it's done:

This is a war. . . . But since these play, before they die,
Like puppies with their puppy; since, a man,
I did as these have done, but did not die—
I will content the people as I can
And give up these to them: Behold the man!

I have suffered, in a dream, because of him,
Many things; for this last saviour, man,
I have lied as I lie now. But what is lying?
Men wash their hands, in blood, as best they can:
I find no fault in this just man.

A Pilot from the Carrier

Strapped at the center of the blazing wheel,
His flesh ice-white against the shattered mask,
He tears at the easy clasp, his sobbing breaths
Misting the fresh blood lightening to flame,
Darkening to smoke; trapped there in pain
And fire and breathlessness, he struggles free
Into the sunlight of the upper sky—
And falls, a quiet bundle in the sky,
The miles to warmth, to air, to waking:
To the great flowering of his life, the hemisphere
That holds his dangling years. In its long slow sway
The world steadies and is almost still. . . .
He is alone; and hangs in knowledge
Slight, separate, estranged: a lonely eye
Reading a child's first scrawl, the carrier's wake—
The travelling milk-like circle of a miss
Beside the plant-like genius of the smoke
That shades, on the little deck, the little blaze
Toy-like as the glitter of the wing-guns,
Shining as the fragile sun-marked plane
That grows to him, rubbed silver tipped with flame.

The Sick Nought

Do the wife and baby travelling to see
Your grey pajamas and sick worried face
Remind you of something, soldier? I remember
You convalescing washing plates, or mopping
The endless corridors your shoes had scuffed;
And in the crowded room you rubbed your cheek
Against your wife's thin elbow like a pony.

But you are something there are millions of.
How can I care about you much, or pick you out
From all the others other people loved
And sent away to die for them? You are a ticket
Someone bought and lost on, a stray animal:
You have lost even the right to be condemned.
I see you looking helplessly around, in histories,
Bewildered with your terrible companions, Pain
And Death and Empire: what have you understood, to die?
Were you worth, soldiers, all that people said
To be spent so willingly? Surely your one theory, to live,
Is nonsense to the practice of the centuries.
What is demanded in the trade of states
But lives, your lives?—the one commodity.

The Truth

When I was four my father went to Scotland.
They *said* he went to Scotland.

When I woke up I think I thought that I was dreaming—
I was so little then that I thought dreams
Are in the room with you, like the cinema.
That's why you don't dream when it's still light—
They pull the shades down when it is, so you can sleep.
I thought that then, but that's not right.
Really it's in your head.

And it was light then—light at *night*.
I heard Stalky bark outside.
But really it was Mother crying—
She coughed so hard she cried.
She kept shaking Sister,

She shook her and shook her.
I thought Sister had had her nightmare.
But he wasn't barking, he had died.
There was dirt all over Sister.
It was all streaks, like mud. I cried.
She didn't, but she was older.

                        I thought she didn't
Because she was older, I thought Stalky had just gone.
I got *everything* wrong.
I didn't get one single thing right.
It seems to me that I'd have thought
It didn't happen, like a dream,
Except that it was light. At night.

They burnt our house down, they burnt down London.
Next day my mother cried all day, and after that
She said to me when she would come to see me:
"Your father has gone away to Scotland.
He will be back after the war."

The war then was different from the war now.
The war now is *nothing*.

I used to live in London till they burnt it.
What was it like? It was just like here.
No, that's the truth.
My mother would come here, some, but she would cry.
She said to Miss Elise, "He's not himself";
She said, "Don't you love me any more at all?"
I was *my*self.
Finally she wouldn't come at all.
She never said one thing my father said, or Sister.
Sometimes she did,
Sometimes she was the same, but that was when I dreamed it.
I could tell I was dreaming, she was just the same.

That Christmas she bought me a toy dog.

I asked her what was its name, and when she didn't know
I asked her over, and when she didn't know
I said, "You're not my mother, you're not my mother.
She *hasn't* gone to Scotland, she is dead!"
And she said, "Yes, he's dead, he's dead!"
And cried and cried; she *was* my mother,
She put her arms around me and we cried.

Well Water

What a girl called "the dailiness of life"
(Adding an errand to your errand. Saying,
"Since you're up . . ." Making you a means to
A means to a means to) is well water
Pumped from an old well at the bottom of the world.
The pump you pump the water from is rusty
And hard to move and absurd, a squirrel-wheel
A sick squirrel turns slowly, through the sunny
Inexorable hours. And yet sometimes
The wheel turns of its own weight, the rusty
Pump pumps over your sweating face the clear
Water, cold, so cold! you cup your hands
And gulp from them the dailiness of life.

The Refugees

In the shabby train no seat is vacant.
        The child in the ripped mask
        Sprawls undisturbed in the waste

Of the smashed compartment. Is their calm extravagant?
They had faces and lives like you. What was it they possessed,
That they were willing to trade for this?

The dried blood sparkles along the mask
Of the child who yesterday possessed
A country welcomer than this.
Did he? All night into the waste
The train moves silently. The faces are vacant.
Have none of them found the cost extravagant?

How could they? They gave what they possessed.
Here all the purses are vacant.
And what else could satisfy the extravagant
Tears and wish of the child but this?
Impose its cancelling terrible mask
On the days and faces and lives they waste?

What else are their lives but a journey to the vacant
Satisfaction of death? And the mask
They wear tonight through their waste
Is death's rehearsal. Is it really extravagant
To read in their faces: What is there that we possessed
That we were unwilling to trade for this?

The Woman at the Washington Zoo

The saris go by me from the embassies.

Cloth from the moon. Cloth from another planet.
They look back at the leopard like the leopard.

And I. . . .

    this print of mine, that has kept its color
Alive through so many cleanings; this dull null
Navy I wear to work, and wear from work, and so
To my bed, so to my grave, with no
Complaints, no comment: neither from my chief,
The Deputy Chief Assistant, nor his chief—
Only I complain. . . . this serviceable
Body that no sunlight dyes, no hand suffuses
But, dome-shadowed, withering among columns,
Wavy beneath fountains—small, far-off, shining
In the eyes of animals, these beings trapped
As I am trapped but not, themselves, the trap,
Aging, but without knowledge of their age,
Kept safe here, knowing not of death, for death—
Oh, bars of my own body, open, open!

The world goes by my cage and never sees me.
And there come not to me, as come to these,
The wild beasts, sparrows pecking the llamas' grain,
Pigeons settling on the bears' bread, buzzards
Tearing the meat the flies have clouded. . . .

      Vulture,
When you come for the white rat that the foxes left,
Take off the red helmet of your head, the black
Wings that have shadowed me, and step to me as man:
The wild brother at whose feet the white wolves fawn,
To whose hand of power the great lioness
Stalks, purring. . . .

    You know what I was,
You see what I am: change me, change me!

WILLIAM CARLOS WILLIAMS

(1883–1963)

Consultant in Poetry (offered, but never served, 1952)

I have been outspoken all my life, but honestly outspoken. I try to say it straight, whatever is to be said.

William Carlos Williams was appointed consultant in poetry but never served. His relationship with the Library of Congress was vexed from the time he was first offered the consultancy in 1948, after he had the first in a series of strokes that would mar the last fifteen years of his life. In the early summer of 1952 he was again tapped and this time accepted; a month later he had a second, more severe stroke, leaving him unable to speak for several weeks. The Library encouraged him to rest at home and come to Washington three months into his term. A week after the press release announcing his appointment went out, an anticommunist newsletter circulated a list of accusations against Williams, ushering in one of the most senseless and damaging chapters in McCarthy-era history. As a result, Williams, one of our nation's greatest literary innovators and a poet-pediatrician who had delivered over two thousand children, was bullied and distracted from writing just after a period of grave illness. The toll on his health and creativity was devastating.

In response to the allegations against Williams, the Library of Congress initiated its own investigation and found that only one minor charge stood. The Librarian at the time, Luther H. Evans, responded cagily to Williams's accusers, saying his staff had not yet questioned Williams because he was seriously ill. Soon senators and congressmen joined the fray, lambasting the Library as "an employment service for indigent Left-wingers." By the time Williams and his wife were notified, the FBI had begun an investigation. Williams retained a lawyer and fought back, stating he would in no way waive "his right to assume his position . . . nor his right to any salary or other payment due him." The Librarian then canceled his appointment, citing Williams's poor health rather than the Communist allegations. Writers and publishers rallied to Williams's defense, and charges were dropped. The Librarian then reoffered Williams his post in April for the remaining six weeks of his term, and Williams accepted, thinking he would stay on for the following year. However, a new chief Librarian was appointed during this time,

L. Quincy Mumford, who failed to extend the appointment (or to appoint another poet) for the 1953–54 term. About the only thing Williams did in Washington was to pose in the Library's poetry office for the photograph included in this book.

A steadfast practitioner of a plain, deceptively simple American style, Williams wrote poetry that reflected his daily life as a doctor, writer, husband, and resident of Paterson, New Jersey. Toward the end of his career he shifted from the minimalism he is best known for to a longer, more rhythmically complex verse form he devised called the "variable foot," breaking up long lines into three "steps" that resemble the ambling pace of thoughtful walking.

Danse Russe

If I when my wife is sleeping
and the baby and Kathleen
are sleeping
and the sun is a flame-white disc
in silken mists
above shining trees,—
if I in my north room
dance naked, grotesquely
before my mirror
waving my shirt round my head
and singing softly to myself:
"I am lonely, lonely.
I was born to be lonely,
I am best so!"
If I admire my arms, my face,
my shoulders, flanks, buttocks
against the yellow drawn shades,—

Who shall say I am not
the happy genius of my household?

The Red Wheelbarrow

so much depends
upon

a red wheel
barrow

glazed with rain
water

beside the white
chickens

It Is a Living Coral

a trouble

archaically fettered
to produce

E Pluribus Unum an
island

in the sea a Capitol
surmounted

by Armed Liberty—
painting

sculpture straddled by
a dome

eight million pounds
in weight

iron plates constructed
to expand

and contract with
variations

of temperature
the folding

and unfolding of a lily.
And Congress

authorized and the
Commission

was entrusted was
entrusted!

a sculptured group
Mars

in Roman mail placing
a wreath

of laurel on the brow
of Washington

Commerce Minerva
Thomas

Jefferson John Hancock
at

the table Mrs. Motte
presenting

Indian burning arrows
to Generals

Marion and Lee to fire
her mansion

and dislodge the British—
this scaleless

jumble is superb

and accurate in its
expression

of the thing they
would destroy—

Baptism of Poca-
hontas

with a little card
hanging

under it to tell
the persons

in the picture.

It climbs

it runs, it is Geo.
Shoup

of Idaho it wears
a beard

it fetches naked
Indian

women from a river
Trumbull

Varnum Henderson
Frances

Willard's corset is
absurd—

Banks White Columbus
stretched

in bed men felling trees

The Hon. Michael
C. Kerr

onetime Speaker of
the House

of Representatives
Perry

in a rowboat on Lake
Erie

changing ships the
dead

among the wreckage
sickly green

Poem

As the cat
climbed over
the top of

the jamcloset
first the right
forefoot

carefully
then the hind
stepped down

into the pit of
the empty
flowerpot

This Is Just to Say

I have eaten
the plums
that were in
the icebox

and which
you were probably
saving
for breakfast

Forgive me
they were delicious
so sweet
and so cold

Item

This, with a face
like a mashed blood orange
that suddenly

would get eyes
and look up and scream
War! War!

clutching her
thick, ragged coat
A piece of hat

broken shoes
War! War!
stumbling for dread

at the young men
who with their gun-butts
shove her

sprawling—
a note
at the foot of the page

The Locust Tree in Flower

Among
of
green

stiff
old
bright

broken
branch
come

white
sweet
May

again

The Term

A rumpled sheet
of brown paper
about the length

and apparent bulk
of a man was
rolling with the

wind slowly over
and over in
the street as

a car drove down
upon it and
crushed it to

the ground. Unlike
a man it rose
again rolling

with the wind over
and over to be as
it was before.

The Last Words of My English Grandmother

There were some dirty plates
and a glass of milk
beside her on a small table
near the rank, disheveled bed—

Wrinkled and nearly blind
she lay and snored
rousing with anger in her tones
to cry for food,

Gimme something to eat—
They're starving me—
I'm all right I won't go
to the hospital. No, no, no

Give me something to eat
Let me take you
to the hospital, I said
and after you are well

you can do as you please.
She smiled, Yes
you do what you please first
then I can do what I please—

Oh, oh, oh! she cried
as the ambulance men lifted
her to the stretcher—
Is this what you call

making me comfortable?
By now her mind was clear—
Oh you think you're smart
you young people,

she said, but I'll tell you
you don't know anything.
Then we started.
On the way

we passed a long row
of elms. She looked at them
awhile out of
the ambulance window and said,

What are all those
fuzzy-looking things out there?
Trees? Well, I'm tired
of them and rolled her head away.

The Dance

In Brueghel's great picture, The Kermess,
the dancers go round, they go round and
around, the squeal and the blare and the
tweedle of bagpipes, a bugle and fiddles
tipping their bellies (round as the thick-
sided glasses whose wash they impound)
their hips and their bellies off balance
to turn them. Kicking and rolling about
the Fair Grounds, swinging their butts, those
shanks must be sound to bear up under such
rollicking measures, prance as they dance
in Brueghel's great picture, The Kermess.

A Sort of a Song

Let the snake wait under
his weed
and the writing
be of words, slow and quick, sharp
to strike, quiet to wait,
sleepless.

—through metaphor to reconcile
the people and the stones.
Compose. (No ideas
but in things) Invent!
Saxifrage is my flower that splits
the rocks.

The Maneuver

I saw the two starlings
coming in toward the wires.
But at the last,
just before alighting, they

turned in the air together
and landed backwards!
that's what got me—to
face into the wind's teeth.

The Mind Hesitant

Sometimes the river
becomes a river in the mind
or of the mind
or in and of the mind

Its banks snow
the tide falling a dark
rim lies between
the water and the shore

And the mind hesitant
regarding the stream
senses
a likeness which it

will find—a complex
image: something
of white brows
bound by a ribbon

of sooty thought
beyond, yes well beyond
the mobile features
of swiftly

flowing waters, before
the tide will
change
and rise again, maybe

The Sparrow

(To My Father)

This sparrow
  who comes to sit at my window
    is a poetic truth
more than a natural one.
  His voice,
    his movements,
his habits—
  how he loves to
    flutter his wings
in the dust—
  all attest it;
    granted, he does it
to rid himself of lice
  but the relief he feels
    makes him
cry out lustily—
  which is a trait
    more related to music

than otherwise.
       Wherever he finds himself
              in early spring,
on back streets
       or beside palaces,
              he carries on
unaffectedly
       his amours.
              It begins in the egg,
his sex genders it:
       What is more pretentiously
              useless
or about which
       we more pride ourselves?
              It leads as often as not
to our undoing.
       The cockerel, the crow
              with their challenging voices
cannot surpass
       the insistence
              of his cheep!
Once
       at El Paso
              toward evening,
I saw—and heard!—
       ten thousand sparrows
              who had come in from
the desert
       to roost. They filled the trees
              of a small park. Men fled
(with ears ringing!)
       from their droppings,
              leaving the premises
to the alligators
       who inhabit
              the fountain. His image

is familiar
         as that of the aristocratic
                  unicorn, a pity
there are not more oats eaten
         nowadays
                  to make living easier
for him.
         At that,
                  his small size,
keen eyes,
         serviceable beak
                  and general truculence
assure his survival—
         to say nothing
                  of his innumerable
brood.
         Even the Japanese
                  know him
and have painted him
         sympathetically,
                  with profound insight
into his minor
         characteristics.
                  Nothing even remotely
subtle
         about his lovemaking.
                  He crouches
before the female,
         drags his wings,
                  waltzing,
throws back his head
         and simply—
                  yells! The din
is terrific.
         The way he swipes his bill
                  across a plank

to clean it,
      is decisive.
           So with everything
he does. His coppery
      eyebrows
           give him the air
of being always
      a winner—and yet
           I saw once,
the female of his species
      clinging determinedly
           to the edge of
a water pipe,
      catch him
           by his crown-feathers
to hold him
      silent,
           subdued,
hanging above the city streets
      until
           she was through with him.
What was the use
      of that?
           She hung there
herself,
      puzzled at her success.
           I laughed heartily.
Practical to the end,
      it is the poem
           of his existence
that triumphed
      finally;
           a wisp of feathers
flattened to the pavement,
      wings spread symmetrically
           as if in flight,

the head gone,
    the black escutcheon of the breast
        undecipherable,
an effigy of a sparrow,
    a dried wafer only,
        left to say
and it says it
    without offense,
        beautifully;
This was I,
    a sparrow.
        I did my best;
farewell.

CONRAD AIKEN

(1889–1973)

Consultant in Poetry (1950–1952)

It's largely a matter of receiving visitors and answering peculiar questions and turning down invitations to speak or read. And . . . the wretched business of being introduced facetiously as the Lib's "short-haired poet" to the Staff of the Library assembled in the Library theater, standing up and making a bow to the multitude. Painful. But I survived. The best thing is my office, generally reputed to be the handsomest in the city, top floor, overlooking Capitol on one side and Supreme Court on the other, with view out to river and country too—all Washington. A fine balcony on which to perch, too . . . I disregard office hours, drifting in a[t] 9-15 in the morning, out for nigh two hours for lunch, then vamoose at 5 to the awaiting orange blossoms. Washington is dull, I think, like something abandoned by a World's Fair.

"The best-known unread poet of the twentieth century" (Louis Untermeyer). "The buried giant of twentieth-century American writing" (Malcolm Cowley). "When the tide of aesthetic sterility which is slowly engulfing us has withdrawn, our first great poet will be left. Perhaps he [Aiken] is the man" (William Faulkner). Conrad Aiken never seemed to mind that his famously difficult writing attracted few readers and critics. He said in many ways, at many times throughout his long writing life, that it was best for writers to be left alone, to enjoy one's inviolate privacy, to defend oneself from critical reception and the influence of other writers—exile, he believed, was crucial for the development of genius. His lack of a wide readership certainly did not hinder his productivity: he published nearly fifty books of verse, fiction, and criticism during his lifetime; another twenty books have appeared posthumously.

A tragedy of Faulknerian scale marked Aiken's childhood and became the psychological force behind much of his writing. When he was eleven and at home alone with his parents, his father calmly walked downstairs and murdered Aiken's mother and then shot himself. Aiken describes the scene in his autobiography, *Ushant* (much of which was written during his consultancy): "After the desultory early-morning quarrel, came the half-stifled scream, and the sound of his father's voice counting three, and the two loud pistol shots and he [Aiken] tiptoed into the dark room, where the two bodies lay motionless, and apart, and, finding them dead, found himself possessed of them forever."

Freudian psychoanalysis and the notion of finding ways to give voice to unspeakable trauma underpin much of Aiken's writing. His early works are books full of dense, ornate interconnected verse cycles obliquely charting a speaker's quest for self-knowledge. He loathed public appearances, wishing to let his work speak for itself on the page, and his first official letter as consultant in poetry established his "no-speaking" rule: "Unhappily, I am one of those wretches who simply cannot speak—three attempts at it in as many decades have taught me that the net result is to inflict great and needless suffering on others as well as myself." But he was a convivial friend to many poets, and his letters and autobiography are filled with reminiscences of time spent carousing with the great writers of his day, such as T. S. Eliot, William Carlos Williams, and Robert Penn Warren.

The Habeas Corpus Blues

In the cathedral the acolytes are praying,
in the tavern the teamsters are drinking booze,
in his attic at dusk the poet is playing,
the poet is playing the Habeas Corpus Blues.

The poet prefers the black keys to the white,
he weaves himself a shroud of simple harmonics;
across the street a house burns, in its light
he skeins more skillfully his bland ironics.

All down the block the windows bloom with faces,
the paired eyes glisten in the turning glare;
and the engines throb, and up a ladder races
an angel with a helmet on his hair.

He cracks the window in with a golden axe,
crawls through the smoke and disappears forever;
the roof whams in, and the whole city shakes;
the faces at the windows say *ah!* and *never!*

And then the hour. And near and far are striking
the belfry clocks; and from the harbour mourn
the tugboat whistles, much to the poet's liking,
smoke-rings of bronze to the fevered heavens borne.

The hydrants are turned off, the hose rewound,
the dirty engines are no longer drumming;
the angel's golden helmet has been found,
the fire is out, the insurance man is coming.

And in the cathedral the acolytes are praying,
and in the tavern the teamsters are drinking booze,
and in his attic the poet is still playing,
the poet is playing the Habeas Corpus Blues.

Exile

These hills are sandy. Trees are dwarfed here. Crows
Caw dismally in skies of an arid brilliance,
Complain in dusty pine-trees. Yellow daybreak
Lights on the long brown slopes a frost-like dew,
Dew as heavy as rain; the rabbit tracks
Show sharply in it, as they might in snow.
But it's soon gone in the sun—what good does it do?
The houses, on the slope, or among brown trees,
Are grey and shrivelled. And the men who live here
Are small and withered, spider-like, with large eyes.

Bring water with you if you come to live here—
Cold tinkling cisterns, or else wells so deep
That one looks down to Ganges or Himalayas.
Yes, and bring mountains with you, white, moon-bearing,
Mountains of ice. You will have need of these
Profundities and peaks of wet and cold.

Bring also, in a cage of wire or osier,
Birds of a golden colour, who will sing
Of leaves that do not wither, watery fruits
That heavily hang on long melodious boughs
In the blue-silver forests of deep valleys.

I have now been here—how many years? Years unnumbered.
My hands grow clawlike. My eyes are large and starved.
I brought no bird with me, I have no cistern
Where I might find the moon, or river, or snow.
Some day, for lack of these, I'll spin a web
Between two dusty pine-tree tops, and hang there
Face downward, like a spider, blown as lightly
As ghost of leaf. Crows will caw about me.
Morning and evening I shall drink the dew.

from *Time in the Rock*

IV

Woman, woman, let us say these things to each other
as slowly as if we were stones in a field
with centuries of rain in which to say them—
let us say in the morning
            'we do not hear each other'
and in the evening
            'we do not hear each other'
and let us be bewildered by the yes and the no,
the plus and minus, the where and there,
the hour in the thistledown, the acre in the seed—

and walk distracted in the world of men,
bow to all voices,
see ourselves in the mirrors of all minds,
smile at all faces,
and in the beneficent evening, once more, always,
sleep in all peacefulness.

from *Time in the Rock*

XLVII

Not with the noting of a private hate,
as if one put a mark down in a book;
nor with the chronicling of a private love,
as if one cut a vein and let it bleed;
nor the observing of peculiar light,
ringed round with what refractions peace can bring—
give it up, phrase-maker! your note is nothing:
the sum is everything.

Who walks attended by delight will feel it,
whom sudden sorrow hushes, he will know.
But you, who mark the drooping of an eyelid
or in a wrinkled cheek set out a reason—
sainted! But only if you see—

        and only then—

why, that the sum of all your notes is nothing . . .
Make a rich note of this—and start again.

from *Time in the Rock*

LXXVII

The great one who collects the sea shells I beheld
he was like the fog with long fingers he was like a cloud
stooping over the mean fields and the salt beaches

brushing the sad trees with kind shoulders
but again he had no shape, his shape was my imagination
and I beneath his foot like a dry pebble.

The fog went above me with long hands and a soft face
above the ships with a cold breath above the sails
what he loved he took and kept well, beyond death,
but I noticed that especially he loved little things
the seaweed, the starflower, the mussel, the bones of a small fish on the sand

I separate from him, but not separate, because I loved him
thinking of him among the marshes, the wet woodpaths, the grasses,
thinking of him who was myself but who was more loving than myself
alas that the pebble cannot move or be moved
nevertheless I imagined him, he was my creation

O god of my imagination, god of my creation,
whom thus I impersonate, my father, my mother,
whom I create out of the visible world, as you created me
out of the invisible, let me be the one
who loves the seaweed, the starflower, the mussel, the bones of a small
    fish on the beach
and I among them like a smooth pebble.

The Whippoorwill

Last night, as I lay half awake,
A whippoorwill was in this tree,
And sang, for the three-quarters moon,
Another whippoorwill, and me.

At first, I heard him far away—
A ghostly whiplash. Then I heard,
From the tall tree beneath the moon,
What seemed indeed a different bird—

So near, so loud, so sweet he sang;
And what, far off, seemed harsh and strange,
Grew to a beauty in the moon,
Even as I listened seemed to change.

"Why? Why?" he asked. . . . And then was gone
Without a sound of wing or leaf.
And the tall tree stood carved in stone;
The moonlight night as still as grief.

Music

The calyx of the oboe breaks,
silver and soft the flower it makes.
And next, beyond, the flute-notes seen
now are white and now are green.

What are these sounds, what daft device,
mocking at flame, mimicking ice?
Musicians, will you never rest
from strange translation of the breast?

The heart, from which all horrors come,
grows like a vine, its gourd a drum;
the living pattern sprawls and climbs
eager to bear all worlds and times:

trilling leaf and tinkling grass
glide into darkness clear as glass
then the musicians cease to play
and the world is waved away.

Summer

Absolute zero: the locust sings:
summer's caught in eternity's rings:
the rock explodes, the planet dies,
we shovel up our verities.

The razor rasps across the face
and in the glass our fleeting race
lit by infinity's lightning wink
under the thunder tries to think.

In this frail gourd the granite pours
the timeless howls like all outdoors
the sensuous moment builds a wall
open as wind, no wall at all:

while still obedient to valves and knobs
the vascular jukebox throbs and sobs
expounding hope propounding yearning
proposing love, but never learning

or only learning at zero's gate
like summer's locust the final hate
formless ice on a formless plain
that was and is and comes again.

When You Are Not Surprised

When you are not surprised, not surprised,
nor leap in imagination from sunlight into shadow
or from shadow into sunlight
suiting the color of fright or delight
to the bewildering circumstance
when you are no longer surprised
by the quiet or fury of daybreak
the stormy uprush of the sun's rage
over the edges of torn trees
torrents of living and dying flung
upward and outward inward and downward to space
or else
peace peace peace peace
the wood-thrush speaking his holy holy
far hidden in the forest of the mind
while slowly
the limbs of light unwind
and the world's surface dreams again of night
as the center dreams of light
when you are not surprised
by breath and breath and breath
the first unconscious morning breath
the tap of the bird's beak on the pane
and do not cry out come again
blest blest that you are come again
o light o sound o voice of bird o light
and memory too o memory blest
and curst with the debts of yesterday
that would not stay, or stay

when you are not surprised
by death and death and death
death of the bee in the daffodil
death of color in the child's cheek
on the young mother's breast
death of sense of touch of sight
death of delight
and the inward death the inward turning night
when the heart hardens itself with hate and indifference
for hated self and beloved not-self
when you are not surprised
by wheel's turn or turn of season
the winged and orbèd chariot tilt of time
the halcyon pause, the blue caesura of spring
and solar rhyme
woven into the divinely remembered nest
by the dark-eyed love in the oriole's breast
and the tides of space that ring the heart
while still, while still, the wave of the invisible world
breaks into consciousness in the mind of god
then welcome death and be by death benignly welcomed
and join again in the ceaseless know-nothing
from which you awoke to the first surprise.

The Grasshopper

Grasshopper
grasshopper
all day long
we hear your scraping
summer song
      like
          rusty
              fiddles
                  in
          the
        grass
as through
        the meadow
           path
              we pass
such funny legs
such funny feet
and how we wonder
what you eat
maybe a single blink of dew
sipped from a clover leaf would do
then high in air
      once more you spring
        to fall in grass again
              and sing.

ELIZABETH BISHOP

(1911–1979)

Consultant in Poetry (1949–1950)

I've always felt I've written poetry more by *not* writing it than by writing it, and now this Library business makes me really feel like the "poet by default." At 1st I felt a little overcome and inclined to wire you a frantic "no," but having thought about it for a day or two I've concluded that it is something I *could* do (there isn't much, heaven knows) and that even if I haven't nearly enough poetry to warrant it that maybe it will be all right . . . particularly if I work hard from now until then.

An intensely private person, shy by nature and plagued for most of her life by asthma and other health issues that were inflamed by stress, Elizabeth Bishop had misgivings about coming to Washington right from the start. She soldiered through her year as consultant, doing much to build up the Library's Archive of Recorded Poetry and Literature, giving the obligatory readings, and presiding over a blowout seventy-fifth birthday party for Robert Frost (though it turned out to have been his seventy-sixth) at the White House. She kept up a cheerful front for her friends in letters, writing to one that she seemed to do nothing all day but serve sherry to visitors.

In truth, the public demands of the job took a great toll on Bishop's health and work, and it would take her well over a year to recover. Bishop was thirty-eight and had published only one book of poems when she accepted the post in Washington. She was one of the youngest consultants in poetry and didn't yet know how to defend and nurture her writing life.

Bishop was exacting, spending long periods of time revising and polishing her work. She published only 101 poems during her lifetime, and they are among the most celebrated in the English language. Her verse is marked by vivid, surprising descriptions of the physical world and her at once formal yet intimate tone. Her underlying themes include the struggle to feel at home, grief, longing, and celebrating visionary moments in the natural world.

Bishop was born in Worcester, Massachusetts. Her father died before her first birthday, and her mother was committed to a mental asylum several years later. She spent her childhood shuttling from relative to relative, a formative experience that echoes in the patterns of loss and displacement throughout her poetry and short stories. She began publishing poems in high school and knew she wanted to devote her life to poetry when she went to Vassar College, where she started a literary magazine with Mary McCarthy and initiated a lifelong correspondence with Marianne Moore, who helped publish her acclaimed first book, *North and South*, in 1946.

Not long after she left Washington, Bishop traveled to South America, where she had a violent allergic reaction to a cashew fruit she ate in Rio, just before she was scheduled to leave for a tour of the Amazon. She was nursed back to health by the architect Lota de Macedo Soares, a friend of a friend who became the great love of Bishop's life. The two set up a home in the mountain town of Petrópolis. From her perch in Brazil, Bishop created many of her best-loved poems, which appeared with regularity in *The New Yorker* and were collected in her second book, *Poems: North and South—A Cold Spring*, which won the 1956 Pulitzer Prize.

Sandpiper

The roaring alongside he takes for granted,
and that every so often the world is bound to shake.
He runs, he runs to the south, finical, awkward,
in a state of controlled panic, a student of Blake.

The beach hisses like fat. On his left, a sheet
of interrupting water comes and goes
and glazes over his dark and brittle feet.
He runs, he runs straight through it, watching his toes.

—Watching, rather, the spaces of sand between them,
where (no detail too small) the Atlantic drains
rapidly backwards and downwards. As he runs,
he stares at the dragging grains.

The world is a mist. And then the world is
minute and vast and clear. The tide
is higher or lower. He couldn't tell you which.
His beak is focused; he is preoccupied,

looking for something, something, something.
Poor bird, he is obsessed!
The millions of grains are black, white, tan, and gray,
mixed with quartz grains, rose and amethyst.

The Imaginary Iceberg

We'd rather have the iceberg than the ship,
although it meant the end of travel.
Although it stood stock-still like cloudy rock
and all the sea were moving marble.
We'd rather have the iceberg than the ship;
we'd rather own this breathing plain of snow
though the ship's sails were laid upon the sea
as the snow lies undissolved upon the water.
O solemn, floating field,
are you aware an iceberg takes repose
with you, and when it wakes may pasture on your snows?

This is a scene a sailor'd give his eyes for.
The ship's ignored. The iceberg rises
and sinks again; its glassy pinnacles
correct elliptics in the sky.
This is a scene where he who treads the boards
is artlessly rhetorical. The curtain
is light enough to rise on finest ropes
that airy twists of snow provide.
The wits of these white peaks
spar with the sun. Its weight the iceberg dares
upon a shifting stage and stands and stares.

This iceberg cuts its facets from within.
Like jewelry from a grave
it saves itself perpetually and adorns
only itself, perhaps the snows
which so surprise us lying on the sea.
Good-bye, we say, good-bye, the ship steers off
where waves give in to one another's waves
and clouds run in a warmer sky.

Icebergs behoove the soul
(both being self-made from elements least visible)
to see them so: fleshed, fair, erected indivisible.

Casabianca

Love's the boy stood on the burning deck
trying to recite "The boy stood on
the burning deck." Love's the son
      stood stammering elocution
      while the poor ship in flames went down.

Love's the obstinate boy, the ship,
even the swimming sailors, who
would like a schoolroom platform, too,
      or an excuse to stay
      on deck. And love's the burning boy.

The Unbeliever

> *He sleeps on the top of a mast.*
> —Bunyan

He sleeps on the top of a mast
with his eyes fast closed.
The sails fall away below him
like the sheets of his bed,
leaving out in the air of the night the sleeper's head.

Asleep he was transported there,
asleep he curled
in a gilded ball on the mast's top,
or climbed inside
a gilded bird, or blindly seated himself astride.

"I am founded on marble pillars,"
said a cloud. "I never move.
See the pillars there in the sea?"
Secure in introspection
he peers at the watery pillars of his reflection.

A gull had wings under his
and remarked that the air
was "like marble." He said: "Up here
I tower through the sky
for the marble wings on my tower-top fly."

But he sleeps on the top of his mast
with his eyes closed tight.
The gull inquired into his dream,
which was, "I must not fall.
The spangled sea below wants me to fall.
It is hard as diamonds; it wants to destroy us all."

The Fish

I caught a tremendous fish
and held him beside the boat
half out of water, with my hook
fast in a corner of his mouth.
He didn't fight.
He hadn't fought at all.

He hung a grunting weight,
battered and venerable
and homely. Here and there
his brown skin hung in strips
like ancient wallpaper,
and its pattern of darker brown
was like wallpaper:
shapes like full-blown roses
stained and lost through age.
He was speckled with barnacles,
fine rosettes of lime,
and infested
with tiny white sea-lice,
and underneath two or three
rags of green weed hung down.
While his gills were breathing in
the terrible oxygen
—the frightening gills,
fresh and crisp with blood,
that can cut so badly—
I thought of the coarse white flesh
packed in like feathers,
the big bones and the little bones,
the dramatic reds and blacks
of his shiny entrails,
and the pink swim-bladder
like a big peony.
I looked into his eyes
which were far larger than mine
but shallower, and yellowed,
the irises backed and packed
with tarnished tinfoil
seen through the lenses
of old scratched isinglass.
They shifted a little, but not
to return my stare.

—It was more like the tipping
of an object toward the light.
I admired his sullen face,
the mechanism of his jaw,
and then I saw
that from his lower lip
—if you could call it a lip—
grim, wet, and weaponlike,
hung five old pieces of fish-line,
or four and a wire leader
with the swivel still attached,
with all their five big hooks
grown firmly in his mouth.
A green line, frayed at the end
where he broke it, two heavier lines,
and a fine black thread
still crimped from the strain and snap
when it broke and he got away.
Like medals with their ribbons
frayed and wavering,
a five-haired beard of wisdom
trailing from his aching jaw.
I stared and stared
and victory filled up
the little rented boat,
from the pool of bilge
where oil had spread a rainbow
around the rusted engine
to the bailer rusted orange,
the sun-cracked thwarts,
the oarlocks on their strings,
the gunnels—until everything
was rainbow, rainbow, rainbow!
And I let the fish go.

At the Fishhouses

Although it is a cold evening,
down by one of the fishhouses
an old man sits netting,
his net, in the gloaming almost invisible,
a dark purple-brown,
and his shuttle worn and polished.
The air smells so strong of codfish
it makes one's nose run and one's eyes water.
The five fishhouses have steeply peaked roofs
and narrow, cleated gangplanks slant up
to storerooms in the gables
for the wheelbarrows to be pushed up and down on.
All is silver: the heavy surface of the sea,
swelling slowly as if considering spilling over,
is opaque, but the silver of the benches,
the lobster pots, and masts, scattered
among the wild jagged rocks,
is of an apparent translucence
like the small old buildings with an emerald moss
growing on their shoreward walls.
The big fish tubs are completely lined
with layers of beautiful herring scales
and the wheelbarrows are similarly plastered
with creamy iridescent coats of mail,
with small iridescent flies crawling on them.
Up on the little slope behind the houses,
set in the sparse bright sprinkle of grass,
is an ancient wooden capstan,
cracked, with two long bleached handles
and some melancholy stains, like dried blood,
where the ironwork has rusted.
The old man accepts a Lucky Strike.
He was a friend of my grandfather.
We talk of the decline in the population

and of codfish and herring
while he waits for a herring boat to come in.
There are sequins on his vest and on his thumb.
He has scraped the scales, the principal beauty,
from unnumbered fish with that black old knife,
the blade of which is almost worn away.

Down at the water's edge, at the place
where they haul up the boats, up the long ramp
descending into the water, thin silver
tree trunks are laid horizontally
across the gray stones, down and down
at intervals of four or five feet.

Cold dark deep and absolutely clear,
element bearable to no mortal,
to fish and to seals . . . One seal particularly
I have seen here evening after evening.
He was curious about me. He was interested in music;
like me a believer in total immersion,
so I used to sing him Baptist hymns.
I also sang "A Mighty Fortress Is Our God."
He stood up in the water and regarded me
steadily, moving his head a little.
Then he would disappear, then suddenly emerge
almost in the same spot, with a sort of shrug
as if it were against his better judgement.
Cold dark deep and absolutely clear,
the clear gray icy water . . . Back, behind us,
the dignified tall firs begin.
Bluish, associating with their shadows,
a million Christmas trees stand
waiting for Christmas. The water seems suspended
above the rounded gray and blue-gray stones.
I have seen it over and over, the same sea, the same,
slightly, indifferently swinging above the stones,

icily free above the stones,
above the stones and then the world.
If you should dip your hand in,
your wrist would ache immediately,
your bones would begin to ache and your hand would burn
as if the water were a transmutation of fire
that feeds on stones and burns with a dark gray flame.
If you tasted it, it would first taste bitter,
then briny, then surely burn your tongue.
It is like what we imagine knowledge to be:
dark, salt, clear, moving, utterly free,
drawn from the cold hard mouth
of the world, derived from the rocky breasts
forever, flowing and drawn, and since
our knowledge is historical, flowing, and flown.

View of the Capitol from the Library of Congress

Moving from left to left, the light
is heavy on the Dome, and coarse.
One small lunette turns it aside
and blankly stares off to the side
like a big white old wall-eyed horse.

On the east steps the Air Force Band
in uniforms of Air Force blue
is playing hard and loud, but—queer—
the music doesn't quite come through.

It comes in snatches, dim then keen,
then mute, and yet there is no breeze.
The giant trees stand in between.
I think the trees must intervene,

catching the music in their leaves
like gold-dust, till each big leaf sags.
Unceasingly the little flags
feed their limp stripes into the air,
and the band's efforts vanish there.

Great shades, edge over,
give the music room.
The gathered brasses want to go
boom—boom.

Letter to N.Y.

For Louise Crane

In your next letter I wish you'd say
where you are going and what you are doing;
how are the plays, and after the plays
what other pleasures you're pursuing:

taking cabs in the middle of the night,
driving as if to save your soul
where the road goes round and round the park
and the meter glares like a moral owl,

and the trees look so queer and green
standing alone in big black caves
and suddenly you're in a different place
where everything seems to happen in waves,

and most of the jokes you just can't catch,
like dirty words rubbed off a slate,
and the songs are loud but somehow dim
and it gets so terribly late,

and coming out of the brownstone house
to the gray sidewalk, the watered street,
one side of the buildings rises with the sun
like a glistening field of wheat.

—Wheat, not oats, dear. I'm afraid
if it's wheat it's none of your sowing,
nevertheless I'd like to know
what you are doing and where you are going.

The Shampoo

The still explosions on the rocks,
the lichens, grow
by spreading, gray, concentric shocks.
They have arranged
to meet the rings around the moon, although
within our memories they have not changed.

And since the heavens will attend
as long on us,
you've been, dear friend,
precipitate and pragmatical;
and look what happens. For Time is
nothing if not amenable.

The shooting stars in your black hair
in bright formation
are flocking where,
so straight, so soon?
—Come, let me wash it in this big tin basin,
battered and shiny like the moon.

Song for the Rainy Season

Hidden, oh hidden
in the high fog
the house we live in,
beneath the magnetic rock,
rain-, rainbow-ridden,
where blood-black
bromelias, lichens,
owls, and the lint
of the waterfalls cling,
familiar, unbidden.

In a dim age
of water
the brook sings loud
from a rib cage
of giant fern; vapor
climbs up the thick growth
effortlessly, turns back,
holding them both,
house and rock,
in a private cloud.

At night, on the roof,
blind drops crawl
and the ordinary brown

owl gives us proof
he can count:
five times—always five—
he stamps and takes off
after the fat frogs that,
shrilling for love,
clamber and mount.

House, open house
to the white dew
and the milk-white sunrise
kind to the eyes,
to membership
of silver fish, mouse,
bookworms,
big moths; with a wall
for the mildew's
ignorant map;

darkened and tarnished
by the warm touch
of the warm breath,
maculate, cherished,
rejoice! For a later
era will differ.
(O difference that kills,
or intimidates, much
of all our small shadowy
life!) Without water

the great rock will stare
unmagnetized, bare,
no longer wearing
rainbows or rain,
the forgiving air
and the high fog gone;
the owls will move on

and the several
waterfalls shrivel
in the steady sun.

> *Sitio da Alcobaçinha*
> *Fazenda Samambaia*
> *Petrópolis*

Manners

For a Child of 1918

My grandfather said to me
as we sat on the wagon seat,
"Be sure to remember to always
speak to everyone you meet."

We met a stranger on foot.
My grandfather's whip tapped his hat.
"Good day, sir. Good day. A fine day."
And I said it and bowed where I sat.

Then we overtook a boy we knew
with his big pet crow on his shoulder.
"Always offer everyone a ride;
don't forget that when you get older,"

my grandfather said. So Willy
climbed up with us, but the crow
gave a "Caw!" and flew off. I was worried.
How would he know where to go?

But he flew a little way at a time
from fence post to fence post, ahead;
and when Willy whistled he answered.
"A fine bird," my grandfather said,

"and he's well brought up. See, he answers
nicely when he's spoken to.
Man or beast, that's good manners.
Be sure that you both always do."

When automobiles went by,
the dust hid the people's faces,
but we shouted "Good day! Good day!
Fine day!" at the top of our voices.

When we came to Hustler Hill,
he said that the mare was tired,
so we all got down and walked,
as our good manners required.

In the Waiting Room

In Worcester, Massachusetts,
I went with Aunt Consuelo
to keep her dentist's appointment
and sat and waited for her
in the dentist's waiting room.
It was winter. It got dark
early. The waiting room
was full of grown-up people,
arctics and overcoats,
lamps and magazines.
My aunt was inside

what seemed like a long time
and while I waited I read
the *National Geographic*
(I could read) and carefully
studied the photographs:
the inside of a volcano,
black, and full of ashes;
then it was spilling over
in rivulets of fire.
Osa and Martin Johnson
dressed in riding breeches,
laced boots, and pith helmets.
A dead man slung on a pole
—"Long Pig," the caption said.
Babies with pointed heads
wound round and round with string;
black, naked women with necks
wound round and round with wire
like the necks of light bulbs.
Their breasts were horrifying.
I read it right straight through.
I was too shy to stop.
And then I looked at the cover:
the yellow margins, the date.

Suddenly, from inside,
came an *oh!* of pain
—Aunt Consuelo's voice—
not very loud or long.
I wasn't at all surprised;
even then I knew she was
a foolish, timid woman.
I might have been embarrassed,
but wasn't. What took me
completely by surprise

was that it was *me:*
my voice, in my mouth.
Without thinking at all
I was my foolish aunt,
I—we—were falling, falling,
our eyes glued to the cover
of the *National Geographic,*
February, 1918.

I said to myself: three days
and you'll be seven years old.
I was saying it to stop
the sensation of falling off
the round, turning world
into cold, blue-black space.
But I felt: you are an *I,*
you are an *Elizabeth,*
you are one of *them.*
Why should you be one, too?
I scarcely dared to look
to see what it was I was.
I gave a sidelong glance
—I couldn't look any higher—
at shadowy gray knees,
trousers and skirts and boots
and different pairs of hands
lying under the lamps.
I knew that nothing stranger
had ever happened, that nothing
stranger could ever happen.

Why should I be my aunt,
or me, or anyone?
What similarities—
boots, hands, the family voice

I felt in my throat, or even
the *National Geographic*
and those awful hanging breasts—
held us all together
or made us all just one?
How—I didn't know any
word for it—how "unlikely"...
How had I come to be here,
like them, and overhear
a cry of pain that could have
got loud and worse but hadn't?

The waiting room was bright
and too hot. It was sliding
beneath a big black wave,
another, and another.

Then I was back in it.
The War was on. Outside,
in Worcester, Massachusetts,
were night and slush and cold,
and it was still the fifth
of February, 1918.

Sestina

September rain falls on the house.
In the failing light, the old grandmother
sits in the kitchen with the child
beside the Little Marvel Stove,
reading the jokes from the almanac,
laughing and talking to hide her tears.

She thinks that her equinoctial tears
and the rain that beats on the roof of the house
were both foretold by the almanac,
but only known to a grandmother.
The iron kettle sings on the stove.
She cuts some bread and says to the child,

It's time for tea now; but the child
is watching the teakettle's small hard tears
dance like mad on the hot black stove,
the way the rain must dance on the house.
Tidying up, the old grandmother
hangs up the clever almanac

on its string. Birdlike, the almanac
hovers half open above the child,
hovers above the old grandmother
and her teacup full of dark brown tears.
She shivers and says she thinks the house
feels chilly, and puts more wood in the stove.

It was to be, says the Marvel Stove.
I know what I know, says the almanac.
With crayons the child draws a rigid house
and a winding pathway. Then the child
puts in a man with buttons like tears
and shows it proudly to the grandmother.

But secretly, while the grandmother
busies herself about the stove,
the little moons fall down like tears
from between the pages of the almanac
into the flower bed the child
has carefully placed in the front of the house.

Time to plant tears, says the almanac.
The grandmother sings to the marvellous stove
and the child draws another inscrutable house.

One Art

The art of losing isn't hard to master;
so many things seem filled with the intent
to be lost that their loss is no disaster.

Lose something every day. Accept the fluster
of lost door keys, the hour badly spent.
The art of losing isn't hard to master.

Then practice losing farther, losing faster:
places, and names, and where it was you meant
to travel. None of these will bring disaster.

I lost my mother's watch. And look! my last, or
next-to-last, of three loved houses went.
The art of losing isn't hard to master.

I lost two cities, lovely ones. And, vaster,
some realms I owned, two rivers, a continent.
I miss them, but it wasn't a disaster.

—Even losing you (the joking voice, a gesture
I love) I shan't have lied. It's evident
the art of losing's not too hard to master
though it may look like (*Write* it!) like disaster.

Five Flights Up

Still dark.
The unknown bird sits on his usual branch.
The little dog next door barks in his sleep
inquiringly, just once.
Perhaps in his sleep, too, the bird inquires
once or twice, quavering.
Questions—if that is what they are—
answered directly, simply,
by day itself.

Enormous morning, ponderous, meticulous;
gray light streaking each bare branch,
each single twig, along one side,
making another tree, of glassy veins . . .
The bird still sits there. Now he seems to yawn.

The little black dog runs in his yard.
His owner's voice arises, stern,
"You ought to be ashamed!"
What has he done?
He bounces cheerfully up and down;
he rushes in circles in the fallen leaves.

Obviously, he has no sense of shame.
He and the bird know everything is answered,
all taken care of,
no need to ask again.
—Yesterday brought to today so lightly!
(A yesterday I find almost impossible to lift.)

———————

It is marvellous to wake up together
At the same minute; marvellous to hear
The rain begin suddenly all over the roof,
To feel the air suddenly clear
As if electricity had passed through it
From a black mesh of wires in the sky.
All over the roof the rain hisses,
And below, the light falling of kisses.

An electrical storm is coming or moving away;
It is the prickling air that wakes us up.
If lightning struck the house now, it would run
From the four blue china balls on top
Down the roof and down the rods all around us,
And we imagine dreamily
That the whole house caught in a bird-cage of lightning
Would be quite delightful rather than frightening;

And from the same simplified point of view
Of night and lying flat on one's back
All things might change equally easily,
Since always to warn us there must be these black
Electrical wires dangling. Without surprise
The world might change to something quite different,
As the air changes or the lightning comes without our blinking,
Change as our kisses are changing without our thinking.

Dear, my compass
still points north
to wooden houses
and blue eyes,

fairy-tales where
flaxen-headed
younger sons
bring home the goose,

love in hay-lofts,
Protestants, and
heavy drinkers . . .
Springs are backward,

but crab-apples
ripen to rubies,
cranberries
to drops of blood,

and swans can paddle
icy water,
so hot the blood
in those webbed feet.

Cold as it is we'd
go to bed, dear,
early, but never
to keep warm.

LÉONIE ADAMS

(1899–1988)

Consultant in Poetry (1948–1949)

Send forth the high falcon flying after the mind
To topple it from its cold cloud:
The beak of the falcon to pierce it till it fall
Where the simple heart is bowed.

éonie Adams, a poet of lapidary and metaphysical verse, was born in Brooklyn, New York, in 1899. She attended Barnard College and published her first poems before she graduated in 1922. Adams was among the most diligent poets to serve as consultant. She took the job at a time when there was a considerable amount of work to be done, and she viewed the post as a job, not merely a title. Her work was the object of critical acclaim—she won numerous awards, and was corecipient of the Bollingen Prize along with Louise Bogan, who was a close friend of Adams. Throughout her writing life she remained an editor and tireless educator. She taught at many institutions, including Columbia University and Sarah Lawrence College. At Columbia, Adams served as a mentor to future poet laureate Louise Glück. In 1924 she became one of the editors of the poetry magazine *The Elect*, and in 1928 she was awarded a Guggenheim Fellowship for creative writing. She lived in Paris in the late 1920s.

Allen Tate praised her Romantic sensibility, writing about her second volume: "Even if she never issued another book, her reputation is secure as one of the best American poets. More than anyone else writing today, she continues at the highest level the great lyrical tradition of the English romantics, with whom, in her time, she would have held her own." Adams herself wrote: "My work has been sometimes described as 'metaphysical' and sometimes as 'romantic.' It is perhaps some sort of fusion. Its images are largely from nature (and the tradition of Nature) and I have tended in my better work toward a contemplative lyric articulated by some sort of speech music."

Magnificat in Little

I was enriched, not casting after marvels,
But as one walking in a usual place,
Without desert but common eyes and ears,
No recourse but to hear, power but to see,
Got to love you of grace.

Subtle musicians, that could body wind,
Or contrive strings to anguish, in conceit
Random and artless strung a branch with bells,
Fixed in one silver whim, which at a touch
Shook and were sweet.

And you, you lovely and unpurchased note,
One run distraught, and vexing hot and cold
To give to the heart's poor confusion tongue,
By chance caught you, and henceforth all unlearned
Repeats you gold.

Recollection of the Wood

Light at each point was beating then to flight,
The sapling bark flushed upward, and the welling
Tips of the wood touched, touched at the bound,

And boughs were slight and burdened beyond telling
Toward that caress of the boughs a summer's night,
Illimitable in fragrance and in sound.

Here were the blue buds, earlier than hope,
Unnumbered, beneath the leaves, a breath apart,
Wakening in root-dusk. When the air went north,
Lifting the oakleaves from the northern slope,
Their infinite young tender eyes looked forth.
Here all that was, was frail to bear a heart.

The Summer Image

(From a Persian Carpet)

Ash and strewments, the first moth-wings, pale
Ardour of brief evenings, on the fecund wind;
Or all a wing, less than wind,
Breath of low herbs upfloats, petal or wing,
Haunting the musk precincts of burial.
For the season of newer riches moves triumphing,
Of the evanescence of deaths. These potpourris
Earth-tinctured, jet insect-bead, cinder of bloom—
How weigh while a great summer knows increase,
Ceaselessly risen, what there entombs?—
Of candour fallen from the slight stems of Mays,
Corrupt of the rim a blue shades, pensively:
So a fatigue of wishes will young eyes.
And brightened, unpurged eyes of revery, now
Not to glance to fabulous groves again;
For now deep presence is, and binds its close,

And closes down the wreathed alleys escape of sighs.
And now rich time is weaving, hidden tree,
The fable of orient threads from bough to bough.
Old rinded wood, whose lissomeness within
Has reached from nothing to its covering
These many corymbs' flourish!—And the green
Shells which wait amber, breathing, wrought
Towards the still trance of summer's centering,
Motives by ravished humble fingers set,
Each in a noon of its own infinite.
And here is leant the branch and its repose
Of the deep leaf to the pilgrim plume. Repose,
Inflections brilliant and mute of the voyager, light!
And here the nests, and freshet throats resume
Notes over and over found, names
For the silvery ascensions of joy. Nothing is here
But moss and its bells now of the root's night;
But the beetle's bower, and arc from grass to grass
For the flight in gauze. Now its fresh lair,
Grass-deep, nestles the cool eft to stir
Vague newborn limbs, and the bud's dark winding has
Access of day. Now on the subtle noon
Time's image, at pause with being, labours free
Of all its charge, for each in coverts laid,
Of clement kind; and everlastingly,
In some elision of bright moments is known,
Changed wide as Eden, the branch whose silence sways
Dazzle of the murmurous leaves to continual tone;
Its separations, sighing to own again
Being of the ignorant wish; and sways to sight,
Waked from it knighted, the marvelous foundlings of light;
Risen and weaving from the ceaseless root
A divine ease whispers toward fruitfulness,
While all a summer's conscience tempts the fruit.

Sundown

This is the time lean woods shall spend
A steeped-up twilight, and the pale evening drink,
And the perilous roe, the leaper to the west brink,
Trembling and bright to the caverned cloud descend.

Now shall you see pent oak gone gusty and frantic,
Stooped with dry weeping, ruinously unloosing
The sparse disheveled leaf, or reared and tossing
A dreary scarecrow bough in funeral antic.

Then, tatter you and rend,
Oak heart, to your profession mourning; not obscure
The outcome, not crepuscular; on the deep floor
Sable and gold match lustres and contend.

And rags of shrouding will not muffle the slain.
This is the immortal extinction, the priceless wound
Not to be staunched. The live gold leaks beyond,
And matter's sanctified, dipped in a gold stain.

Early Waking

Four hooves rang out and now are still.
In the dark wall the casements hold
Essential day above each sill,
Just light, and colored like thin gold.
Behind those hooves a drowsy course
All night I rode where hearts were clear,
And wishes blessed at the source,
And for no shape of time stop here.

No more to raise that lively ghost
Which ran quicksilver to the bone:
By a whim's turn the whole was lost
When all its marrow worth was known.
Ghosts can cast shadows in the breast,
And what was present tears to weep,
Not heart nor mind would bid from rest
As fast as sorrow's, ten years deep.

I travel, not for a ghost's sake,
One step from sleep, and not for one
Left sleeping at my side I wake.
Before bricks rosy with the dawn,
The hooves will sound beyond the light:
There are dark roads enough to go
To last us through the end of night,
And I will make my waking slow.

It was for unconcerning light
That has not fallen on earth, to stare
An instant only out of night
And with night's cloudy character,
Before the laden mind shall slip
Past dream and on to brightmost dream
And fetterless high morning dip
Her two cold sandals in the stream.

Song from a Country Fair

When tunes jigged nimbler than the blood
And quick and high the bows would prance
And every fiddle string would burst
To catch what's lost beyond the string,

While half afraid their children stood,
I saw the old come out to dance.
The heart is not so light at first,
But heavy like a bough in spring.

The Mount

Now I have tempered haste,
The joyous traveller said,
The steed has passed me now
Whose hurrying hooves I fled.
My spectre rides thereon,
I learned what mount he has,
Upon what summers fed;
And wept to know again,
Beneath the saddle swung,
Treasure for whose great theft
This breast was wrung.
His bridle bells sang out,
I could not tell their chime,
So brilliantly he rings,
But called his name as Time.
His bin was morning light,
Those straws which gild his bed
Are of the fallen West.
Although green lands consume
Beneath their burning tread,
In everlasting bright
His hooves have rest.

Thought's End

I'd watched the hills drink the last colour of light,
All shapes grow bright and wane on the pale air,
Till down the traitorous east there came the night
And swept the circle of my seeing bare;
Its intimate beauty like a wanton's veil
Tore from the void as from an empty face.
I felt at being's rim all being fail,
And my one body pitted against space.
O heart more frightened than a wild bird's wings
Beating at green, now is no fiery mark
Left on the quiet nothingness of things.
Be self no more against the flooding dark;
There thousandwise, sown in that cloudy blot,
Stars that are worlds look out and see you not.

ROBERT LOWELL

(1917–1977)

Consultant in Poetry (1947–1948)

This job reminds me of Kafka's castle. But I think it will work well.

The year 1947 was auspicious and in many respects overwhelming for Robert Lowell, who at twenty-nine became the sixth consultant in poetry. He was far younger than any of his predecessors, and was tapped based on the merit and acclaim of his Pulitzer Prize–winning second book, *Lord Weary's Castle*. In that same year, he received cash awards from both the American Academy of American Poets and the Guggenheim Foundation, was approached by several universities with offers to teach, and was featured in a *Life* magazine spread with photographs that prompted a film producer in Hollywood to contact him about acting. Aside from a stir caused by Lowell's six months in federal prison as a conscientious objector to the Second World War, which occurred five years before he came to Washington, his term was uneventful. He was dismayed by the state of the Library's poetry recording archives and informed the Librarian that "the selection of poets is idiosyncratic. Four or five of the inclusions are absurd." He advised bringing major poets like Frost and Eliot in to record whole albums, and successfully negotiated a complicated contract with Eliot to this end.

After leaving Washington, Lowell went to Yaddo, the artists' colony in Saratoga Springs, after which he was was hospitalized for the first of many manic episodes that would thereafter interrupt his life. During this volatile period, his third volume of poems appeared to mixed reviews. This gave Lowell pause to look at his career in relation to rapid changes in postwar America and his mental health. He became interested in Beat culture and Allen Ginsberg's self-revelations, compared to which, he wrote, his poems seemed "distant, symbol-ridden, and willfully difficult ... dragged down into the bog and death by their ponderous armor."

Lowell emerged from this crisis by turning inward, a reaction that would radically influence the course of American poetry in the second half of the twentieth century. His next book, *Life Studies*, published in 1959, is written in a much looser style that narrates Lowell's

personal and ancestral history, which had intrigued his readers since he
first started publishing his poems. His poetry and "91 Revere Street,"
the prose sketch that forms an important part of *Life Studies*, recounts
a childhood marked by conflict between his cowering father and his
imperious mother. Boston Brahmins of the highest order, both par-
ents traced their roots back to the early days of New England. Stanley
Kunitz called *Life Studies*, which won the 1960 National Book Award,
"the most influential book of modern verse since [T. S. Eliot's] *The
Waste Land*." The term "confessional" was coined by the critic M. L.
Rosenthal in reviewing the volume and has since been used to describe
obvious autobiographical elements in American poetry. Much of the
book's emotional power comes from Lowell's attempts to find a writ-
ten form that was compatible with his mood swings. During the period
of the book's composition, he suffered from mania and depression and
for a while found it difficult to write. "When I was working on *Life
Studies*," he wrote in an essay, "I found I had no language or meter that
would allow me to approximate what I saw or remembered. Yet in prose
I had already found what I wanted, the conventional style of autobi-
ography and reminiscence. So I wrote my autobiographical poetry in a
style I thought I had discovered in Flaubert. . . . I did all kinds of tricks
with meter and the avoidance of meter. . . . I didn't have to bang words
into rhyme and count."

Later in life Lowell would have a brief but decisive falling-out with
his friend Elizabeth Bishop over both the amount of personal infor-
mation he included and the lack of formal rigor in many of his late
poems, some of which contained passages of letters from family mem-
bers and friends (Bishop among them) transcribed almost verbatim and
turned into verse merely by inserting line breaks. Bishop was famously
reticent about her difficult childhood, and she was a painstaking crafts-
person who could revise a poem for a decade before sending it out for
publication. In the early 1970s, as Lowell was preparing to publish *The
Dolphin*, in which he included passages of letters from his ex-wife, Eliza-
beth Hardwick, he sent the manuscript to Bishop, saying, "I am going to
publish, and don't want any advice, except for yours." Bishop began her
letter back with, "It's Hell to write this," and then launched into one of
her most direct rebukes: "One can use one's life as material—one does

anyway—but these letters—aren't you violating a trust? IF you were given permission—IF you hadn't changed them . . . etc. *But art just isn't worth that much.*" This exchange marks a defining point in American poetry. Lowell made a few minor changes but published the book anyway. A year later he would write to Bishop, "I couldn't bear to have my book (my life) wait hidden inside me like a dead child."

Man and Wife

Tamed by *Miltown*, we lie on Mother's bed;
the rising sun in war paint dyes us red;
in broad daylight her gilded bed-posts shine,
abandoned, almost Dionysian.
At last the trees are green on Marlborough Street,
blossoms on our magnolia ignite
the morning with their murderous five days' white.
All night I've held your hand,
as if you had
a fourth time faced the kingdom of the mad—
its hackneyed speech, its homicidal eye—
and dragged me home alive. . . . Oh my *Petite*,
clearest of all God's creatures, still all air and nerve:
you were in your twenties, and I,
once hand on glass
and heart in mouth,
outdrank the Rahvs in the heat
of Greenwich Village, fainting at your feet—
too boiled and shy
and poker-faced to make a pass,
while the shrill verve
of your invective scorched the traditional South.

Now twelve years later, you turn your back.
Sleepless, you hold
your pillow to your hollows like a child;
your old-fashioned tirade—
loving, rapid, merciless—
breaks like the Atlantic Ocean on my head.

The Exile's Return

There mounts in squalls a sort of rusty mire,
Not ice, not snow, to leaguer the Hôtel
De Ville, where braced pig-iron dragons grip
The blizzard to their rigor mortis. A bell
Grumbles when the reverberations strip
The thatching from its spire,
The search-guns click and spit and split up timber
And nick the slate roofs on the Holstenwall
Where torn-up tilestones crown the victor. Fall
And winter, spring and summer, guns unlimber
And lumber down the narrow gabled street
Past your gray, sorry and ancestral house
Where the dynamited walnut tree
Shadows a squat, old, wind-torn gate and cows
The Yankee commandant. You will not see
Strutting children or meet
The peg-leg and reproachful chancellor
With a forget-me-not in his button-hole
When the unseasoned liberators roll
Into the Market Square, ground arms before
The Rathaus; but already lily-stands
Burgeon the risen Rhineland, and a rough
Cathedral lifts its eye. Pleasant enough,
Voi ch'entrate, and your life is in your hands.

Inauguration Day: January 1953

The snow had buried Stuyvesant.
The subways drummed the vaults. I heard
the El's green girders charge on Third,
Manhattan's truss of adamant,

that groaned in ermine, slummed on want. . . .
Cyclonic zero of the word,
God of our armies, who interred
Cold Harbor's blue immortals, Grant!
Horseman, your sword is in the groove!

Ice, ice. Our wheels no longer move.
Look, the fixed stars, all just alike
as lack-land atoms, split apart,
and the Republic summons Ike,
the mausoleum in her heart.

Father's Bedroom

In my Father's bedroom:
blue threads as thin
as pen-writing on the bedspread,
blue dots on the curtains,
a blue kimono,
Chinese sandals with blue plush straps.
The broad-planked floor
had a sandpapered neatness.
The clear glass bed-lamp
with a white doily shade
was still raised a few
inches by resting on volume two
of Lafcadio Hearn's
Glimpses of Unfamiliar Japan.
Its warped olive cover
was punished like a rhinoceros hide.
In the flyleaf:
"Robbie from Mother."
Years later in the same hand:

"This book has had hard usage
on the Yangtze River, China.
It was left under an open
porthole in a storm."

Skunk Hour

(For Elizabeth Bishop)

Nautilus Island's hermit
heiress still lives through winter in her Spartan cottage;
her sheep still graze above the sea.
Her son's a bishop. Her farmer
is first selectman in our village;
she's in her dotage.

Thirsting for
the hierarchic privacy
of Queen Victoria's century,
she buys up all
the eyesores facing her shore,
and lets them fall.

The season's ill—
we've lost our summer millionaire,
who seemed to leap from an L. L. Bean
catalogue. His nine-knot yawl
was auctioned off to lobstermen.
A red fox stain covers Blue Hill.

And now our fairy
decorator brightens his shop for fall;
his fishnet's filled with orange cork,
orange, his cobbler's bench and awl;
there is no money in his work,
he'd rather marry.

One dark night,
my Tudor Ford climbed the hill's skull;
I watched for love-cars. Lights turned down,
they lay together, hull to hull,
where the graveyard shelves on the town. . . .
My mind's not right.

A car radio bleats,
"Love, O careless Love. . . ." I hear
my ill-spirit sob in each blood cell,
as if my hand were at its throat. . . .
I myself am hell;
nobody's here—

only skunks, that search
in the moonlight for a bite to eat.
They march on their soles up Main Street:
white stripes, moonstruck eyes' red fire
under the chalk-dry and spar spire
of the Trinitarian Church.

I stand on top
of our back steps and breathe the rich air—
a mother skunk with her column of kittens swills the garbage pail.
She jabs her wedge-head in a cup
of sour cream, drops her ostrich tail,
and will not scare.

Water

It was a Maine lobster town—
each morning boatloads of hands
pushed off for granite
quarries on the islands,

and left dozens of bleak
white frame houses stuck
like oyster shells
on a hill of rock,

and below us, the sea lapped
the raw little match-stick
mazes of a weir,
where the fish for bait were trapped.

Remember? We sat on a slab of rock.
From this distance in time,
it seems the color
of iris, rotting and turning purpler,

but it was only
the usual gray rock
turning the usual green
when drenched by the sea.

The sea drenched the rock
at our feet all day,
and kept tearing away
flake after flake.

One night you dreamed
you were a mermaid clinging to a wharf-pile,
and trying to pull
off the barnacles with your hands.

We wished our two souls
might return like gulls
to the rock. In the end,
the water was too cold for us.

For the Union Dead

"Relinquunt Omnia Servare Rem Publicam."

The old South Boston Aquarium stands
in a Sahara of snow now. Its broken windows are boarded.
The bronze weathervane cod has lost half its scales.
The airy tanks are dry.

Once my nose crawled like a snail on the glass;
my hand tingled
to burst the bubbles
drifting from the noses of the cowed, compliant fish.

My hand draws back. I often sigh still
For the dark downward and vegetating kingdom
of the fish and reptile. One morning last March,
I pressed against the new barbed and galvanized

fence on the Boston Common. Behind their cage,
yellow dinosaur steamshovels were grunting
as they cropped up tons of mush and grass
to gouge their underworld garage.

Parking spaces luxuriate like civic
sandpiles in the heart of Boston.
A girdle of orange, Puritan-pumpkin colored girders
braces the tingling Statehouse,

shaking over the excavations, as it faces Colonel Shaw
and his bell-cheeked Negro infantry
on St. Gaudens' shaking Civil War relief,
propped by plank splint against the garage's earthquake.

Two months after marching through Boston,
half the regiment was dead;
at the dedication,
William James could almost hear the bronze Negroes breathe.

Their monument sticks like a fishbone
in the city's throat.
Its Colonel is as lean
as a compass-needle.

He has an angry wren like vigilance,
a greyhound's gentle tautness;
he seems to wince at pleasure,
and suffocate for privacy.

He is out of bounds now. He rejoices in man's lovely,
peculiar power to choose life and die—
when he leads his black soldiers to death,
he cannot bend his back.

On a thousand small town New England greens,
the old white churches hold their air
of sparse, sincere rebellion; frayed flags
quilt the graveyards of the Grand Army of the Republic.

The stone statues of the abstract Union Solider
grow slimmer and younger each year—
wasp-waisted, they doze over muskets
and muse through their sideburns . . .

Shaw's father wanted no monument
except the ditch,
where his son's body was thrown
and lost with his "niggers."

The ditch is nearer.
There are no statues for the last war here;
on Boylston Street, a commercial photograph
shows Hiroshima boiling

over a Mosler Safe, the "Rock of Ages"
that survived the blast. Space is nearer.
When I crouch to my television set,
the drained faces of Negro school-children rise like balloons.

Colonel Shaw
is riding on his bubble,
he waits
for the blessèd break.

The Aquarium is gone. Everywhere,
giant finned cars nose forward like fish;
a savage servility
slides by on grease.

The Old Flame

My old flame, my wife!
Remember our lists of birds?
One morning last summer, I drove
by our house in Maine. It was still
on top of its hill—

Now a red ear of Indian maize
was splashed on the door.
Old Glory with thirteen stars
hung on a pole. The clapboard
was old-red schoolhouse red.

Inside, a new landlord,
a new wife, a new broom!
Atlantic seaboard antique shop
pewter and plunder
shone in each room.

A new frontier!
No running next door
now to phone the sheriff
for his taxi to Bath
and the State Liquor Store!

No one saw your ghostly
imaginary lover
stare through the window,
and tighten
the scarf at his throat.

Health to the new people,
health to their flag, to their old
restored house on the hill!

Fall 1961

Back and forth, back and forth
goes the tock, tock, tock
of the orange, bland, ambassadorial
face of the moon
on the grandfather clock.

All autumn, the chafe and jar
of nuclear war;
we have talked our extinction to death.
I swim like a minnow
behind my studio window.

Our end drifts nearer,
the moon lifts,
radiant with terror.
The state
is a diver under a glass bell.

A father's no shield
for his child.
We are like a lot of wild
spiders crying together,
but without tears.

Nature holds up a mirror.
One swallow makes a summer.
It's easy to tick
off the minutes,
but the clockhands stick.

Back and forth!
Back and forth, back and forth—
my one point of rest
is the orange and black
oriole's swinging nest!

July in Washington

The stiff spokes of this wheel
touch the sore spots of the earth.

On the Potomac, swan-white
power launches keep breasting the sulphurous wave.

Otters slide and dive and slick back their hair,
raccoons clean their meat in the creek.

On the circles, green statues ride like South American
liberators above the breeding vegetation—

prongs and spearheads of some equatorial
backland that will inherit the globe.

The elect, the elected . . . they come here bright as dimes,
and die disheveled and soft.

We cannot name their names, or number their dates—
circle on circle, like rings on a tree—

but we wish the river had another shore,
some further range of delectable mountains,

distant hills powdered blue as a girl's eyelid.
It seems the least little shove would land us there,

that only the slightest repugnance of our bodies
we no longer control could drag us back.

New York 1962: Fragment

(For E.H.L.)

This might be nature—twenty stories high,
two water tanks, tanned shingle, corseted
by stapled pasture wire, while bed to bed,
we two, one cell here, lie
gazing into the ether's crystal ball,
sky and a sky, and sky, and sky, till death—
my heart stops . . .
This might be heaven. Years ago,
we aimed for less and settled for
a picture, out of style then and now in,
of seven daffodils. We watched them blow:
buttercup yellow were the flowers, and green
the stems as fresh paint, over them the wind,
the blousy wooden branches of the elms,
high summer in the breath that overwhelms
the termites digging in the underpinning . . .
Still over us, still in parenthesis,
this sack of hornets sopping up the flame,
still over us our breath,
sawing and pumping to the terminal,
and down below, we two, two in one waterdrop
vitalized by a needle drop of blood,
up, up, up, up and up,
soon shot, soon slugged into the overflow
that sets the wooden workhorse working here below.

Night Sweat

Work-table, litter, books and standing lamp,
plain things, my stalled equipment, the old broom—
but I am living in a tidied room,
for ten nights now I've felt the creeping damp
float over my pajamas' wilted white . . .
Sweet salt embalms me and my head is wet,
everything streams and tells me this is right;
my life's fever is soaking in night sweat—
one life, one writing! But the downward glide
and bias of existing wrings us dry—
always inside me is the child who died,
always inside me is his will to die—
one universe, one body . . . in this urn
the animal night sweats of the spirit burn.

Behind me! You! Again I feel the light
lighten my leaded eyelids, while the gray
skulled horses whinny for the soot of night.
I dabble in the dapple of the day,
a heap of wet clothes, seamy, shivering,
I see my flesh and bedding washed with light,
my child exploding into dynamite,
my wife . . . your lightness alters everything,
and tears the black web from the spider's sack,
as your heart hops and flutters like a hare.
Poor turtle, tortoise, if I cannot clear
the surface of these troubled waters here,
absolve me, help me, Dear Heart, as you bear
this world's dead weight and cycle on your back.

Randall Jarrell 2

I grizzle the embers of our onetime life,
our first intoxicating disenchantments,
dipping our hands once, not twice in the newness . . .
coming back to Kenyon on the Ohio local—
the view, middle distance, back and foreground, shifts,
silos shifting squares like chessmen—a wheel
turned by the water buffalo through the blue
of true space before the dawn of days. . . .
Then the night of the caged squirrel on his wheel,
lights, eyes, peering at you from the overpass;
black-gloved, black-coated, you plod out stubbornly
as if in lockstep to grasp your blank not-I
at the foot of the tunnel . . . as if asleep, Child Randall,
greeting the cars, and approving—your harsh luminosity.

The Nihilist as Hero

"All our French poets can turn an inspired line;
who has written six passable in sequence?"
said Valéry. That was a happy day for Satan. . . .
I want words meat-hooked from the living steer,
but a cold flame of tinfoil licks the metal log,
beautiful unchanging fire of childhood
betraying a monotony of vision. . . .
Life by definition breeds on change,
each season we scrap new cars and wars and women.
But sometimes when I am ill or delicate,
the pinched flame of my match turns unchanging green,
a cornstalk in green tails and seeded tassel. . . .
A nihilist wants to live in the world as is,
and yet gaze the everlasting hills to rubble.

Symptoms

I fear my conscience because it makes me lie.
A dog seems to lap water from the pipes,
life-enhancing water brims my bath—
(the bag of waters or the lake of the grave . . . ?)
from the palms of my feet to my wet neck—
I have no mother to lift me in her arms.
I feel my old infection, it comes once yearly:
lowered good humor, then an ominous
rise of irritable enthusiasm. . . .
Three dolphins bear our little toilet-stand,
the grin of the eyes rebukes the scowl of the lips,
they are crazy with the thirst. I soak,
examining and then examining
what I really have against myself.

KARL SHAPIRO

(1913–2000)

Consultant in Poetry (1946–1947)

The poet is in exile whether he is or he is not. Because of what every-body knows about society's idea of the artist as a peripheral character and potential bum. Or troublemaker. . . . And so I always thought of myself as being both in and out of society at the same time. Like the way most art-ists probably feel in order to survive—you have to at least pretend that you are "seriously" in the world. Or actually perform in it while you know that in your own soul you are not in it at all. You are outside observing it.

Karl Shapiro wrote much of the verse in his popular first volume, *V-Letter and Other Poems*, as a young combat soldier in the Second World War. A consummate and outspoken autodidact, Shapiro studied at the University of Virginia and Johns Hopkins University but never earned a college degree, despite going on to teach with distinction at a number of colleges and universities throughout the country before settling at UC Davis, where he taught from 1968 to 1985.

His early work was traditional in form and focused on themes of war and loss. In the latter half of his career he loosened up, finding a voice that is by turns ironic, incisive, and populist. Later in his career, Shapiro fell out of fashion with critics and the public (in large part because of his public denunciation of Ezra Pound and T. S. Eliot) and was even reported dead (listed famously in the *New York Times* crossword puzzle under the clue "deceased poet"), to which he responded, with characteristic humor, by titling his subsequent autobiography *Reports of My Death*.

Shapiro served as poetry consultant at the very outset of his career, immediately upon returning from armed service. While in office, he deliberately neglected to record Ezra Pound for the Library's recording series. Pound had become involved in Fascist politics while living in Italy between 1924 and 1945, when he was arrested on the charge of treason for broadcasting Fascist propaganda by radio to the United States during the Second World War. In 1946 Pound was acquitted but declared mentally ill and committed to St. Elizabeths Hospital in Washington, D.C. In 1948 the Fellows in American Letters of the Library of Congress chose to overlook Pound's political career in the interest of recognizing his poetic achievements and awarded him the Library's first Bollingen Prize in Poetry for the *Pisan Cantos*.

Shapiro publicized his opposition to giving Pound the first Bollingen Prize, criticizing both Pound's politics and his anti-Semitism. Shapiro remembered this as a turning point in his career: "I was suddenly forced into a conscious decision to stand up and be counted as a Jew." He titled his next volume *Poems of a Jew*, defining "the free modern Jew" as "neither hero nor victim" but rather as "man left over, after everything that can happened has happened."

Lower the Standard

Lower the standard: that's my motto. Somebody is always putting the food out of reach. We're tired of falling off ladders. Who says a child can't paint? A pro is somebody who does it for money. Lower the standards. Let's all play poetry. Down with ideals, flags, convention buttons, morals, the scrambled eggs on the admiral's hat. I'm talking sense. Lower the standards. Sabotage the stylistic approach. Let weeds grow in the subdivision. Putty up the incisions in the library façade, those names that frighten grade-school teachers, those names whose U's are cut like V's. Burn the *Syntopicon* and *The Harvard Classics*. Lower the standard on classics, battleships, Russian ballet, national anthems (but they're low enough). Break through to the bottom. Be natural as an American abroad who knows no language, not even American. Keelhaul the poets in the vestry chairs. Renovate the Abbey of cold-storage dreamers. Get off the Culture Wagon. Learn how to walk the way you want. Slump your shoulders, stick your belly out, arms all over the table. How many generations will this take? Don't think about it, just make a start. (You have made a start.) Don't break anything you can step around, *but don't pick it up.* The law of gravity is the law of art. You first, poetry second, the good, the beautiful, the true come last. As the lad said: We must love one another or die.

The Fly

O hideous little bat, the size of snot,
With polyhedral eye and shabby clothes,
To populate the stinking cat you walk
The promontory of the dead man's nose,
Climb with the fine leg of a Duncan-Phyfe
    The smoking mountains of my food
        And in a comic mood
    In mid-air take to bed a wife.

Riding and riding with your filth of hair
On gluey foot or wing, forever coy,
Hot from the compost and green sweet decay,
Sounding your buzzer like an urchin toy—
You dot all whiteness with diminutive stool,
    In the tight belly of the dead
        Burrow with hungry head
    And inlay maggots like a jewel.

At your approach the great horse stomps and paws
Bringing the hurricane of his heavy tail;
Shod in disease you dare to kiss my hand
Which sweeps against you like an angry flail;
Still you return, return, trusting your wing
    To draw you from the hunter's reach
        That learns to kill to teach
    Disorder to the tinier thing.

My peace is your disaster. For your death
Children like spiders cup their pretty hands
And wives resort to chemistry of war.
In fens of sticky paper and quicksands
You glue yourself to death. Where you are stuck
    You struggle hideously and beg,
        You amputate your leg
    Imbedded in the amber muck.

But I, a man, must swat you with my hate,
Slap you across the air and crush your flight,
Must mangle with my shoe and smear your blood,
Expose your little guts pasty and white,
Knock your head sidewise like a drunkard's hat,
  Pin your wings under like a crow's,
   Tear off your flimsy clothes
And beat you as one beats a rat.

Then like Gargantua I stride among
The corpses strewn like raisins in the dust,
The broken bodies of the narrow dead
That catch the throat with fingers of disgust.
I sweep. One gyrates like a top and falls
  And stunned, stone blind, and deaf
   Buzzes its frightful F
And dies between three cannibals.

Poet

Il arrive que l'esprit demande la poesie

Left leg flung out, head cocked to the right,
Tweed coat or army uniform, with book,
Beautiful eyes, who is this walking down?
Who, glancing at the pane of glass looks sharp
And thinks it is not he—as when a poet
Comes swiftly on some half-forgotten poem
And loosely holds the page, steady of mind,
  Thinking it is not his?

And when will *you* exist?—Oh, it is I,
Incredibly skinny, stooped, and neat as pie,
Ignorant as dirt, erotic as an ape,
Dreamy as puberty—with dirty hair!
Into the room like kangaroo he bounds,
Ears flopping like the most expensive hound's;
His chin receives all questions as he bows
      Mouthing a green bon-bon.

Has no more memory than rubber. Stands
Waist-deep in heavy mud of thought and broods
At his own wetness. When he would get out,
To his surprise he lifts in air a phrase
As whole and clean and silvery as a fish
Which jumps and dangles on his damned hooked grin,
But like a name-card on a man's lapel
      Calls him a conscious fool.

And child-like he remembers all his life
And cannily constructs it, fact by fact,
As boys paste postage stamps in careful books,
Denoting pence and legends and profiles,
Nothing more valuable.—And like a thief,
His eyes glassed over and congealed with guilt,
Fondles his secrets like a case of tools,
      And waits in empty doors.

By men despised for knowing what he is,
And by himself. But he exists for women.
As dolls to girls, as perfect wives to men,
So he to women. And to himself a thing,
All ages, epicene, without a trade.
To girls and wives always alive and fated;
To men and scholars always dead like Greek
      And always mistranslated.

Towards exile and towards shame he lures himself,
Tongue winding on his arm, and thinks like Eve
By biting apple will become most wise.
Sentio ergo sum: he feels his way
And words themselves stand up for him like Braille
And punch and perforate his parchment ear.
All language falls like Chinese on his soul,
      Image of song unsounded.

This is the coward's coward that in his dreams
Sees shapes of pain grow tall. Awake at night
He peers at sounds and stumbles at a breeze.
And none holds life less dear. For as a youth
Who by some accident observes his love
Naked and in some natural ugly act,
He turns with loathing and with flaming hands,
      Seared and betrayed by sight.

He is the business man, on beauty trades,
Dealer in arts and thoughts who, like the Jew,
Shall rise from slums and hated dialects
A tower of bitterness. Shall be always strange,
Hunted and then sought after. Shall be sat
Like an ambassador from another race
At tables rich with music. He shall eat flowers,
Chew honey and spit out gall. They shall all smile
      And love and pity him.

His death shall be by drowning. In that hour
When the last bubble of pure heaven's air
Hovers within his throat, safe on his bed,
A small eternal figurehead in terror,
He shall cry out and clutch his days of straw
Before the blackest wave. Lastly, his tomb
Shall list and founder in the troughs of grass
      And none shall speak his name.

Elegy for a Dead Soldier

I

A white sheet on the tail gate of a truck
Becomes an altar; two small candlesticks
Sputter at each side of the crucifix
Laid round with flowers brighter than the blood
Red as the red of our apocalypse,
Hibiscus that a marching man will pluck
To stick into his rifle or his hat,
And great blue morning-glories pale as lips
That shall no longer taste or kiss or swear.
The wind begins a low magnificat,
The chaplain chats, the palmtrees swirl their hair,
The columns come together through the mud.

II

We too are ashes as we watch and hear
The psalm, the sorrow, and the simple praise
Of one whose promised thoughts of other days
Were such as ours, but now wholly destroyed,
The service record of his youth wiped out,
His dream dispersed by shot, must disappear.
What can we feel but wonder at a loss
That seems to point at nothing but the doubt
Which flirts our sense of luck into the ditch?
Reader of Paul who prays beside this fosse,
Shall we believe our eyes or legends rich
With glory and rebirth beyond the void?

III

For this comrade is dead, dead in the war,
A young man out of millions yet to live,
One cut away from all that war can give,
Freedom of self and peace to wander free.
Who mourns in all this sober multitude
Who did not feel the bite of it before
The bullet found its aim? This worthy flesh,
This boy laid in a coffin and reviewed—
Who has not wrapped himself in this same flag,
Heard the light fall of dirt, his wound still fresh,
Felt his eyes closed, and heard the distant brag
Of the last volley of humanity?

IV

By chance I saw him die, stretched on the ground,
A tattooed arm lifted to take the blood
Of someone else sealed in a tin. I stood
During the last delirium that stays
The intelligence a tiny moment more,
And then the strangulation, the last sound,
The end was sudden, like a foolish play,
A stupid fool slamming a foolish door,
The absurd catastrophe, half-prearranged,
And all the decisive things still left to say.
So we disbanded, angrier and unchanged,
Sick with the utter silence of dispraise.

V

We ask for no statistics of the killed,
For nothing political impinges on
This single casualty, or all those gone,

Missing or healing, sinking or dispersed,
Hundreds of thousands counted, millions lost.
More than an accident and less than willed
Is every fall, and this one like the rest.
However others calculate the cost,
To us the final aggregate is *one*,
One with a name, one transferred to the blest;
And though another stoops and takes the gun,
We cannot add the second to the first.

VI

I would not speak for him who could not speak
Unless my fear were true: he was not wronged,
He knew to which decision he belonged
But let it choose itself. Ripe in instinct,
Neither the victim nor the volunteer,
He followed, and the leaders could not seek
Beyond the followers. Much of this he knew;
The journey was a detour that would steer
Into the Lincoln Highway of a land
Remorselessly improved, excited, new,
And that was what he wanted. He had planned
To earn and drive. He and the world had winked.

VII

No history deceived him, for he knew
Little of times and armies not his own;
He never felt that peace was but a loan,
Had never questioned the idea of gain.
Beyond the headlines once or twice he saw
The gathering of a power by the few
But could not tell their names; he cast his vote,
Distrusting all the elected but not law.

He laughed at socialism; *on mourrait*
Pour les industriels? He shed his coat
And not for brotherhood, but for his pay.
To him the red flag marked the sewer main.

VIII

Above all else he loathed the homily,
The slogan and the ad. He paid his bill,
But not for Congressmen at Bunker Hill.
Ideals were few and those there were not made
For conversation. He belonged to church
But never spoke of God. The Christmas tree,
The Easter egg, baptism, he observed,
Never denied the preacher on his perch,
And would not sign Resolved That or Whereas.
Softness he had and hours and nights reserved
For thinking, dressing, dancing to the jazz.
His laugh was real, his manners were homemade.

IX

Of all men poverty pursued him least;
He was ashamed of all the down and out,
Spurned the panhandler like an uneasy doubt,
And saw the unemployed as a vague mass
Incapable of hunger or revolt.
He hated other races, south or east,
And shoved them to the margin of his mind.
He could recall the justice of the Colt,
Take interest in a gang-war like a game.
His ancestry was somewhere far behind
And left him only his peculiar name.
Doors opened, and he recognized no class.

X

His children would have known a heritage,
Just or unjust, the richest in the world,
The quantum of all art and science curled
In the horn of plenty, bursting from the horn,
A people bathed in honey, Paris come,
Vienna transferred with the highest wage,
A World's Fair spread to Phoenix, Jacksonville,
Earth's capital, the new Byzantium,
Kingdom of man—who knows? Hollow or firm,
No man can ever prophesy until
Out of our death some undiscovered germ,
Whole toleration or pure peace is born.

XI

The time to mourn is short that best becomes
The military dead. We lift and fold the flag,
Lay bare the coffin with its written tag,
And march away. Behind, four others wait
To lift the box, the heaviest of loads.
The anesthetic afternoon benumbs,
Sickens our senses, forces back our talk.
We know that others on tomorrow's roads
Will fall, ourselves perhaps, the man beside,
Over the world the threatened, all who walk:
And could we mark the grave of him who died
We would write this beneath his name and date:

EPITAPH

Underneath this wooden cross there lies
A Christian killed in battle. You who read,
Remember that this stranger died in pain;

And passing here, if you can lift your eyes
Upon a peace kept by a human creed,
Know that one soldier has not died in vain.

The Living Rooms of My Neighbors

The living rooms of my neighbors are like beauty parlors, like night-
    club powder rooms, like international airport first-class lounges.
    The bathrooms of my neighbors are like love nests—Dufy prints,
    black Kleenex, furry towels, toilets so highly bred they fill and fall
    without a sigh (why is there no bidet in so-clean America?). The
    kitchens of my neighbors are like cars: what gleaming dials, what
    toothy enamels, engines that click and purr, idling the hours away.
    The basements of my neighbors are like kitchens; you could eat
    off the floor. Look at the furnace, spotless as a breakfront, stand-
    ing alone, prize piece, the god of the household.

But I'm no different. I arrange my books with a view to their appear-
    ance. Some highbrow titles are prominently displayed. The desk
    in my study is carefully littered; after some thought I hang a
    diploma on the wall, only to take it down again. I sit at the
    window where I can be seen. What do my neighbors think of
    me—I hope they think of me. I fix the light to hit the books. I
    lean some rows one way, some rows another.

A man's house is his stage. Others walk on to play their bit parts. Now
    and again a soliloquy, a birth, an adultery.

The bars of my neighbors are various, ranging from none at all to the
    nearly professional, leather stools, automatic coolers, a naked
    painting, a spittoon for show.
The businessman, the air-force captain, the professor with tenure—it's a
    neighborhood with a sky.

Editing *Poetry*

Next to my office where I edit poems ("Can poems be edited?") there
 is the Chicago Models Club. All day the girls stroll past my door
 where I am editing poems, behind my head a signed photo-
 graph of Rupert Brooke, handsomer than any movie star. I edit,
 keeping one eye peeled for the models, straining my ears to hear
 what they say. In there they photograph the girls on the bam-
 boo furniture, glossies for the pulsing façades of night spots. One
 day the manager brings me flowers, a huge and damaged bou-
 quet: hurt gladiolas, overly open roses, long-leaping ferns (least
 hurt), and bruised carnations. I accept the gift, remainder of last
 night's opening (where?), debut of lower-class blondes. I distrib-
 ute the flowers in the other poetry rooms, too formal-looking
 for our disarray.

Now after every model's bow to the footlights the manager brings more
 flowers, hurt gladiolas, overly open roses, long-leaping ferns and
 bruised carnations. I edit poems to the click of sharp high heels,
 flanked by the swords of lavender debut, whiffing the cinnamon
 of crepe-paper-pink carnations of the bruised and lower-class
 blondes.

Behind me rears my wall of books, most formidable of human barriers.
 No flower depresses me like the iris but these I have a fondness
 for. They bring stale memories over the threshold of the street.
 They bring the night of cloth palm trees and soft plastic leop-
 ard chairs, night of sticky drinks, the shining rhinestone hour in
 the dark-blue mirror, the peroxide chat of models and photo-
 genic morn.

Today the manager brings all gladioli. A few rose petals lie in the corri-
 dor. The mail is heavy this morning.

Manhole Covers

The beauty of manhole covers—what of that?
Like medals struck by a great savage khan,
Like Mayan calendar stones, unliftable, indecipherable,
Not like the old electrum, chased and scored,
Mottoed and sculptured to a turn,
But notched and whelked and pocked and smashed
With the great company names
(Gentle Bethlehem, smiling United States).
This rustproof artifact of my street,
Long after roads are melted away will lie
Sidewise in the grave of the iron-old world,
Bitten at the edges,
Strong with its cryptic American,
Its dated beauty.

A Drawerful of Eyeglasses

I have a drawerful of eyeglasses
Which Spinoza or Galileo would have given their eyeteeth for:
Green-black prescription glasses,
Glasses for reading or driving,
Even a reading lens for proofreading poems.
What if a tornado ground them up with brick?
What if they were melted by the master-bomb
As the sands of the desert were melted to balls of glass?
What if I couldn't read the latest book
On metaphor or guilt?
What if I had to make up poems in my head
Like Milton or Homer?

Man on Wheels

Cars are wicked, poets think.
Wrong as usual. Cars are part of man.
Cars are biological.
A man without a car is like a clam without a shell.
Granted, machinery is hell,
But carless man is careless and defenseless.
Ford is skin of present animal.
Automobile is shell.
You get yourself a shell or else.

The Piano Tuner's Wife

That note comes clear, like water running clear,
Then the next higher note, and up and up
And more and more, with now and then a chord,
The highest notes like tapping a tile with a hammer,
Now and again an arpeggio, a theme,
As if the keyboard spoke to the one key,
Saying, No interval is exactly true,
And the note whines slightly and then truly sings.

She sits on the sofa reading a book she has brought,
A ray of sunlight on her white hair.
She is here because he is blind. She drives.
It is almost a platitude to say
That she leads him from piano to piano.

And this continues for about an hour,
Building bridges from both sides of the void,
Coasting the chasms of the harmonies.

And in conclusion,
When there is no more audible dissent,
He plays his comprehensive keyboard song,
The loud proud paradigm,
The one work of art without content.

LOUISE BOGAN

(1897–1970)

Consultant in Poetry (1945–1946)

Now that the time draws near that I shall leave (a bad translation from the Sanskrit, that last!) I am feeling rather warmly toward Washington, Georgetown, the L. of C.... The Library machinery still baffles me; but I have leaned over backwards to be cool and detached and cheerful and obliging. As a matter of fact, it has all been v., v. pleasant, and I have learned a lot; and the Library has learned a few things, too. Such as the fact that R. M. Rilke is a man, not a woman, and writes in German, not Italian.

L ouise Bogan was born in Livermore Falls, Maine, and spent most of her childhood in Boston. She began writing and studying poetry in elementary school, discovering early that writing about certain images helped counteract the destabilizing effects of her parents' unhappy marriage and her mother's frequent illnesses. She wrote that a vision of a vase of marigolds seen in a hospital room was her call to poetry: "Suddenly I *recognized* something at once simple and full of the utmost richness of design and contrast that was mine."

Bogan's first book of poetry, *Body of Death*, appeared in 1923, a year after T. S. Eliot's *The Waste Land*. It was hailed by critics as a spare, minimalist alternative to Eliot's brand of sprawling, fragmented modernism. Bogan's poems are ample proof that economy of line can convey abundance of emotion. Grief is most often the emotional center of poems that explore conflicts between desire and the intellect.

During the 1930s when many of her poet friends were writing about their left-leaning politics, Bogan staunchly defended the historical remove of lyric poetry, referring to political poets as "time-servers." From 1931 until 1969 she was *The New Yorker's* chief poetry critic, setting a standard for fair and penetrating criticism (often of the work of close friends) and expressing her disdain for the trend toward confessional poetry by poets like Robert Lowell.

Bogan thrived during her term as consultant in poetry: "The work at the Library is delightful: I have an assistant who treats me like a Mandarin." During her tenure she compiled a bibliography of literary works published in Great Britain from 1939 to 1946, evaluated and listed all of the smaller magazines devoted to publishing poetry, and oversaw the first stages of the Library's long-term project of recording the best twentieth-century poetry in English. Bogan herself was a celebrated poetry reader. Fellow laureate William Jay Smith praised "her rich contralto voice," saying, "she has the most perfect enunciation that you will ever encounter among poets today: every consonant, every vowel, every syllable is given its proper value, and then there are the pauses around which the poems are constructed, all carefully observed."

The Daemon

Must I tell again
In the words I know
For the ears of men
The flesh, the blow?

Must I show outright
The bruise in the side,
The halt in the night,
And how death cried?

Must I speak to the lot
Who little bore?
It said *Why not?*
It said *Once more.*

Medusa

I had come to the house, in a cave of trees,
Facing a sheer sky.
Everything moved,—a bell hung ready to strike,
Sun and reflection wheeled by.

When the bare eyes were before me
And the hissing hair,

Held up at a window, seen through a door.
The stiff bald eyes, the serpents on the forehead
Formed in the air.

This is a dead scene forever now.
Nothing will ever stir.
The end will never brighten it more than this,
Nor the rain blur.

The water will always fall, and will not fall,
And the tipped bell make no sound.
The grass will always be growing for hay
Deep on the ground.

And I shall stand here like a shadow
Under the great balanced day,
My eyes on the yellow dust, that was lifting in the wind,
And does not drift away.

Knowledge

Now that I know
How passion warms little
Of flesh in the mould,
And treasure is brittle,—

I'll lie here and learn
How, over their ground,
Trees make a long shadow
And a light sound.

Second Song

I said out of sleeping:
Passion, farewell.
Take from my keeping
Bauble and shell,

Black salt, black provender.
Tender your store
To a new pensioner,
To me no more.

Several Voices Out of a Cloud

Come, drunks and drug-takers; come, perverts unnerved!
Receive the laurel, given, though late, on merit; to whom
     and wherever deserved.

Parochial punks, trimmers, nice people, joiners true-blue,
Get the hell out of the way of the laurel. It is deathless
     And it isn't for you.

Question in a Field

Pasture, stone wall, and steeple,
What most perturbs the mind:
The heart–rending homely people,
Or the horrible beautiful kind?

Solitary Observation Brought Back from a Sojourn in Hell

At midnight tears
Run into your ears.

The Dream

O God, in the dream the terrible horse began
To paw at the air, and make for me with his blows.
Fear kept for thirty-five years poured through his mane,
And retribution equally old, or nearly, breathed through his nose.

Coward complete, I lay and wept on the ground
When some strong creature appeared, and leapt for the rein.
Another woman, as I lay half in a swound,
Leapt in the air, and clutched at the leather and chain.

Give him, she said, something of yours as a charm.
Throw him, she said, some poor thing you alone claim.
No, no, I cried, he hates me; he's out for harm,
And whether I yield or not, it is all the same.

But, like a lion in a legend, when I flung the glove
Pulled from my sweating, my cold right hand,
The terrible beast, that no one may understand,
Came to my side, and put down his head in love.

Cartography

As you lay in sleep
I saw the chart
Of artery and vein
Running from your heart,

Plain as the strength
Marked upon the leaf
Along the length,
Mortal and brief,

Of your gaunt hand.
I saw it clear:
The wiry brand
Of the life we bear

Mapped like the great
Rivers that rise
Beyond our fate
And distant from our eyes.

The Dragonfly

You are made of almost nothing
But of enough
To be great eyes
And diaphanous double vans;
To be ceaseless movement,
Unending hunger
Grappling love.

Link between water and air,
Earth repels you.
Light touches you only to shift into iridescence
Upon your body and wings.

Twice-born, predator,
You split into the heat.
Swift beyond calculation or capture
You dart into the shadow
Which consumes you.

You rocket into the day.
But at last, when the wind flattens the grasses,
For you, the design and purpose stop.

And you fall
With the other husks of summer.

Night

The cold remote islands
And the blue estuaries
Where what breathes, breathes
The restless wind of the inlets,
And what drinks, drinks
The incoming tide;

Where shell and weed
Wait upon the salt wash of the sea,
And the clear nights of stars
Swing their lights westward
To set behind the land;

Where the pulse clinging to the rocks
Renews itself forever;
Where, again on cloudless nights,
The water reflects
The firmament's partial setting;

—O remember
In your narrowing dark hours
That more things move
Than blood in the heart.

ALLEN TATE

(1899–1979)

Consultant in Poetry (1943–1944)

It seems to me that my verse or anybody else's is merely a way of knowing something: if the poem is a real creation, it is a kind of knowledge that we did not possess before. It is not knowledge "about" something else; the poem is the fullness of that knowledge. We know the particular poem, not what it says that we can restate. In a manner of speaking, the poem is its own knower, neither poet nor reader knowing anything that the poem says apart from the words of the poem.

R egionalist, agrarian, New Critic, Roman Catholic apologist, and groundbreaking modernist, Allen Tate was born at the turn of the twentieth century and grew up in Kentucky and Tennessee, the son of a brutal father and an unstable mother who glorified her aristocratic Southern ancestors. Tate's preoccupation with the romantic past of the Old South, his distrust of Northern industrialism, and his disillusionment with the country's materialistic values in the aftermath of World War I fueled his twenty-some volumes of verse, criticism, and fiction, all studded with allusions to antebellum lore and classical antiquity. He rose to a position of literary prominence in the 1940s as an editor at the *Kenyon Review* and later as the editor in chief of the *Sewanee Review*, and held professorships at Princeton, the University of Minnesota, and Southwestern College in Memphis. One of the twentieth century's most influential critics, Tate was an early and staunch proponent of New Criticism, an "art for art's sake" approach to reading poetry, without reference to historical or biographical context.

During his tenure at the Library, Tate was a curatorial force. He undertook a survey of the collections in American and English poetry, resulting in the anthology *Sixty American Poets, 1896–1944,* and edited the Library's *Quarterly Journal of Current Acquisitions.* In an essay he wrote while in Washington, however, Tate expressed his reservations about such projects: "it is my impression that poets in the past, before the era of Teutonic efficiency in letters, had to make their own way, and they did it without the benefit of library science." He went on to say that he didn't believe libraries could do much "for literature unless the society sustaining the literature has already done it or is doing it, and the 'science' is a mere instrument of that deeper will." At the end of his term, Tate helped found the Fellows in American Letters of the Library of Congress.

Ode to the Confederate Dead

Row after row with strict impunity
The headstones yield their names to the element,
The wind whirrs without recollection;
In the riven troughs the splayed leaves
Pile up, of nature the casual sacrament
To the seasonal eternity of death;
Then driven by the fierce scrutiny
Of heaven to their election in the vast breath,
They sough the rumour of mortality.

Autumn is desolation in the plot
Of a thousand acres where these memories grow
From the inexhaustible bodies that are not
Dead, but feed the grass row after rich row.
Think of the autumns that have come and gone!—
Ambitious November with the humors of the year,
With a particular zeal for every slab,
Staining the uncomfortable angels that rot
On the slabs, a wing chipped here, an arm there:
The brute curiosity of an angel's stare
Turns you, like them, to stone,
Transforms the heaving air
Till plunged to a heavier world below
You shift your sea-space blindly
Heaving, turning like the blind crab.

Dazed by the wind, only the wind
The leaves flying, plunge

You know who have waited by the wall
The twilight certainty of an animal,
Those midnight restitutions of the blood
You know—the immitigable pines, the smoky frieze
Of the sky, the sudden call: you know the rage,
The cold pool left by the mounting flood,
Of muted Zeno and Parmenides.
You who have waited for the angry resolution
Of those desires that should be yours tomorrow,
You know the unimportant shrift of death
And praise the vision
And praise the arrogant circumstance
Of those who fall
Rank upon rank, hurried beyond decision—
Here by the sagging gate, stopped by the wall.

     Seeing, seeing only the leaves
     Flying, plunge and expire

Turn your eyes to the immoderate past,
Turn to the inscrutable infantry rising
Demons out of the earth—they will not last.
Stonewall, Stonewall, and the sunken fields of hemp,
Shiloh, Antietam, Malvern Hill, Bull Run.
Lost in that orient of the thick-and-fast
You will curse the setting sun.

     Cursing only the leaves crying
     Like an old man in a storm.

You hear the shout, the crazy hemlocks point
With troubled fingers to the silence which
Smothers you, a mummy, in time.

                    The hound bitch
Toothless and dying, in a musty cellar
Hears the wind only.

                    Now that the salt of their blood
Stiffens the saltier oblivion of the sea,
Seals the malignant purity of the flood,
What shall we who count our days and bow
Our heads with a commemorial woe
In the ribboned coats of grim felicity,
What shall we say of the bones, unclean,
Whose verdurous anonymity will grow?
The ragged arms, the ragged heads and eyes
Lost in these acres of the insane green?
The gray lean spiders come, they come and go;
In a tangle of willows without light
The singular screech-owl's tight
Invisible lyric seeds the mind
With the furious murmur of their chivalry.

                    We shall say only the leaves
                    Flying, plunge and expire

We shall say only the leaves whispering
In the improbable mist of nightfall
That flies on multiple wing;
Night is the beginning and the end
And in between the ends of distraction
Waits mute speculation, the patient curse
That stones the eyes, or like the jaguar leaps
For his own image in a jungle pool, his victim.
What shall we say who have knowledge
Carried to the heart? Shall we take the act
To the grave? Shall we, more hopeful, set up the grave
In the house? The ravenous grave?

                                        Leave now
The shut gate and the decomposing wall:
The gentle serpent, green in the mulberry bush,
Riots with his tongue through the hush—
Sentinel of the grave who counts us all!

Mr. Pope

When Alexander Pope strolled in the city
Strict was the glint of pearl and gold sedans.
Ladies leaned out more out of fear than pity
For Pope's tight back was rather a goat's than man's.

Often one thinks the urn should have more bones
Than skeletons provide for speedy dust,
The urn gets hollow, cobwebs brittle as stones
Weave to the funeral shell a frivolous rust.

And he who dribbled couplets like a snake
Coiled to a lithe precision in the sun
Is missing. The jar is empty; you may break
It only to find that Mr. Pope is gone.

What requisitions of a verity
Prompted the wit and rage between his teeth
One cannot say. Around a crooked tree
A moral climbs whose name should be a wreath.

The Wolves

There are wolves in the next room waiting
With heads bent low, thrust out, breathing
At nothing in the dark; between them and me
A white door patched with light from the hall
Where it seems never (so still is the house)
A man has walked from the front door to the stair.
It has all been forever. Beasts claw the floor.
I have brooded on angels and archfiends
But no man has ever sat where the next room's
Crowded with wolves, and for the honor of man
I affirm that never have I before. Now while
I have looked for the evening star at a cold window
And whistled when Arcturus spilt his light,
I've heard the wolves scuffle, and said: So this
Is man; so—what better conclusion is there—
The day will not follow night, and the heart
Of man has a little dignity, but less patience
Than a wolf's, and a duller sense that cannot
Smell its own mortality. (This and other
Meditations will be suited to other times
After dog silence howls his epitaph.)
Now remember courage, go to the door,
Open it and see whether coiled on the bed
Or cringing by the wall, a savage beast
Maybe with golden hair, with deep eyes
Like a bearded spider on a sunlit floor
Will snarl—and man can never be alone.

The Mediterranean

Quem das finem, rex magne, dolorum?

Where we went in the boat was a long bay
A slingshot wide, walled in by towering stone—
Peaked margin of antiquity's delay,
And we went there out of time's monotone:

Where we went in the black hull no light moved
But a gull white-winged along the feckless wave,
The breeze, unseen but fierce as a body loved,
That boat drove onward like a willing slave:

Where we went in the small ship the seaweed
Parted and gave to us the murmuring shore,
And we made feast and in our secret need
Devoured the very plates Aeneas bore:

Where derelict you see through the low twilight
The green coast that you, thunder-tossed, would win,
Drop sail, and hastening to drink all night
Eat dish and bowl to take that sweet land in!

Where we feasted and caroused on the sandless
Pebbles, affecting our day of piracy,
What prophecy of eaten plates could landless
Wanderers fulfil by the ancient sea?

We for that time might taste the famous age
Eternal here yet hidden from our eyes
When lust of power undid its stuffless rage;
They, in a wineskin, bore earth's paradise.

Let us lie down once more by the breathing side
Of Ocean, where our live forefathers sleep
As if the Known Sea still were a month wide—
Atlantis howls but is no longer steep!

What country shall we conquer, what fair land
Unman our conquest and locate our blood?
We've cracked the hemispheres with careless hand!
Now, from the Gates of Hercules we flood

Westward, westward till the barbarous brine
Whelms us to the tired land where tasseling corn,
Fat beans, grapes sweeter than muscadine
Rot on the vine: in that land were we born.

Aeneas at Washington

I myself saw furious with blood
Neoptolemus, at his side the black Atridae,
Hecuba and the hundred daughters, Priam
Cut down, his filth drenching the holy fires.
In that extremity I bore me well,
A true gentleman, valorous in arms,
Disinterested and honourable. Then fled:
That was a time when civilization
Run by the few fell to the many, and
Crashed to the shout of men, the clang of arms:
Cold victualing I seized, I hoisted up
The old man my father upon my back,
In the smoke made by sea for a new world
Saving little—a mind imperishable
If time is, a love of past things tenuous
As the hesitation of receding love.

(To the reduction of uncitied littorals
We brought chiefly the vigor of prophecy,
Our hunger breeding calculation
And fixed triumphs.)

                I saw the thirsty dove
In the glowing fields of Troy, hemp ripening
And tawny corn, the thickening Blue Grass
All lying rich forever in the green sun.
I see all things apart, the towers that men
Contrive I too contrived long, long ago.
Now I demand little. The singular passion
Abides its object and consumes desire
In the circling shadow of its appetite.

There was a time when the young eyes were slow,
Their flame steady beyond the firstling fire,
I stood in the rain, far from home at nightfall
By the Potomac, the great Dome lit the water,
The city my blood had built I knew no more
While the screech-owl whistled his new delight
Consecutively dark.

               Struck in the wet mire
Four thousand leagues from the ninth buried city
I thought of Troy, what we had built her for.

The Meaning of Life

A Monologue

Think about it at will: there is that
Which is the commentary; there's that other,
Which may be called the immaculate
Conception of its essence in itself.
It is necessary to distinguish the weights
Of the two methods lest the first smother
The second, the second be speechless (without the first).
I was saying this more briefly the other day
But one must be explicit as well as brief.
When I was a small boy I lived at home
For nine years in that part of old Kentucky
Where the mountains fringe the Blue Grass,
The old men shot at one another for luck;
It made me think I was like none of them.
At twelve I was determined to shoot only
For honor; at twenty not to shoot at all;
I know at thirty-three that one must shoot
As often as one gets the rare chance—
In killing there is more than commentary.
One's sense of the proper decoration alters
But there's a kind of lust feeds on itself
Unspoken to, unspeaking; subterranean
As a black river full of eyeless fish
Heavy with spawn; with a passion for time
Longer than the arteries of a cave.

To the Lacedemonians

> An old soldier on the night before the veterans' reunion talks partly to himself, partly to imaginary comrades:

The people—people of my kind, my own
People but strange with a white light
In the face: the streets hard with motion
And the hard eyes that look one way.
Listen! the high whining tone
Of the motors, I hear the dull commotion:
I am come, a child in an old play.

I am here with a secret in the night;
Because I am here the dead wear gray.

It is a privilege to be dead; for you
Cannot know what absence is nor seize
The odour of pure distance until
From you, slowly dying in the head,
All sights and sounds of the moment, all
The life of sweet intimacy shall fall
Like a swift at dusk.

       Sheer time! Stroke of the heart
Towards retirement. . . .

        Gentlemen, my secret is
Damnation: where have they, the citizens, all
Come from? They were not born in my father's
House, nor in their fathers': on a street corner
By motion sired, not born; by rest dismayed.
The tempest will unwind—the hurricane
Consider, knowing its end, the headlong pace?
I have watched it and endured it, I have delayed
Judgement: it warn't in my time, by God, so
That the mere breed absorbed the generation!

Yet I, hollow head, do see but little;
Old man: no memory: aimless distractions.

I was a boy, I never knew cessation
Of the bright course of blood along the vein;
Moved, an old dog by me, to field and stream
In the speaking ease of the fall rain;
When I was a boy the light on the hills
Was there because I could see it, not because
Some special gift of God had put it there.
Men expect too much, do too little,
Put the contraption before the accomplishment,
Lack skill of the interior mind
To fashion dignity with shapes of air.
Luxury, yes—but not elegance!
Where have they come from?

                              Go you tell them
That we their servants, well-trained, gray-coated
Gray-haired (both foot and horse) or in
The grave, them obey . . . obey them,
What commands?

                    My father said
That everything but kin was less than kind.
The young men like swine argue for a rind,
A flimsy shell to put their weakness in;
Will-less, ruled by what they cannot see;
Hunched like savages in a rotten tree
They wait for the thunder to speak: Union!
That joins their separate fear.

                    I fought
But did not care; a leg shot off at Bethel,
Given up for dead; but knew neither shell-shock
Nor any self-indulgence. Well may war be

Terrible to those who have nothing to gain
For the illumination of the sense:
When the peace is a trade route, figures
For the budget, reduction of population,
Life grown sullen and immense
Lusts after immunity to pain.

There is no civilization without death;
There is now the wind for breath.

Waken, lords and ladies gay, we cried,
And marched to Cedar Run and Malvern Hill,
Kinsmen and friends from Texas to the Tide—
Vain chivalry of the personal will!

Waken, we shouted, lords and ladies gay,
We go to win the precincts of the light,
Unshadowing restriction of our day . . . .
Regard now, in the seventy years of night,

Them, the young men who watch us from the curbs:
They hold the glaze of wonder in their stare—
Our crooked backs, hands fetid as old herbs,
The tallow eyes, wax face, the foreign hair!

Soldiers, march! we shall not fight again
The Yankees with our guns well-aimed and rammed—
All are born Yankees of the race of men
And this, too, now the country of the damned:

Poor bodies crowding round us! The white face
Eyeless with eyesight only, the modern power—
Huddled sublimities of time and space,
They are the echoes of a raging tower

That reared its moment upon a gone land,
Pouring a long cold wrath into the mind—
Damned souls, running the way of sand
Into the destination of the wind!

The Swimmers

SCENE: Montgomery County,
Kentucky, July 1911

Kentucky water, clear springs: a boy fleeing
  To water under the dry Kentucky sun,
  His four little friends in tandem with him, seeing

Long shadows of grapevine wriggle and run
  Over the green swirl; mullein under the ear
  Soft as Nausicaä's palm; sullen fun

Savage as childhood's thin harmonious tear:
  O fountain, bosom source undying-dead
  Replenish me the spring of love and fear

And give me back the eye that looked and fled
  When a thrush idling in the tulip tree
  Unwound the cold dream of the copperhead.

—Along the creek the road was winding; we
  Felt the quicksilver sky. I see again
  The shrill companions of that odyssey:

Bill Eaton, Charlie Watson, 'Nigger' Layne
  The doctor's son, Harry Duèsler who played
  The flute; and Tate, with water on the brain.

Dog-days: the dusty leaves where rain delayed
      Hung low on poison-oak and scuppernong,
      And we were following the active shade

Of water, that bells and bickers all night long.
      'No more'n a mile,' Layne said. All five stood still.
      Listening, I heard what seemed at first a song;

Peering, I heard the hooves come down the hills.
      The posse passed, twelve horse; the leader's face
      Was worn as limestone on an ancient sill.

Then, as sleepwalkers shift from a hard place
      In bed, and rising to keep a formal pledge
      Descend a ladder into empty space,

We scuttled down the bank below a ledge
      And marched stiff-legged in our common fright
      Along a hog-track by the riffle's edge:

Into a world where sound shaded the sight
      Dropped the dull hooves again; the horsemen came
      Again, all but the leader: it was night

Momently and I feared: eleven same
      Jesus-Christers unmembered and unmade,
      Whose Corpse had died again in dirty shame.

The bank then leveling in a speckled glade,
      We stopped to breathe above the swimming-hole;
      I gazed at its reticulated shade

Recoiling in blue fear, and felt it roll
      Over my ears and eyes and lift my hair
      Like seaweed tossing on a sunk atoll.

I rose again. Borne on the copper air
    A distant voice green as a funeral wreath
    Against a grave:'That dead nigger there.'

The melancholy sheriff slouched beneath
    A giant sycamore; shaking his head
    He plucked a sassafras twig and picked his teeth:

'We come too late.' He spoke to the tired dead
    Whose ragged shirt soaked up the viscous flow
    Of blood in which It lay discomfited.

A butting horse-fly gave one ear a blow
    And glanced off, as the sheriff kicked the rope
    Loose from the neck and hooked it with his toe

Away from the blood.—I looked back down the slope:
    The friends were gone that I had hoped to greet.—
    A single horseman came at a slow lope

And pulled up at the hanged man's horny feet;
    The sheriff noosed the feet, the other end
    The stranger tied to his pommel in a neat

Slip-knot. I saw the Negro's body bend
    And straighten, as a fish-line cast transverse
    Yields to the current that it must subtend.

The sheriff's Goddamn was a murmured curse
    Not for the dead but for the blinding dust
    That boxed the cortège in a cloudy hearse

And dragged it towards our town. I knew I must
    Not stay till twilight in that silent road;
    Sliding my bare feet into the warm crust,

I hopped the stonecrop like a panting toad
      Mouth open, following the heaving cloud
      That floated to the court-house square its load

Of limber corpse that took the sun for shroud.
      There were three figures in the dying sun
      Whose light were company where three was crowd.

My breath crackled the dead air like a shotgun
      As, sheriff and the stranger disappearing,
      The faceless head lay still. I could not run

Or walk, but stood. Alone in the public clearing
      This private thing was owned by all the town,
      Though never claimed by us within my hearing.

Ode to Our Young Pro-consuls of the Air

To St.-John Perse

Once more the country calls
From sleep, as from his doom,
      Each citizen to take
      His modest stake
Where the sky falls
With a Pacific boom.

Warm winds in even climes
Push southward angry bees
      As we, with tank and plane,
      Wrest land and main
From yellow mimes,
The puny Japanese.

Boys hide in lunging cubes
Crouching to explode,
    Beyond Atlantic skies,
    With cheerful cries
Their barking tubes
Upon the German toad.

Marvelling day by day
Upon the human kind
    What might I have done
    (A poet alone)
To balk or slay
These enemies of mind?

I sought by night to foal
Chimeras into men—
    Decadence of power
    That, at late hour,
Untimed the soul
To live the past again:

Toy sword, three-cornered hat
At York and Lexington—
    While *Bon-Homme* whipped at sea
    This enemy
Whose roar went flat
After George made him run;

Toy rifle, leather hat
Above the boyish beard—
    And in that Blue renown
    The Gray went down,
Down like a rat,
And even the rats cheered.

In a much later age
(Europe had been in flames)
  Proud Wilson yielded ground
  To franc and pound,
Made pilgrimage
In the wake of Henry James.

Where Lou Quatorze held *fête*
For sixty thousand men,
  France took the German sword
  But later, bored,
Opened the gate
To Hitler—at Compiègne.

In this bad time no part
The poet took, nor chance:
  He studied Swift and Donne,
  Ignored the Hun,
While with faint heart
Proust caused the fall of France.

Sad day at Oahu
When the Jap beetle hit!
  Our Proustian retort
  Was Kimmel and Short,
Old women in blue,
And then the beetle bit.

It was defeat, or near it!
Yet all that feeble time
  Brave Brooks and lithe MacLeish
  Had sworn to thresh
Our flagging spirit
With literature made Prime!

Cow Creek and bright Bear Wallow,
Nursing the blague that dulls
   Spirits grown Eliotic,
   Now patriotic
Are: we follow
The Irresponsibles!

Young men, Americans!
You go to win the world
   With zeal pro-consular
   For our whole star—
You partisans
Of liberty unfurled!

O animal excellence,
Take pterodactyl flight
   Fire-winged into the air
   And find your lair
With cunning sense
On some Arabian bight

Or sleep your dreamless sleep
(Reptilian bomber!) by
   The Mediterranean
   And like a man
Swear you to keep
Faith with imperial eye:

Take off, O gentle youth,
And coasting India
   Scale crusty Everest
   Whose mythic crest
Resists your truth;
And spying far away

Upon the Tibetan plain
A limping caravan,
      Dive, and exterminate
      The Lama, late
Survival of old pain.
Go kill the dying swan.

Winter Mask

        To the memory of W. B. Yeats

I

Towards nightfall when the wind
Tries the eaves and casements
(A winter wind of the mind
Long gathering its will)
I lay the mind's contents
Bare, as upon a table,
And ask, in a time of war,
Whether there is still
To a mind frivolously dull
Anything worth living for.

II

If I am meek and dull
And a poor sacrifice
Of perverse will to cull
The act from the attempt,
Just look into damned eyes

And give the returning glare;
For the damned like it, the more
Damnation is exempt
From what would save its heir
With a thing worth living for.

III

The poisoned rat in the wall
Cuts through the wall like a knife,
Then blind, drying, and small
And driven to cold water,
Dies of the water of life:

Both damned in eternal ice,
The traitor become the boor
Who had led his friend to slaughter,
Now bites his head—not nice,
The food that he lives for.

IV

I supposed two scenes of hell,
Two human bestiaries,
Might uncommonly well
Convey the doom I thought;
But lest the horror freeze
The gentler estimation
I go to the sylvan door
Where nature has been bought
In rational proration
As a thing worth living for.

V

Should the buyer have been beware?
It is an uneven trade
For man has wet his hair
Under the winter weather
With only fog for shade:
His mouth a bracketed hole
Picked by the crows that bore
Nature to their hanged brother,
Who rattles against the bole
The thing that he lived for.

VI

I asked the master Yeats
Whose great style could not tell
Why it is man hates
His own salvation,
Prefers the way to hell,
And finds his last safety
In the self-made curse that bore
Him towards damnation:
The drowned undrowned by the sea,
The sea worth living for.

JOSEPH AUSLANDER

(1897–1965)

Consultant in Poetry (1937–1941)

Having been appointed to the task of building in our national Library for the People of the United States a permanent sanctuary for the manuscripts and memorabilia of the poets of our tongue, I take the liberty of inviting your cooperation. Such a room, dedicated to the best and noblest utterances of the best and noblest minds, is intended not only as a storehouse of treasures to inspire and instruct the multitude that daily throng our doors; it is to serve as one more heartening sign, in a confused and darkened world, of the power of the poets and dramatists, the glory of our ideals and aspirations.

The poetry of Joseph Auslander, who was in 1937 the first poet to hold the official post at the Library of Congress, then called the "poetry chair," is dark and ornate and imitative of an earlier period of Gothic romanticism in American poetry. Auslander was born in 1897 in what he described as the slums of Philadelphia, and spent three years as a boy working in a sweatshop before distinguishing himself in a Brooklyn high school as a student with literary promise. He went on to study at Harvard and the Sorbonne and started teaching poetry at Columbia in 1929. He wrote six large volumes of poetry during his lifetime and two novels, which he coauthored with his second wife, the poet Audrey Wurdemann, who was his assistant throughout his nearly four years at the Library.

Auslander wrote many poems about war, and his poetry was used to sell U.S. war bonds during World War II. Marie Bullock, who founded the Academy of American Poets, was a student of Auslander's at Harvard; she recalled that her former teacher "rather resembled Poe, and he fancied he did. . . . He liked to strike poses when he read [and] was notably kind about helping untalented poets, chiefly ladies, with their verses." Auslander was a keen fund-raiser and spent much of his three years focusing on the acquisition of rare manuscripts. In 1941 he launched, with the third Librarian of Congress, Archibald MacLeish, the first recorded readings at the Library called "The Poet in a Democracy," which is one of the oldest poetry reading series in the country. The inaugural reader was Robinson Jeffers, who, in the first public appearance he had ever agreed to make, gave a short speech declaring, "It may be the destiny of America to carry culture and freedom across the twilight of another dark age" and to "keep alive, through everything, our ideal values, of freedom and courage, mercy and tolerance."

Protest

I will not make a sonnet from
Each little private martyrdom;
Nor out of love left dead with time
Construe a stanza or a rhyme.

We do not suffer to afford
The searched for and the subtle word:
There is too much that may not be
At the caprice of prosody.

Dawn at the Rain's Edge

The drowsy, friendly, comfortable creak
        Of axles arguing and wet spokes gleaming,
When old empty tumbrels blunder dreaming, too sleepy to speak,
        Blunder down the road in the rain dreaming.

And the house-lights rub at the shining dripping shadows
        Over the windows; through the drenched silver willows;
                everywhere:
In the sulphurous fluctuant marsh this side the steaming meadows
        Where black weeds trouble the moon's drowned hair.

There is a sudden fuss of draggled feathers and the swing
      Of winds in a hissing burst of raindrops; then a cry
Of color at the hill's rim; a strange bright glimmering;
      And a lark talking madness in some corner of the sky.

Home-Bound

The moon rims the wavering tide where one fish slips,
      The water makes a quietness of sound,
Night is an anchoring of many ships
      Home-bound.

There are strange tunnelers in the dark, and whirs
      Of wings that die, and hairy spiders spin
The silence into nets, and tenanters
      Move softly in.

I step on shadows gliding through the grass
      And feel the night lean cool against my face:
      And challenged by the sentinel of space—
I pass.

Upper Park Avenue

The pavement ringing under my heels is hard
As bell-metal; and the houses on the street
Stare at the passer-by from their retreat
Of steel: this is the sanctity they guard,
This grim domestic fortress, double-barred,

Where only the anointed and elite
May purr and agitate on papal feet
And your admission flutters in a card.

What are these walls that cut into the sun,
Scissor the sky in little cubes and squares,
Rhomboids and arcs beyond which no blue dares
Penetrate and no casual radiance run? . . .
Dawn, crash into this plaything with your hoof
And send white daylight roaring through the roof!

Severus to Tiberius Greatly Ennuyé

In places the water had thumbed the thick sunglow to patches
Of oil bloom, peacock flare, adroit black bronze;
And I was a diver, slime-silkened, hot with hot gold scratches
Of hammered glitter, slipping from hammered bastions
Down under dense foam slaver, down under tons
Of weed trash, polyp, down to the cool uncluttered deep sea garrisons.

There I blundered through smoke of dim turquoise, corroded old
Quinquiremes and galleons and Chinese
Junks and swan ships of Egypt crazy with gold;
Every vessel that had ever brawled with the seas;
Green wrecks, and there went out a glittering vapour from these;
And blunt inquisitive fishes vexed their beauty with vacant
    solemnities.

Tiberius, I tell you it would have seriously pleased your flesh,
It would have curiously delighted the bone of your thighs

Testament

To see a dream
Reduced to rust
Is a bitter theme,
Yet it leaves a gleam—
It must . . .
But to lose trust
In a simple thing
Like the golden dust
On a miller's wing
Or the smell of spring
In the air—
That I could never bear.

Target for Tonight

Serenely through a sea of stars
The moon of autumn rides,
Blind to our wounds, deaf to our wars,
But tyrant of our tides.

From her indifferent wrist depends
A silver punctual chain
That harnesses to restless ends
The rhythms of the rain.

Upon unholy calendars
Men mark their blood-drenched Ides. . . .
Serenely through a sea of stars
The moon of autumn rides.

NOTES AND SOURCES

ABBREVIATIONS EMPLOYED IN THE NOTES

PCB: William McGuire, *Poetry's Catbird Seat* (Washington, DC: Library of Congress, 1988)

PR: *Paris Review*

NYT: *New York Times*

NYTBR: *New York Times Book Review*

PF: Poetry Foundation

NAMP: *The Norton Anthology of Modern Poetry*, 2nd ed. (New York: Norton, 1988)

INTRODUCTION

xlv **Plato quotes:** Plato, *The Republic*, Book X, trans. Benjamin Jowett. Available at http://classics.mit.edu/Plato/republic.html.

xlvi **Gibbon quotes:** Edward Gibbon, *The History of the Decline and Fall of the Roman Empire*, vol. 7 (London: Methuen, 1900), 256.

xlvi **"you shall have nothing required":** Sir Robert Peel quoted in John Stringer, "Poems of the Week: Poets Laureate," The Mediadrome, http://www.themediadrome.com/content/articles/words_articles/poems_poets_laureate.htm.

xlvii **"hired applauder . . . President's Cat":** Elizabeth Schmidt, "Ill Paid, Ill Defined and Nearly Irresistible," *NYTBR*, December 17, 1995.

xlvii **"best in Washington":** *PCB*, 135.

xlviii **"lighting poetry bonfires":** Laura Secor, "Interview: Billy Collins— Mischievous Laureate," *Mother Jones*, March/April 2002, 84.

xlviii **John F. Kennedy on Frost:** "Remarks Recorded for the Television Program 'Robert Frost: American Poet.' February 26, 1961," in John T. Woolley and Gerhard Peters, The American Presidency Project, http://www.presidency.ucsb.edu/ws/index.php?pid=8507.

xlix **"The eye was placed":** Ralph Waldo Emerson, "Self-Reliance," in *Selections from Ralph Waldo Emerson*, ed. Stephen E. Whicher (Boston: Houghton Mifflin, 1957), 148.

xlix **Aristotle's definition of poetry:** Aristotle, *The Poetics of Aristotle*, Book XXV, trans. S. H. Butcher (London: Macmillan, 1902). Available at http://www.sacred-texts.com/cla/ari/index.htm.

W. S. MERWIN

2 **Epigraph:** W. S. Merwin, interview by Academy of Achievement, July 3, 2008, http://www.achievement.org/autodoc/page/meroint-1.

3 **"I can't imagine":** W. S. Merwin, interview by Bill Moyers, *Bill Moyers Journal*, PBS, June 6, 2009. Transcript available at http://www.pbs.org/moyers/journal/06262009/transcript1.html.

3 **"As soon as I could write":** Ibid.

4 **"I think there's a kind of desperate hope":** W. S. Merwin quoted in PF biography, http://www.poetryfoundation.org/archive/poet.html?id=4676.

KAY RYAN

22 **Epigraph:** Kay Ryan, interview by Sarah Fay, "The Art of Poetry No. 94," *PR*, Winter 2008.

23 **Introduction:** All quotes are from ibid. and Elizabeth Lund, "Poet Kay Ryan: A Profile," *Christian Science Monitor*, August 25, 2004, http://www.csmonitor.com/2004/0825/p25s01-bogn.html.

CHARLES SIMIC

37 **Epigraph:** Charles Simic, interview by Jeffrey Brown, *PBS NewsHour*, PBS, September 26, 2007. Transcript available at http://www.pbs.org/newshour/bb/entertainment/july-dec07/simic_09-26.html.

38 **"touched and honored":** Charles Simic quoted in Poets.org biography, http://www.poets.org/poet.php/prmPID/27.

38 **"Hitler and Stalin":** Charles Simic, interview by J. M. Spalding, *Cortland Review*, August 1994, http://www.cortlandreview.com/issuefour/interview4.htm.

38 **"not rapturous about nature":** Charles Simic, interview by Deborah Solomon, "In-Verse Thinking," *New York Times Magazine*, February 3, 2008. Available at http://www.nytimes.com/2008/02/03/magazine/03wwln-q4-t.html.

39 **"tasty can of American corned beef":** Charles Simic, "In the Beginning . . . ," Wonderful Words, Silent Truth (Ann Arbor: University of Michigan Press, 2000), 12.

39 **"the vulnerability of those participating in tragic events":** Charles Simic, "Notes on Poetry and History," *The Uncertain Certainty: Interviews, Essays, and Notes on Poetry* (Ann Arbor: University of Michigan Press, 1985), 126.

DONALD HALL

54 **Epigraph:** Donald Hall, "The One Day" in *White Apples and the Taste of Stone* (New York: Houghton-Mifflin Company, 2006), 178.

55 **"so much of his poetry has emerged":** Verlyn Klinkenborg, "Donald Hall, Poet Laureate," *NYT*, June 15, 2006.

55 **"the most important thing":** Donald Hall, interview by Robert Birnbaum, "Donald Hall," Identity Theory, December 18, 2006, http://www.identitytheory.com/interviews/birnbaum178.php.

55 **"Contentment . . . is work so engrossing":** Bob Thompson, "Set to Verse: Donald Hall Is New Poet Laureate," *Washington Post*, June 14, 2006.

TED KOOSER

74 **Epigraph:** Angel Gurria Quintana, "Enjoying a Poem Shouldn't Be Hard," *Financial Times*, January 11, 2006. Available at http://www.ft.com/cms/s/2/697d095c-8246-11da-aea0-0000779e2340.html.

75 **"pick up and understand":** Ted Kooser, "Q and A: Kooser's American Life in Poetry," *Poets and Writers*, March/April 2005.

75 **"You can tweak a poem":** Elizabeth Lund, "Retired Insurance Man Puts a Premium on Verse," *Christian Science Monitor*, November 16, 2004, http://www.csmonitor.com/2004/1116/p15s02-bogn.html.

LOUISE GLÜCK

85 **Epigraph:** Louise Glück, "Education of the Poet," *Proofs and Theories* (New York: Ecco, 1994), 16.

86 **"no concern with widening audience":** Justin Pope, "A Quiet Path for New Poet Laureate," *Los Angeles Times*, October 20, 2003. Available at http://articles.latimes.com/2003/oct/20/entertainment/et-pope20.

86 **"to each individual's personality":** Laura Secor, "Interview: Billy Collins—Mischievous Laureate," *Mother Jones*, March/April 2002, 84.

86 **"The discipline gave me a place to use my mind":** Glück, *Proofs and Theories*, 13.

87 **"Persephone is having sex in hell":** Louise Glück, "Persephone the Wanderer," in *Averno* (New York: Farrar, Straus & Giroux, 2006), 17.

87 **"simple language":** Glück, *Proofs and Theories*, 4.

BILLY COLLINS

112 **Epigraph:** Billy Collins, Commencement Address at Choate Rosemary Hall, June 3, 2001. Available at http://www.bestcigarette.us/2004/09/commencement_ad.html.

113 **"the man I held the door for":** Billy Collins, "Dear Reader," in *The Art of Drowning* (Pittsburgh, PA: Pittsburgh University Press, 1995), 3.

113 **"the face behind the wheel":** Ibid.

113 **"designed to make it easy for students":** Billy Collins, Poetry 180, http://www.loc.gov/poetry/180.

113 **"I ask them":** Billy Collins, "Introduction to Poetry," in *Sailing Around the Room: New and Selected Poems* (New York: Random House, 2001), 16.

STANLEY KUNITZ

130 **Epigraph:** Stanley Kunitz, "Instead of a Foreword, Speaking on Poetry," *Passing Through: The Later Poems* (New York: Norton, 1995), 11.

131 **"In my youth . . . the adversary":** Stanley Kunitz quoted in PF biography, http://www.poetryfoundation.org/archive/poet.html?id=3869.

132 **"I don't know of another":** Robert Lowell quoted in ibid.

132 **"By its nature":** Stanley Kunitz quoted in ibid.

ROBERT PINSKY

152 **Epigraph:** Elizabeth Mehren, "The Meter in Running," *Los Angeles Times,* June 10, 1997.

153 **"I think poetry is a vital part":** Robert Pinksy, interview by *Christian Science Monitor,* quoted in PF biography, http://www.poetryfoundation.org/archive/poet.html?id=5406.

154 **"a technology for remembering":** Robert Pinksy, "A Man Goes Into a Bar," *NYTBR,* September 25, 1994.

154 **"Our greatness consists":** Robert Pinsky, "Poetry and American Memory," *Atlantic Monthly,* October 1999. Available at http://www.theatlantic.com/issues/99oct/9910pinsky.htm.

ROBERT HASS

171 **Epigraph:** Robert Hass, interview, "An Informal Occasion with Robert Hass," *Iowa Review,* vol. 21, no. 3 (1991), 126.

172 **"the first time I went to Washington":** Tony Perry, "Poetry Man," *Los Angeles Times,* October 20, 1996.

172 **"values come from the imagination":** Elizabeth Schmidt, "Ill Paid, Ill Defined and Nearly Irresistible," *NYTBR,* December 17, 1995.

RITA DOVE

195 **Epigraph:** Rita Dove, interview by M. W. Thomas, "An Interview with Rita Dove," Modern American Poetry, http://www.english.illinois.edu/maps/poets/a_f/dove/mwthomas.htm. Originally published in *Swansea Review,* August 12, 1995.

196 **"It'll ruin my life":** David Streitfeld, "Laureate for New Age," *Washington Post,* May 19, 1993.

196 **"like beads on a necklace":** Ibid.

196 **"I was working":** Ibid.

197 **"music and poetry":** Ibid.

197 **"reluctance with being labeled":** Ibid.

MONA VAN DUYN

212 **Epigraph:** David Streitfeld, "Van Duyn Named New Poet Laureate," *Washington Post,* June 15, 1992.

213 **"I use domestic imagery":** Matt Schudel, "Poet Laureate Mona Van Duyn Dies at 83," *Washington Post*, December 4, 2004.

213 **"I have not found the subject for my poems in my illness":** Ibid.

213 **"run kicking and screaming":** Editorial, *Washington Post*, May 22, 1993.

JOSEPH BRODSKY

229 **Epigraph:** Joseph Brodsky, Nobel Lecture, December 8, 1987, http://nobelprize.org/nobel_prizes/literature/laureates/1987/brodsky-lecture-e.html.

230 **Trial transcript:** W. L. Webb, "Poet Against an Empire," *The Guardian*, January 29, 1996.

231 **"I'm a government worker, as it were":** Karen de Witt, "Washington at Work," *NYT*, December 10, 1991.

231 **"survives like a fish in the sand":** Joseph Brodsky quoted in PF biography, http://www.poetryfoundation.org/archive/poet.html?id=822.

MARK STRAND

245 **Epigraph:** Bill Thomas, "What's A Poet Laureate to Do?", *Los Angeles Times*, January 31, 1991.

246 **"When I was a child":** Mark Strand, in *Ecstatic Occasions, Expedient Forms*, ed. David Lehman (Ann Arbor: University of Michigan Press, 1996), 197.

246 **"Lots of poets I admired":** Katharine Coles, "In the Presence of America: A Conversation with Mark Strand," *Weber Studies*, vol. 9.3 (Fall 1992).

247 **"I look to be moved":** Mark Strand, interview by Elizabeth Farnsworth, *PBS NewsHour*, PBS, April 15, 1999. Transcript available at http://www.pbs.org/newshour/bb/entertainment/jan-june99/pulitzer_4-15.html.

HOWARD NEMEROV

262 **Epigraph:** Howard Nemerov, interview by Grace Cavalieri, October 1988, Library of Congress.

263 **"Poetry and Nonsense":** Michael Wines and Philip Shenon, "Washington Talk: Briefing," *NYT*, October 12, 1988.

263 **"It's such blessed relief":** Elizabeth Kastor, "New Poet Laureate Contemplates an Odd Job," *Gainesville Sun*, October 12, 1988.

RICHARD WILBUR

281 **Epigraph:** Richard Wilbur, interview by Helen McCloy Ellison, Ellesa Clay High, and Peter A. Stitt, "The Art of Poetry," *PR*, Winter 1977.

282 **"In a nation famously composed of immigrants":** Dana Gioia, "Richard Wilbur: A Critical Survey of His Career," http://www.dana gioia.net/essays/ewilbur.htm.

282 **"One does not use poetry for":** Richard Wilbur, interview by David Curry, "An Interview with Richard Wilbur," *Trinity Review*, December 1962, 21–32.

283 **"Limitation makes for power":** *The Oxford Book of American Poetry* (New York: Oxford University Press, 2006), 667.

283 **"I feel that the universe is full":** Wilbur, "The Art of Poetry."

ROBERT PENN WARREN

297 **Epigraph:** Robert Penn Warren, interview by Eugene Walter, "The Art of Fiction No. 18," *PR*, Spring–Summer 1957, 4.

298 **"hired applauder":** Elizabeth Schmidt, "Ill Paid, Ill Defined and Nearly Irresistible," *NYTBR*, December 17, 1995.

298 **"Between the ages of sixty-one and eighty-one":** Harold Bloom, foreword to *The Collected Poems of Robert Penn Warren*, ed. John D. Burt (Baton Rouge: Lousiana State University Press, 1988), xxiii.

GWENDOLYN BROOKS

314 **Epigraph:** Gwendolyn Brooks, interview by Susan Elizabeth Howe and Jay Fox, *Literature and Belief*, vol. 12 (1992), 1–12.

315 **"bookish and lonely":** *Milwaukee Sentinel*, March 10, 1977.

315 **"You're talented, keep writing":** Langston Hughes quoted in Gwendolyn Brooks, interview by Alan Jabbour and Ethelbert Miller, "A Conversation with Gwendolyn Brooks," 1986, in *Conversations with Gwendolyn Brooks*, ed. Gloria Wade Gayles (Jackson: University Press of Mississippi, 2003), 128.

315 **"folksy narrative":** Gwendolyn Brooks quoted in PF biography, http://www.poetryfoundation.org/archive/poet.html?id=843.

316 **"a powerful, beautiful dagger of a book":** David Littlejohn quoted in ibid.

316 **"No matter what the theme is":** Mel Watkins, "Gwendolyn Brooks, 83, Passionate Poet, Dies," *NYT*, December 5, 2000.

317 **"Thank you for your funny note":** *PCB*, 420.

317 **"I'd love to come":** *PCB*, 421.

ROBERT FITZGERALD

332 **Epigraph:** Herbert Mitgand, Robert Fitzgerald obituary, *NYT*, January 17, 1985.

ANTHONY HECHT

343 **Epigraph:** Benjamin Ivry, "Poet of Sorrow, and of Wit," *Wall Street Journal*, October 26, 2004.

344 **Introduction:** All quotes are from *PCB*, 402–4.

MAXINE KUMIN

357 **Epigraph:** Maxine Kumin, interview by Steven Ratiner, in *Giving their Word: Conversations with Contemporary Poets*, ed. Steven Ratiner (Amherst: University of Massachusetts Press, 2002), 134–35.

358 **"very safe, heterosexual, middle-class":** *PCB*, 389.

358 **"among all those éminences grise":** Albin Krebs and David Bird, "Symposium Becomes a Battleground of the Sexes," *NYT*, Nov 21, 1980.

359 **"I have been twitted":** Maxine Kumin quoted in PF biography, http://www.poetryfoundation.org/archive/poet.html?id=3866.

WILLIAM MEREDITH

381 **Epigraph:** William Meredith, interview by Edward Hirsch, "The Art of Poetry No. 34," *PR*, Spring 1985, 4.

382 **"I know it . . . but I can't say the words":** Edward Hirsch, William Meredith obituary, *Washington Post*, January 18, 2004.

382 **"I see the need":** Meredith, "The Art of Poetry No. 34," 6.

382 **"Astonishing experience":** Ibid., 3.

383 **"Looking back":** *PCB*, 368.

ROBERT HAYDEN

397 **Epigraph:** Norma R. Jones, "Robert Hayden (1913–1980)," in *Dictionary of Literary Biography*, vol. 76, *Afro-American Writers, 1940–1955* (Detroit, MI: Gale, 1988), 84.

398 **"my dark nights of the soul":** Mark A. Sanders, "About Hayden's Life and Career," Modern American Poetry, http://www.english.illinois .edu/maps/poets/g_l/hayden/life.htm. Originally published in *The Oxford Companion to African American Literature* (New York: Oxford University Press, 1997).

398 **"Hayden declared himself":** William Meredith, introduction to *Collected Poems*, by Robert Hayden, quoted in PF biography of Robert Hayden, http://www.poetryfoundation.org/archive/poet.html?id=3014.

399 **"a real testament":** Michael Harper quoted in Sanders, "About Hayden's Life and Career."

399 **"As the first African-American to become Consultant":** *PCB*, 355.

DANIEL HOFFMAN

419 **Epigraph:** Daniel Hoffman, *Words to Create a World: Interviews, Essays, and Reviews of Contemporary Poetry* (Ann Arbor: University of Michigan Press, 1993), 151.

420 **"a new direction":** W. H. Auden, foreword to *An Armada of Thirty Whales*, by Daniel Hoffman (New Haven: Yale University Press, 1954), cited in PDF biography of Daniel Hoffman, http://www.poetryfoundation.org/archive/poet.html?id=3195.

420 **"Nature always wears":** Ralph Waldo Emerson, "Nature," *Selections from Ralph Waldo Emerson*, ed. Stephen E. Whicher (Boston: Houghton Mifflin, 1957), 25.

420 **"As long as man was subject to Nature":** Hoffman, *Words to Create a World*, 151.

JOSEPHINE JACOBSEN

432 **Epigraph:** *PCB*, 334.

433 **"Each had a fine quiddity":** Josephine Jacobsen, *The Instant of Knowing* (Ann Arbor: University of Michigan Press, 1997), 29.

433 **"The atmosphere has totally changed":** *PCB*, 331.

434 **"Often the poet brings back very little":** Jacobsen, *The Instant of Knowing*, 43.

WILLIAM STAFFORD

447 **Epigraph:** William Stafford, interview by American Poems, 1971, http://www.americanpoems.com/poets/William-Stafford.
449 **"I've purposely rambled":** *PCB*, 319.

WILLIAM JAY SMITH

457 **Epigraph:** William Jay Smith quoted in PF biography, http://www .poetryfoundation.org/archive/poet.html?id=6388.
458 **"one of the oddest childhoods ever lived":** Dana Gioia, "The Journey of William Jay Smith," http://www.danagioia.net/essays/esmith .htm.
458 **"master work":** Harold Bloom quoted on back cover of *The Cherokee Lottery*, by William Jay Smith (Jackson, TN: Curbstone Press, 2000).

JAMES DICKEY

470 **Epigraph:** James Dickey, interview by Francis Roberts, in *The Voiced Connections of James Dickey: Interviews and Conversations*, ed. Ronald Baughman (Columbia: University of South Carolina Press, 1989), 12–27.
471 **"country surrealism":** James Dickey quoted in PF biography, http:// www.poetryfoundation.org/archive/poet.html?id=1772.
471 **"the most inept":** Henry Hart, *James Dickey: World as a Lie* (New York: Picador, 2000), 355.
471 **"to get every guy":** Ibid.

STEPHEN SPENDER

494 **Epigraph:** Stephen Spender, *Journals 1939–1983*, ed. John Goldsmith (London: Faber, 1985), 265.
495 **"The idealist expects":** Stephen Spender, *World Within World: The Autobiography of Stephen Spender* (New York: Modern Library, 2001), 28.
495 **"I myself am":** Stephen Spender quoted in PF biography, http://www .poetryfoundation.org/archive/poet.html?id=6465.

REED WHITTEMORE

505 **Epigraph:** *PCB*, 280.

506 **"The author, critic":** Reed Whittemore, "The Cultural Conference," in *The Past, the Future, the Present: Poems Selected and New* (Fayetteville: University of Arkansas Press, 1990), 30.

506 **"cultural storm":** *PCB*, 279.

LOUIS UNTERMEYER

516 **Epigraph:** *PCB*, 632.

517 **"mr u will not be missed":** Ian Hamilton, ed., *The Oxford Companion to Twentieth-Century Poetry* (New York: Oxford University Press, 1994), 555.

RICHARD EBERHART

527 **Epigraph:** Richard Eberhardt, interview, 1979, quoted in "A Life Lived for Poetry," *Vox of Dartmouth*, http://www.dartmouth.edu/~vox/0506/0627/eberhart.html.

528 **"Looks as unlike Byron as you can get":** *PCB*, 217.

ROBERT FROST

541 **Epigraph:** *PCB*, 214.

542 **"Somebody said to me that New England's in decay":** *PCB*, 213.

543 **"I have to say that my Frost":** Lawrance Thompson and R. H. Winnick, *Robert Frost: The Later Years* (New York: Henry Holt, 1977), 268.

543 **"You made my birthday party a surprise party":** Ibid., 269.

RANDALL JARRELL

554 **Epigraph:** Randall Jarrell, "A Verse Chronicle," *The Nation*, February 1946. Reprinted as "Bad Poets," in *Poetry and the Age* (New York: Knopf, 1953).

555 **"The public has an unusual relationship to the poet":** "Randall Jarrell, Poet, Killed by Car in Carolina," *NYT*, October 15, 1965.

555 **"have spent their lives in card-indexes":** Randall Jarrell, *No Other Book: Selected Essays*, ed. Brad Leithauser (New York: HarperCollins, 1999), 293.

556 **"had a deadly hand for killing what he despised"**: Robert B. Silvers and Barbara Epstein, *The Company They Kept* (New York: New York Review of Books, 2006), 14.

556 **"A wicked fairy"**: Dana Gioia essay on Randall Jarrell, first published in the *Washington Post*, October 10, 1999, http://www.danagioia.net/essays/ejarrell.htm.

556 **"We've been going to the zoo here ... I've had to do lots. . . spontaneous minutes"**: Mary Jarrell, ed., *Randall Jarrell's Letters* (Charlottesville: University of Virginia Press, 2002), 414.

WILLIAM CARLOS WILLIAMS

571 **Epigraph:** William Carlos Williams, *I Wanted to Write a Poem*, reported and edited by Edith Heal (Boston: Beacon Press, 1958), 10.

572 **Introduction:** All references and quotes are from *PCB*, 148–61.

CONRAD AIKEN

591 **Epigraph:** *PCB*, 135.

592 **"The best-known unread poet"**: Louis Untermeyer quoted in "Conrad Aiken," *Dictionary of Literary Biography*, Gale Literary Database.

592 **"The buried giant"**: Malcolm Cowley quoted in ibid.

592 **"When the tide"**: William Faulkner quoted in ibid.

592 **"After the desultory"**: Conrad Aiken quoted in PF biography, http://www.poetryfoundation.org/archive/poet.html?id=61.

592 **"Unhappily, I am one of those wretches"**: *PCB*, 136.

ELIZABETH BISHOP

604 **Epigraph:** Elizabeth Bishop, letter to Robert Lowell, January 21, 1949, in *One Art: Letters of Elizabeth Bishop* (New York: Farrar, Straus & Giroux, 1995), 180.

LÉONIE ADAMS

630 **Epigraph:** Léonie Adams, "Send Forth the High Falcon," *High Falcon and Other Poems* (The John Day Company, 1929), 43.

631 **"Even if she never issued another book"**: *PCB*, 107.

631 **"My work has been"**: Léonie Adams quoted in PF biography, http://
www.poetryfoundation.org/archive/poet.html?id=41.

ROBERT LOWELL

639 **Epigraph:** Robert Lowell, letter to Gertrude Buckman, in *The Letters
of Robert Lowell*, ed. Saskia Hamilton (New York: Farrar, Straus & Giroux,
2005), 70.

640 **"the selection of poets"**: *PCB*, 102.

640 **"distant, symbol-ridden, and willfully difficult"**: Troy Jollimore,
"Robert Lowell:'Skunk Hour,'" PF, http://www.poetryfoundation.org/
learning/poem-guide.html?guide_id=179983.

641 **"the most influential book"**: Stanley Kunitz quoted in PF biogra-
phy of Robert Lowell, http://www.poetryfoundation.org/archive/poet
.html?id=4181.

641 **"When I was working on *Life Studies*"**: Robert Lowell in an essay in
Salmagundi, quoted in PF biography, http://www.poetryfoundation.org/
archive/poet.html?id=4181.

641 **"It's Hell to write this"**: Elizabeth Bishop, letter to Robert Lowell,
February 1972, quoted in Thomas Mallon, "Theirs Truly: The Lowell-
Bishop Letters," *Atlantic Monthly*, April 2009. Available at http://www
.theatlantic.com/doc/200904/lowell-bishop-letters.

642 **"I couldn't bear"**: Robert Lowell, letter to Elizabeth Bishop, 1973,
quoted in ibid.

KARL SHAPIRO

659 **Epigraph:** Karl Shapiro, interview by Robert Phillips, "The Art of
Poetry No. 36," *PR*, Spring 1986.

660 **Background on Ezra Pound and the 1948 Bollingen Prize and
"I was suddenly forced"**: *PCB*, 112–13.

LOUISE BOGAN

677 **Epigraph:** Louise Bogan, letter to William Maxwell, 1946, quoted in
PCB, 96.

678 **"Suddenly I *recognized* something"**: Wendy Hirsch, "Louise Bogan's
Life and Career," Modern American Poetry, http://www.english.illinois

.edu/maps/poets/a_f/bogan/life.htm. Originally published in *American National Biography* (New York: Oxford University Press, 1999).

678 **"time-servers":** *PCB*, 91.

678 **"The work at the Library is delightful":** Louise Bogan, letter to William Maxwell, September 23, 1945, in *What the Woman Lived: Selected Letters of Louise Bogan*, ed. Rith Limner (New York: Harcourt, 1973), 250.

679 **"her rich contralto voice":** *PCB*, 94.

ALLEN TATE

687 **Epigraph:** Allen Tate, *Reason in Madness: Critical Essays* (New York: G.P. Putnam and Sons, 1941), 135.

688 **"it is my impression that poets in the past":** *PCB*, 78.

JOSEPH AUSLANDER

711 **Epigraph:** *PCB*, 48.

712 **"rather resembled Poe":** *PCB*, 46.

712 **"It may be the destiny of America":** *PCB*, 57.

PERMISSIONS
ACKNOWLEDGMENTS

Photo credits: W. S. Merwin, by Mark Hanauer; Kay Ryan, by Christina Koci Hernandez; Charles Simic, courtesy of the Poetry Office, Library of Congress; Donald Hall, by Brian Crowley; Ted Kooser, by Charles W. Guildner; Louise Glück, by Sigrid Estrada; Billy Collins, by Joann Carney; Stanley Kunitz, courtesy of the Manuscript Division, Library of Congress; Robert Pinsky, by Sigrid Estrada; Robert Hass, courtesy of the Poetry Office, Library of Congress; Rita Dove, by Fred Viebahn; Mona Van Duyn, courtesy of the Poetry Office, Library of Congress; Joseph Brodsky, courtesy of the Publishing Office, Library of Congress; Mark Strand, by Mary Noble Ours; Howard Nemerov, courtesy of the Publishing Office, Library of Congress; Richard Wilbur, courtesy of the Poetry Office, Library of Congress; Robert Penn Warren, courtesy of the Poetry Office, Library of Congress; Gwendolyn Brooks, permission courtesy of the Publishing Office, Library of Congress; Robert Fitzgerald, courtesy of Harvard University News, Cambridge, MA; Anthony Hecht, courtesy of the Publishing Office, Library of Congress; Maxine Kumin, by Kelly Weiss; William Meredith, courtesy of the Poetry Office, Library of Congress; Robert Hayden, by Jill Krementz; Daniel Hoffman, courtesy of the Publishing Office, Library of Congress; Josephine Jacobsen, by William Klender; William Stafford, courtesy of the Poetry Office, Library of Congress; William Jay Smith, by Robert Turney; James Dickey, courtesy of the Poetry Office, Library of Congress; Stephen Spender, by Imogen Cunningham, Prints

Kay Ryan: "A Hundred Bolts of Satin," "Bad Day," and "Crown" from *Say Uncle*, copyright © 1991 by Kay Ryan. Used by permission of Grove/Atlantic, Inc. "This Life," "Flamingo Watching," "Paired Things," "Force," and "Turtle" from *Flamingo Watching*, © 1994 by Kay Ryan. Used by permission of Copper Beech Press. "Odd Blocks." First printed in *The Threepenny Review*. Reprinted by permission of Kay Ryan. "Doubt," "Mirage Oases," "That Vase of Lilacs," "Relief," and "A Plain Ordinary Steel Needle Can Float on Pure Water" from *Elephant Rocks*, copyright © 1996 by Kay Ryan. Used by permission of Grove/Atlantic, Inc. "Home to Roost," "Sharks' Teeth," "Things Shouldn't Be So Hard," and "Hide and Seek" from *The Niagara River*, copyright © 2005 by Kay Ryan. Used by permission of Grove/Atlantic, Inc.

Charles Simic: "My mother was . . . ," "I was stolen . . . ," and "My father loved . . ." from *The World Doesn't End: Prose Poems*, copyright © 1987 by Charles Simic, reprinted by permission of Houghton Mifflin Harcourt Publishing Company. "Evening Talk" and "In the Library" from *The Book of Gods and Devils*, copyright © 1990 by Charles Simic, reprinted by permission of Houghton Mifflin Harcourt Publishing Company. "Cameo Appearance," "An Address with Exclamation Points," "Entertaining the Canary," and "Against Winter" from *Walking the Black Cat*, copyright © 1996 by Charles Simic, reprinted by permission of Houghton Mifflin Harcourt Publishing Company. "Prodigy," "Empire of Dreams," "My Beloved," and "My Weariness of Epic Proportions" from *Selected Early Poems* (New York: George Braziller, 1999). "The Return of the Invisible Man" and "Love Poem" from *Jackstraws*, copyright © 1999 by Charles Simic, reprinted by permission of Houghton Mifflin Harcourt Publishing Company. "Couple at Coney Island" from *Night Picnic*, copyright © 2001 by Charles Simic, reprinted by permission of Houghton Mifflin Harcourt Publishing Company. "Listen" from *That Little Something*, copyright © 2007 by Charles Simic, reprinted by permission of Houghton Mifflin Harcourt Publishing Company. Originally published in *The New Yorker*.

Donald Hall: "Ardor," "Safe Sex," "The Ship Pounding," "Kill the Day," "Her Garden," "Maple Syrup," "Gold," "To a Waterfowl," "White Apples," "Names of Horses," and "Affirmation" from *White Apples and the Taste of Stone: Selected Poems, 1946–2006* by Donald Hall. Copyright © 2006 by Donald Hall. Reprinted by permission of Houghton Mifflin Harcourt Publishing Company. All rights reserved. "After Love" and "Nymph and Shepherd." Copyright © by Donald Hall. Used by permission of Donald Hall. Originally published in *The New Yorker*.

Ted Kooser: "Selecting A Reader," "So This Is Nebraska," "Carrie," "My Grandfather Dying," and "Highway 30" from *Sure Signs: New and Selected Poems,* by Ted Kooser, © 1980. Reprinted by permission of the University of Pittsburgh Press. "Flying at Night" and "The Fan in the Window" from *One World at a Time,* by Ted Kooser, © 1985. Reprinted by permission of the University of Pittsburgh Press. "December 15," "February 10," and "February 21" from *Winter Morning Walks.* First published by Carnegie Mellon University Press. Copyright © 2000 by Ted Kooser. Reprinted by permission of Ted Kooser. "Tattoo," "At the Cancer Clinic," "A Jar of Buttons," and "Grasshoppers" from *Delights & Shadows.* Copyright © 2004 by Ted Kooser. Reprinted with the permission of Copper Canyon Press, www.coppercanyonpress.org.

Louise Glück: "The Drowned Children" and "Mock Orange" from *The First Four Books of Poems* by Louise Glück. Copyright © 1968, 1971, 1972, 1973, 1974, 1975, 1976, 1977, 1978, 1979, 1980, 1985, 1995 by Louise Glück. Reprinted by permission of HarperCollins Publishers and Carcanet Press Limited. "A Novel," "Celestial Music," and "First Memory" from *Ararat* by Louise Glück. Copyright © 1990 by Louise Glück. Reprinted by permission of HarperCollins Publishers and Carcanet Press Limited. "Penelope's Song," "Telemachus' Guilt," "Telemachus' Fantasy," and "Telemachus' Detachment" from *Meadowlands* by Louise Glück. Copyright © 1996 by Louise Glück. Reprinted by permission of HarperCollins Publishers and Carcanet Press Limited. "Nest" from *Vita Nova* by Louise Glück. Copyright © 1999 by Louise Glück. Reprinted by permission of HarperCollins Publishers and Carcanet Press Limited. "Eros," "Time," and "Memoir" from *The Seven Ages* by Louise Glück. Copyright © 2001 by Louise Glück. Reprinted by permission of HarperCollins Publishers and Carcanet Press Limited. "October" from *Averno.* Copyright © 2006 by Louise Glück. Used by permission of Farrar, Straus & Giroux, LLC and Carcanet Press Limited. "At the River." Originally appeared in *The New Yorker.* Reprinted by permission of Farrar, Strauss, & Giroux, LLC and Carcanet Press Limited from *A Village Life.* Copyright © 2009 Louise Glück. Reprinted by permission of Louise Glück.

Billy Collins: "Another Reason I Don't Keep a Gun in the House," "Advice to Writers," and "Introduction to Poetry" from *The Apple That Astonished Paris.* Copyright © 1988, 1996 by Billy Collins. Used by permission of the University of Arkansas Press, www.uapress.com. "Forgetfulness" from *Questions About Angels,* by Billy Collins, © 1991. Reprinted by permission of the University of Pittsburgh Press. "Pinup" and "Man in Space" from *The Art of Drowning,* by Billy Collins, © 1995. Reprinted by permission of the University of Pitts-

Alfred A. Knopf, a division of Random House, Inc. "Falling in Love at Sixty-Five" and "The Burning of Yellowstone" from *Near Changes* by Mona Van Duyn, copyright © 1990 by Mona Van Duyn. Used by permission of Alfred A. Knopf, a division of Random House, Inc. "Death By Aesthetics," "The Gentle Snorer," "A Kind of Music," "Notes from a Suburban Heart," "Earth Tremors Felt in Missouri," "Late Loving," "The Block," and "Sonnet for Minimalists" from *Selected Poems of Mona Van Duyn* by Mona Van Duyn, copyright © 2002 by Mona Van Duyn. Used by permission of Alfred A. Knopf, a division of Random House, Inc. "For William Clinton, President-Elect." First printed in *The Washington Post*. Copyright © 2009 by The Literary Estate of Mona Van Duyn at Washington University. Reprinted by permission of J. D. McClatchy.

Joseph Brodsky: "Six Years Later," "Anno Domini," "Autumn in Norenskaia," "For E.R.," "A Part of Speech," "Folk Tune," "Törnfallet," "Bosnia Tune," "Once More by the Potomac," "Love Song," and "To the President-Elect," from *Collected Poems in English* by Joseph Brodsky. Copyright © 2000 by the Estate of Joseph Brodsky. Reprinted by permission of Farrar, Straus & Giroux, LLC and Carcanet Press Limited.

Mark Strand: "Keeping Things Whole," "Eating Poetry," "The Remains," "Coming to This," "The Coming of Light," "Lines for Winter," and "Pot Roast" from *Selected Poems* by Mark Strand, copyright © 1979, 1980 by Mark Strand. Used by permission of Alfred A. Knopf, a division of Random House, Inc. "The Continuous Life" from *The Continuous Life* by Mark Strand, copyright © 1990 by Mark Strand. Used by permission of Alfred A. Knopf, a division of Random House, Inc. "The Night, the Porch," "Our Masterpiece Is the Private Life," "A Piece of the Storm," and "The View" from *Blizzard of One* by Mark Strand, copyright © 1998 by Mark Strand. Used by permission of Alfred A. Knopf, a division of Random House, Inc. "My Name," "Black Sea," and "Mirror" from *Man and Camel* by Mark Strand, copyright © 2006 by Mark Strand. Used by permission of Alfred A. Knopf, a division of Random House, Inc. "For Jessica, My Daughter" from *New Selected Poems* by Mark Strand, copyright © 2007 by Mark Strand. Used by permission of Alfred A. Knopf, a division of Random House, Inc.

Howard Nemerov: "Money," "Storm Windows," "The Blue Swallows," "To D——, Dead by Her Own Hand," "I Only Am Escaped Alone to Tell Thee," "The Goose Fish," "Boy With Book of Knowledge," "Style," and "Elegy for a Nature Poet" from *The Collected Poems of Howard Nemerov*. Copyright © 1977 by Howard Nemerov. Reprinted with the permission of University of Chicago

right © 2002 by Daniel Hoffman. Reprinted with the permission of Louisiana State University Press. "The Seals in Penobscot Bay," "Owed to Dejection," "In the Days of Rin Tin Tin," and "Power" from *Beyond Silence: Selected Shorted Poems*. Copyright © 2003 by Daniel Hoffman. Reprinted with the permission of Louisiana State University Press.

Josephine Jacobsen: "Arrival of Rain," "Landscape Finally with Human Figure," from *The Animal Inside* by Josephine Jacobsen. Reprinted with permission of Ohio University Press, Athens, Ohio (www.ohioswallow.com) and with permission of Erlend Jacobsen. "The Arrivals," p. 18, "Language as an Escape from the Discreet," p. 41, "How We Learn," p. 50, and "The Monosyllable," p. 51, from *The Chinese Insomniacs*. Copyright © 1981 by the University of Pennsylvania Press. Reprinted with permission of the University of Pennsylvania Press. "The Edge" from *The Sisters: New and Selected Poems*. Copyright © 1987 by Josephine Jacobsen. Reprinted by permission of Erlend Jacobsen. "Lines to a Poet," "Gentle Reader," "Over Timberline," "The Dogs," "The Blue-Eyed Exterminator," "First Woman," and "Hourglass" from *In the Crevice of Time: New and Collected Poems*, pp. 3, 140, 190, 220, 234, 252, 257–258. © 1995 Josephine Jacobsen. Reprinted with permission of The Johns Hopkins University Press.

William Stafford: "Ask Me," "Level Light," "A Ritual to Read to Each Other," "Traveling Through the Dark," "An Introduction to Some Poems," "The Little Ways that Encourage Good Fortune," "Just Thinking," "Objector," "For My Young Friends Who Are Afraid," "When I Met My Muse," and "Security" from *The Way It Is: New and Selected Poems*. Copyright © 1973, 1976, 1977, 1984, 1987, 1991, 1998, by William Stafford and the Estate of William Stafford. Reprinted with the permission of Graywolf Press, Saint Paul, Minnesota, www.graywolfpress.org.

William Jay Smith: "Persian Miniature" from *Celebration at Dark*. Copyright © 1950 by William Jay Smith. Reprinted by permission of William Jay Smith. "The World Below the Window" from *Collected Poems 1939–1989*. Copyright © 1990 by William Jay Smith. Reprinted by permission of William Jay Smith. "American Primitive" from *The World Below the Window: Poems 1937–1997*, p. 91. © 1998 William Jay Smith. Reprinted with permission of The Johns Hopkins University Press. "Morels," from *The World Below the Window: Poems 1937–1997*, pp. 143–144. © 1998 William Jay Smith. Reprinted with permission of The Johns Hopkins University Press. "The Pumpkin Field" from *The Cherokee Lottery* by William Jay Smith. Curbstone Press, 2002. Reprinted with permission of Curbstone Press. "The Atoll" and "Invitation to Ground Zero" from

Company. "Six Epigrams" from *Selected Poems and Parodies* by Louis Untermeyer, copyright 1935 by Harcourt, Inc., and renewed 1963 by Louis Untermeyer, reprinted by permission of Houghton Mifflin Harcourt Publishing Company. "Jerusalem Delivered" from *Long Feud: Selected Poems*, copyright 1935 and renewed 1962 by Louis Untermeyer, reprinted by permission of Houghton Mifflin Harcourt Publishing Company. (Originally appeared in *The New Yorker.*) "Upon Washington Bridge" from *Long Feud: Selected Poems*, copyright 1935 and renewed 1963 by Louis Untermeyer, reprinted by permission of Houghton Mifflin Harcourt Publishing Company. (Originally appeared in *The New Yorker.*) "A Side Street" from *Long Feud: Selected Poems* by Louis Untermeyer, copyright 1962, reprinted by permission of Houghton Mifflin Harcourt Publishing Company.

Richard Eberhart: "21st Century Man," "The Groundhog," "The Fury of Aerial Bombardment," "The Hard Structure of the World," "The Swallows Return," "As If You Had Never Been," "Gnat on My Paper," "Man's Type," "Long Term Suffering," and "You Think They Are Permanent But They Pass" from *Collected Poems 1930–1986.* Copyright © 1960, 1976, 1987 by Richard Eberhart. Reprinted by permission of Oxford University Press and the Richard Eberhart Estate. "Coast of Maine" from *Maine Poems.* Copyright © 1988 by Richard Eberhart. Reprinted by permission of Oxford University Press and the Richard Eberhart Estate.

Robert Frost: "The Gift Outright," "The Pasture," "Mending Wall," "The Road Not Taken," "The Oven Bird," "Birches," "Fire and Ice," "Dust of Snow," "Nothing Gold Can Stay," "Stopping by Woods on a Snowy Evening," "Design," "The Silken Tent," and "Never Again Would Birds' Song Be the Same" from *The Poetry of Robert Frost* edited by Edward Connery Lathem. Copyright © 1916, 1923, 1930, 1939, 1967, 1969, by Henry Holt and Company, copyright © 1964, 1967, 1970 by Lesley Frost Ballantine, copyright © 1936, 1942, 1944, 1951, 1958 by Robert Frost. Reprinted by arrangement with Henry Holt and Company, LLC.

Randall Jarrell: "A Girl in the Library," "Children Selecting Books in a Library," "The Snow Leopard," "Eighth Air Force," "Losses," "A Pilot from the Carrier," "A Front," "The Sick Nought," "1945: The Death of the Gods," "The Truth," "The Refugees," and "The Woman at the Washington Zoo" from *The Complete Poems* by Randall Jarrell. Copyright © 1969, renewed 1997 by Mary von S. Jarrell. Reprinted by permission of Farrar, Straus & Giroux, LLC.

"Well Water" from *The Lost World*. Copyright 1965. Reprinted by permission of Alleyne Boyette, Executor of the Estate of Randall Jarrell.

William Carlos Williams: "Danse Russe," "It Is a Living Coral," "Item," "Pastoral," "Poem (As the cat)," "The Last Words of My English Grandmother [Second Version]," "The Locust Tree In Flower [Second Version]," "The Red Wheelbarrow," "The Term," "This Is Just to Say," and "Young Sycamore," by William Carlos Williams, from *The Collected Poems: Volume I, 1909–1939*, copyright © 1938 by William Carlos Williams. Reprinted by permission of New Directions Publishing Corp. "Porous," by William Carlos Williams, from *The Collected Poems: Volume I, 1909–1939*, copyright © 1939 by William Carlos Williams. Reprinted by permission of New Directions Publishing Corp. "A Sort of Song," "The Dance (In Brueghel's)," and "The Graceful Bastion," by William Carlos Williams, from *The Collected Poems: Volume II, 1939–1962*, copyright © 1944 by William Carlos Williams. Reprinted by permission of New Directions Publishing Corp. "The Maneuver" and "The Mind Hesitant," by William Carlos Williams, from *The Collected Poems: Volume II, 1939–1962,* copyright © 1948 by William Carlos Williams. Reprinted by permission of New Directions Publishing Corp. "The Sparrow," by William Carlos Williams, from *The Collected Poems: Volume II, 1939–1962*, copyright © 1953 by William Carlos Williams. Reprinted by permission of New Directions Publishing Corp. "The Woodthrush," by William Carlos Williams, from *The Collected Poems: Volume II, 1939–1962*, copyright © 1962 by William Carlos Williams. Reprinted by permission of New Directions Publishing Corp.

Conrad Aiken: "Exile," Section IV from "Time in the Rock," Section XLVII from "Time in the Rock," Section LXXVII from "Time in the Rock," "The Habeas Corpus Blues," "Music," "Summer," and "When You Are Not Surprised" from Conrad Aiken, *Collected Poems*, Oxford University Press. Copyright © 1925, 1942, 1949, 1953, 1958, 1970 by Conrad Aiken. Copyright renewed © 1977, 1981, 1986 by Mary Hoover Aiken. Reprinted by permission of Brandt and Hochman Literary Agents, Inc., and Joseph Killorin, Executor of the Estate of Conrad Aiken. "The Grasshopper" from *Cats and Bats and Things with Wings* by Conrad Aiken. Copyright © 1965 by Conrad Aiken. Copyright renewed © 1993 by Joan Aiken and Jane Aiken Hodge. Reprinted by permission of Brandt & Hochman Literary Agents, Inc. All rights reserved. "The Whippoorwill" from *The New Yorker*. Copyright © 1941 by Conrad Aiken. Reprinted by permission of Joseph Killorin, Executor of the Estate of Conrad Aiken.

INDEX